Serapion Sister

Northwestern University Press
Studies in Russian Literature and Theory

Founding Editor
  Gary Saul Morson

General Editor
  Caryl Emerson

Consulting Editors
  Carol Avins
  Robert Belknap
  Robert Louis Jackson
  Elliott Mossman
  Alfred Rieber
  William Mills Todd III
  Alexander Zholkovsky

Serapion Sister

THE POETRY OF ELIZAVETA POLONSKAJA

Leslie Dorfman Davis

NORTHWESTERN UNIVERSITY PRESS / EVANSTON, ILLINOIS

Northwestern University Press
Evanston, Illinois 60208-4210

Copyright © 2001 by Northwestern University Press.
Published 2001. All rights reserved.

Printed in the United States of America
10 9 8 7 6 5 4 3 2 1

ISBN 0-8101-1579-4

Library of Congress Cataloging-in-Publication Data

Davis, Leslie Dorfman.
    Serapion sister : the poetry of Elizaveta Polonskaja / Leslie Dorfman Davis.
      p. cm. — (Studies in Russian literature and theory)
    Includes bibliographical references and index.
    ISBN 0-8101-1579-4 (alk. paper)
    1. Polonskaia, Elizaveta, b. 1890—Criticism and interpretation. I. Title.
II. Series.
PG3476.P617 Z88 2001
891.71′42—dc21

                                                                                                       00-011659

The paper used in this publication meets the minimum requirements of the American National Standard for Information Sciences—Permanence of Paper for Printed Library Materials, ANSI Z39.48-1984.

Contents

Introduction		1
Chapter One	Polonskaja's Life	18
Chapter Two	Early Verse	46
Chapter Three	Under a Stone Rain, 1921–23	76
Chapter Four	The NEP Period	106
Chapter Five	Poetry in the Stalinist Period	135
Chapter Six	Poetry in the Post-Stalinist Period	174
Conclusion		208
Notes		213
Bibliography		243
Index		263

Introduction

ELIZAVETA GRIGOR'EVNA POLONSKAJA (1890–1969), the Russian poet, translator, children's writer, journalist, and noted memoirist, is chiefly remembered as an enigmatic minor figure, the only woman in the Petrograd literary circle known as the Serapion Brothers. As an insider in that group, Polonskaja had close ties with some of the most important literary figures of her day, including satirist Mixail Zoščenko, formalist critics Viktor Šklovskij and Jurij Tynjanov, novelists Konstantin Fedin and Vsevolod Ivanov, and critic and children's writer Kornej Čukovskij. In the past few decades, her quiet but persistent presence in Russian literature has been felt mainly in her capacity as memoirist; her recollections have appeared in several recent collections, and excerpts from her archive have been published in a few journals. She has, in turn, also made some brief but memorable appearances in the memoirs of other writers, such as Il'ja Erenburg, Veniamin Kaverin, and Evgenij Švarc. Polonskaja, an active member of the Leningrad literary community, is still remembered and respected by the older generation; at the same time, she is almost completely unknown among those too young to recall the publication of her last collection of verse in 1966.

Polonskaja's career as a poet began before the Russian Revolution and spanned five decades of the Soviet regime. A 1921 review by Boris Ejxenbaum contains these words of praise for the "muscular tension" and "oratorical pathos" of her verse: "Polonskaja's verse is distinguished by its expression: in it, we feel a muscular tension, there are strong speech gestures in it. . . . She does not sing, she speaks—with strength, with oratorical pathos."[1] In 1926, D. S. Mirskij called Polonskaja "the most gifted of the young poetesses" of Petersburg,[2] and critics in the 1960s lauded her as one of the founders of Soviet poetry. However, no events or publications in Russia marked Polonskaja's centennial; the only scholarly work on her to appear in 1990 was a master's thesis at the University of Zurich.[3] There has never been a critical edition of her poetry. Thirty years after her death, Polonskaja has just begun to attract scholarly attention in Russia. Aside from a few encyclopedia entries and a mention where the Serapion Brothers are listed by name, almost nothing has been written about her, either in Russia or in the West, since her death in 1969.

Such obscurity is a common fate for women writers, but in Polonskaja's case it may also be explained by her ambiguous political status. It was in the postwar period that she experienced the greatest difficulty in publishing her work; in the wake of the Communist Party's attack on Zoščenko in 1946, her association with him and the other Serapions was not propitious. Neither was the fact that she had been a pupil of Nikolaj Gumilev, the first writer executed by the Bolsheviks as a counterrevolutionary. The fact that, in her youth, she had served as technical secretary and propagandist to an underground Bolshevik group in St. Petersburg and had to flee the country to avoid arrest in 1908 was actually no help. Indeed, Polonskaja kept this information to herself during the Stalinist period, since she understood that her association with prominent figures among the original Bolsheviks was a liability. After returning to Russia, she never did officially join the Party, although she was a prominent member of the Leningrad Writers' Union.[4] Furthermore, as a non-Party member, a Jew, and, incidentally, a doctor, she was affected by the postwar wave of anti-Semitism.[5]

The Serapion Brothers were a controversial group. Although they weathered critical attacks in the 1920s and went on to become some of the most important and successful Soviet writers, in the 1930s they were required to recant publicly their earlier insistence on the autonomy of art from prescribed ideology. In the 1940s, past membership in the Serapions became a dangerous attribute. It was, for example, one of several charges leveled at Zoščenko in Ždanov's 1946 attack. As A. Metčenko pointed out in 1956, the phrase "Serapion Brothers" became a term of abuse; in attempts to "redeem" certain writers (Fedin, Kaverin, Tixonov, Vsev. Ivanov) from this taint, every flaw in their works was attributed to the Serapion influence, while every virtue was attributed to that of Gor'kij.[6]

If, as a onetime Serapion, Polonskaja was suspect to the Soviets, she seems to have been equally so among Western scholars, who also tend either to relegate her to the footnotes entirely or to gloss over the political aspects of her work. All but ignored during the cold war period, she is portrayed respectfully but not entirely accurately in Wolfgang Kasack's *Dictionary of Russian Literature since 1917:* "Polonskaya's poetry is clear and beautiful.... Polonskaya, who never stooped to propaganda, is seldom published (1960, 1966), certainly less than she deserves, but she is regarded benignly by official critics."[7] Polonskaja did indeed write what many would call propaganda, though not as crudely as many others did. Her verse is often overtly political, though in the 1920s she maintained her independence as to the shade of ideology she expressed. In the 1930s and 1940s she did what was required of all Soviet writers who wished to remain active during the Stalinist period, surviving mainly on journalism and translation and trying to apply her poetic gift as much as possible to politically safe material. Thus she has, perhaps, been doubly compromised by political circumstances: not Communist enough for the Marxist critics, yet still somehow too "Red" for non-Soviet readers.

Kasack's characterization of Polonskaja may make her more appealing to Western (and post-Soviet Russian) readers, but it distorts the image of a writer whose profound humanism is hardly contradicted by an enduring commitment to the goal of socialism. An idealist raised on Nekrasov and Hugo, she regarded ideology as not only compatible with but even necessary to art. Born in a Jewish intelligentsia family with progressive leanings (her mother had attended the Bestužev courses for women at St. Petersburg University and had friends among the Narodovol'cy), Polonskaja was attracted from childhood to the Russian revolutionary movement. Her disillusionment with the Soviet regime, which can be traced to the early 1920s, has more to do with the use of terror and systematic repression than it does with underlying political ideology.

Aside from its political aspects, Polonskaja's work is also characterized by a preoccupation with two of the most controversial social issues in Russian history: the "woman question" and the "Jewish question." She was a socialist before she was a feminist, but her vision of socialism, like that of Aleksandra Kollontai, included the liberation of women as well as men from the injustices of autocracy and capitalism. A significant portion of Polonskaja's poetry is concerned with the conflict between women's freedom and their traditional roles, and she created a number of poetic portraits of women who are heroic and/or noteworthy in entirely untraditional ways. Although herself an atheist, she never lost her sense of cultural identity with the Jewish people, particularly in the face of anti-Semitism. Not only Jewish motifs but also the rhythms and cadences of the Old Testament in the Church Slavonic translation (she read no Hebrew) can be found in her poetry, as well as an occasional word of Yiddish. As the old woman in her poem "Vstreča" ("The Meeting") solemnly pronounces, "And though you may have forgotten your faith and your kin, / A *id iz immer a id!*" (A Jew is always a Jew!)[8]

Even in the past decade, when changes in the Russian social and political climate have made possible more thorough and objective study of early Soviet literature in Russia itself, Polonskaja's name still appears only occasionally. In 1991 Aleksandr Rubaškin lamented the fact that not a single periodical marked the centennial of this "noteworthy figure in the literary life of the twenties and early thirties." He attributes this omission to the fact that Polonskaja "did not leave, was not repressed, but died quietly in her communal apartment." In other words, in contemporary Russia she lacks the cachet of dissidence (and distance) which can make even such a writer as the émigré Villi Tokarev a celebrity in his homeland.[9]

Although she deserves detailed study as an individual writer, for most readers Polonskaja's name is a mere footnote to the larger text of the Serapion Brothers. Furthermore, the group itself was so maligned and misrepresented during the Stalinist period that its members felt compelled to recant their artistic principles and downplay their membership, thus marginalizing Polonskaja even further. It is only in recent years that serious scholarship on the Serapions has begun to appear in Russia, in part due also to the fact that, until recently, the archives of certain members have been officially closed.[10] Thus, in order to contextualize Polonskaja's work properly, it is necessary to clarify not only her role in the brotherhood but also the brotherhood's role in the history of Soviet literature. Polonskaja's role within the group will be discussed in the body of this book. This introduction outlines and evaluates the larger history of the Serapions in order to establish a proper context.

Although commonly linked with the rebirth of Russian prose after the Revolution, the Serapion Brothers were a heterogeneous group, consisting of six prose writers (Konstantin Fedin, Vsevolod Ivanov, Veniamin Kaverin, Nikolaj Nikitin, Mixail Slonimskij, and Mixail Zoščenko), one dramatist (Lev Lunc), one critic (Il'ja Gruzdev), and two poets (Polonskaja and Nikolaj Tixonov). Furthermore, there were also pronounced stylistic and theoretical differences among them. What united them was a unique blend of personal friendship, political irreverence, and commitment to artistic freedom. They came together, in Slonimskij's words, "without rules . . . and above all [they] feared losing [their] independence, that suddenly there would be a Society of the Serapion Brothers under the auspices of the People's Commissariat of Education."[11] Though accused by Marxist critics of professing a bourgeois creed of "art for art's sake" and of taking a counterrevolutionary position, the Serapions rejected neither the Revolution nor political ideology per se. What they objected to was any attempt to regulate art according to the demands of political ideology, a position which could still be argued in the 1920s but which was to cost some of them dearly decades hence.

Literary historians differ as to the precise duration of the active period of the brotherhood's existence, but most will agree that it was relatively short, from 1921 to some time in the mid-1920s. Long after they ceased to function as an active group, however, the Serapions remained a potent symbol of resistance to Party control of literature. This symbolic image has given the group a kind of "afterlife" which has taken on a significance of its own in Soviet literary-political discourse, from the Party's Resolution on the journals *Zvezda* and *Leningrad* in 1946 to the publication of the unauthorized anthology *Metropol* in 1976. Even after Stalin's death, for conservatives the Serapion Brotherhood was synonymous with "rotten apoliticism" and imitation of the West, while for liberals they represented an ideal of artistic freedom and personal integrity. Furthermore, in the period of the

Introduction

post-Stalinist "thaws," the division between liberal and conservative became evident within the group itself, some members having attained high enough professional and social rank to be wary of jeopardizing their own positions. Their ambivalence about examining their own past was exacerbated in the 1960s by the attention of émigré and American "bourgeois literary scholars"[12] such as Edward Brown, Hongor Oulanoff, and Gary Kern, whose work on the Serapions was reviled in Russia as anti-Soviet. It is only now, in the post-Soviet period, seventy years after the group ceased to function, that some Russian scholars have begun to evaluate the phenomenon of the Serapion Brothers with some objectivity, neither idealizing nor demonizing them, but seeking to understand both their role in the development of Soviet literature and the forces which shaped their individual fates.

Membership in this group was no small distinction, for the Serapions were considered among the most talented new writers to emerge in the early Soviet period. In 1923, Maksim Gor'kij wrote: "I am following the development and spiritual growth of the Serapions with great hopes. These young people seem to me capable of creating a new literature in Russia."[13] Several of the Serapions did in fact create masterpieces of early Soviet literature, which were acknowledged as such even by their ideological enemies. These acknowledged masterpieces include Ivanov's *Bronepoezd 14-69* (*Armored Train No. 14-69*) and *Partizany* (*The Partisans*), Tixonov's ballads, and Fedin's *Goroda i gody* (*Cities and Years*). In Gary Kern's words, the Serapions were among the first Soviet writers "to develop revolutionary themes, to satirize the Soviet state, to depict the NEPman and the doubting intellectual, and to depart from the metaphysical pretensions of Symbolist prose."[14] Among those who recognized their talent while attacking them for their political nonconformity was Lev Trotskij, who wrote in 1923: "We know very well the political limitations, the instability and unreliability of the fellow-travelers. But if we should eliminate Pilnyak, with his *The Bare Year*, the Serapion Fraternity with Vsevolod Ivanov, Tikhonov, and Polonskaya, if we should eliminate Mayakovskij and Yessenin, is there anything that will remain for us but a few unpaid promissory notes of a future proletarian literature?"[15]

The Serapions came together in the cultural hothouse created by Gor'kij in civil war Petrograd. Gor'kij, whom Viktor Šklovskij called "the Noah of the Russian intelligentsia,"[16] used his political influence, stemming largely from his personal friendship with Lenin, to establish a network of state-supported institutions to shelter and support writers, scholars, and artists. These institutions, which Šklovskij called "concentration camps for the intelligentsia,"[17] provided essentials such as housing, food (the *pajok*, or academic ration), and work. They also brought artists and writers together to create a matrix for the growth of a new literature, one which would reflect the collective historical experience of the period.

Serapion Sister

One such "camp" was the Translators' Studio at the publishing house Vsemirnaja Literatura (World Literature), one of Gor'kij's many projects to create meaningful work for intellectuals. The studio opened in 1919, under the supervision of Kornej Čukovskij. Initially intended to provide a pool of trained translators, the studio attracted an unexpected number of students interested in much more than translation and was quickly expanded to offer a range of subjects. The first studio was held in the offices of World Literature, on Nevskij Prospekt; it was later moved to separate quarters in the Muruzi House, a former merchant's residence on Litejnyj Prospekt. The three-month courses offered included poetry, taught by Gumilev; literary criticism, taught by Čukovskij; poetic translation, taught by Mixail Lozinskij; prose, taught by Zamjatin; and theory of literature, taught by Šklovskij. Among the students at this first studio were several of the future Serapions, including Polonskaja.

On December 19, 1919, Gor'kij opened Dom Iskusstv (the House of Arts), one of several intelligentsia dormitories in the city; others included Dom Pisatelej (the House of Writers) and Dom Učenyx (the House of Scholars). Centrally located in the former Eliseev mansion, at the corner of Nevskij and the Mojka Canal, the House of Arts soon became a center of intellectual life in the city, particularly for new, young talents. Gor'kij sent the most promising students from the first Literary Studio to a new studio in the House of Arts, which opened in the spring of 1920. By the fall, Šklovskij and Zamjatin were among those lecturing there, Šklovskij on theory of prose, and Zamjatin on the craft of prose writing. Their students included Polonskaja, Gruzdev, Zoščenko, Lunc, Slonimskij, Kaverin, Nikitin, and Vladimir Pozner.

These students began meeting regularly on Saturday evenings in Slonimskij's room at the House of Arts to read each other their work. At Lunc's suggestion, they half-jokingly christened themselves the Serapion Brothers, after the heroes of E. T. A. Hoffmann's novel. As Polonskaja recalled decades later, "we all rejoiced at the word 'brotherhood,' forgetting about the hermit Serapion, whom the German Romantic Ernst Theodore Amadeus Hoffmann had invented. Jesting, we called ourselves brothers and, mercilessly criticizing each other, like Hoffmann's characters, we helped each other in all the difficult circumstances of our lives. . . . Aleksej Maksimovič Gor'kij accepted the name of our circle, and then it became official and subsequently caused us more than one unpleasant moment."[18] The first "official" meeting (if anything connected with the Serapions can be called official) took place on February 1, 1921. Later that spring, Gor'kij sent them two new members, Fedin and Ivanov, and Tixonov joined in the summer. Pozner emigrated to France with his family; thus, the roster of the Serapions was complete, and their life as a publicly recognized literary circle began. Their meetings were attended by *gostiški* (little guests), who included various friends, girlfriends, and their teachers, Šklovskij and Zamjatin, as well as Anna Axmatova and Osip Mandel'štam.

In his article "Serapionovy Brat'ja" ("The Serapion Brothers"), Zamjatin divided the group into "eastern" and "western" camps; the westerners (Lunc, Kaverin, and Slonimskij) "tend to operate predominantly with architectural masses, with plot, but with relatively little ear or love for the Russian language itself, its music and its color."[19] These were students of Šklovskij, whose special area of interest was plot structure. Language itself was more the province of the easterners (Nikitin, Ivanov, Zoščenko, and, to some degree, Fedin), whom Zamjatin describes as "folklorists and painters."[20] Their favorite device was *skaz,* the use of highly stylized first-person narration. This tendency reflects the influence of Zamjatin himself, whose early works, such as *Uezdnye* (*A Provincial Tale,* 1913), are distinguished by the author's mastery of provincial dialect. Zamjatin does not concern himself with poetry in this article, and his scheme is more easily applied to prose; however, since both Polonskaja and Tixonov wrote plot-driven ballads, they may be considered closer to the westerners.

Aside from Zamjatin's "east-west" scheme, there was another, potentially more serious division within the group. Easterners and westerners alike were encouraged by their mentors, Šklovskij and Zamjatin, to experiment with style and structure. The teachings of the two were complementary: Šklovskij proposed a method of understanding literature, while Zamjatin offered a rigorous approach to the craft of prose. With the arrival of Fedin, a protégé of Gor'kij's, a conflict arose.[21] Gor'kij prized psychological realism and formal simplicity over literary experimentation, and Fedin was one of his most loyal followers. He was put off at first by what he regarded as the Serapions' flippant manner of discussing "the holiest of holies—literature" and by their treatment of works of art as "things," to be judged by how well or how poorly they were made. In his memoir, *Gor'kij sredi nas* (*Gor'kij among Us*), Fedin describes his own passionate debate with Lunc over the primacy of content over form, of the "what" over the "how." Nevertheless, as he himself acknowledges in the same passage, despite different approaches to the process of creation, the Serapions did share a common goal: "In our constant skirmishes we groped for the goal of our mutual voyage, and in the final instance we all inwardly admitted that it was one and the same: the creation of the new literature for the epoch of war and revolution. This understanding of the historicity of our task, which came to us slowly, made us the same, despite all our differences."[22]

The Serapions' first literary success came in May 1921, when the House of Writers announced the six winners of a prestigious short story contest. Five out of six were Serapions: Fedin, Nikitin, Kaverin, Lunc, and Tixonov, who had submitted entries months before the actual formation of the group.[23] Soon after, Ivanov published his novella *Partizany* (*Partisans*)

Serapion Sister

in the first issue of *Krasnaja nov'* (*Red Virgin Soil*), the first Soviet "thick" journal. Polonskaja's first collection of poetry, *Znamen'ja* (*Omens*) and Zoščenko's first collection of stories, *Rasskazy Nazara Il'iča gospodina Sinebrjuxova* (*The Stories of Nazar Il'ič, Mr. Bluebelly*), also appeared in 1921. Already in 1921, Gor'kij had taken an interest in the group; as Zamjatin remarked, Gor'kij "felt like a happy father; he fussed over them like a hen over her chicks."[24] The Serapions were clearly becoming a presence in literary Petrograd, reading their works to large audiences at both the House of Arts and the House of Writers.

As Kern points out, certain of the controversies provoked by the Serapions were linked to their association with both the House of Writers and the House of Arts. The tension between the two institutions was considerable, since, as Fedin wrote in his memoir, "Gor'kij founded the House of Arts in conscious opposition to the House of Writers,"[25] whose tenants, Kern writes, "he considered infertile in literature and reactionary in politics."[26] According to a 1922 article in *Literaturnye zapiski* (*Literary Notes*), the journal of the House of Writers, several of the Serapions took part in the "literary Wednesdays" there.[27] Furthermore, their participation in 1922 in two publications under the auspices of the House of Writers sparked a polemic with Marxist critics which was to have serious political repercussions.

The first incident was the appearance of *Peterburgskij sbornik 1922* (*Petersburg Collection 1922*), an anthology published by the House of Writers containing fiction and poetry by thirty Petersburg writers, including both well-established names and new young talents. In the poetry section, Polonskaja, Tixonov, and other young poets from the House of Arts published verse alongside Axmatova, Kuzmin, Xodasevič, Sologub, and others. In the section titled "Belletrists," stories by Zoščenko, Ivanov, Nikitin, Slonimskij, Fedin, and other young writers appeared with pieces by Zamjatin and Remizov. Intended as a showcase for the "poetic forces of Petersburg,"[28] the collection—more specifically, the presence of the Serapions in the collection—provoked a complaint on ideological grounds. Sergej Gorodetskij, a former Acmeist poet who had recently joined the Bolshevik Party, published an article in *Izvestija* in which he simultaneously praised the Serapions as promising writers and castigated them for "ideological emptiness." Gorodetskij blamed this emptiness on the harmful influence of such "bourgeois" writers as Zamjatin, who, he claimed, belonged to the past.[29]

The Serapions responded to Gorodetskij in a collective letter, signed by all the members of the group, which they published in the first issue of *Novaja Rossija* (*New Russia*). In it, they categorically rejected what they saw as the critic's demand that literature express "political tendency, not simply ideology, but a truly 'hidebound' ideology (his very word)." Gorodetskij, they felt, demanded not only the presence of a discernible ideology in a work of literature but also the presence of a particular ideology acceptable to the Party. They dismissed this demand with contempt: "There have always been enough tradesmen pledged to that type of 'creation.' Art needs an artistic and not a tendentious ideology, just as governmental power needs open agitation and not agitation masked by bad literature."[30] This collective assertion of artistic freedom from the demands of the state expresses one of the main principles uniting the Serapion Brotherhood.

The second controversy erupted several months later, in August 1922. After the appearance of their first (and only) anthology, *Serapionovy Brat'ja: Almanax pervyj* (*The Serapion Brothers: Almanac the First*),[31] which was favorably reviewed by the critics Tynjanov and Voronskij,[32] the Serapions were invited by the editors of *Literaturnye zapiski* to publish short autobiographies.[33] Their irreverent tone, as well as the perceived audacity of writers publishing autobiographies when they had scarcely begun to publish at all, were not well received, but worst of all was the essay published by Lev Lunc in lieu of an autobiography. "Počemu My Serapionovy Brat'ja" ("Why We Are the Serapion Brothers") is a passionate defense of the writer's freedom to choose his own style, subject, and political ideology. "It is time to say," wrote Lunc, "that a non-Communist story may be worthless, but it also may be brilliant."[34] Furthermore, Lunc argued that art does not merely copy life but has a life of its own, which cannot be regulated; it is an end in itself, not an ideological tool. All of the Serapions were, in fact, receptive to the Revolution, but they reserved the right to be writers first and Communists second. This attitude, eloquently expressed in Lunc's essay and echoed in some of the other pieces, provoked a heated polemic in the Soviet press, in which Marxist critics such as Polyanskij, Trotskij, and Arvatov labeled the brothers petty-bourgeois intellectuals and advocates of (horribile dictu!) art for art's sake.[35]

The battle between the Serapions and their critics during the autumn of 1922 concentrated attention on the broader question of how all literary "fellow travelers" would be regarded by the Party and to what extent they would be tolerated. Despite the objections of many hard-line Marxist critics, throughout most of the 1920s the Party itself largely refrained from issuing any concrete directives in the realm of art and culture. As Trotskij wrote in 1923, "The domain of art is not one in which the Party is called upon to command. It can and must protect and help it, but it can only lead it indirectly. . . . Because it prepares consciously and step by step the ground for a new culture and therefore for a new art, it regards the literary fellow-travelers not as the competitors of the writers of the working class, but as the real or potential helpers of the working class in the big work of reconstruction."[36] In fact, the Central Committee had issued a protocol in January of that year, specifically promising the support of the State Publishing House, Goslitizdat, to the Serapions, "conditional upon their nonparticipation in such reactionary publications as *Žurnal* [*The Journal*] and *A Petersburg Collection*."³⁷ The 1925 "Resolution on Party Policy in the Field of Belles-Lettres" reaffirms this position, stating that "Communist criticism must struggle relentlessly against counter-revolutionary manifestations in literature . . . but at the same time, display the greatest tact, caution and tolerance in its relations with all those literary stratifications that can march with the proletariat and will march with it. Communist criticism must banish from practice the tone of literary command."³⁸ Although aggressive political pressure from the Russian Association of Proletarian Writers (RAPP) began in earnest in 1928, with the beginning of the First Five-Year Plan, it was not until 1932 that the Party itself would begin dictating literary policy from on high.

The furor over the autobiographies and Lunc's manifesto did not prevent the Serapions from flourishing, though they never again published as a group. Indeed, in December 1922, Lunc read them an essay, "Na Zapad!" ("Go West!"), in which he chastised them for succumbing to the lure of easy success and turning away from what he saw as the original goal of the group: to create a literature of plot, modeled on the literature of the West.³⁹ As Šklovskij observed, however, there was another, more practical problem which had also united the Serapions: the difficulty of publishing in Petrograd, where paper was scarce and typesetting expensive.⁴⁰ In 1922, it was easier for a young unknown writer to pool resources with a group and publish an anthology than to publish independently. By 1924, ties among the group had already loosened as some of the brothers (most notably Nikitin, Fedin, and Ivanov) were pulled by their success into the orbit of Moscow. Their works were appearing in *Krasnaja nov'*, and they were also co-founders, along with Voronskij, the editor of *Krasnaja nov'*, of an important new Moscow publishing house, Krug (Circle). In December 1922, both the House of Arts and the House of Writers were officially closed, bringing to an end the weekly meetings in Slonimskij's room. The Serapions continued to celebrate their anniversary on February 1, but attendance at meetings grew spotty.

Lunc himself left Russia in the spring of 1923. After taking his degree in Romance languages and literatures, he decided to pursue further studies in Spain. However, he never got farther than Hamburg, where he stopped to visit his parents. Already in poor health for some time, he became even more ill during the visit, and he died in a Hamburg sanatorium in 1924, at the age of twenty-two. Mourning for a dear friend strengthened the personal bond among the Serapions, but it could not slow the dissolution of the group as a literary entity. As Fedin wrote to Gor'kij in July 1924, "we are connected now by the past and by personal friendship, but not by that literary bond that held the brotherhood together in its time."⁴¹ Thus, in 1925, when the Party Central Committee formally announced its resolution to

Introduction

follow a policy of tolerance toward fellow travelers, the Serapions, one of the most prominent and controversial fellow-traveler groups, had already ceased to function in any active way.

In 1932 the Party imposed the doctrine of Socialist Realism in art, at which point the surviving Serapions were forced at last to conform in order to survive. Like all Soviet writers who wished to continue publishing, they joined the newly created Writers' Union. Two years later, at the First Congress of Soviet Writers, Vsevolod Ivanov explicitly renounced on behalf of the entire group their original position on tendentiousness in literature: "I affirm that, without exception, all who signed or sympathized with the declarations of the Serapion Brothers—against tendentiousness—have undergone such a growth in consciousness during the last twelve years that there is no longer even one of us who would not accept with all sincerity Comrade Ždanov's formulation, that we are *for* Bolshevik tendentiousness in literature."[42] Both their work and their behavior in the 1930s and 1940s reflect political compromise and justifiable fear. According to Vjačeslav Ivanov,[43] during the Terror, Fedin, Ivanov, and Tixonov were all under attack, which included attempts by the NKVD to fabricate a counterrevolutionary writers' organization, headed by Tixonov. Their self-protective measures included signing letters demanding the execution of "enemies of the people," writing testimonials filled with praise for the "vast work" accomplished on the Baltic–White Sea Canal (without mentioning the role of forced labor), and even serving as correspondents for *Izvestija* at the show trials.[44] The former Serapions were particularly vulnerable after the death, in 1936, of their longtime friend and patron, Gor'kij. They were fortunate not only to survive the purges but also to go on, in some cases, to high positions in the Writers' Union; Ivanov and Tixonov both served in the Secretariat during Stalin's lifetime, Tixonov as first secretary, and Fedin attained that post in the late 1950s. In Vjačeslav Ivanov's words, the epoch stifled the Serapions, "some with persecution, others—with the seduction of rank and money, still others with a peculiar blend of whips and gingerbread."[45]

Despite the outward conformity of the Serapion Brothers to Party demands, however, "Comrade Ždanov" would not so easily forget the circumstances of their literary debut, as Zoščenko learned when his story "Priključenija ob'jezjany" ("Adventures of an Ape"), which appeared in the journal *Zvezda,* became a target for Party condemnation. In his 1946 speech denouncing the journals *Zvezda* and *Leningrad,* Ždanov used the brothers' own words, taken from their scandalous 1922 "autobiographies," to brand Zoščenko an "unprincipled literary hooligan."[46] Zoščenko's ironic depiction of himself as "not a Communist, a socialist or a monarchist, but simply a Russian and moreover politically immoral"[47] is quoted alongside Lunc's assertion that "art is as real as life itself, and like life it exists without aim or reason, exists because it cannot help existing."[48] Ždanov thus accuses Zoščenko both

11

of individual heresy and of heresy by association, a charge which could logically be extended to other former Serapions. In addition, Ždanov draws particular attention in his speech to "the enormous harm of substituting literary relations based on friendship for relations based on principle,"[49] which could also be construed as an attack on the Serapions. Not only was Zoščenko expelled from the Writers' Union, but Tixonov, then first secretary, was removed from his position for having failed to exercise his authority to prevent objectionable works from appearing in the two journals. His removal was both a punishment and a warning.

Ždanov's speech signaled the beginning of a severe postwar crackdown on any deviation from Party-sanctioned norms in art. This new wave of intensified repression was accompanied by the campaign against "rootless cosmopolitans," a thinly veiled program of anti-Semitism which was to culminate in the fabrication of a "doctors' plot" in 1953 and the arrest and execution of the last generation of Yiddish writers and artists in Russia. For the Jews among the former Serapions (Polonskaja, Kaverin, and Slonimskij), this factor compounded the precariousness of their situation. In the years between 1946 and the death of Stalin, they published little new work, relying heavily on new editions of older pieces, translation, and journalism. The only former Serapion to publish a successful major work in those years was Fedin, whose two socialist realist novels, *Pervye radosti* (*Early Joys*, 1946) and *Neobyknovennoe leto* (*No Ordinary Summer*, 1948), won him a Stalin Prize.

In the period following Stalin's death, starting around 1956, the Serapions became the focus of a reevaluation meant to correct some of the excesses of the Stalinist era. A. Metčenko, A. Dement'jev, G. Lomidze, K. D. Muratova, and others began calling for more balanced and historically accurate representation of a group which had, after all, included such major figures as Tixonov, Fedin, and Ivanov, and which had been lavishly praised and guided by Gor'kij. These critics did not dispute Ždanov's characterization of Zoščenko's late works as ideologically harmful. However, they rejected the dogmatic reception of Ždanov's attacks on the Serapions as a group. According to Metčenko, following Ždanov's speech, "the phrase 'Serapion Brothers' turned into a term of abuse. No facts were taken into account. The only useful work that was done was an attempt to "rescue" from censure such writers as Fedin, Kaverin, Ivanov, Tixonov, and others who had joined the group at one time. Everything bad in the works of these writers was attributed to the 'Serapion Brothers,' and everything good was attributed to Gor'kij's influence."[50] Fedin, Ivanov, Tixonov, and Kaverin were treated by the authors of *Očerk istorii russkoj sovetskoj literatury* (*Outline of the History of Russian Soviet Literature*, 1954) as the only significant members of the Serapions.[51] Muratova draws attention to the disdainful tone, unwarranted in her opinion, with which the others were dismissed as "not having left any noticeable trace in literature."[52] The Serapions, it seemed, were being officially welcomed back into Soviet literature; in 1958, Konstantin Fedin was appointed first secretary of the Writers' Union.

The chief method of rehabilitation used by these critics was to discount the idea that there was any sort of unity among the Serapions and attribute any objectionable views primarily to Lunc. In an article by Metčenko, Dement'jev, and Lomidze, we find the statement that the Serapions "included not only Zoščenko and Lunc, but also Tixonov, Fedin, Ivanov and others not mentioned in Ždanov's report."[53] Their works, the authors assert, played a positive role in the development of Soviet literature, "in spite of the erroneous theoretical directives of the group."[54] Ždanov judged the group primarily by their declarations, particularly Lunc's essay, "Why We Are the Serapion Brothers," rather than by their literary works, which, as Metčenko points out, even their ideological enemies in the 1920s did not do. Metčenko and his colleagues avoid this approach. According to Muratova, the real manifesto of the Serapions was not "Why We Are the Serapion Brothers," but their letter to Gorodetskij, which was actually signed by all the members. She distinguishes between the kind of apoliticism expressed in the letter, which she defines as "a rejection of primitive propaganda," and Lunc's declared "apoliticism," which "meant withdrawal from treatment of complex ideological problems, a refusal to reproduce actual contemporary themes."[55] Although several other Serapions spoke of their disillusionment with politics in their autobiographies, according to Muratova, their statements are belied by their works, which reveal their deep commitment to the Revolution. In this series, she names only Fedin, Ivanov, Tixonov, Nikitin, and Slonimskij.[56] Lunc's profoundly philosophical and, indeed, political, dramas apparently do not qualify as ideological, since his ideology is much more ambivalent and disturbing.

This use of Lunc as the scapegoat for the Serapions was predictable, given the fact that he was certainly the most outspoken and provocative proponent of artistic freedom in the group. His early death removed him from the scene before he could be confronted by the same dilemmas which led his "brothers" to compromise, to varying degrees, their earlier principles. Touched by neither the whips nor the gingerbread, he remains frozen in memory as the iconoclast who named the group and called upon its members to follow not the Communist Party but the Hermit Serapion. It is also clear from his essay "Go West!" that Lunc had been at odds with most of the brothers on aesthetic and formal grounds; only Kaverin was known to have shared his views on the importance of plot and of Western models. Lunc's apparent isolation does not, in fact, contradict his and the group's basic premise, which was their mutual respect and tolerance of each other's individual views and approaches. Their highest values were artistic freedom and honesty. Thaw-era critics gloss over this fact. The Serapions' rehabili-

ature had something in common with faith and a sense of duty."[70] The reticence with which the brothers approached the very fact of Lunc's presence in the group, let alone his role in the polemic, illustrates the degree to which the terror induced by Ždanov's speech still held sway in the 1960s.

Kaverin, who outlived all the other Serapions, published several more memoirs in the 1970s and 1980s, and he returned each time in increasing degrees of detail to the role and fate of Lunc. First, briefly, in his autobiographical trilogy *Osveščennye okna* (*Lighted Windows,* 1970–75),[71] and in greater detail in *Epilog* (1989), Kaverin told the story of the ill-fated Commission to Preserve the Legacy of Lev Lunc, which was created in 1967 with the aim of publishing an anthology of Lunc's writings. The commission, whose members consisted of Slonimskij (as president), Kaverin, Tixonov, Šklovskij, and S. S. Podol'skij (as secretary), had a manuscript ready for publication in January 1968; the collection was to include not only Lunc's fiction but also his publicistic works, "Why We Are the Serapion Brothers" and "Go West!"[72] As Kaverin points out, however, the last "thaw" was in its final stages in 1968, particularly after the Soviet invasion of Czechoslovakia, and some members of the commission began backing away from the project. Even Fedin's personal intervention as first secretary of the Writers' Union could not persuade the publisher, Sovetskij pisatel' (Soviet Writer), to approve the manuscript.[73] It was not until 1989 that Kaverin was able to publish his detailed account of the commission in *Epilog*, and it was in only 1994 that the first collection of Lunc's works appeared in Russia.[74]

Kaverin was initially heartened by the appearance in 1976 of the unofficial, uncensored anthology *Metropol,* whose introduction, with its demands for the right to variety and individuality and rejection of all regulation, reminded him instantly of Lunc's declarations;[75] in 1981, however, he wrote of a "thick layer of dirty lies, hypocrisy and terror" which still hampered the expression of public opinion.[76] It was not until after Kaverin's death, in the post-Soviet period (1995), that a scholarly conference devoted exclusively to the Serapions was held in Russia (specifically, in newly "renamed" St. Petersburg). Even then, out of twenty-two papers, only three were devoted to Lunc, and of those, two were presented by visitors from abroad.[77]

The prolonged controversy over Lunc and the continued reticence concerning his importance, both as an individual writer and within the Serapion Brothers, indicates the degree to which he and the brotherhood have remained relevant in literary-political discourse throughout the Soviet period and beyond. The Serapions are a major part of the legacy of early Soviet literature, which is still in the process of being reclaimed by a later generation. After half a century of Soviet censorship and repression, they remain an important and inspiring model of creative and ideological independence. This model is no less important for having been compromised

Introduction

under the extreme political pressures of the Soviet period. The suppression of the very memory of Lev Lunc violates both historical truth and the "serapionic" principle of artistic truth, and it must be corrected in order to establish a historically faithful record of Soviet literature.

The same is true for the other members of this most egalitarian of all groups, in which some members may have been more outspoken but all were equally valued and respected. Elizaveta Polonskaja not only played her own important and unique role in the group but also shared certain artistic and philosophical views with Lunc, views which she was later forced to mask in order to survive. Her self-censorship was one of several factors which contributed to the obscuring and distortion of her image. Dispelling the misrepresentation of both Polonskaja and Lunc is an essential step in completing the picture of the Serapions, both during their active period and in subsequent decades. Until Russian literary scholarship has dealt thoroughly and objectively with all of the Serapion Brothers, traces of the web of falsehood and fear created by Ždanov and his followers will remain in place.

Due to the scarcity of even the most general information about Polonskaja, it will be necessary to begin with a biographical chapter, in which I will trace both the major events of her life and the evolution of her thought and work. The chapters that follow constitute a general introduction to Polonskaja's poetry; themes, influences, stylistic features, and historical context will be considered. I will also devote some attention to critical reception of the poetry and the ways in which Polonskaja's strategies for keeping her work in circulation have affected long-range critical evaluation.

Chapter One

Polonskaja's Life

CHILDHOOD AND YOUTH

Elizaveta Grigor'evna Movšenson was born on June 27/14, 1890. Her father, Grigorij L'vovič Movšenson, was a Jewish engineer who graduated with high honors from the Riga Polytechnical Institute. Because of his high professional status, he was granted the right to live outside the Jewish Pale of Settlement, in any city in the Russian Empire. Her mother, Charlotta Il'inična Movšenson (née Mejlax), came from a large Jewish merchant family in Białystok. Three of the five Mejlax sisters managed to escape their father's watchful eye long enough to establish independent lives for themselves. One, Berta, ran off to Italy, where she lived for many years under bohemian and slightly mysterious circumstances. Two of the younger sisters, Sofija and Charlotta, made their way to St. Petersburg, where Sofija enrolled in a gymnasium. Charlotta attended the Bestužev courses for women at St. Petersburg University and received her training as a tutor, authorized to teach members of her own faith. Sofija went on to become, at a very young age, a well-known Moscow obstetrician and patroness of the arts. Thus, Elizaveta was born into a family with a history on both sides of strong-willed, independent, and highly educated people.

Russian was the main language used in the Movšenson household, but Elizaveta was also taught French, German, Italian, and English.[1] She was drawn to Russian poetry at an early age under the influence of her mother and aunts, and her early experience of poetry was as a vehicle for expressing outrage at social injustice. In a passage from her unpublished autobiography, she writes: "The poems that Mama and her sisters read passed into my memory and remained there forever, although often I did not understand the meaning of a word or a stanza. In our house, Nekrasov's 'Hey, Ivan!' was often declaimed, and from the age of four I read with a feeling of deep sympathy for this incomprehensible Ivan."[2] She wrote her first poem at the age of eight, in French, under the influence of her governess, Jeanne Nicault, apparently herself a poet. The poem was, in Polonskaja's words, "devoted to Alsace-Lorraine; it conveyed the idea of French revenge for the Franco-Prussian war."³

The family moved often in connection with Grigorij L'vovič's career. When Elizaveta was born, they were living in Warsaw, but shortly thereafter they moved to Łodz. She entered the Łodz women's gymnasium, where the language of instruction was Russian, at a time of repression and social ferment. Many of her classmates frequented various *kružki* (circles), in which they read subjects unavailable to them in the gymnasium. Charlotta Il'inična Movšenson secretly organized such a circle for her daughter's fourth-year class; a young student was found to lead the girls in studying Belinskij. The following year, Elizaveta joined a group reading political economy. In 1905, she narrowly escaped expulsion because of an aborted strike by gymnasium pupils, the demands of which were to have included the use of Polish in the schools and a general call for "the overthrow of autocracy."⁴ During this period, she was not writing verse, but rather "composing dramas of 'garrison life,'" and her preferred poets were Nekrasov, Nadson, and Heine.⁵

Another important influence in her childhood years was the language of Scripture. Although the Movšenson household was strictly secular, observing a bare minimum of Jewish customs in deference to Charlotta Il'inična's parents, the women's gymnasium required its pupils to study the "Law of God" according to their faith. In "Lodz," Polonskaja recalls her teacher, Rabbi Dončin, with great affection and describes the extraordinarily strong impression made on her by his stories of the Jewish people. It is clear that not only the stories themselves but also the biblical language (albeit in Russian translation) made a deep impression on her; her solemn, rhetorical verse is often marked by Slavonicisms. In the 1920s she wrote to Pavel Medvedev, "Of all my subjects, I liked the 'Law of God' best, and in the 'Law of God,' what I loved were the splendid words. . . . And to this day I prefer the Bible to all other books."⁶

In 1905 the threat of pogroms led Grigorij Movšenson to send his wife and children (Elizaveta and her brother Aleksandr) for several months to the relative safety of Berlin, where Charlotta Il'inična's sister Fanny lived with her husband. There was a large community of Russian speakers in Berlin at that time, many of them also Jews fleeing westward from pogroms. Among these refugees Elizaveta found another young people's reading group where, under the guidance of one Rozalija Grigorievna Lemberg, she first read Marx.

The following year, the family was transferred to St. Petersburg, and Elizaveta graduated from a women's gymnasium there in 1907.⁷ After a chance encounter with Lemberg, she became involved with an underground youth group, which seems to have been more of a social circle than a serious political body. Most were classmates, and their activities consisted mainly of raising money for the cause by means of lectures, readings, and concerts, often with dancing. Elizaveta apparently found these young people frivolous and their parties a waste of time, and after a prolonged illness (measles with complications and pneumonia) followed by intensive preparation for a set of external high-school finishing exams, she drifted out of the circle.

For a time she occupied herself in the public library, reading Hauptmann, Shakespeare, and Ibsen. It was there that she ran into Rozalija Samojlovna Zemljačka, who was also connected with the Berlin Marxist reading group. Zemljačka sent her to a Bolshevik cell in a workers' district (Semjannikov) to serve as a technical secretary. Elizaveta later worked as a propagandist and technical secretary in the Nevskij district, during which time she was even sent to Finland to pick up leaflets from Lenin for distribution in Petersburg.

In 1908 she applied to the Women's Medical Institute, but, as she had not reached the minimum age required for admittance (nineteen), she was not accepted. Her father suggested she go abroad to study as was then accepted among the middle-class Jewish intelligentsia, largely due to the *numerus clausus* limiting the number of Jews admitted to universities. At the same time, the family servant warned her that she was under police surveillance; she had no alternative but to go abroad immediately. Her father offered her a choice: Paris or Geneva. She chose Paris and left shortly afterward. On arriving, she enrolled at the Sorbonne, where she received her medical degree in 1914.

PARIS: STUDENT LIFE

So it was that, at eighteen, Elizaveta Movšenson found herself on her own in Paris. Although most of her time was taken up with medical studies, she nevertheless managed to attend meetings of the Russian Social Democratic Party, having brought a letter of reference from her Petersburg comrades sewn into the lining of her coat. Among the younger members of the Party, she found a circle of people who shared her love of poetry, and it was through them that she was introduced to the work of the Russian Symbolists, which made a profound impression on her. In her memoir "1908: Medical Studies, New Friends," she writes: "I completely stopped writing verse, because I felt that one ought to write in an entirely different way than those authors I was mad about at one time. Neither Nadson nor Nekrasov spoke to me now, yet there was so much that was new in poetry, so much that was being said in our own, contemporary language! So much that stirred and touched us! We greeted every new poem by Blok with delight, and for us, the most desired of all journal issues or almanacs were those which contained these poems."[8]

Through these friends in the Party she met Il'ja Erenburg in 1909. It was a significant event in both of their lives. In his autobiography, *Ljudi, gody, žizn'* (*People, Years, Life*), Erenburg recalls: "Liza loved poetry with a passion; she would read me poems by Bal'mont, Brjusov, Blok. I made fun of Nad'ja L'vova when she said that Blok was a great poet. I did not dare contradict Liza. Returning home from her place, I would mutter: 'The bright wind falls silent, gray evening falls. . . .' Why was the wind bright? I could not explain this to myself, but I felt that it really was bright. I began borrowing the work of contemporary poets from the Turgenev Library, and I suddenly understood that you can say in verse what you cannot say in prose. And I needed to say a great deal to Liza."[9] According to Marija Kireeva, a member of their circle, Liza's close Party connections and poetic gift made her the center around which the group revolved, and she describes Erenburg as a "constant pupil . . . who greedily caught her every word; all his thoughts were taken up with poems and with Liza's appraisal of his attempts at poetry."[10]

Aside from poetry, Erenburg and Movšenson shared a a satirical impulse which provoked disapproval from some of their older comrades. Both were involved in a production of Andreev's play *Dni našej žizni* (*Days of Our Life*) at a Party fund-raiser in 1909; during rehearsals, several of Andreev's expressions became catchphrases among the young people. "Former people," for example, became an epithet they used to deride their elders. As Movšenson later recalled: "We began using these expressions often in our far from jolly life, and they helped lighten that life for us. When our stern Party comrades looked askance at our youthful merriment, without a moment's thought we called them former people. By that name we meant: if such a person joins the 'former people,' he loses both charm and authority, although he may perhaps possess a multitude of worthy qualities."[11] Movšenson and Erenburg collaborated on a satirical poem along these lines, and together they published two journals, *Byvšie ljudi* (*Former People*) and *Tixoe semejstvo* (*A Quiet Family*), in which they "rather caustically, without any sort of reverence, mocked the manners of the Bolshevik circle, insulting even the 'chiefs' (Plexanov, Lenin, Trotskij), and therefore had a sensational response. . . . The publishers of the journal[s] had to choose between literature and politics, and they preferred literature."[12] Polonskaja says little in her memoirs about the aftermath of this affair, but Kireeva recalls that Erenburg so provoked some of the right Mensheviks that they refused to greet him.[13]

Although they quarreled and Erenburg fell in love with another woman, Ekaterina Schmidt, he and Movšenson remained friends and corresponded until his death. Aside from their complex personal relations, they had a profound effect on each other's writing. Long after his reputation was established, he often sent her copies of his work and requested her opinion; in 1939, he wrote: "Dear Liza, world events have allowed Erenburg-Joslen some leisure time; in view of this, Erenburg has recalled old times and, after a seventeen-year break, is writing verse. Just as in his day he would show you his first poems, so now he felt he would like to send his second debut to you and no one else. Write when you have a chance, and tell me what you think about it."[14] Later, in 1960, he wrote, even more significantly, "Now you can read the whole first part of *People, Years, Life.* Much in this work, as is generally the case with my life, is dedicated inwardly to you."[15] He, in turn, was both the addressee of many of her lyrics and her first publisher; in June 1914, her first published poems appeared in the second issue of his monthly poetry review, *Večera (Evenings).* Finally, Erenburg's memoirs stimulated her to think, and later to write, about her own past, as evidenced in their correspondence from the early 1960s. In a letter from September 1961, she reminisces about a lecture she gave in 1921 on his novel, *Julio Jurenito,* at a meeting of the Free Philosophical Society and remarks, "Pardon me, but reminiscences are contagious."[16]

By 1913, Movšenson was reading her poetry regularly to appreciative audiences at the Russian Academy, an enclave of Russian writers and artists who rented studio and living space in a house on the Boulevard Montparnasse. They had a communal dining room, where gatherings took place every Saturday. In her memoir of the Russian Academy, she mentions having known, among others, Vera Inber, Marija Škapskaja, Oscar Lesinski, Mixail Gerasimov, Mark Talov, Anatolij Lunačarskij, and Nikolaj Minskij.[17] In another memoir, she also mentions having known the French writers Appollinaire, Francis Jammes, Paul Fort, and Charles Peguy.[18] Although her poetry from this period consists mostly of rather imitative love lyrics and some translations of French poets (Verlaine, Moréas), she nevertheless made a mark on the literary scene of Paris, and she also developed some close friendships with other writers, for example, Erenburg and Škapskaja.

Her Party connections appear to have loosened during the Paris years. As fondly as she recalled her early days in the Bolshevik movement, and as much as she admired her comrades, she began to see them from a certain distance. They remained in the tightly knit émigré community, speaking only Russian and consumed by a single idea. Movšenson, on the other hand, was fluent in French and entranced by Paris—its museums, its street musicians, and the ferment of its intellectual and artistic life. The Russian Academy replaced the Party as her primary affiliation. In her "Proščal'naja Oda" ("Farewell Ode," 1926), dedicated privately to Erenburg, the poet recalls these years as a heady whirl of "iambs, love and idleness."[19] She later wrote to Pavel Medvedev, "I fell in love with Paris forever. Emigration alienated me from the Party."[20]

WAR AND REVOLUTION: RETURN TO RUSSIA

In 1914, graduation and the outbreak of war put an end to the idyllic student life Movšenson had been leading. When the Germans invaded Lorraine in the autumn of 1914, she joined a group of several dozen doctors, mostly women and last-year male medical students, who served as replacements for those mobilized in the province's defense. She worked for several months at a convent hospital in the city of Nancy, where she tended a constant stream of wounded soldiers. Upon returning to Paris in December 1914, she found work in a newly organized military hospital in Neuilly. Less than a year out of medical school, Movšenson was essentially running the new hospital, with a staff of volunteers from the Association of French Women.

She remained at the hospital until March 1915. A telegram from her parents informed her that all Russian doctors who had trained abroad were being urged to return, and government qualifying exams would be held shortly so that the foreign-trained doctors could receive Russian diplomas and serve on the Russian front. Movšenson acted quickly; having obtained all the necessary documents, she made the dangerous wartime journey back to Russia, crossing the Mediterranean by steamship and traveling by train through Greece, Serbia, Bulgaria, and Romania. Arriving in Petersburg, she found her family mourning her father's death.

The qualifying exams were held in the spring at the university in Jur'ev, now known by its Estonian name, Tartu. After a few months of intense preparation, Movšenson, still in mourning, received her diploma and the title of *lekar'* (physician) in July 1915. She went on to supervise an epidemiological division of the Zemskij Sojuz (Rural District Union) on the Southwestern Front in Galicia, where she remained until April 1917.

It was during the period of her service, while in Kiev, that Movšenson met Lev Davidovič Polonskij, an engineer who became her lover and the father of her son Mixail. Their union, never formalized, ended unhappily when Polonskij was confronted by a woman to whom he was, apparently, already engaged.[21] Polonskaja, as she now called herself, withdrew from the relationship, taking Mixail back to Petrograd. She left him in the care of her mother and brother and returned to the front, where she continued to serve for several months.[22]

On her return from the front, Polonskaja had little time either for poetry or for political activity. The ideals of her youth gave way to the realities of caring for her son and supporting her family. Her father's death had left the family deep in debt, her brother was still a student, and her relatives had fled German-occupied Białystok and were living in the Movšenson apartment. Thus, she was grateful to find work as assistant to a municipal charity doctor on Vasil'jevskij Island and spent most of her time shuttling between her family and her patients. When the Bolshevik Revolution actually occurred, Polonskaja, the former Party activist, was a spectator. As she remarked ruefully to her friend, the sculptor Nadežda Ostrovskaja, in 1917, medical work and motherhood took up all her time: "I am not writing or publishing, I am working as a doctor in the Harbor. . . . It's very difficult with a child, it's impossible to do anything."[23]

By the winter of 1918 to 1919, Polonskaja was writing in her spare moments, for example, on night duty at a military hospital, where, unlike in her apartment, there was a warm room lit by electric lamps. She also regularly attended meetings of the Poets' Union. It was in this period that Polonskaja began writing the civic lyrics, beautiful in their austerity, for which she is best remembered. Her work from this period has little in common with the poems she wrote in Paris. It reflects, in stark and powerful language, the grim realities of the civil war period: cold, hunger, fear, and loss. As Ejxenbaum wrote in his review of her first collection, "Here are poems about our severe, comfortless, terrible life. Here is our Petersburg—'a solid vision of smoke and stone.'"[24]

THE HOUSE OF ARTS AND THE SERAPION BROTHERS

In her memoirs, Polonskaja wrote that she first learned of the Translators' Studio from an advertisement in a streetcar. That very evening she went to the Muruzi House to enroll, choosing Gumilev's poetry class and Šklovskij's class on theory of literature. As she was leaving the building she struck up an acquaintance with Il'ja Gruzdev and Mixail Zoščenko, two of her future classmates. They were also two of her future Serapion "Brothers."

Polonskaja was an active member of the Serapion Brotherhood from the very beginning and one of the first to publish; her poems had appeared in Paris, and her first collection, *Znamen'ja (Omens)*, was published in 1921.[25] Indeed, among the Serapions, she was the oldest and, perhaps, the most experienced *literator*. It was she who invited Zoščenko to take part in a publishing venture, "Erato," which produced not only her *Omens* but also his first published collection of stories.[26] In their correspondence, Erenburg turned to her constantly for help in handling his literary business. If, as Šklovskij has stated, one of the main reasons for the existence of the Serapions was collective support in publishing their work, then Polonskaja's contributions are hardly insignificant.[27]

Polonskaja had a playful, irreverent side which was entirely in keeping with the spirit of the brotherhood. She described herself thus in print: "I was a good student at the gymnasium, but there were three things that I never could learn—not to be late to the first lesson, not to look sullen, and not to speak insolently."[28] She took part in the "children's club" at the House of Arts, where the Serapions and their friends enacted their famous "films," and she composed satirical verses and fairy tales to commemorate the Serapion anniversaries.[29] Satire came easily to Polonskaja. She was known to her contemporaries as a wit,[30] and her archive contains ample evidence of her talent for epigrams and satirical fables.³¹ According to her son, she also published satirical prose in the 1920s under the pseudonym Elizaveta Bertram (incidentally, the same name under which she published her first poems in *Večera*).³²

This literary playfulness reflects, at least in part, Šklovskij's influence on all of the Serapions; he is often credited with instilling the sort of literary "impudence" which marked their boisterous debates and the scandalous autobiographies. Polonskaja appears to have been particularly close in spirit and philosophy to Lunc, who was the main advocate of formalism among the Serapions and one of Šklovskij's most promising pupils.³³ Not long after Lunc published an article, "Detskij smex" ("Children's Laughter"), in *Žizn' iskusstva* (*The Life of Art*),³⁴ Polonskaja published "O detskix avtorax, detskix p'jesax, i detskom teatre" ("On Children's Authors, Children's Plays, and Children's Theater") in the same journal.³⁵ In this article, she expresses views similar to those later expressed by Lunc in his controversial essay "Go West!"³⁶ There are a number of common threads running through these three articles, all of which can be traced to Šklovskij's teachings: the importance of plot in good literature; Russians' tendency to denigrate the Western adventure novel, which has a strong plot tradition, as "light reading" or "children's literature"; the superiority of children's unspoiled, fresh appreciation of art to the jaded judgments of adults; and the idea of art as "play" in which the reader or spectator actively participates: "For children, theater is, above all, play. Play . . . removes them from the realm of the ordinary. For children, the transition to the extraordinary is attainable at any moment. For this, they need neither sets nor props. . . . An adult needs the complete illusion of the 'other.' It is he who needs the costumier, the lighting designer and set decorator, and musical *divertissement.*"³⁷

Known chiefly as a lyric poet, Polonskaja is not often included in the east-west schemes used by critics to characterize the Serapions. Neither was she always an active participant in their literary debates, often preferring to voice her opinions privately.³⁸ In this instance, however, she makes it clear that she is firmly in the camp of the westerners, led by Lunc, whom she called "the most serapionic."³⁹ Polonskaja dedicated a drama to Lunc in 1924. "I have already burned my play," she told him in a letter, "but the dedication remains—I will transfer it to a new play, seven times if need be."⁴⁰ Her archive contains manuscripts of two plays written in the early 1920s, one of which, *Prepirat' ɑ-Sketč v 5 narečijax* (*Prepirat ɑ 23—a Sketch in 5 Dialects*), is dedicated to Lunc.

As S. I. Timina points out, Polonskaja shared with Lunc not only his formalism, but also his fear that Russian culture would "deviate from the general course of European culture due to an apologia of Russian exclusivity, 'Scythianism.' She shared the idea of western orientation, seeing in it another possibility for the liberation and independence of the creative personality, supported by the postulates of western free-thinking (not many of the Serapions chose this path)."[41] Her Western orientation is especially evident in ballads modeled on those of Kipling, which she also translated. She was subsequently to use her considerable command of foreign languages as a translator of German, French, English, and other literatures. Furthermore, in the 1930s she also used translation as a means of veiled political expression, as I shall demonstrate in a later chapter.

As Timina also notes, Polonskaja's poetry from the 1920s perfectly embodies the ideal of artistic freedom articulated by Lunc in his manifesto, "Why We Are the Serapion Brothers." Far from following a prescribed ideological line, Polonskaja directly challenged Bolshevik policies in such provocative poems as "O Revoljucija, o kniga meždu knig" ("O Revolution, O Book among Books"), "Smešalos' vse. Goda vojny" ("All Was Confusion: The Years of War"), and "Tak, značit ty dumaeš'—eto konec!" ("So, Then, You Think It Is Over!"). Throughout the 1920s, Polonskaja continued to "speak insolently" in her poetry, drawing fire from hard-line Marxist critics. Even after the 1920s, the worst excesses of Stalinist repression could not quash Polonskaja's impudence entirely; driven underground, it surfaced wherever possible in veiled allusions and dark ironies, for example, in a narrative poem of 1938, "Portret" ("The Portrait").

According to Evgenij Švarc, one of the "little guests" frequently present at the Serapions' meetings, Polonskaja participated little in the group: "Elizaveta Polonskaja, the only sister among the 'Serapion Brothers,' kept apart from them for many years. She did not publish poetry. She mostly did translations and practiced medicine; she worked in a clinic somewhere."[42] Švarc's portrait of Polonskaja as a marginal Serapion is simply not an accurate representation. It is true that she was most active at the Serapion meetings during the period from 1920 to 1922, but the same could also be said of other members; Ivanov and Nikitin were the first to move to Moscow, missing meetings frequently, and Lunc left Russia in 1923. Although Kaverin reported to Lunc in a letter from December 1923 that Polonskaja had been ill and had not read her work at the Serapion meetings for some time,[43] she published poetry that year in numerous journals and in the Moscow almanac *Nedra* (*Depths*); her second collection, *Pod kamennym doždem* (*Under a Stone Rain*), was also published in 1923.[44] She continued in this vein throughout the 1920s. The period to which Švarc refers, during which Polonskaja published mostly translations and no original poetry, was much later, after the Second World War, at which point the Serapions no longer had any active existence and she had given up practicing medicine. Furthermore, it cannot be said that she ever "withdrew completely from them [the Serapions]," as Švarc maintains.[45] In the 1920s they met from time to time in her apartment (as Švarc himself notes),[46] and their gala fifth anniversary evening was held there.[47] Even toward the end of her life, Polonskaja maintained a warm correspondence with a number of the Serapions and their friends, particularly Kaverin and Čukovskij, as attested by their letters in her archive.

NEW DIRECTIONS IN THE 1920S

With the publication of her second verse collection, *Under a Stone Rain*, in 1923, Polonskaja was well established as a lyric poet. By the time her third collection, *Uprjamyj kalendar'* (*A Stubborn Calendar*), appeared in 1929, there had been a marked change in her poetry. She had begun to move from strictly lyric poetry to ballads, narrative poems, and literary portraits. This change was in keeping with the general trend in Russian literature, which was shifting from an emphasis on poetry to prose and in prose from fiction to the "literature of fact." It was at this time that, under the guidance of Čukovskij, she began to publish in several other genres, including satirical prose, translation, and poetry for children. During the early 1920s she also began writing sketches for several journals, traveling as a correspondent for *Leningradskaja pravda* and other periodicals, and in 1927 she published a collection, *Poezdka na Ural* (*A Trip to the Urals*).[48]

Polonskaja's career as a translator of poetry began with Kipling's "Ballad of East and West," which she heard for the first time at one of Čukovskij's lectures. On her own she translated it and brought it to him. To her surprise and delight, he published it in the first issue of a new journal, *Sovremennyj zapad* (*Contemporary West*).[49] Polonskaja went on to become an extremely prolific and highly regarded translator of poetry, but, as she stresses in "To My Readers," her choice was "always only that which I really liked."[50] It also included material which could convey a political message, as we shall see in subsequent chapters. Polonskaja read widely in Western literatures; among the many authors she translated are Molière, Calderón, Shakespeare, Browning, Ibsen, and Brecht, and in her later years she made a name for herself as a translator of poetry from the languages of the various Soviet republics.

Čukovskij also helped Polonskaja establish herself as a poet for children. She had been writing humorous verses since childhood, and in the course of raising her son she began writing to entertain him. Čukovskij introduced her to the publishing house Raduga (Rainbow), which published her first children's book, *Zajčata* (*Baby Rabbits*), in 1923.[51] She subsequently published twelve more, eight in verse and four in prose. Her poems for children also appeared in various periodicals, such as *Novyj Robinzon* (*New Robinson*), *Vorobej* (*Sparrow*), and *Leninskie iskry* (*Lenin's Sparks*), and one of her children's books, *Časy* (*Clocks*), was set to music by the composer Ljubov' Štrejxer in 1927.[52]

Official critical reception of Polonskaja was always mixed. Certain of her poems on Jewish themes were treated with hostility by some critics, especially *"Ja ne mogu terpet' mladenca Iisusa"* ("I Cannot Abide the Infant Jesus"), which appeared in *Omens*.[53] After *Omens*, the Jewish theme in Polonskaja's published poetry is broached less often and with more restraint; it continues to appear in poems which were never published and which will be discussed further in a subsequent chapter. As mentioned earlier, Polonskaja was the subject of some stinging reviews for her clearly expressed opposition to the New Economic Policy (NEP). Her narrative poem "V petle: Liričeskij fil'm" ("In the Noose—a Lyric Film"),[54] provoked a series of horrified reactions from critics who deplored what they saw as a romanticized portrayal of "hooliganism." "Thus history has already brought us to this," wrote one critic, "that petty-bourgeois literary filth, with the best will in the world, can see nothing in the revolution besides pillaging." The same critic is particularly alarmed by the popularity of "In the Noose" among young people, who, he says, are standing in line for it in libraries and singing the refrain in the streets: "Len'ka Panteleev— / The terror of detectives: / Bracelet on his arm, / Deep blue eyes."[55]

LOVE AND THE WOMAN QUESTION

Another piece from 1924 considered in dubious taste by official critics was "Karmen" ("Carmen"), the heroine of which is an attractive and promiscuous proletarian woman liberated by the Revolution.[56] In the words of another critic, "If we are to declare a holy war on hooliganism, shouldn't we consider Sel'vinskij, Inber, and Polonskaja, who have taken to romanticizing criminals and—prostitutes? We must open fire on the entire front of decadence, beginning with weeping lyrics and ending with the criminal romanticism of sharply honed knives, the spirit of daring, and the incitement of unhealthy instincts."[57] The character Carmen, however, is not actually a prostitute; she is the embodiment of women's sexual freedom, a theme which appears repeatedly in Polonskaja's work in the 1920s. Although in her first two collections the theme of motherhood is prominent, both as sacred duty and as metaphor for the creation of the new society, there is also another prominent theme: traditional marriage and motherhood as a burden imposed on women. Carmen, the child of an illicit union, loves "without bargaining" and is described emphatically as "no mother and no wife." She is last seen marching with her lover (not her husband) against General Kolčak. Polonskaja's treatment of the theme of the independent woman reaches its highest intensity in *A Stubborn Calendar*.

Polonskaja's own life reflects this ideal of independence. She never did marry, although she remained in contact with Lev Polonskij; her travels as a correspondent occasionally took her to Kiev, and her archive contains evidence of a long correspondence between them. After the death of his wife, Anna, he apparently asked her to marry him, but she refused. Two unpublished poems in the archive eloquently express her ambivalence about this complex and painful relationship. In "Конец" ("The End," 1932–34), she writes:

> Враг мой, друг мой, муж мой невенчанный
> Снова, снова, снова про тебя.
> Нет кольца на пальце безымянном,
> Но кольцом свивается судьба.
>
> Сколько писем шло тебе вдогонку
> Годы, годы, годы напролет,
> Теплых как ладонь у нашего ребенка,
> Ледяных, как ненависти лед.
>
> А теперь,—через года и версты
> Вдруг ответ, как черный водоем:—
> Возвращайся, друг, запальчивый и черствый,—
> Дни до смерти вместе проживем.
>
> И внезапной злобою объята
> Я кричу в окно, в пространство: -Нет!
> Господин, низка у вас зарплата,
> Не умею я варить обед!
>
> Не умею утешать и холить,
> И делиться, и давать отчет
> За платок, за воротник соболий,
> Ворковать над мужниным плечом. . . .
>
> My enemy, my friend, my uncrowned husband,
> Again, again, again, I speak of you.
> There is no ring on my finger,
> But our fate is wound into a ring.
>
> How many letters have pursued you,
> Years, years, and years running,
> Warm, like the palm of our child,
> Frigid, like the ice of hatred.
>
> And now—across years and versts,
> Suddenly, an answer, like a black reservoir:—
> Come back, my quick-tempered, callous friend—
> Let us live out our days together until death.
>
> And seized by a sudden malice,
> I cry out the window, into space: No!
> Sir, your salary is low,
> I don't know how to cook your dinners.
>
> I don't know how to comfort and nurture,
> And share, and give an account
> For a scarf or a sable collar,
> Or to bill and coo at my husband's shoulder. . . . [58]

In the beautiful and moving "Povest'" ("Tale," 1937), she addresses the dead wife:

> Не стала я с тобою спорить, Анна,
> Я сына молча увезла на Север.
> Взамен любви - судьба дала мне песни
> И смерть твоя разняла руки, Анна.
> Я не сержусь, ты можешь спать спокойно,
> Ты тоже не была счастливой, Анна.
>
> I did not quarrel with you, Anna,
> In silence I bore my son off to the north.
> In place of love, fate gave me song
> And your death has unbound my hands, Anna.
> I am not angry, you may sleep in peace,
> You also were unhappy, Anna.[59]

Though painful, the loss of Polonskij had forced her to find fulfillment elsewhere than in love. Polonskaja was subsequently to have many relationships, but her work as a writer remains the central fact of her life. She thus became a living example of Kollontai's "New Woman," for whom "attraction, infatuation, passion, love—these are only a part of life. Its true substance consists of that 'holy' which the new woman serves: a social idea, science, a calling, creative work. . . . And her occupation, her goal—for her, for the new woman, it is often more important, more precious, more sacred than all the joys of the heart, all the pleasures of passion."[60] Polonskij's proposal came too late. By this time, her independence had become so accustomed and so important to her that she was not willing to give it up.

As though to avoid submerging her identity in marriage, Polonskaja formed several close emotional attachments to married men. Her continued friendship with Erenburg during the 1920s and 1930s is attested by his letters (her side of the correspondence from this period has been lost). Although there is nothing overtly romantic in these letters, they are extremely warm. He addresses her throughout with the informal *ty* (thou) and often ends with "I kiss you firmly." The tone of the many poems she dedicated to Erenburg throughout her life indicates that she retained deep feelings for him. A new addressee also appears during the 1920s: Mixail Ferberg, the husband of her cousin Sofija, with whom she had an affair. Ferberg is the "thou" of some of Polonskaja's most passionate love poetry from the 1920s and 1930s, particularly her unfinished poema "Plennik" ("The Prisoner"), and her archive contains many of his letters. Given the complexity of these relationships, as well as several others more fleeting, it is not surprising that a generally positive review of the 1935 collection *Goda: Izbrannye stixi* (*Years: Selected Poems*) contains the following statement: "Poems about love occupy a fairly large place in the collection. But these poems are not marked by joy or a sense of the fullness of being. These are gloomy, even feeble poems of parting, last farewells, painful backward glances, and so on."[61] The confident and exuberant eroticism in some of her earlier love poems, such as "B'jet dožd' v lico, i veter brodit p'janyj" ("Rain Lashes My Face, and the Drunken Wind Wanders"),[62] is replaced by resignation to the inevitability of loss and stoic willingness to find happiness not in love, but in the writer's craft. *Years* contains, along with "gloomy poems" about love, the following lines in a poem called "Sčast'je" ("Happiness"):

> Так пусть оно движеньем станет
> Колес, кружащих на осях,
> Пусть долгим изойдет дыханьи,
> Вздохом и выдохом стиха.

> So, let it become the motion
> Of wheels turning on their axles,
> Let it come out in a long breath,
> The inhale and exhale of verse.[63]

THE PROFESSIONAL PERIOD: 1931–41

In "To My Readers," Polonskaja called the period before 1931, when she worked "combining literature with medicine," "nonprofessional" "because I wrote verse only when I was especially moved by something, when the image of a person or an event arose in my imagination so clearly and persistently that I experienced a physical need to free myself from it."[64] In the period of the First Five-Year Plan, amid the growing regimentation and professionalization of writers and the emphasis on literature as "product," such an approach was becoming less and less feasible. In order to remain a part of the Soviet literary scene, the writer had to become a professional in every sense of the word; there was no room for amateurs. Also, as Robert Maguire points out, the professionalization of the writer's craft was intimately connected not only with politics but also with economics; for all but the major figures, becoming a professional writer "meant moving into journalism, where the rates of pay were not high, but where one could turn out more."[65]

In 1931 Polonskaja stopped practicing medicine and became a full-time writer. Aleksandr Rubaškin attributes this move to caution and a shrewd appraisal of the changing position of the writer in Soviet Russia: "People lived in such a confused political atmosphere.... They tried to find some kind of application for their talents.... But, of course, no one had any idea how it would all develop, although Elizaveta Grigor'evna was smarter and more far-sighted than many others, because, first of all, at the beginning of the thirties she stopped practicing medicine. Secondly, she did not generally reveal her revolutionary past."⁶⁶ The fate of so many old Bolsheviks, including her old friends Kirov and Kamenev, revealed the wisdom of Polonskaja's reticence about her political past. Giving up medicine was a statement that, for Polonskaja, literature had become her profession, and she practiced it like a professional. By the end of the 1920s, she had become "literary consultant" to a circle of beginning writers connected with the proletarian women's journal *Rabotnica i krest'janka* (*Worker Woman and Peasant Woman*). She also took part in literary brigades, traveling and recording her observations, and she continued to publish her sketches regularly in *Leningradskaja Pravda, Leningrad, Zvezda,* and *Večernaja Krasnaja Gazeta* (*Evening Red Gazette*). Her second collection of sketches, *Ljudi sovetskix budnej* (*Everyday Soviet People*), appeared in 1934.⁶⁷

As Barbara Heldt points out, the shift from creative writing to journalism was especially common among women writers in the 1920s; Škapskaja, for example, published her last collection of poems in 1925 and was known thereafter for her journalism.⁶⁸ Unlike Škapskaja, however, Polonskaja continued writing and publishing both journalism and poetry. As she wrote in "To My Readers," "I got to know the country and wrote sketches about features of what was new, which I perceived with particular sharpness. And if I could not put it into prose, I wrote verse."⁶⁹ In 1935, Polonskaja published a collection of poetry, *Goda* (*Years*), which was largely retrospective.⁷⁰ The last section, however, contained new pieces, followed by five translations. *Years* was followed in 1937 by *Novye stixi* (*New Poems*).⁷¹

Aside from journalism and poetry, Polonskaja was also active in the musical and theatrical life of Leningrad in the 1930s. Her translation from Molière, "Sumasbrod, ili vse nevpopad" ("The Madcap, or, Everything Out of Place"), appeared in 1935,⁷² and her translations of two Offenbach librettos, *Doč' Tambur-mažora* (*The Drum-Major's Daughter*, 1936) and *Žustina Favar* (1940), were commissioned and performed by the Musical Comedy Theater.⁷³ She also translated Shakespeare's *Measure for Measure* in 1935, but that play did not fare as well; it was held up in 1936 due to "some sort of internal complications" at Gosdrama, the state committee on drama.⁷⁴ The play became the object of a lawsuit against the Alexandrinskij Theater and was eventually staged by the Novyj Theater in 1937.⁷⁵

Many of Polonskaja's lyrics were set to music during this period. For example, the composer Ljubov' Štrejxer, who had earlier composed a "children's opera" based on Polonskaja's text *Clocks,* collaborated with her on *Uzbekskaja simfonija* (*An Uzbek Symphony*), for which Polonskaja wrote texts.⁷⁶ Štrejxer had also set to music the poem "Ottorvan ot ruk moix" ("Torn from My Arms"), which appears as part of the cycle "Ešče ljubov'" ("More Love") in *A Stubborn Calendar,* and it was performed in concert programs as a romance.⁷⁷ Among the many other songs for which Polonskaja provided texts was "Djadja El'ja" ("Uncle El'ja"), a translation of a

Yiddish folk song, "Der Rebbe Elimelech," which was recorded by the jazz singer Leonid Utesov in 1939.[78]

"REMAIN YOURSELF . . ."

With the growth of the various literary organizations and the need for ever greater conformity, the writer's career became more and more a public matter. It was not enough simply to produce literary work in keeping with the Party line; one had to be a conspicuous participant in the process of developing a collective attitude toward art and its function in society. Thus Polonskaja, who had chided Šaginjan in 1926, calling her "you, who have danced a *pas de quatre* with Averbax,"[79] herself became a member of the Leningrad Association of Proletarian Writers (LAPP) in 1931.

Polonskaja had never been a solitary writer; from the very beginning, literary friendships and circles were vital to her development, especially the studios at World Literature and the House of Arts, of which she wrote: "Here I found a literary milieu—which is necessary for the beginning of any literary work."[80] The studios, however, were a setting in which young writers were allowed to be original, even shocking, and to develop their own voices.

The originality and irreverence which made Polonskaja a cherished member of the Serapions was not always appreciated in more formal settings, such as the Poets' Union. Having been accepted as a candidate for membership, she made her debut by reading "I Cannot Abide the Infant Jesus," which was greeted by a stunned silence; Gumilev, her teacher at the studio, very pointedly stood up and left the room.[81] Despite this inauspicious beginning, however, Polonskaja did go on to become a member, and by 1924 her name appears on reports of the admissions committee.[82] In one memoir, she wrote with pride that she had been a member of a literary organization since the very beginning of Soviet literary organizations: "from the formation of the All-Russian Poets' Union."[83] Nevertheless, the Poets' Union was an organization whose criteria for selection were based on literary quality; neither class origin nor precise shadings of political ideology played any role, although a stated prerequisite for admission was "the author's living connection with questions of the revolutionary present (*sovremennost'*)."[84] The Writers' Union was another matter. As mentioned in the introduction, Ivanov's public recantation at the First Congress of Soviet Writers in 1934 illustrates the extent to which the former Serapions were required to distance themselves in the 1930s from their former stand against tendentiousness in art.

Polonskaja's private attitude toward the development of the literary bureaucracy may be inferred from various comments in her correspondence. In a 1931 letter to Šaginjan, she remarked:

Serapion Sister

> Marietta. I share your repulsion toward writers. They are parasites in the hair of the epoch. With a good shaking they fall out, but then everything quiets down and they multiply.
> They are time-servers who take on the color of the epoch. There are people who believe that life without parasites is impossible—they're snobs.
> Unfortunately, there are even more snobs than there are parasites.[85]

Yet her contempt was apparently reserved for those who used the system cynically for personal gain, not for those who sincerely believed they were serving the state and literature. As she wrote to Škapskaja in February 1941: "I love union workers, I've loved them from my youth. I am not joking. There are many good, selfless people among them. They are not bewitched by head-spinning glory, indeed, you won't find it among their kind. . . . And even the driest of them, if you know how to approach him, turns out to be much loftier than the 'juiciest' literary figures."[86]

Perhaps the most telling statement to be found in Polonskaja's letters is the following, written to Šaginjan at the end of 1938, the culmination of the purges, the year in which, among many others, one of her dearest friends, the writer David Vygodskij, was arrested. Her lover, Mixail Ferberg, had been arrested the year before. She begins with an allegory concerning "iguanodons," a species of "huge herbivores, not without beauty in their native landscape." Among these creatures are those of a special category, "degenerates," who shock their fellows by their originality. The species is eventually crowded out by new, carnivorous creatures, "dogs, or something":

> The "original" iguanodons, because of their originality, saw themselves in the camp of the dogs, and even "barked up" to them. . . . The dogs, as a young class, listened to the original iguanodons, though they also tore hunks of filet from the sides of their relatives. They [the dogs] were also flattered to have such a weight of argument on their side.

Although the "degenerate" iguanodons try to adapt, they are simply unable; "their teeth were of a different type and their digestion incompatible with that of the dogs." The letter ends on the following note of resignation:

> My angel, I have long since admitted to myself that I am a degenerate, and this buoys me up a bit in my own existence. Will there be sanctuaries judiciously created for iguanodons? I hardly think so. Must an iguanodon feel like a split personality? It must. But somewhere in the pastures of the old tertiary or quaternary epoch, a precious herb has been preserved—irony. Once having nibbled it, the iguanodon must, by the laws of chemistry, feel his digestion settling. . . .
> What should be the slogan of the healed iguanodon? "Remain yourself," "Don't try to bark and believe quietly in God." There is nothing on earth stronger than that faith.[87]

Polonskaja's Life

Polonskaja's own attempts to remain herself throughout the years of the Five-Year Plans and the purges are a study in creative adaptation. Her work with *Rabotnica i krest'janka,* for example, was a way of finding a niche for herself in the new literary order while at the same time continuing to pursue a subject which was close to her heart: the "woman question." As literary consultant, she advised and nurtured budding proletarian women writers; she also wrote for the journal. As she wrote in her memoirs, "The following topics were close to my heart: the establishment and strengthening of women's roles in the productive and social spheres of society, the appearance of offshoots of the new in family relations and daily life, women's friendship, and the international solidarity of women. And I wrote about these things."[88] Much of her poetry and many of her sketches from the 1930s contain images and examples of "the New Soviet Woman." An entire section of *Everyday Soviet People,* "Kak oni rosli" ("How They Grew") consists of sketches about women liberated by the Revolution from domestic slavery. *New Poems* contains a section called "Portraits," which consists of five poetic portraits of women, among them two poems about Muslim women Communists, "Sestra s vostoka" ("Sister from the East") and "Jangi Kišlak," as well as "Sokolenok" ("The Falcon Chick"), dedicated to the memory of the young parachutist Nata Babuškina.

The growth of fascism in Spain and Germany also provided Polonskaja with ample material which was both politically correct and about which she could write with sincerity. Along with a handful of other Leningrad writers, she began learning Spanish in December 1936, not long after the outbreak of the Spanish Civil War. She subsequently translated a number of Spanish authors; "Spain," she writes in a memoir, "was, at that time, an antifascist theme."[89] Aside from translating such classics as Calderón, however, Polonskaja also used her Spanish to take part in meetings and presentations with visiting Spanish intellectuals.[90] Her "Pesnja o Line Odene" ("Song about Lina Odena"), about the heroic death of a Spanish Communist, was written in 1938, and she also reviewed *Govorit Ispanija (This Is Spain Speaking),* a translated collection of writings on the war, in *Literaturnoe obozrenie (Literary Review).*[91] Furthermore, the Spanish Civil War was also an occasion for demonstrations of the aforementioned "international solidarity of women": in *Literaturnaja gazeta (Literary Gazette)* on September 26, 1936, a notice appears addressed to "the women of Spain," stating that the signers are sending one thousand rubles, taken from their literary honoraria, as a contribution to the organization of a children's feeding station in Madrid. Of the eight signers, Elizaveta Polonskaja's name appears first. Her fluency in German also made her a natural link with German antifascist writers, with whom she corresponded and whose work she translated, for example, Erich Weinert and Bertolt Brecht.

Irreverent as Polonskaja was toward the Stalinist literary apparatus, she was, naturally, circumspect in her comments regarding the leader himself. In her memoir on Tynjanov, many years later, she wrote (somewhat disingenuously): "Understanding little about politics, I believed blindly in Stalin, and in his fairness and infallibility."[92] The poem "Sadovnik" ("The Gardener"), which appeared in *Literaturnyj Leningrad* in 1936 and also in *New Poems*, portrays him as a wise teacher and defender of the Soviet people.[93] However, Polonskaja distances herself, if only slightly, by attributing this vision of Stalin to folk legend:

> Но достаточно разве зерно посадить, чтобы плод появился?
> И встает из народных глубин молодая легенда—
> Молодая и древняя сказка о садовнике мудром...
>
> ... Но враги,—повествует легенда,—замышляли другое,
> Притаились они в ожиданьи удобного часа.
>
> But is it really enough just to plant the seed for the fruit to appear?
> And from the depths of the people a young legend arises—
> A young and ancient tale of a wise gardener...
>
> But enemies—the legend goes—have thought up something else,
> They have hidden, waiting for a convenient time.[94]

Allegorical portrayal of Russia as a garden tended by the wise hand of an all-powerful gardener gives way to folk-tinged epic portrayal of heroic events, written in a shifting but predominantly ternary meter. The narrative voice merges with that of the people, which leaves the poem open to interpretation and the poet herself obscured from view in the general chorus.

Letters and notes reveal that "The Gardener" was a difficult poem for Polonskaja to write. She confided her nervousness about its reception to Šaginjan in a letter from October 1936: "I don't know how it will sound—it was very difficult to find the right tone; I was afraid of slipping into a false epic, but without epos I could not approach such a theme.... I read it to Čumandrin and Libedinskij and reworked it completely on their advice, but I am still not sure that it's come out right. If only I weren't such a fool!"[95] Polonskaja's son confirms that, despite their close friendship, she and Šaginjan often differed politically, Šaginjan being a "fervent Stalinist"; however, both women being "fairly smart and experienced," there is no written evidence to corroborate this assertion.[96] If "The Gardener" was an attempt to meet the political demands of the literary apparatus, it must be understood in the context of its time and as, perhaps, an attempt at deflecting attention away from many doubtful and potentially dangerous aspects of Polonskaja's past: her bourgeois Jewish origins, her foreign ties, her association with certain of the old Bolsheviks, membership in the Serapions, and her anti-NEP poetry. If so, it appears to have helped. Polonskaja and her family escaped the purges shaken but essentially unharmed.

Polonskaja's Life

Whatever "blind faith" she may have had in Stalin, however, did not escape the purges unscathed. Her private misgivings are attested by a draft, in her archive, of a poem which appeared in her last collection, *Izbrannoe* (*Selected Poems,* 1966). "Byvaet mat' nespravedliva" ("At Times a Mother Can Be Unjust") is dated 1957 in its published form. This poem about the tortured but indissoluble bond between mother and child, despite whatever wounds she may inflict, cannot help but lend itself to political interpretation, especially given the clear linkage of the theme of motherhood with that of the birth of the new society in Polonskaja's early poetry. In 1966, long after Stalin's death and the Twentieth Party Congress, such a poem could appear in print. An early draft, however, appears in one of Polonskaja's notebooks from 1938, dedicated to the exiled Mixail Ferberg. It contains a fifth stanza, which is missing from the printed version:

> Пред далью ледяной могилы
> Склоняема притворно-ль иль скорбя
> Отчизна, я бы не простила
> Ни за него, ни за себя.

> Before the expanse of an icy grave,
> Grieving or feigning a bow,
> Fatherland, I would not forgive you,
> Neither on his nor on my own behalf.[97]

THE 1940S: WAR AND EVACUATION

Polonskaja's letters to Marija Škapskaja reveal that, as the 1930s drew to a close, she was suffering from a worrisome heart condition, which interfered with her work and contributed to recurring bouts of despair. In August 1940, she wrote to her friend, "Write to me about yourself, dear. You write such good letters, they strengthen my will to live. And it has been failing somehow."[98] At about the same time, Polonskaja's sixth volume of poetry, *Vremena mužestva* (*Times of Courage*),[99] appeared. Although she was dissatisfied with the editorial changes, Polonskaja seems to have revived somewhat by the following March, when she wrote, again to Škapskaja:

> I am very glad that you liked my little book. What is surprising is that I am writing verse. It seems to me that this is my real calling, and only in vain did I exchange it for various "lentils and corn in tomato sauce" [the moral equivalent of the biblical "mess of pottage"]. That is why my senses have somehow begun to rust, which they must not do. For rust renders up everything completely.
> At one time I had the feeling that this little book would be my last; it has passed, and I want to write many more. If I could just live and feel healthy. . . .[100]

In August 1941, not long after the war began, Polonskaja, still ill, was obliged to leave Leningrad with her family for the relative safety of the

Urals, and it was almost three years before she was able to return. The decision to join the evacuation was a difficult one, and it had to be made literally overnight. Polonskaja's brother Aleksandr, a theater critic, was at that time teaching in a choreographic institute closely associated with the Mariinskij Theater. The entire student body, about three hundred children, along with their teachers and a few mothers, were evacuated to Polazna, a small town on the river Kama, not far from Molotov, and the school was reestablished there. Fearing that she would not be able to move her ailing mother herself if the need should arise later, Polonskaja accepted the position of school doctor, and thus the entire family (except for her son, Mixail, who was already in the army) set out with the students on August 19, 1941. Their journey was interrupted a week later when Charlotta Il'inična fell ill with dysentery and had to be taken off the train. The family found lodging in a peasant hut and, despite the primitive conditions, she managed to recover sufficiently to continue on to Polazna by November.

The life Polonskaja describes in her letters from this period is one of extreme hardship. Not only were the living conditions in Polazna primitive but also she was forced to resist local authorities who, on more than one occasion, tried to transfer her to remote hospitals in other places, which would have meant separation from her mother and brother. The nadir of this period was November 1942, when the ballet school moved yet again and she found herself in Molotov sharing a dormitory cot with her mother, which they were in danger of losing. Unable to secure any lodging in Molotov, she sent desperate telegrams to Škapskaja, Fadeev, and Erenburg, and between them they were able to intervene with local authorities to keep the two women from being turned out into the street.[101] Amid all these worries, Mixail was never far from her thoughts, particularly when she learned that he had been wounded in 1941.

Aside from keeping body and soul (and her family) together, Polonskaja also struggled to remain active as a writer. Isolated from the centers of Russian literary life, she was forced to rely heavily on friends in Moscow to pass on her texts to possible publishers, and in some cases to radio stations for broadcast. Many other writers, including Kaverin, Tynjanov, and Slonimskij, were also evacuated to Molotov, and on her periodic trips into the city she was able to pass on letters to friends who traveled back and forth to Moscow.

Polonskaja managed to keep her hand in, publishing poetry in the Perm' newspaper *Zvezda*, in the journal *Prikam'je* (*By the Kama*), and also in *Rabotnica*.[102] She continued writing sketches for various collections and journals and composing song lyrics, one of which was set to music by the composer Fardi for a performance by the ballet school in Molotov. She also negotiated a contract with the publishing house Molotovgiz for a collection of poetry, *Kamskaja tetrad'* (*A Kama Notebook*), which eventually appeared in 1945.[103]

As her literary activity increased, Polonskaja began experiencing more and more conflict between her obligations as a doctor and her calling as a writer. In July 1942 she wrote to Škapskaja:

> I wasted eighteen days in Molotov and at last got permission not to work in the hospital. At times it seemed to me that I was behaving disgracefully by refusing such work, but I did it all the same. Now I am back in Polazna and have taken up my literary specialty. After all, I have more experience in and better understanding of literary work than surgical. Of course, if it's really necessary, I'll go to the hospital, but then goodbye, book!
>
> My dear, be my conscience and tell me if I did the right thing. For it's still not too late, and I could still change everything. I don't know what I should do.[104]

Despite these struggles, she did remain with the ballet school as both a doctor and a teacher of anatomy. Upon returning to Leningrad in 1944, however, she ceased medical work entirely and became, once again, a full-time professional writer.

THE POSTWAR PERIOD

After returning home, Polonskaja was caught up in the task of rebuilding the city, which began almost as soon as the siege was lifted in January 1944. Like most people, she was required to do a certain amount of physical labor, but she also contributed inspirational verse for periodicals and propaganda posters. In September 1944 she wrote to Škapskaja with her characteristic irony:

> I have worked as both a plasterer and a poet. My posters flaunt themselves here and there around Leningrad. The texts are of this sort:
>
> > Друзья,
> >   С Урала
> >   или
> >   с Алтая,
> > Откуда б ни вернулись вы
> > Закон -
> >   На берегах Невы
> >   Работать рук не покладая.
>
> > Friends,
> >   From the Urals
> >   or
> >   From Altaj,
> > From wherever you have returned
> >   It's the law—
> >   On the banks of the Neva
> >   You must work indefatigably.[105]

The joy of returning home and of the victory over Germany were soon overshadowed for Polonskaja by personal loss and a serious professional setback. In December 1945, Charlotta Il'inična Movšenson suffered a stroke, and on January 13, 1946, she died. On the day of the funeral, Polonskaja's adopted grandson, Igor', was hospitalized with scarlet fever.[106] Igor' recovered and returned home some six weeks later, but the loss of her mother was a devastating blow for Polonskaja. Their relationship had always been remarkably close. Charlotta Il'inična had encouraged the growth of her daughter's social conscience and exposed her to Russian poetry at an early age, and despite debilitating illness, she had been the center around which the family revolved, especially during their evacuation. Polonskaja's memoirs begin with a long, loving portrait of her mother's childhood and youth, which ends with her decline into childlike helplessness in her old age. Perhaps most moving, however, are the many unpublished poems, one of which, written in April 1946, begins, "Not for any lover on earth / Could I ever leave you."[107]

In the professional sphere as well, the immediate postwar years were to prove extremely difficult for Polonskaja. Her major project was *Gorod* (*The City*), a novel about the rebuilding of Leningrad.[108] It was an enormous undertaking, on a much larger scale than anything she had previously attempted. It was never published, and Polonskaja's struggles with the publisher, Sovetskij pisatel', took an ugly turn when, having missed her deadline, she was forced to return an advance she had already spent. According to M. L. Polonskij, debt collectors actually came to the apartment to assess the family's possessions.[109] Polonskaja's major difficulty in completing this manuscript, aside from its ambitious scope, was apparently related to the political sensitivity of her topic and her predilection for portraying actual and recognizable individuals, in particular the main character, the architect who headed the reconstruction project.[110] When the prototype for this character was arrested, it became obvious that substantial revisions would be required. According to Brett-Harrison, it is not clear whether the manuscript was already finished or whether Sovetskij pisatel' returned it to Polonskaja unfinished.[111] At any rate, it was not deemed acceptable, and she was ordered to repay the advance. She managed to do so with the help of the *Litfond*, which agreed to settle the debt in return for literary work.[112] This disastrous sequence of events took place in 1949. Despite attempts to revive the project in 1950 with the help of Šaginjan, who attempted to persuade the publisher to reconsider supporting it, *The City* remained unfinished.[113] Brett-Harrison suggests that Polonskaja may have felt it prudent to let this controversial work die, especially with the memory of the 1946 attacks on Zoščenko and Axmatova still relatively fresh.

A more successful project during this period was *Na svoix plečax* (*On Their Own Shoulders*), a collection of short prose pieces about the heroism

Polonskaja's Life

of the young Red Cross nurses in Leningrad during the war, which appeared in two editions, with some minor differences in content, in 1948. The Moscow edition, sponsored by the Executive Committee of the Union of Societies of the Soviet Red Cross and Red Crescent, is handsomely illustrated and is subtitled *Očerki* (*Sketches*); the Leningrad version, published by the Leningrad Periodical and Book Publishing House, is subtitled *Rasskazy* (*Short Stories*). The question of genre raised by this difference in subtitles indicates that the collection marks a transition in Polonskaja's published prose from journalism to fiction, the next stage of which was to have been her novel. *On Their Own Shoulders* was favorably reviewed by R. Fedorov: "E. Polonskaja's book recounts truthfully one of the most stirring pages of the epic of Leningrad—the part played during the war by our city's girls. Most of the stories successfully re-create the events of recent years, clearly portraying typical people, their noble feelings and actions. The reader cannot help feeling pride in heroic Soviet youth who, together with the older generation, courageously took upon their own shoulders the heavy burden of war."[114]

Polonskaja continued working in journalism; however, from 1950 until the end of her life, she appears to have published her sketches almost exclusively in one journal, *Gudok* (*Train Whistle*). She was also extremely active as a translator during the postwar period. Her projects included Marlowe's "Tamburlaine the Great"; Longfellow's "The Building of the Ship," "The Lighthouse," and "Seaweed"; various poems by Verhaeren and the Armenian poet Tsaturjan; and works of various Latvian, Estonian, and Bulgarian poets, to name only a few. She was heavily involved with the Translators' Section of the Leningrad Writers' Union and, in fact, headed it for a few years until she was unceremoniously removed from that position.[115]

LATE POETRY

According to M. L. Polonskij, Polonskaja's primary affiliation with the Translators' Section cost her the support of other poets during the postwar period and thus made it especially difficult for her to publish her own poetry: "I think she wanted to [publish a collection], but somehow her collections didn't fare well after the war, especially since she left the Poetry Section [of the Writers' Union] and began to work on translations and in the Translators' Section. For some reason she had little support from the poets, although she still had friends."[116] Her private archive contains ample evidence that Polonskaja was extremely prolific after the war, but after the appearance of *A Kama Notebook* in 1945, fifteen years passed before she was able to publish another collection of her own poetry, *Stixotvorenija i poema* (*Poems and a Narrative Poem*).[117] *Izbrannoe* (*Selected Poems*), her last collection, followed in 1966. Both of these are mostly retrospective; some new poetry is included along with a sampling of previously published work.

Of all the previously unpublished poems in these last two collections, only a handful were actually written after 1960. *Poems and a Narrative Poem* contains nothing written later than 1958, and *Selected Poems* contains only seven poems dating from the 1960s. Almost all of the current poetry published by Polonskaja during the 1960s appeared in journals and almanacs. She published in the almanacs *Den' poeta* (*Day of the Poet*) and *Priboj* (*Surf*) between 1956 and 1959, and beginning in 1961, she published in *Den' poezii* (*Day of Poetry*) every year through 1967. Illness forced Polonskaja to cease writing in 1967, and she died on January 11, 1969.

Polonskaja's poetry from this last period has been celebrated by a number of her critics as a return of her powers after a definite weakening during the 1930s and 1940s.[118] As A. Galuškin points out, the lyric hero of this late poetry is closer to that of her earliest lyrics than to anything in between. Rather than the exalted patriotism of the war years, we find here a return to the thoughtful, meditative, philosophical poetry of Polonskaja's youth, with the broadened perspective of age. She did not become an apolitical poet, but her politics were no longer a matter of national or party loyalties. "Rodina" (homeland) became humanity. There is even an unpublished poem in her archive, "Ubili prezidenta" ("They Killed a President," 1963), in which she laments the murder of John F. Kennedy; as she wrote to Erenburg, "Kennedy's death distressed me very much. You see how easily Dame History moves from farce to tragedy."[119] In "Madonna Rembrandta" ("Rembrandt's Madonna," 1965), a seventeenth-century Dutch painting inspires somewhat gloomy reflections on the fate of a twentieth-century child in the wake of war and totalitarianism. Other dark meditations on history include the previously mentioned "At Times a Mother Can Be Unjust," which, although published in truncated form, is still a powerful statement on the emotional torments of the abused children of the "Motherland."[120]

THE POET AS ORPHEUS

Major themes in Polonskaja's late poetry include reflections on aging, illness, and death; the future as embodied in younger generations; and nature. She also wrote autobiographical reminiscences and memorials to lost friends and relatives, most importantly her brother, Aleksandr, who died in 1965. She felt his loss deeply. He was, by all accounts, an extraordinarily gifted and erudite man who often collaborated with his sister on translations. Like her, he never married, and the two siblings remained in the family's apartment on Zagorodnyj Prospekt to the end of their lives, vacationing together every summer in Estonia during the last two decades. Mixail L'vovič Polonskij recalls his parental generation as a triumvirate consisting of his mother, his uncle, and his nurse, Anastasja Petrovna, a peasant woman from Tula who came to work for the family some time in the 1920s and remained as a family member for the rest of her life. She, too, is affectionately portrayed in a poem, "Golubka naša" ("Our Darling"), which appeared in *Zvezda* in 1963.

Many of the people Polonskaja remembered in her verse were not simply loved ones but also fellow artists, a reflection of her position that it is the duty of the artist to preserve and pass on both personal and cultural memory. A. Anatol'jev, in his review of *Selected Poems*, points out one of the guiding principles expressed in Polonskaja's poetry as a whole: "One must live on. Survive the battle. Why? To continue life. To help one's home or, in a larger sense, one's homeland. The voice of a mother can be heard in this call to 'remain among the living.' We must, so that the species survives, the house is not depopulated, so that our native speech does not die out."[121] If the younger Polonskaja's emphasis was on physical survival, on carrying on the life of one's family, nation, and ultimately species, her final preoccupation is with metaphysical survival. Polonskaja saw herself and her entire generation as witnesses and, as such, she felt obliged to testify to what she had seen during her lifetime. "Vospominanija" ("Memories"), written in 1958 and published in both of Polonskaja's last collections, eloquently expresses the poet's sense of duty to the forgotten past:

> Воспоминанья давных лет,
> Скажите, что мне делать с вами?
> Я слышу: «Нас на свете нет.
> Наш мир—твоя скупая память.
>
> Откажешься, и мы уйдем
> Куда-нибудь навек, за угол,
> А позовешь, и мы живем,
> Покуда ты жива, подруга.
>
> Захочешь, мы в небытие,
> Как все прекрасное на свете,
> Уйдем, и дело не твое,
> И ты за это не в ответе.
>
> Но если любишь ты смелей,
> Превозмогая сон покоя,
> Из царства мертвых, как Орфей,
> Ты уведешь нас за собою».

> Memories of bygone years,
> Tell me, what shall I do with you?
> I hear: "We are no longer on earth.
> Our world is your meager memory.
>
> Refuse us, and we will go
> Somewhere forever, out of sight,
> But call us, and we live
> As long as you are alive, our friend.

> If you wish it, we will go into oblivion,
> Like everything beautiful on earth,
> And it is no affair of yours,
> And you are not to blame.
>
> But if you love more bravely,
> Overcoming the dream of peace,
> From the kingdom of the dead,
> Like Orpheus, you shall lead us."[122]

This sense of duty led Polonskaja to devote her last years to resurrecting shades of the past, not only in verse, but also in prose.

Letters dating as far back as the 1930s reveal both a sense of responsibility to record her experiences in prose and understandable ambivalence about doing so. In 1939, Polonskaja wrote to Škapskaja, "Someday I would really like to write a tale about our youth, to write an open, straightforward account. We have seen so much, that I doubt any other generation can compare with us. It's true that now is not yet the time to write it, but I am afraid of forgetting. More and more, one forgets the details."[123] This mix of desire and fear remains long after the death of Stalin. She began her memoir of her mother before the latter's death, but it was only after Erenburg had begun publishing his memoirs in *Novyj mir* in 1961 that she overcame her reluctance and began writing memoirs in earnest. As she admitted in a letter to Erenburg in September 1960, "I admit, when I heard that you were writing about the past I was secretly uneasy. . . . You know, I am afraid of rough hands, of curious glances. You can write openly about what is invented, but never about what is experienced, or else you must write it in a sonnet. That form will contain it."[124]

Polonskaja's first published memoirs were enormously successful. Her 1963 piece on Zoščenko in particular was greeted with expressions of gratitude from the other Serapions; one friend of the Serapions, Zoja Nikitina, wrote: "In your memoir I felt his nature, so pure, a bit naive and unusually talented, but mainly, as he was in life. And the part about the 'Reds' is very good in your article on Fedin. It seems to me also that you are the first to succeed in writing, if only in brief, 'the truth about the Serapions.' Everyone else always takes such an 'official' approach to this question."[125] Polonskaja published several more memoirs over the following three years, which included reminiscences of Fedin, Tixonov, Ivanov, Čukovskij, Forš, Šklovskij, Reisner, Maršak, Gumilev, Čikovani, and various other writers. These memoirs, particularly the piece on Zoščenko, have been cited as influential both by Polonskaja's contemporaries (for example, Čukovskij, who wrote, "You have revived in my memory 'those mythic years'—'the House of Arts,' 'the House of Writers,' 'the Studio.' Thank you, dear friend.")[126] and a younger generation of literary scholars, most notably Marietta Čudakova, whose *Poetika Mixaila Zoščenko* (*Mixail Zoščenko's Poetics*) was inspired by Polonskaja's "My Acquaintance with Mixail Zoščenko."[127]

The published pieces, however, represent a small portion of Polonskaja's actual output. At her death, she left behind a vast body of unpublished memoir material which she had hoped to publish as a collection, *Vstreči* (*Meetings*). It consists of both autobiographical chapters and portraits of various literary figures. The unpublished autobiographical chapters begin with her parents and cover her childhood and gymnasium days in Łodz and her family's flight from pogroms to Berlin. Polonskaja's memoir of her early experiences in the Bolshevik underground in St. Petersburg was published in Zvezda in 1965.[128] One short piece on her life as an émigré student in Paris was published posthumously in *Neva*;[129] however, her archive contains much more material on this period. The outbreak of war, Polonskaja's medical service in France, and her return to Russia are described in the unpublished material, as are the years of the civil war in Petrograd. Polonskaja was able to publish a significant amount of material on the early 1920s, in particular concerning the Serapion Brothers and the House of Arts, as mentioned before, and a few more pieces from the archive have been published since her death. There is, however, a great deal of interesting unpublished material in her archive on Esenin, Lunc, Lozinskij, Nikitin, Šaginjan, Škapskaja, David and Emma Vygodskij, and Čerubina de Gabriak.

Had Polonskaja lived to finish and publish *Meetings*, there is no question that it would have been a valued contribution to the memoir literature of the 1960s. Her friends and colleagues, among them Čukovskij, Erenburg, Kaverin, Šklovskij, and Šaginjan, praised and encouraged her, and even after her death, various pieces reappeared several times in collections of reminiscences on certain writers. However, the manuscript is fragmented and in need of extensive editing. Also, Polonskaja was first and foremost a poet, and there was much she felt she could not express in prose. As valuable as the memoirs are in forming an understanding of Polonskaja and the milieu in which she developed, the fact that they are written in prose and that she hoped to publish them could not fail to inhibit her. Her reluctance to discuss Lunc has been noted earlier. As she wrote to Erenburg in 1966, although her friends were encouraging her to publish *Meetings*, "the censor's muse stands guard, and I never forget about her."[130]

Thus it is Polonskaja's poetry which remains the central document of her life and thought, and it is to her poetry that I devote the body of this book. Thanks to the generous cooperation of the late Mixail Polonskij and other members of his family, I have been able to draw upon the entire range of Polonskaja's verse, both published and unpublished.

Chapter Two

Early Verse

POLONSKAJA'S CONCEPTION of the poet's role evolved from a nineteenth-century vision of inspired social leadership to that of the poet as inspired singer and, finally, as chronicler, interpreter, and preserver of historical truth and cultural memory. This idea, particularly as expressed in her poetry of the early 1920s, clearly reflects the influence of Mandel'štam and Axmatova, for whom the task of the poet in history became "the reconstruction of history under conditions in which 'the share value of the personality in history is falling' (*The End of the Novel*). . . . *Memory, reminiscence,* not just as something in a person which allows us to correlate him with history, but also as a deeply *moral* principle, opposing unconsciousness, oblivion, and chaos as the basis for art, faith, and loyalty. . . . The preservation of memory is a pledge of the continuity of life; it becomes an affirmation of the reality of existence. . . . By contrast, oblivion is a betrayal of life, its interruption and its destruction . . . to destroy memory means to destroy life. After this, one must learn to live again."[1]

The themes of survival and continuity are central in Polonskaja's verse, in both the physical and the metaphysical sense. As she came to realize with increasing certainty in the 1920s, however, survival in the new state would require ingenuity, caution, and frequent compromises. Thus, her literary biography consists not only of a progression of themes, genres, and stylistic choices, but also of tricky maneuvering between the demands of her personal muse and those of an increasingly regimented and punitive literary apparatus. As she wrote in "Vedu opasnuju igru" ("I Am Playing a Dangerous Game," 1923):

> Так на канате танцовщик,-
> На тонкой ниточке мечтаний,—
> Скользить уверенно привык
> Под марш и плеск рукоплесканий.
>
> Но есть закон для ремесла
> И есть судьба у лицедея:
> Мой друг, такого то числа
> Сломаю непременно шею.

Early Verse

> Thus, a dancer on a rope,—
> On a slender thread of dreams,—
> Is used to gliding deftly
> To a march and the splash of applause.
>
> But there is a law to the craft,
> And a fate for one who dissembles:
> My friend, someday
> I will certainly break my neck.[2]

By the 1930s Polonskaja, like many others, had adapted herself to the role of professional Soviet writer, which demanded orthodox treatment of an approved range of subject matter. She had become, at least publicly, a member of the "tribe of writers" described with such scorn by Mandel'štam in his *Četvertaja proza* (*Fourth Prose*). Yet, paradoxically, even in the early 1920s, when she was at her most scandalous, shocking critics with blasphemy and a disreputable assortment of underworld heroes, she began to understand where some of the political dangers lay and to use both self-censorship and camouflage, whereas in the 1930s she managed to weave some strikingly subversive threads into outwardly orthodox poetry. The resulting impression is of a constant tension between her native caution and a wayward, rebellious impulse which led her to write, if not always to publish, poetry of a stubbornly irreverent and individualistic cast.

Polonskaja's native defiance is often expressed in her choice of a controversial theme or point of view, such as anti-Semitism and Russian-Jewish cultural identity, or criticism of Bolshevik policies. For example, in the early 1920s, emboldened by the spirit of radical break with tradition, she actually achieved a certain notoriety for her "Jewish" poems, which were not simply affirmations of her own identity but attacks on Christianity. Like her satire, however, the more audacious features of her serious poetry were gradually driven underground, confined to inside references and subtle subterfuges which escaped the censors but not her close associates. The suppression of the Jewish theme in Polonskaja's poetry is a particularly poignant example, since it represents a hope for greater freedom which was raised in 1917 and subsequently dashed by the continued existence of anti-Semitism. Similarly, as a Communist, an intellectual, and an independent-minded woman, Polonskaja was initially heartened and then bitterly disillusioned by the Bolshevik Revolution. In the development of her poetry and her publication history we can trace an increasing awareness of her decreasing freedom, which reached its culmination in the 1940s.

Polonskaja's subsequent reprintings of her early poetry—by means of both selection and editing, often involving changed dates—substantially altered the tone of many poems and thus fostered an illusion of conformity among readers not familiar with the original versions. Even in her last two collections, published in the post-Stalinist period, changes made in the 1930s were retained, and new ones introduced, which obscured her earlier boldness. Thus, a chronological examination of her poetry, with close attention to publication history and textological details, is essential to a balanced picture of her work.

STUDENT YEARS: THE PARISIAN PERIOD (1908–14)

Very little poetry from Polonskaja's student years has survived. As attested in her memoirs, as well as in those of Erenburg and Kireeva, she wrote satirical pieces, which appeared in the two journals she published with Erenburg in 1909.[3] Aside from the lyrics she published in Erenburg's *Evenings* in 1914, there is one poem dated 1913, "Davno eto bylo" ("It Was Long Ago"), which, however, was first published in 1966 in her last collection, *Selected Poems*. Otherwise, all that remains in her archive are a few unpublished poems and translations from French Symbolist poets. The dating of these poems is imprecise, making an exact chronology of their composition impossible.

As she recalls in her memoirs, it was in Paris that Polonskaja first became acquainted with the poetry of the Russian Symbolists, and it had a profound effect upon her. She was also translating French Symbolist poetry; her unpublished translations of Verlaine and Moréas are preserved in her archive, and Kireeva mentions an incident when Polonskaja expressed interest in translating Baudelaire.[4] The influence of Blok and his contemporaries in Polonskaja's early verse makes itself felt in various ways. The poems display formal affinities with Symbolist poetry. For example, "U nix byla verbnaja subbota" ("For Them It Was Pussy Willow Saturday") is written in accentual verse, with as many as four syllables between stresses; "Ja kogda-to byla veseloj" ("At One Time I Was Merry") is also written in *taktoviki*, accentual verse lines with intervals ranging from one to three syllables. "V okne starevščika Ekateringofskoj" ("In the Window of an Antiques Dealer on Ekaterinhof Street") is a sonnet, a form revived and practiced extensively by the Symbolists. Polonskaja's rhymes also reflect the experimental tendencies of the period, ranging from canonically exact masculine and feminine and even rich masculine open rhymes to such approximate dactylic rhymes as *veselaja/volosy* or *plakala/makami*.

An example of Blok's influence is the unpublished "For Them It Was Pussy Willow Saturday," in which Polonskaja uses a catachresis typical of Blok, as described by Žirmunskij:[5] her lyric heroine buys a dream from an old woman, as though it were a fragrant blue flower:

> И когда ты ушел поцеловав мою перчатку,
> Я купила на улице у старухи сон.
> Синий сон, дурманющий [sic] и сладкий
> Словно мартовский вербный ветренный звон.

Early Verse

> And when you left, having kissed my glove,
> I bought a dream from an old woman on the street.
> An azure dream, intoxicating and sweet
> Like the willowy, windy March ringing.[6]

The dream is not simply treated as an object which can be bought and sold; its color and fragrance are also likened synaesthetically to the sound of church bells. The epithets applied to the word *zvon* (ringing), *martovskij* (March), *verbnyj* (willowy), and *vetrennyj* (windy) appear to be derived from alliteration and the semantic development of the poem rather than any external logic of similarity: "Verbnaja subbota," or "Pussy Willow Saturday," is in March, just before Palm Sunday; in the first strophe, young girls with their *kavalery* (swains) have bought pussy willow branches (*verby*); in the second strophe the beloved appears sad, as though in love "with a passing girl, with the wind (*veter*), with the gilding / Of the red sunset on the glass of the windows." Furthermore, "For Them It Was Pussy Willow Saturday" has a subtext in Blok's own "Verbnaja subbota" ("Pussy Willow Saturday," 1903), in which the dream is also a central image:

> На улице праздник, на улице свет,
> И свечки, и вербы встречают зарю.
> Дремотная сонь, неуловленный бред—
> Заморские гости приснились царю ...
>
> In the street it's a holiday, in the street there is light,
> And candles, and pussy willows greet the sunset.
> A dreamy sleep, an elusive delirium—
> The tsar was dreaming of guests from across the sea.[7]

Indeed, the *dremotnaja son'* (dreamy sleep) in Blok's poem is curiously linked with Polonskaja's *sinij son, durmanjuščij i sladkij* (azure dream, intoxicating and sweet) through the hidden intermediary word *son-drema*, the blue anemone flower (Pulsatilla patens).[8] Both Blok and Polonskaja use the occasion of Pussy Willow Saturday, a holiday associated in Russia with young courting couples,[9] as the setting for a love poem. In her later poems, Polonskaja recalled her student years as the time when she discovered both love and poetry, apparently simultaneously:

> А помнишь, как начинались
>   стихи?
> Подстриженных парков Версаля
>   зеленые мхи ...
>
> ... Ямбы, любовь, безделье ...
> Ямбы, безделье, лень ...
>
> ("Прощальная Ода," 1926)

> And do you remember how the poems began?
> The green mosses of Versailles' clipped parks . . .
>
> . . . Iambs, love, idleness . . .
> Iambs, idleness, laziness . . .
>
> ("Farewell Ode," 1926)[10]

> Мой первый друг . . . он мне одной известен.
> Он жил в плену, в плену у звонких слов,
> Поэзию мы открывали вместе,
> И вместе с ней открыли мы любовь.
>
> ("На швейной фабрике," 1935)

> My first friend . . . he is known to me alone.
> He was a captive, a captive of ringing words,
> We discovered poetry together,
> And with it, we discovered love.
>
> ("At the Garment Factory," 1935)[11]

The "first friend" is Erenburg, who, as Kireeva recalls, was at this time completely absorbed with poetry and with "Liza's opinion of his efforts in verse."[12] He was also, according to M. L. Polonskij, the unofficial addressee of her "Farewell Ode," in which she bids farewell to youth, love, idleness, and Paris.[13]

Characteristic of Polonskaja's early love lyrics is a decadent eroticism akin to that of Mirra Loxvitskaja, the "poetess of Bacchic sensuality,"[14] whose poetry "frequently and characteristically reflects the sunlit and mysterious Orient, with its intoxicating types of incense, bright flowers, and narcotics; the Orient with its instantaneous passion and sensual love."[15] The rich, sensual quality of Loxvitskaja's love poetry is particularly evident in Polonskaja's "Polden' l'jetsja v komnatu kak sladkij med" ("Noon Pours into the Room Like Sweet Honey"), in which the memory and expectation of passion is mingled with warm sunlight, the fragrance of linden and roses, and the sweetness of plums and grapes brought, with the roses, by the beloved; all of the senses are engaged:

> Розы смялись, розы пожелтели,
> Розы пахнут на моей постели . . .
> Сливы темносиние и виноград,
> Как рассыпали под вечер, так лежат . . .
> Мы одну лишь сливу надкусили,
> Мы других не тронули, мы о них забыли . . .
> Полдень греет, полдень нежит плечи мне . . .
> Хорошо лежать в таком ленивом полусне.
> Я глаза закрою, стану вспоминать . . .
> Знаю, вечером ты будешь, будешь ты опять!

Early Verse

> The roses were crushed, the roses yellowed,
> Roses are giving off fragrance in my bed . . .
> Deep blue plums and grapes are lying
> Just as we scattered them last night . . .
> We nibbled only one plum,
> We did not touch the rest, we forgot them . . .
> Noon warms, noon caresses my shoulders . . .
> How good it is to lie in such a lazy half-sleep.
> I will close my eyes, will start to recall . . .
> I know you will come again tonight, you will be here again![16]

Polonskaja's published cycle of 1914 has a narrative structure and a unified image of author; in the first poem, "Ulybnulsja izdali, možet byt' ne mne" ("He Smiled from a Distance, Perhaps Not at Me"), she describes an ambiguous smile on the face of her beloved. Both the second and the third poem are not so much narrated as spoken to the beloved. The second, "Nad rešetkoj vašego okna" ("Over the Grating of Your Window"), shows the lovers gazing out over Paris at twilight. Here again there is ambiguity, but this time it is the poet whose feelings are not altogether clear. Although they are now close, there is little warmth in the poem. The light is cold and bluish, the beloved weary, and the narrator admires his "sad silhouette." In the third poem, "U tebja pri každom rezkom slove" ("You, at Every Sharp Word"), in which they have progressed from formal *vy* to informal *ty*, she begs him not to be angry with her for smiling at passersby, saying she has been intoxicated by the heavy March rains. In the fourth poem, "Kogda ja budu staroj, ja ujedu" ("When I Am Old, I Will Go"), the poet describes the small French town where she will settle in old age, to remember through the long nights. All mention of the beloved is avoided, implying a rift.[17]

The lyric persona in this cycle, as in several of Polonskaja's unpublished love poems from this period, recalls those of early Axmatova, whom Sonia Ketchian calls "victims of love."[18] She mourns the loss of love but is not necessarily blameless, as she hints in the refrain of the second poem: "In the twilight I am almost faithful to you, / In the twilight we become closer." The lyric persona in "At One Time I Was Merry" is another such victim:

> И я стала совсем пустой,
> Пустой, как бусы стеклянные.
> Ни о ком не помню, никогда не устану я
> Никогда не вернусь домой.
>
> And I have become completely empty,
> Empty as glass beads.
> I remember nothing, I will never grow tired
> I will never return home.[19]

Also reminiscent of Axmatova is the use of concrete details and gestures to convey emotional states, as in "Da, v etot večer ja odna ostalas'" ("Yes, That Evening I Remained Alone"):

> Там, над Парижем, небо было ало ...
> Его поклон насмешлив и глубок.
> Но я не плакала, я только разорвала
> В клочки свой кружевной платок.
>
> There, above Paris, the sky was crimson ...
> His bow mocking and deep.
> But I did not cry, I only tore
> My lace handkerchief into shreds.[20]

Polonskaja was also subsequently to follow Axmatova in the further development of the theme of unhappy love. In the 1920s her lyric persona, like that of Axmatova, transforms the pain of lost love into poetry.

WAR, REVOLUTION, AND CIVIL WAR: *OMENS* (1921)

This period is marked by the development of a mature public voice in Polonskaja's poetry. Although she continued to publish love poems, the majority are civic lyrics reflecting her experience of war and revolution. The earliest published poem dated to this period, "Pod jablonjami Lotaringii" ("Under the Apple Trees of Lorraine," 1915), describes, in energetic quatrains of *dol'niki* approaching 4/3-footed amphibrachs and masculine rhymes, the frenzied activity of her frontline hospital work in Nancy:

> Хрипел санитарный фургон у ворот
> И раненых выгружал ...
> Носилки стояли за рядом ряд,
> Где вход в перевязочный зал ...
>
> Четвертые сутки дежурство несем,
> И свет в глазах потемнел,
> Но не иссякает на белых столах
> Поток окровавленных тел.
>
> The ambulance was wheezing at the gates
> And unloading the wounded ...
> Stretchers were standing row upon row,
> By the entrance to the bandaging room ...
>
> Our shifts run four days round the clock,
> And the world has gone dark in our eyes,
> But on the white tables the stream
> Of bloodied bodies does not run dry.[21]

Alongside this thematic shift is a refinement of poetic technique that Polonskaja attributes to the lessons she learned from Gumilev at the Literary Studio. However, although she admired him, their teacher-student relationship was an antagonistic one. Polonskaja recalls in her memoirs that Gumilev was "very talented, but very haughty" and that he laughed at her poem about the heroic death of an old worker ("V litejnoj masterskoj starik rabočij" ["An Old Worker in the Foundry Workshop," 1921–67]).[22] As Brett-Harrison points out, it is clear from these reminiscences how little teacher and student had in common in their attitudes toward art:

> Whereas Gumilev strove for a harmonious combination of form, intuition and ideas, and saw their perfection realized in musicality ("Music, music above all!"—Polonskaja, "The Early Twenties," 112), for Polonskaja, ideas and rhetoric were in the foreground. Characteristic of her conviction is the remark: "A poem must have a thought in it" (Polonskaja, "The Early Twenties," 112), in connection with which the ideas in her poetry are coupled with strong emotions, whose full extent and effect on her creations she did not always have completely under control.[23]

After her humiliation over Gumilev's reaction to "An Old Worker in the Foundry Workshop," Polonskaja resolved never again to read him any verses written "from the soul," but only those which were well made. "He was an enemy," she later recalled, "but for formal mastery he gave a great deal,—I personally owe him a lot."[24]

Polonskaja's first collection (*Omens*, 1921) contains twenty-three poems, all undated. It begins with a poem written just after Blok's death and dedicated to him, "Ne ispytali korablekrušen'ja" ("We Were Not Shipwrecked"), followed by three titled sections: "Znamen'ja" ("Omens"), "Krov' i plot'" ("Flesh and Blood"), and "Tol'ko v snax" ("Only in Dreams"). The first two sections consist mostly of poems on civic and political themes, while the third contains love poetry.

"We Were Not Shipwrecked" functions in the collection as a programmatic poem, explicitly laying out the worldview and preoccupations of the authorial voice, rendered here not as "I," but as "we." This generalized "we" occurs frequently in Polonskaja's early poems; as one reviewer commented: "How many years has the Russian lyric known only 'I'! In Polonskaja's work there is almost always a stirring 'we,' which we have interpreted thus: she speaks not only from and for herself, but presents, with pathos, some large group, united by a common suffering and consciousness, and has already broken the impasse of the narrowly personal."[25] The identity of the group in question varies. At times it is as broad as the nation, at other times it is specifically feminine. In this poem it is clearly identified with poets. The central image is of a shipwreck, sudden and devastating, which befalls the victims not at sea, in the course of mad adventures, but at home, "in comfortable, domestic rooms." Survivors of the catastrophe are driven by a primal instinct for survival which "blooms in the blood," a stubborn ancestral voice commanding them to live. But if these survivors are like Robinson Crusoe, the "faithful Friday" who does not abandon them is none other than the lyric muse: "And faithful Friday—the Lyric Muse / Does not abandon us in our exile."

Ejxenbaum cites these lines in particular as an echo of Mandel'štam's voice.[26] This echo is not only a matter of the meter and rhyme scheme (variable iambs with masculine/feminine rhymes) or of Polonskaja's syntax, which Ejxenbaum compares in the same review to that of Mandel'štam, or of her similar use of "concluding *pointes*." It is also based upon the central image in Polonskaja's poem, which is similar to that of "time's ship" sinking, in the second strophe of Mandel'štam's "Sumerki svobody" ("The Twilight of Freedom, 1918"):

> Прославим роковое бремя,
> Которое в слезах народный вождь берет.
> Прославим власти сумрачное бремя,
> Ее невыносимый гнет.
> В ком сердце есть—тот должен слышать, время,
> Как твой корабль ко дну идет.
>
> Let us celebrate the fatal burden,
> Which, in tears, the people's chief takes up.
> Let us celebrate the gloomy burden of power,
> Its unbearable weight.
> Whoever has a heart must hear, time,
> How your ship sinks to the bottom.[27]

Both poems are commentaries on the experience of historical upheaval and the new state, and both valorize the survival of memory, the carrier of which is the poetic word. However, when we compare closely, it appears that the subtext in Polonskaja's poem is a polemical treatment of the theme as it appears in Mandel'štam.

In the final strophe of "The Twilight of Freedom," we find a stoic determination to preserve memory (and thus, the poetic word) in the face of one's personal death, to which he alludes in the phrase "in Lethe's cold":

> Ну что ж, попробуем: огромный, неуклюжий,
> Скрипучий поворот руля.
> Земля плывет. Мужайтесь, мужи,
> Как плугом, океан деля,
> Мы будем помнить и в летейской стуже,
> Что десяти небес нам стоила земля.

Early Verse

> Well, let us try: a huge, clumsy
> Creaking turn of the wheel.
> The earth sails on. Have courage, men,
> Furrowing the ocean as with a plow,
> We will remember, in Lethe's cold,
> That earth cost us ten heavens.[28]

As mentioned earlier, Levin et al. point out that memory becomes, for Mandel'štam (and Axmatova), a "deeply moral principle, opposing unconsciousness [*bespamjatstvo*], oblivion, and chaos as the basis of art, faith, and loyalty."[29] They cite the following passage from Mandel'štam's fragmentary essay "Puškin i Skrjabin" ("Puškin and Scriabin," 1915): "memory triumphs—let it cost us our death: to die means to remember, to remember means to die. . . . To remember, at any cost. To fight against oblivion, though it should cost us our death."[30] S. Averincev relates the consciousness of the need for courage to face death ("Mužajtes', muži") with Mandel'štam's developing, strangely prophetic sense of his own destiny as sacrificial victim: "When, as a twenty-year-old, he wrote, before the Revolution, even before the beginning of the war: '*Rossija—ty, na kamne i krovi, / Učastvovat' v tvoej železnoj kare / Xot' tjažest'ju menja blagoslovi!*' ('You—Russia, built on stone and covered with blood / Give your blessing, if only with your heaviness / To my participation in your cruel punishment!'), was this still literature? It is hard to say—for some reason, such words have a way of being fulfilled."[31]

The lyric persona in Polonskaja's poem shows no resignation to such a destiny. Rather than a will to self-sacrifice, she expresses a stubborn will to live:

> Но прадедов суровое упорство
> У внуков ветренных еще цветет в крови,
> И голос родовой, настойчивый и черствый,
> Еще твердит упрямое—живи!—
>
> И мы живем, и Робинзону Крузо
> Подобные—за каждый бьемся час,
> И верный Пятница—Лирическая Муза
> В изгнании не покидает нас.
>
> But the forebears' rugged obstinacy
> Still blooms in the blood of their flighty grandchildren,
> And an ancestral voice, insistent and hard,
> Still stubbornly repeats—live!
>
> And we live, and like Robinson Crusoe
> We struggle for every hour,
> And faithful Friday, the Lyric Muse,
> Does not abandon us in our exile.[32]

It is in living, not in dying, that she preserves memory and the poetic word. Like Mandel'štam's images of poetic memory beyond the grave and himself as an offering to the age, Polonskaja's "rugged obstinacy" is also prophetic, but in a different way. She was fated to survive the worst excesses of the age, choosing internal exile over death by compromising in ways Mandel'štam could not have done. Polonskaja's reviewers often commented upon her preoccupation with biological imagery, with the "kinship principle." In part this orientation may reflect her medical training. It may also reflect the perspective of motherhood; as we shall see in "Vykup" ("Ransom," 1923), some of Polonskaja's maternal personae are capable of any sacrifice for their children.

The first section of the collection, "Omens," contains poetry on World War I and the hardships of life in Petrograd during the civil war. The section's title comes from one of the poems, "1914": "Ne darom znamen'ja grozjaščie dany: / Zatmilos' mrakom solnečnoe leto . . ." (Not in vain are the menacing omens given: / The sunny summer is eclipsed by gloom . . .); these lines echo the opening of the "Lay of Igor's Campaign," which begins with an eclipse, followed by the words: "Spala knjazju um' poxoti, i žalost' emu znamenie zastupi iskusiti Donu velikago . . ." (And the prince's mind was seized by ambition. / And the desire to drink from the great river Don / Concealed the evil omens from him).[33] Other ominous signs in Polonskaja's poem include the appearance of Halley's comet in the heavens and a mysterious and unnatural fertility on and of the earth, coupled with the curious fact that women have begun giving birth only to boys. "Vojna" ("War") gives a similarly ominous twist to the idea of fertility. Here the central image is an inversion of the classical myth of Jason's trial at Colchis: the field of Russia, sown with human bodies, brings forth only a harvest of wolves' teeth:

> Побросали в земные недра
> Не зерно, тела человечьи.
>
> И земля урожай небывалый
> Принесла, но острее желчи:
> Не ячмень, не рожь, не пшеницу,
> Принесла только зубы волчьи.
>
> They scattered into the depths of the earth
> Not seed, but human bodies.
>
> And the earth brought forth a fantastic
> Harvest, but sharper than gall:
> Not barley, not rye, not wheat,
> It brought forth only wolves' teeth.[34]

The most striking indictment of war in this collection is "Mjagkoj gubkoj, teploj vodoj" ("With a Soft Sponge, with Warm Water"), in which a mother grieves for her son, swallowed up in the trenches:

Early Verse

> Мягкой губкой, теплой водой
> Мыла я запыленные ножки,
> Загоревшие в солнечный зной,
> Топотуньи, веселые крошки.
>
> А теперь ты, как загнанный зверь,
> В земляные кроешься норы,
> И тебя по канавам теперь
> Валит сон, беспокойный и скорый.
>
> With a soft sponge, with warm water
> I washed dusty little feet,
> Tanned in the sun's heat,
> Little stampers, merry little things.
>
> But now, like a hunted animal,
> You hide in earthen burrows,
> And you are tossed among ditches
> By a dream, restless and swift.[35]

This poem, one of Polonskaja's most powerful treatments of the theme of motherhood, blends an individual lyric voice with the "stirring we" noted by the aforementioned reviewer:

> Иль не стало в нашей стране
> Сыновьям нашим должного места,
> Что мы отдали их войне
> И дали им смерть в невесты?
>
> Но тебя от меня не возьмет
> Грохот тысячи тысяч орудий;
> Все я чувствую слабый твой рот
> На моей опустевшей груди.
>
> Is there, then, no longer in our land
> Any proper place for our sons,
> That we have given them to war
> And given them death for a bride?
>
> The thunder of a thousand thousand guns
> Shall never take you from me;
> I still feel your feeble mouth
> Upon my emptied breast.[36]

Motherhood is one of Polonskaja's most prominent and complex themes; as we see in this poem, it is treated as simultaneously intimate and universal. Motherhood is a metaphor for the state in Polonskaja's verse, but it is often represented in terms of an intensely physical connection between mother and child; the image of the breast and of nursing appears frequently. As if to emphasize the purely biological, instinctual aspects of motherhood, particularly under the extreme conditions of life in the civil war period, its imagery and vocabulary are often linked to animals, from the mother goat in "Skazka" ("Fairy Tale"), a poetic adaptation of a well-known folktale, to "Ves' etot god byl truden i žestok" ("All That Year Was Difficult and Cruel"), in which "The den bristles with snarls: / They are feeding their young here..."[37] In "Na pamjat' o tjažëlom gode" ("In Memory of a Harsh Year"), we find, "And a gloomy mother feeds / Her child, like a hungry wolf cub, / With a carefully hoarded scrap...."[38] As Aleksandr Voronskij remarked in his review of the Serapion Brothers' 1922 almanac, "A tendency toward the bestial is characteristic of our contemporary literature."[39]

The setting of this fierce struggle for survival, and, indeed, most of Polonskaja's early poetry, is the city of Petrograd, which retains its former majesty in spite of all. The city is the subject of "Peterburg," whose title emphasizes the eternal and mythical qualities of the city, associated both with its physical, architectural beauty and with a bloody history:

> Но ты, источник стольких вдохновений,
> Мечта из камня, город измышлений,
> Ты полон новой, мрачной красоты;
> Ты кровью опален и смертью тронут,
> И над тобой уж плакальщицы стонут...
> О, Петербург, не изменяешь ты!...
>
> ...Так, значит, мы живем, так, значит, смерти нет!
> И чьей то мысли отягченный след
> Останется в веках, как крепкая работа...
>
> But you, the source of so many inspirations,
> A dream of stone, an invented city,
> You are full of new, somber beauty;
> You are singed by blood and touched by death,
> And over you the mourning women are already moaning...
> O, Petersburg, you never change!...
>
> ... So, then, we are alive, so, then, there is no death!
> And the ponderous trace of someone's thought
> Remains in the centuries, as sturdy workmanship...[40]

That remaining "trace of someone's thought," embodied in the physical details of the city, brings us back again to the central values expressed in Polonskaja's verse: the continuity of life and of human memory. Both these values and the architectural imagery of the poem represent a link with Acmeist poetics.

The importance of memory in particular is also expressed in "Ne stranno li, čto my zabudem vse" ("Isn't It Strange That We Shall Forget Everything") and "In Memory of a Harsh Year." Both poems are about the need to remember present suffering long after it has passed in order to

Early Verse

appreciate the cost of freedom. In the first, the poet speaks, in the inclusive "we," of her certainty that, like a mother whose memory of the pain of childbirth fades as her child grows, her people will forget the painful birth of the new state. However, she also voices personal regret at the passing of that memory:

> Но грустно мне, что мы утратим цену
> Друзьям смиренным, преданным, безгласным:
> Березовым поленьям, горсти соли,
> Кувшину с молоком, и небогатым
> Плодам земли, убогой и суровой.
>
> But I find it sad that we shall cease to value
> Our humble, devoted, voiceless friends:
> Birch logs, a handful of salt,
> A pitcher of milk, and the modest
> Fruits of a poor, plain earth.[41]

The second poem, addressed to the people (*narod*), proposes a ritual commemoration of their suffering, to be passed from generation to generation:

> На память о тяжелом годе
> Установи себе, народ,
> Семь дней на память о свободе,
> И передай из рода в род!
>
> In memory of a harsh year
> Establish for yourselves, my people,
> Seven days in memory of freedom,
> And pass them from generation to generation![42]

The proposed weeklong rite of commemoration, complete with dietary restrictions ("You will share your bread in beggars' portions") is strongly reminiscent of Passover, which brings us to the second section of *Omens*, "Flesh and Blood," in which Polonskaja's treatment of the "Jewish" theme is most concentrated.

"KROV' I PLOT'": THE JEWISH THEME

"Flesh and Blood" consists of four poems on the theme of kinship. It begins with the death of the poet's father ("1-oe fevralja" ["February 1"]) and ends with her fear for her child ("Dosyta ne mogu, ditja" ["I Cannot Give You Your Fill, Child"]). Within this frame are the two "Jewish poems" to which critics reacted so strongly, "I Cannot Abide the Infant Jesus" and "Šejlok" ("Shylock"). "February 1," though less obvious and less controversial, can also be considered a "Jewish" poem because of its allusions to Jewish mourning rites which will not be performed:

> На непокрытый пол, без обуви, согбен,
> Не сядет с нами гость, как для молитвы надо.
> Мужчины в доме нет, и, как велит закон,
> В знак траура никто не совершит обряда.
>
> On the uncovered floor, barefoot and bent,
> No guest will sit down with us to pray.
> No men are in the house and, by decree,
> No one will perform the mourning rites.[43]

The absence of ritual is made even more conspicuous by the mention of a mirror, since, according to Jewish custom, mirrors must remain covered during the period of mourning:

> Но в зеркале моем тебя я узнаю,—
> Не тень бескрылую нездешнего предела,—
> Родную кровь, отец, живую плоть твою,
> И ты живешь во мне, душа моя и тело.
>
> But in my mirror I recognize you,—
> No wingless shade of an otherworldly pale,—
> Kindred blood, my father, your living flesh,
> And you live in me, my soul and body.[44]

The ties of blood appear in this poem to be the poet's only real remaining connection with Judaism. However, in the two central poems, she reveals a much less detached attitude. Here kinship is a banner proudly displayed in a direct confrontation with anti-Semitism.

The decade following the Revolution was initially a period of unprecedented freedom and hope for Russian Jews; after years of brutal pogroms and government-sanctioned anti-Semitism, the Pale of Settlement was abolished and equal legal rights established for Jews in 1917. It must be noted that these legal reforms were carried out by the provisional government after the February Revolution, not by the Bolsheviks.[45] However, the change in legal status was maintained after the October Revolution, and although there were many pogroms during the civil war, these were perpetrated mainly by the Whites, not the Bolsheviks. During the 1920s an official campaign against anti-Semitism was carried out, but at the same time the Party made a concerted effort, led by the Jewish Communists of the *Jevsektskija* (Jewish Section) to eradicate the use of Hebrew and the practice of Judaism.[46] Zvi Gitelman describes this antireligious campaign as "to a considerable extent . . . an internal Jewish affair . . . the insecurity of the Jewish Communists drove them to prove their fidelity to the cause and their ability to transcend kinship in order to serve ideology."[47]

Yiddish survived somewhat longer than Hebrew, being a secular language, but it was used in print mainly to bombard the Jewish population with Soviet propaganda. As Maurice Friedberg points out, "Because Judaism is closely interwoven with Jewish folkways and customs (and is professed only by a single ethnic group), a campaign against the former could not but weaken the Jewish social fabric as a whole. As a result, renunciation of Judaism was—as was becoming increasingly apparent—ultimately a threat to Jewish survival as a distinct cultural and ethnic community."[48] Moreover, as Alice Nakhimovsky states, activists in the Jewish Section itself, after managing "to destroy the foundations of Jewish life," were purged in the mid-1930s, and as for Yiddish, "The audience for Yiddish literature would be destroyed by the Nazis, and, a few years later, the major writers would be killed by Stalin."[49]

In the early 1920s, however, there was still a sense of euphoria among many Russian Jews. L'vov-Rogačevskij's *History of Russian Jewish Literature*, published in Moscow in 1922, ends on an optimistic note: "The thrice-fettered people has created a literature in which its bondage was too much in evidence. A free people of a free country shall have new bards and they shall sing new songs. Instead of lamentation and mourning and woe and the constant refrain 'it's terrible to live,' these songs will reverberate with a joyous, 'Lord, now lettest thou thy servant to depart in peace' [Luke 2:29], and there will rise up to lead a new life 'the last generation given to slavery and the first experiencing joyous freedom.' And this shall come to pass. It must!"[50] This sense of liberation is also vividly expressed in the defiantly Jewish self-assertion in the two poems by Polonskaja under discussion. "I Cannot Abide the Infant Jesus" is a direct address by the poetic "I" to her God, infinitely more powerful than the infant Jesus, "with his crowd of saints, beggars, and cripples."[51] Despite the fact that she praises her God "in a strange language," she disavows any connection with Christ or Christianity, emphasizing both her blood relation to the patriarchs of ancient Israel and the covenant which extends even to her Russian-born son:

> Я кровью связана, не с этим желторусым
> Чужим покидышем, распятым на кресте.
> С Тобою, Саваоф,—не с бедным Иисусом
> Мой предок, патриарх, боролся в темноте.
>
> И сыну моему, рожденному в России,
> Ты подтвердишь, Господь, заветный договор:
> Для нас, неверящих, пришествие Мессии
> Подделанное тем, среди Ливанских гор.
>
> I am linked by blood, not with that yellow-haired
> Alien foundling, nailed upon a cross.
> With Thee, Sabaoth,—not with poor Jesus
> Did my ancestor wrestle in darkness.
>
> And to my son, born in Russia,
> Thou shalt affirm, Lord, the cherished covenant:

> For us, unbelievers, the coming of the Messiah
> Which was falsely proclaimed by him [Jesus], among
>   the hills of Lebanon.[52]

In "Shylock," the outraged cry of Shakespeare's villain is taken up by a proud chorus:

> Мы знаем точный вес, мы твердо помним счет;
> Мы научаемся, когда нас научают.
> Когда вы бьёте нас, кровь разве не идёт?
> И разве мы не мстим, когда нас оскорбляют?
>
> We know the precise weight, we keep close account;
> We learn when we are taught.
> When you beat us, do we not bleed?
> And do we not avenge when we are insulted?[53]

The Zionist overtones of "I Cannot Abide the Infant Jesus" in particular could not fail to be politically provocative in 1921; the Zionist movement in Russia was largely anti-Bolshevik, and, as Gitelman notes, "The Zionist Central Office was closed in September 1919, and in April 1920 the delegates to an All-Russian Zionist conference were arrested. In the following years thousands of Zionists were arrested as 'counter-revolutionaries.'"[54] However, Polonskaja's fervent identification with the Jewish people, and "I Cannot Abide the Infant Jesus" in particular, is also linked to another dynamic noted by R. D. Timenčik in his observations on Jewish themes in early-twentieth-century Russian poetry. Timenčik specifically mentions, as "one of the more extreme episodes" of the "dialogue and confrontation of two principles,"[55] the incident when Polonskaja read "I Cannot Abide the Infant Jesus" at a public gathering; she was greeted by a stunned silence, after which, as she later wrote in a memoir, "Gumilev rose and demonstratively walked out."[56] According to Timenčik, the Jewish theme is "interiorized through the motif of personal genealogy," which moves it "away from descriptiveness, exoticism, and moralizing towards a search for internal dramatism."[57] Genealogy, Timenčik suggests, can be used by poets to give an etiologic basis for the makeup of a personality or be the motivation for a poetics; also based on such autogenealogical projections was the motif, popular at the time, of "eternal return." The theme is further developed in categories of rejection and of ambivalence and attraction to Russia. As Timenčik also points out, these turns to genealogical sources arise in the context of growing "doubt in the right to a fully valued presence of Jews in Russian literature," which he connects to a perception among some critics that the Russian language itself cannot be mastered and has even been somehow corrupted by Jewish writers.[58] Clare Cavanagh also describes this phenomenon in the critical reception of Mandel'štam by, among others, Sergej Gorodetskij, for whom "Mandel'štam's poetry, like the poet himself, is an awkward, if not unwelcome, newcomer

Early Verse

to the Russian tradition it seeks to adopt. The true insider, the truly Russian writer will not, however, be easily misled by its seeming fluency; the verses speak with an accent that the discerning, native ear will readily recognize."[59]

Aside from Gumilev's reaction, many reviews of *Omens* also reveal the hostility which greeted Polonskaja's Jewish poems. P. Guber calls "I Cannot Abide" an attempt to attract attention through "unbelievable blasphemy or some other cynical trick."[60] This is, no doubt, the subject of a cryptic reference by Kuzmin to the "fireworks" (*lopnuvšie petardy*) which greeted the appearance of *Omens*.[61] Most significant, however, in light of Timenčik's and Cavanagh's observations, are the negative reviews, specifically mentioning the Jewish poems, in which critics imply that Polonskaja's Russian is somehow impure, alien, foreign. For example, Georgij Ivanov, in a rather literal interpretation of a line in "I Cannot Abide" ("In a foreign language I awkwardly praise him"), calls Polonskaja's language "the Achilles' heel of her art": "The poet herself acknowledges that the Russian language is an alien element for her."[62] Another reviewer, Mixail Pavlov, had the following reaction: "These poems are written in Russian, but only by chance: so alien are they to Russian. They should have been written in the language of the Prophets and of Bialik, and then perhaps they would have sounded different. But here there is such a rift between the meaning and spirit of the verse and its language that they sound false. We—Russians—can also blaspheme, perhaps even more and more terribly, but we blaspheme differently."[63]

Also revealing are the following two positive reviews by admirers of Polonskaja's (including, curiously, Erenburg) who attempt to minimize the importance of the Jewish poems, treating them as aberrations. The first is from A. Baxrax, the second from Erenburg.

> There is something else in the book. There are poems with a particular ideology. ("I Cannot Abide the Infant Jesus," "Shylock.") There is much ecstatic pathos in them, much genuine pain, much suffering, but they are clearly superfluous in the collection, for they take the book onto an entirely different plane. This is no good. Let us pass over them, drawing no conclusions and let us not search out any sort of dogmatic truths in the poet. The true weight is outside them.[64]

> Russian critics have, of course, found an ideology in Polonskaja's poems, and they have begun criticizing her on this plane: Judaism, the kinship principle and so on. I think that the few poems which give rise to such digressions are actually the weakest in the collection (the one about Jesus, or "Shylock"). On the other hand, Polonskaja attains a rare strength when she speaks about the majesty of our devastated days.[65]

Artistically, the poems in question are not the strongest in the collection. They do, however, express what is clearly a major concern of the poet: her cultural identity. Their placement in the very center of the middle section reinforces the centrality of the subject. That Erenburg and Baxrax, themselves Jews, would attempt to deflect attention from these poems suggests their own sensitivity on this point. It is likely that what they objected to was the arrogance and naïveté in Polonskaja's presentation and that their comments were meant as a caution to her. As Vera Alexandrova points out, one need only remember the chapter of Erenburg's 1921 novel *The Adventures of Julio Jurenito* entitled "Prophesy of the Teacher concerning the Destiny of the Judean Tribe," in which Jurenito predicts "in addition to the traditional pogroms so dear to the hearts of the esteemed public some events conceived in the spirit of the age: The burning of Jews, their burial alive in the earth, the sprinkling of the fields with Jewish blood, and new methods of 'evacuation,' 'cleansing of suspicious elements,' and so on" to recognize his prescience.[66] He understood that, despite the political, legal, and social gains made by Jews after the Revolution, there were limits to public tolerance, and a backlash was always possible. Polonskaja's poems were so provocative as to be potentially dangerous, both to her and to other Jews.

Polonskaja's attitude was actually more ambivalent than "I Cannot Abide" and "Shylock" would suggest. A more comprehensive understanding can be gained from examining some of her unpublished poems from the same period, namely, "Izrail'" ("Israel," 1919); "O, deti naroda moego" ("O, Children of My People," 1921), and "O Rossija, zlaja Rossija" ("O Russia, Cruel Russia," 1922). These poems reflect the inner struggle of a writer divided between loyalty to Israel, with which she is connected by blood and memory, and love for Russia, her "stepmotherland," drab, cold, and hostile, but still almost inexpressibly dear.

"Israel," a cycle of four short lyrics, begins with a contrast between the luxuriant, somewhat exotic physical beauty of Israel and the cold drabness of the Russian countryside:

> Таких больших изсиня черных глаз,
> Таких ресниц, стрелчатых и тяжелых
> Не может появиться среди Вас,
> В холодных и убогих Ваших селах.
>
> Such large blue-black eyes,
> Such lashes, arrowlike and heavy,
> Such beauty could not appear among You,
> In Your cold and indigent villages.

This beauty, the poet asserts, can only be given by the God Sabaoth to his sons, "under the burning sky of Palestine." In the second poem, the heavy lashes are lowered in intense study of the "square letters" on "yellow pages": the Jew is seen here studying God's law. There is already a note of ambivalence here in the scholar's narrow focus; the window is low, the street narrow, and

Early Verse

> Над городом сурова и тяжка,—
> Надгробным камнем встала синагога.
>
> Above the city, stern and heavy,—
> The synagogue rose like a gravestone.

The intensely claustrophobic feeling of the second poem is relieved in the third, which moves out of the study to a mountainside, where the shepherd's horn sounds merrily as the flocks are driven home at evening. The reader is asked a rhetorical question: who is the swarthy woman lavishing the well's coolness on the traveler, leading him to her ivory-bearded father's laden table? We do not need to be told that this is Rebecca, greeting the servant of Abraham. The fourth poem, a single quatrain, speaks explicitly of a land of exile, where the Torah is still a source of strength:

> Не будет жалок и унижен тот,
> Кем избрана высокая опора.
>
> He shall not be pitiful and debased,
> Who has chosen a lofty support.[67]

"O, Children of My People" is specifically about the sadness and humiliation of the Jews in exile, mourning their lost homeland and despised by the natives of their new one. The poem, written in blank iambic pentameter, predicts the coming of those who can speak for the exiles, but even these can only articulate their sorrows in song:

> В них оживет внезапный гнев пророков,
> И древней скорби - безудержный плач,
> Века, века, заговорят пред ними
> И сердце детское наполнит ужас . . .
> Их опьянит божественный восторг
> И острой болью, жалость их пронзит.
> И проклянут они, и умилятся—
> Под обреченным жить, и умереть.
> И будет горло, как струна тугая,
> Напряжено одним желанием звука,—
> И лютнею Давида прозвучит,
> На языке чужом, их грустный голос.
>
> In them the sudden wrath of prophets will be revived,
> And the uncontrollable cry of ancient sorrow,
> Centuries, centuries will begin to speak before them
> And horror will fill the childish heart . . .
> And they shall be intoxicated by divine ecstasy
> And compassion, like a sharp pain, shall pierce them.
> And they shall curse, and shall be moved—
> To live under a seal of doom, to die.
> And the throat will be like a taut string,

Strained only by the desire for sound,—
And like David's lute, in a strange language,
Their sad voice will ring out.[68]

The cry of *drevnej skorbi* (ancient sorrow), as well as the generally gloomy tone of the poem and its imagery, places "O, Children of My People" firmly in the tradition of the nineteenth-century poet Semen Frug, the self-proclaimed "gravedigger-singer" whose melancholy lyrics express the bitterness and disillusionment of the assimilated Russian-speaking Jew after the pogroms of 1881 and 1882. The word *skorb'* (sorrow, grief) in particular occurs frequently in Frug's poetry. He looked for hope in the growing Zionist movement but was unable to trust fully in its future. According to Lvov-Rogačevskij, "The poet was unable to surrender himself spontaneously and blindly to the charm of legends and tales of the past; he was unable to find oblivion. While resurrecting old tales, he sadly realized that the world of legends, the voice of prophets, the sound of warriors—'these people, these forces, had come and gone.' He understood perfectly well that about him was 'neither the wrath nor malice of indignant people, but only from time to time the rattle of bones from the darkness of the grave.'"[69]

Also characteristic of Frug is a tormenting split between loyalty to his people and deep love for the Ukrainian landscape. His early poetry is filled with lyrical descriptions of the fields and steppes of his native Kherson, of willows and cherry blossoms. Yet after the shocking events of 1881 and 1882, he was unable to give free rein to this impulse. "The poet was never able to renounce his poignant, tender love for the chastely, [*sic*] shy beauty of his native landscape, and it was this anguish which caused him to weep and moan."[70] A similar anguish can be felt in Polonskaja's powerful "O, Russia, Cruel Russia," in which she bemoans the hostility of her native country toward her, despite her helpless love for the land and its language:

Разве я для тебя - чужая,
Отчего я так горько люблю—
Небо скудное скучного края
И непышную землю твою?

Разве я не взяла добровольно
Слов твоих тяготеющий груз,
Как бы не было [sic] трудно и больно,
Только с жизнью от них отрекусь!

Что ж, убей, но враждебное тело
Средь твоей закопают земли,
Чтоб зеленой травою—допела
Я неспетые песни твои.

Early Verse

> Am I really a stranger to you,
> Why do I love so bitterly
> The pale sky of a dull land
> And your drab earth?
>
> Have I not taken on willingly
> The magnetic burden of your words,
> However difficult and painful,
> I will renounce it only with my life!
>
> Well then, kill me, but they will bury
> My hostile body in your earth,
> So that, as green grass, I may sing
> Out fully all your unsung songs.[71]

For all the studied defiance of her published poems, it is clear that, like many Russian-Jewish intellectuals, Polonskaja was painfully divided in her identity.

This division was not simply a matter of an opposition of two principles, Russian and Jewish. Jews in Russia had always been seen by conservatives as not simply a foreign element, but one linked specifically with the West. As one historian states, in the nineteenth century, "[t]he Jews were identified in the eyes of the Russian public (and eventually in their own eyes) with everything 'western,' i.e., every aspiration to personal and social rights, to rational thought, to any trend considered by the theorists of Russian 'originality' (*samobytnost*) contrary to the 'nature' of Russia and its political and social traditions."[72] After the Russian Revolution, and particularly during the civil war, when American and European troops intervened on the side of the Whites, the taint of Westernism acquired new negative political and social connotations. Several branches of Polonskaja's family were in Poland and Germany. She was fluent from childhood in German and French, educated in Paris, and later closely linked with the so-called western wing of the Serapions; thus, her Jewish identity was accompanied by a deep love of European culture. It is surely no coincidence that those Serapions identified by Zamjatin as "western"—Slonimskij, Lunc, and Kaverin, as well as their mentor, Šklovskij—were all Jewish, while the "easterners"— Nikitin, Ivanov, Zoščenko, and Fedin—were gentiles. In a letter to Polonskaja, Erenburg once remarked: "Give my greetings to the Serapions. They're good, especially their Jewish part + Zoščenko and Tixonov."[73] Furthermore, in describing how Slonimskij, like Lunc, is still wandering from genre to genre, switching constantly, Zamjatin compares him with the Wandering Jew, Ahasuerus.[74] The westerners, writes Zamjatin, tend "to operate predominantly with architectural masses, with plot, but with relatively little ear or love for the Russian word itself, its music and its color,"[75] a curious statement which echoes those of some previously mentioned critics about specifically Jewish writers.

Serapion Sister

Lunc, considered by many the spokesman of the Serapions, published a story, "Rodina" ("Homeland," 1922), in which he grapples with the conflict between his Jewish heritage and his love of both Russian and European culture; the latter two appear to be equated, and both are inimical to his full acceptance of himself as a Jew. In the story, two young assimilated Russian Jews, residents of Petersburg, identified as Leva and Venja (the story is dedicated to Veniamin Kaverin), travel through time to ancient Israel in search of their Jewish identity. Venja, initially reluctant to undertake the journey, is revealed as a prophet, Benjamin, who foretells the liberation of the Judeans from slavery in Babylon and leads them home. Leva is Yehudah, a Judean slave born in Babylon, torn between a desire to return to a homeland he has never seen and love for the city of his birth. He ultimately decides to leave Babylon and follow the Judeans into the desert, but they reject him, stoning him at Benjamin's command. He finds himself alone in Petersburg, under "a native but foreign sky," with the vision of desert sun in his eyes and the cry "Be accursed!" in his ears. Petersburg, the most Western of Russian cities, remains his native land.

The relationship of Lunc's Jewishness to his Westernism is also articulated in the following passage from a draft of a letter he wrote to Gor'kij, dated August 1922. Here Lunc interprets his critics' insistence that "a Jew cannot be a Russian writer" as a reaction chiefly to the Western elements in his work. He also confirms Zamjatin's generalization about his preoccupation with structure rather than linguistic texture, but he makes it clear that this is a matter of literary principle. There is no indication of any lack of love for or fluency in the Russian language:

> But I am a *Jew*. Convinced, steadfast, and glad of it. But I am a *Russian* writer. And then I am a Russian Jew, Russia is my native land, I love Russia above all countries. How can one reconcile this? For myself I have reconciled all, for me this is clear and pure, but others think differently. Others say: "A Jew cannot be a Russian writer." . . . I do not want to write like 9/10 of Russian writers, nor in the final instance like Pil'njak and most of the Serapions. I do not want thick, provincial language, trifling everyday life, tedious play of words, even if it be flowery, even if it be beautiful. I love the great idea and the great, entertaining plot. I can't stand Remizov and Belyj. I love Western literature more than Russian. . . . But around me they say that I am not Russian. And that nothing will come of me.[76]

Lunc, unlike Erenburg, applauded Polonskaja's "prophetic insolence": "And I find it funny when loyal critics are outraged by these 'blasphemous' poems, for I have seen in them the biblical pathos of an uncorrupted and inflexible prophet."[77] Lunc's use of the word "prophetic" underscores an important source of Polonskaja's (and his own) poetics. Brett-Harrison traces the lexical connections between Polonskaja's poem "Trevoga" ("Alarm"), which appears in the first section of *Omens,* and certain verses in Exodus and the first chapter of Ezekiel.[78] The word *truba* (trumpet), used in the poem to characterize the factory sirens sounding the alarm as Judenič approaches the city, is linked with the following passage from Exodus:

> И когда пойдете на войну в земле вашей против врага, наступающего на вас, *трубите тревогу трубами;* и будете воспомянуты перед Господом, Богом вашим, и спасены от врагов ваших.
>
> And when you go to war in your land against an enemy who advances against you, *sound the alarm with trumpets;* and you shall be remembered by the Lord, your God, and saved from your enemies.[79]

Further, the narrative voice in Polonskaja's poem proclaims:

> Враг впустит огонь в ваши темные домы . . .
> Ваш город, он вспыхнет, как связка соломы
>
> The enemy shall set fire to your darkened houses . . .
> Your city shall blaze up like a sheaf of straw

while Exodus contains the line:

> Ты послал гнев Твой, и он попалил их, как солому.
>
> Thou hast sent Thy wrath, and it scorched us, like straw.[80]

Polonskaja's final couplet,

> И в хмурые лица зарницами бьет
> Над Пулковым грозно пылающий свод
>
> And over Pulkovo, in flashes like summer lightning,
> The menacingly flaming firmament strikes gloomy faces.

echoes Ezekiel 1:26–27, both in the use of the word *svod* (firmament), repeated several times in the biblical verses, and the image of deadly fire in the sky, linked explicitly by the word *pylajuščij* (flaming): "I videl ja kak by pylajuščij metall . . ." (And I saw as it were a flaming bronze . . .).

The poem, written in amphibrachs with a varying number of stresses and broken into short lines, is not especially successful; Ejxenbaum calls it "utterly weak . . . not in the spirit of Polonskaja."[81] However, as Brett-Harrison points out, the pathetic undertone which characterizes many of the poems in *Omens* and Polonskaja's second collection, *Under a Stone Rain*, is already perceptible in this poem, written in 1919. Also noteworthy are certain features linking "Alarm" with Lunc's play *Obez'jany idut!* (*The Apes Are Coming!* 1920). The play also describes a situation of imminent invasion; a voice offstage is heard at intervals, repeating the phrase "vrag blizok" (the enemy is near), which is also repeated three times in "Alarm." Toward the end of the play, as the enemy bursts into the city, the stage directions call repeatedly for thunder and lightning, echoing the lightning which fills the flaming firmament (*pylajuščij svod*) at the close of Polonskaja's poem. *The Apes Are Coming!* also has sources in the prophetic tradition. The city's inhabitants are so exhausted and confused that they are not entirely sure whether the invaders are enemies or saviors. A man, identified only as Čelovek (Man), rebukes the crowd for looking to the enemy for salvation. His speech reads like a biblical warning: "It is a lie, a lie, that they shall free you. . . . You expect salvation from them, but they will come and kill you, they will rape you, they will tear you to pieces. . . . Do you hear the blizzard howl? It is they, your saviors, the ones you are waiting for, it is the apes howling, who have laid siege to the city."[82] The motif of God punishing his people by sending wild beasts (*ljutye zveri*) to devour them appears several times in the books of Jeremiah and Ezekiel. Thus, aside from their similarities to each other, both Lunc's play and Polonskaja's poem have important biblical sources in these two books.

"Alarm," with its more subtle interplay of biblical subtext and contemporary thematics, was, in the public sense, a more successful poem than the other "Jewish poems" in *Omens*. It has appeared in every retrospective collection published by Polonskaja, with only minor textual changes. Polonskaja continued to use biblical themes and images in her poetry and, at the same time, began to downplay the overtly Jewish identity of her lyric heroines, as we shall see in discussion of subsequent collections. Her own sense of herself as a Jew was never effaced, however. In her letter of 1925 to critic Pavel Medvedev, who had asked her to write an autobiography, Polonskaja, after the initial formalities in her response, begins thus: "First of all, I must declare my Jewish descent."[83] After several pages of family history, and before beginning an account of her childhood, she apologizes, not without a certain irony, for the digression: "Esteemed Pavel Nikolaevič, I sense that I have strayed from the plan. I have not yet managed to reveal my pettybourgeois and intellectual essence. I have succeeded only in declaring that I feel myself to be a Jew."[84]

"ONLY IN DREAMS": LOVE POETRY

The final section of *Omens*, "Only in Dreams," is devoted almost entirely to love poetry. There is much less originality in these poems. As in the Parisian period, they frequently suggest certain well-known features of Blok and Axmatova; indeed, since they are not dated, it is possible that some were written during that early period and only published here for the first time. The first poem, "Tol'ko v snax ešče ty nastojaščij" ("Only in Dreams Are You Still Real"), even contains a thinly veiled reference to the title of Axmatova's 1916 collection *Belaja staja* (*White Flock*):

> Милый—ты, но кто мне скажет кто ты,
> Что за город здесь, и как я знаю

Early Verse

> Этот дом и сад, и там, у поворота,
> Белых птиц взлетающую стаю . . .
>
> You are dear—but who will tell me who you are,
> What town this is, and how I know
> This house and garden, and there, by the bend,
> A rising flock of white birds . . .[85]

The last, "Ničto už ne volnuet bole" ("Nothing Troubles Me Anymore"), also has a clear subtext in Axmatova's "Skazka o černom kol'ce" ("The Tale of the Black Ring," 1917). In Polonskaja's poem we read:

> Кольцо потеряла . . .
> Пропала любовь . . .
> Нахмурилось сердце,
> Нахмурилась бровь.
>
> I lost the ring . . .
> Love has perished . . .
> My heart clouded over,
> My brow was furrowed.[86]

There is also an allusion in this poem to the smooth ring (*gladkoe kol'co*) in Axmatova's "Ja sošla s uma, o mal'čik strannyj" ("I Have Lost My Mind, O Strange Boy," 1911) in the following lines by Polonskaja:

> Кольцо золотое.
> Гладкое кольцо . . .
> Милое, злое,
> Чужое лицо.
>
> A golden ring.
> A smooth ring . . .
> A dear, cruel
> Stranger's face.[87]

After the heroine has lamented the loss of love, the poem (and, indeed, the collection) ends on a note of hope: that lost love shall be transformed into song:

> Быть может, знаменья чудесней,
> Велишь, явясь на полпути,—
> Скупым губам сказаться песней,
> Жезлу сухому—процвести.
>
> Perhaps, more miraculous than an omen,
> You will command, appearing midway,—
> Miserly lips to bring forth song,
> A dry stick—to blossom.[88]

The idea of unhappy love turned into poetry can be found in Axmatova's poetry as early as 1914, in "Tjažela ty, ljubovnaja pamat'" ("You Are Heavy, Love's Memory"), in which readers warm themselves in the poet's tears, and is further developed in such poems as "Pesnja o pesne" ("Song about Songs," 1916) and "Ja ulybat'sja perestala" ("I Have Stopped Smiling," 1915), in which "There is one less hope, / There will be one more song."[89] All three of these poems were published in *White Flock* (1916), which points us back again to that work as a source of subtexts for Polonskaja. Where Polonskaja differs from Axmatova in her treatment of the theme of lost love turned into poetry is in the optimism and joy she expresses at the idea of sorrow turned to song. For Axmatova's lyric heroine, the process is bitter, and she longs to be free of her compulsion to speak, as in "You Are Heavy":

> Дай мне выпить такой отравы,
> Чтобы сделалась я немой;
> И мою бесславную славу
> Осиянным забвением смой.
>
> Let me drink a poison such
> That I would become mute;
> And wash away my gloryless glory
> With radiant oblivion.[90]

Polonskaja's final image of a dry stick blossoming (a reference to Aaron's rod) is a positive one, and it follows the refrain of the song:

> Шарманка, шарманка,
> Пой, моя душа!
> Поешь или плачешь,
> Жизнь хороша!
>
> Street organ, street organ,
> Sing, my soul!
> Whether you sing or you cry,
> Life is good![91]

For one reviewer, these lines suggest a possible epigraph for the entire collection, expressing as they do the poet's "joy in being," the "joy of sensing her own 'I,'" which is doubly valuable given the grim context of the rest of the collection: "after such a long lethargy the joy of the everyday meeting with the sun, with the world, with oneself, the lyric muse will be able to delight in this for a long time."[92]

As in Polonskaja's earlier love poems, there are echoes of both Loxvitskaja and Blok in the fierce, sensual, and possessive passion of "Revnost'" ("Jealousy"), combined with the image of the snowstorm and wind:

> Над сердцем любовника, злая подруга,
> Ревниво я бодрствую ночь напролет.

Early Verse

> Наушница злобная, зимняя вьюга
> Враждебные, древние песни поет.
>
> Ты дар драгоценный, мне отданный Богом,
> Ты стал безраздельным владеньем моим,—
> Но ты мне изменишь за этим порогом
> Улыбкой и взглядом и телом твоим.
>
> Over the heart of my lover, a cruel girlfriend,
> I jealously keep vigil through the night.
> The winter blizzard, malicious slanderer,
> Sings hostile, ancient songs.
>
> You are a precious gift, given me by God,
> You have become my property, inseparable from me,—
> But you will betray me beyond that threshold
> With your smile and your glance and your body.[93]

Another bow to Blok is "Za oknom nočnogo bara" ("Through the Window of the Night Bar"), with its mysterious and disreputable setting where:

> Дня не будет, будут ночи.
> Ты узнаешь—жизнь проста:
> Подрисованные очи,
> Воспаленные уста.
>
> There will be no day, there will be nights.
> You will learn—life is simple:
> Painted eyes,
> Inflamed lips.[94]

Ejxenbaum dismisses the poems in this last section as weaker than the others; as we have seen, they are, for the most part, imitative and not particularly profound. However, certain of their features should be kept in mind when we examine the further development of Polonskaja's love lyric: the strikingly frank expression of female sensuality, the willfulness of the persona, her resignation to the inevitable loss of love, and the idea of poetry as solace and reward for love's loss.

The one poem in this final section which stands out, and which has been consistently included in all of the retrospective collections, is "My naučaemsja ljubit'" ("We Learn to Love"). In this poem, Polonskaja presents not an individual love lament but an insight into the universal fragility and transitoriness of love:

> Мы научаемся любить
> Мучительно и неумело.
> Так и слепые, может быть,
> Чужое осязают тело.

Так просто кажется сперва
Губами легких губ коснуться;
Но равнодушные слова
Внезапной тяжестью сорвутся.

И будет первый из людей
В ожившей глине создан снова,
И задрожит в руке твоей
Первоначальной жизнью слово,

И для тебя наступит срок
Веселой, горестной науки—
Неповторяемый урок
Любви, и боли, и разлуки.

We learn to love
Agonizingly and clumsily.
Thus do the blind, perhaps,
Feel a stranger's body.

It seems so simple at first
With lips to touch light lips;
But indifferent words
Burst out with sudden heaviness.

And the first human will be
Created anew in clay come to life,
And the word will begin to tremble
In your hand with the first stirring of life,

And there will come a time for you
Of merry, bitter science—
The unrepeated lesson
Of love, and pain, and parting.[95]

Here we find "we" and "you," but no trace of a lyric "I," raising the persona's pronouncement to the status of universal law. The experience of "love, pain, and parting" is raised to the level of a "science" (*nauka*). We also see, once again, the birth of poetry (the word, or *slovo*) following the death of love.

"We Learn to Love" also has a significant subtext in Mandel'štam which is specifically connected with the latter's poetics. In "Slovo i kul'tura" ("The Word and Culture"), Mandel'štam advises poets to

> [w]rite imageless verse, if you can, if you know how. A blind man recognizes a dear face, barely touching it with seeing fingers, and tears of joy, the true joy of recognition, splash from his eyes after a long separation. A poem is alive with an inner image, that sounding mold of form, which anticipates the written poem. There is not yet a single word, and already the poem sounds. It is the inner image sounding, it is that which the poet's ear feels.
> And only the moment of recognition is sweet to us.[96]

Early Verse

This reference to Mandel'štam's poem "Tristia" (1918) leads us to its first line: "Ja izučil nauku razstavan'ja" (I have learned the science of parting), which is echoed in Polonskaja's final quatrain:

> And there will come a time for you
> Of merry, bitter science—
> The unrepeated lesson
> Of love, and pain, and parting.

The synonyms for parting, *razstavan'je* and *razluka,* are also brought together in Mandel'štam's lines: "Kto možet znat' pri slove—razstavan'je, / Kakaja nam razluka predstoit" (Who can know at the word—separation, / What sort of parting lies before us).[97] "Tristia," in the context of the citation in "The Word and Culture," is apparently the inner image which anticipates this poem, one of Polonskaja's finest.

Chapter Three

Under a Stone Rain, 1921–23

GENERAL OUTLINE

During the years 1922 to 1929, which I will call the NEP period in Polonskaja's poetry, she began contributing verse, including verse for children, translations, and sketches, to various periodicals. Much of this work was ephemeral, appearing once and never republished in any of her collections. However, Polonskaja often published variants of a poem in several journals before including the completed version in a collection. Most of the poems she published separately in 1921 to 1922 appeared in her second collection, *Pod kamennym doždem* (*Under a Stone Rain*, 1923).

Polonskaja published in two major anthologies in 1922. "In Memory of a Harsh Year" and "Suxoj i gulkij ščelknul baraban" ("Dry and Resonant Cracked the Drum,") both from *Omens*, appeared in the Berlin edition of *The Serapion Brothers: Almanac the First,* the only collection produced by the brotherhood.[1] The Petrograd edition, which also appeared in 1922, contained only prose fiction. The poetry of Polonskaja and Nikolaj Tixonov, as well as a critical article by Il'ja Gruzdev, "Lico i maska" ("The Face and the Mask"), which had appeared in the Berlin edition, were omitted. Polonskaja also published a new poem, "Smešalos' vse. Goda vojny . . ." ("All Was Confusion. The Years of War . . .") in *A Petersburg Collection,* the 1922 collection produced by the House of Writers.

In the same year, Polonskaja also negotiated a contract with the publisher Poljarnaja Zvezda (Polar Star) to publish a second collection, *Pod smertnym ostriem. Stixotvorenija* (*Under the Fatal Point: Poems*). However, the book did not appear until 1923. It was published under a different title, *Under a Stone Rain: 1921–1923,* with some changes in the order and composition of its contents.

As in *Omens,* there appears to be a general division between civic lyrics and those of a more intimate nature. Part 1 contains fifteen poems on revolution, while parts 2 and 3, with eight and five poems respectively, contain the more personal themes and a greater frequency of the lyric "I," as opposed to the "we" of part 1. However, even these two sections contain some of Polonskaja's most celebrated civic lyrics, such as "Xotja by nas sožgli" ("Though They May Burn Us Up") and "Vykup" ("Ransom"), in which she explores the experience of revolution and civil war specifically by mothers, and does so with particular effectiveness, continuing in the vein of "With a Soft Sponge, with Warm Water" and "Fairy Tale."

The themes of poetry and the poet are also treated in these sections, which contain the aforementioned "I Am Playing a Dangerous Game." The poet's attitude toward her own poetics as it intersects with history is also expressed in "Ne stalo nežnosti živoj" ("There Is No Longer Any Living Tenderness"). She recognizes that the time demands a harsh poetry of "screams and howls" and "words made of oakum":

> Пока не покосится рот,
> И кожа на губах не треснет,
> И кровь соленая пойдет,
> Мешаясь с безобразной песней.

> Until your mouth is twisted,
> And your lips crack,
> And salty blood begins to flow,
> Mingling with a hideous song.[2]

There is also a more intimate dimension to her relationship with her own poetry. In "Pesenka" ("Song"), a mother asks her child to make room by the fire for her muse, the touchy one (*Muza-nedotroga*).[3] The conflict between the demands of muse and child had also been depicted with affectionate, ironic humor in an earlier unpublished poem, "Pojdu ja v magazin Kornilova na Nevskom" ("I Will Go to Kornilov's Shop on Nevskij," 1921), in which the poet vows to buy herself a completely different son, made of porcelain, who would not distract her from her work:

> Уж он не станет разливать чернила
> На рукописи, на мои тетради.
> Без позволения, не будет никогда искать картинок,
> Ни в Брюсове, ни в Белом, ни в Петрарке.
> Играть в подземную железную дорогу
> Под креслом у меня,—он верно не захочет.
> Когда я доскажу шестую сказку,
> Он не потребует:—«Теперь, еще раз.»
> Нет, никогда,—на письменном столе,
> Сидеть он будет чинно, тихо, тихо,
> Играть один, на молчаливой флейте
> И, только иногда,—негромко спросит: «Мама,
> Ты кончила работать? Что, можно целоваться?»

> Surely he will not spill ink
> Onto manuscripts, onto my notebooks.
> He will never, without my permission, look for pictures,
> In Brjusov, Belyj, or Petrarch.
> To play underground railroad under
> My chair—he will certainly not want that.
> When I reach the end of the sixth bedtime story,
> He will not demand: "Now tell me another."
> No, never,—on my desk
> He will sit properly, quietly, quietly,
> And play alone, on a silent flute
> And, only sometimes,—he will softly ask: "Mama,
> Have you finished your work? Can we kiss now?"[4]

The theme of child versus work was to appear once again in "Pro knigi" ("About Books," the first line of which is "Mama, put down those books!") which Polonskaja published in the children's journal *Vorobej* in 1924; the complaint is the same, but here the child is given a direct voice:

> Мама, в этих толстых книгах
> И слоны и обезьяны.
> Целый день ты с ними вместе,
> А меня с тобою нет!

> Mama, in these thick books
> There are elephants and apes.
> You are with them the whole day,
> And I am not with you![5]

"About Books" is the last instance of this theme in Polonskaja's poetry, presumably because, as her son grew older and less dependent, she felt the conflict less painfully.

In "Ne ljubiš' ty, a ja ljublju, i tjažek" ("You Do Not Love, but I Love, and Heavy"), Polonskaja once again takes up Axmatova's theme of unrequited love turned into poetry:

> И выпьют мед, Сафо, тугие пчелы,
> А строки, может быть, другую опьянят:
> С любовью легкой, пряной и веселой
> В нее войдет моей печали яд.
>
> А мне—Нева, великолепье мира,
> Стихов магически определенный счет,
> Да то еще, что золотая лира
> Оттягивает слабое плечо.

> And the miserly bees will drink up all the honey, Sappho,
> But these lines, perhaps, will intoxicate another:
> With light, spicy, merry love,
> The poison of my sorrow shall enter her.

Under a Stone Rain, 1921–23

> And for me—the Neva, splendor of the world,
> A magically determined count of verses,
> And the golden lyre's pull
> At my weak shoulder.[6]

She was to develop it further in her next collection as well. Love poems in general are fewer in this collection (there are only four), and the lyric heroines have a strikingly different character from those in *Omens*. No longer passive "victims of love," more or less resigned to loss, they are self-confident, aggressive, and passionate; the heroine of "Čto mne za delo, kstati il' nekstati" ("What Do I Care If He Welcomes It or Not") vows, "I shall buy you for fifty *červoncy*,"[7] and another declares, "Rain lashes my face, and the drunken wind wanders, / But I want you, and I will have you."[8] These heroines prefigure the strong women in Polonskaja's later narrative poetry; their independence and unabashed eroticism reflect her position with regard to the "woman question" as it developed in the 1920s.

To give some idea of the historical and political context of this subject, 1922 had witnessed the fall from grace of Aleksandra Kollontai, the most radical proponent of women's political and sexual freedom. Kollontai was removed from her post as leader of the Ženotdel (Women's Section) in the wake of the defeat of the Workers' Opposition, which she had championed.[9] She did, however, continue writing on women's emancipation, publishing her essay "Dorogu krylatomu Erosu!" ("Make Way for Winged Eros!") and six works of fiction in 1923.[10] Polonskaja's "Prinesla kukuška čužogo ptenca" ("The Cuckoo Has Brought a Stranger's Chick"), the monologue of a harried single mother struggling to raise her child alone, should be read in the context of Kollontai's ideas on state aid to mothers without regard to their marital status. Thus, even the most apparently intimate of Polonskaja's lyrics during this period can be interpreted as having a political as well as a personal meaning.

Most of the poems in *Under a Stone Rain* are written in tight, finely crafted syllabotonic verse, with a prevalence of quatrains in iambic hexameter and pentameter. Rhyme schemes are generally *AbAb* or *aBaB*. There are a few poems written in looser three-stress or four-stress *dol'niki*, and a few instances of rhyming couplets, both masculine and feminine. In this early period, Polonskaja tends to concentrate not so much on formal innovation as on attaining maximal pathos in her imagery and intonations. However, in a few cases, she forsakes precise meter and strophe for a looser, more flexible form and a narrative rather than a lyric mode. In *Omens* we find an example of this in "Alarm," discussed in the previous chapter. In *Under a Stone Rain*, the most striking case is "Ballada o beglece" ("Ballad of the Fugitive").

Polonskaja's adoption of the ballad form reflects both the general orientation of the "westerners" among the Serapions toward the literature of plot and the formal influence of her fellow Serapion poets, Nikolaj Tixonov and, previously, Vladimir Pozner. Many poets were influenced during the early 1920s by Rudyard Kipling, whose "Ballad of East and West" Polonskaja translated in 1922.[11] The meter of "Ballad of the Fugitive" is a *dol'nik*, with lines of anywhere from two to four stresses and a variable strophe. An impression of speed and motion is created by the exclusively masculine rhymes, repetitions of words, and short syntactical constructions:

> У власти тысяча рук
> И два лица.
> У власти тысяча верных слуг
> Но больше друзей у беглеца.
>   Ветер за ним
>   Закрывает дверь,
>   Вьюга за ним
>   Заметает след;
>   Эхо ему
>   Говорит, где враг,
> Дерзость дает ему легкий шаг.

> Power has a thousand hands
> And two faces.
> Power has a thousand loyal servants
> But the fugitive has more friends.
>   The wind closes
>   The door behind him,
>   The blizzard covers
>   His trail,
>   The echo tells him
>   Where is the foe,
> Insolence gives him a light step.[12]

Comparison with some of Tixonov's ballads reveals similar use of certain types of word repetitions. For example, in Polonskaja's poem we find *za vest'ju vest'* (news upon news), *iz doma v sosednij dom* (from house to neighboring house), *iz serdca v serdce* (from heart to heart); in Tixonov's "Perekop" *k almazu almaz* (diamond to diamond) and *za kapkanom kapkan* (trap after trap), and in his "Ballada o sinem pakete" ("Ballad of the Blue Packet") *Koleso k kolesu, koleso k kolesu* (Wheel to wheel, wheel to wheel) and *Vagon za vagonom* (Car after car).

Unlike Tixonov, however, Polonskaja also uses a form of refrain similar to Kipling's in "The Ballad of East and West" and "Fuzzy Wuzzy." Although the exact wording varies, there are five repetitions of the passage "Power has a thousand hands. . . . Power has a thousand loyal servants. . . ." Also unlike Tixonov, Polonskaja uses the ballad form as the vehicle for a hidden, politically subversive idea, which will be discussed in detail later in this chapter.

Under a Stone Rain, 1921–23

Critical reception of *Under a Stone Rain,* as in the case of *Omens,* was mixed. One reviewer, David Vygodskij, praised Polonskaja's emphasis on strength and placed her on the same artistic level as Mandel'štam and Majakovskij; he found the sources of her civic lyric in Tjutčev's political poetry and the Books of the Prophets.[13] Other reviewers took a more narrowly political stance, however, and although they were quick to point out a change from the "passive tone" (with regard to the Revolution) of *Omens* to a more positive and accepting one in *Under a Stone Rain,* they do not place the poet entirely within the framework of politically acceptable literature. M. Gutner notes with some concern the prevalence of "all sorts of biological images," evidence of the "inertia of primitivism," but he concludes that "by whatever roundabout ways E. Polonskaja has approached the theme of revolution, the main thing in her book *Under a Stone Rain* is that the question of with whom she stands has been decided, and in connection with this, a note has begun to sound in E. Polonskaja's poetry not of biological, but of social optimism."[14] Innokentij Oksenov is also cautious in his praise. On the one hand, he observes that the "passive, minor tone" of *Omens* has given way to a "major, triumphal tone," the "voice of a new 'neoclassical' ode." On the other hand, he asserts that "[t]he theme of revolution is alien to the poet (which does not exclude the possibility of the creation of good poems on the theme), and Polonskaja will enter the history of the contemporary lyric as a lone voice for the ancient, inert and cruel ancestral element."[15]

Polonskaja's ambivalence is perceived by critics in the very structure of the collection. Only the first part is devoted entirely to one theme, revolution, and the second and third parts blend the intimate and the political. This blending of themes reflects the way they are intertwined in Polonskaja's consciousness; love and poetry are closely linked, and motherhood is, as Gutner indicates, both a social and a biological idea. Oksenov identifies the concept of kinship (*rodovoe načalo*) as central to Polonskaja's verse and states that it is in the second and third parts of the collection, where that theme is most concentrated, that we find the poet's true character revealed. Part 1, in which most of the poems on revolution appear, is hastily glossed over by Oksenov. The weight of this theme, he claims, is simply too great for the poet to bear, and her lyric voice in these poems is "unnaturally strained."

Under a Stone Rain does indeed reflect Polonskaja's ambivalence toward the regime, and careful study of the text reveals that her ambivalence was actually considerably greater than the critics indicated. The most compelling evidence, however, lies not in the comparative weight of her treatments of intimate and political themes but within her treatment of the theme of revolution itself, in part 1 of the collection. Polonskaja's response to revolution is not a matter of squeamishness or inability to accept social change; it is a painful realization that the Revolution she and so many of her contemporaries had dreamed of and actively worked for had gone horribly wrong. Furthermore, an ominous indication of the Revolution's failure can be read in Polonskaja's careful encoding of political messages in *Under a Stone Rain* which are not apparent on first reading. Complex webs of subtexts, in some cases from her own unpublished poems, false addressees, and the textual history of the collection reveal both the level of Polonskaja's disillusionment and the constraints on freedom of expression which were already affecting writers as early as 1922.

Polonskaja's essentially Marxist view of human society is evident in the cycle "Oktjabr'" ("October"). The first poem, "Byla li zloba bol'še, čem ljubov'" ("If Malice Were Greater than Love"), is an expression of outrage at the social injustice of the old order, an oath of bloody vengeance by the exploited poor against the rich. However, the poem ends with a curious image of revolution as a ship setting sail into the "leaden air" of the future:

> И в напряженьи распростертых крыл,
> Покинув землю меда, слез и млека,
> Корабль Октябрьский мужественно вплыл
> В свинцовый воздух будущего века.
>
> And in the tension of unfurled wings,
> Having left the land of honey, tears, and milk,
> October's ship courageously set sail
> Into the leaden air of the future age.[16]

The "leaden air" was interpreted by M. Čumandrin as typical of the intelligentsia's ambivalent attitude toward socialism: "socialism—this is something severe, something monotonous, leveling all and everything, perhaps even warping man, but to make up for it, having nothing in common with the screaming, debauched, repulsive world of profit, dirt and philistinism."[17] Yet Čumandrin treats this poem, and specifically the image of the flying ship, as an example of "abstract revolutionary romanticism."[18]

The theme of the flying ship has its own history in Russian poetry, beginning with Lermontov's "Vozdušnyj korabl'" ("The Flying Ship," 1840), in which the ghost of Napoleon returns to France.[19] It was also used by Mandel'štam in his "Admiraltejstvo" ("The Admiralty Building," 1913), in which

> ... в темной зелени фрегат или акрополь
> Сияет издали, воде и небу брат.
>
> Нам четырех стихий приязненно господство,
> Но создал пятую свободный человек.
> Не отрицает ли пространства превосходство,
> Сей целомудренно построенный ковчег?
>
> ... in the dark greenery a frigate or acropolis
> Shines in the distance, brother to water and air.

Under a Stone Rain, 1921–23

> To us was freely given mastery of four elements,
> But a free man created a fifth.
> Does it not negate the superiority of space,
> This chastely constructed ark?[20]

Mandel'štam's airy bark represents a "fifth element" created by another emperor, a "free man," Peter; it is part of the mythology of Petersburg, the invented city, and the idea of human will conquering the elements. Polonskaja's "October's ship" also suggests a relationship with several later poems by Mandel'štam. In "Na štrasnoj vysote bluždajuščij ogon'" ("A Wandering Fire at a Terrible Height," 1918), we also find the image of a "monstrous ship" moving high above the city:

> Чудовищный корабль на страшной высоте
> Несется, крылья расправляет . . .
> Зеленая звезда,—в прекрасной нищете
> Твой брат, Петрополь, умирает.
>
> A monstrous ship at a terrible height
> Floats, spreads its wings . . .
> A green star,—in beautiful poverty
> Your brother, Petropolis, is dying.[21]

Nils Ake Nilsson has posited both phonetic and semantic links between the last lines of Mandel'štam's "The Twilight of Freedom" (1918), discussed in the previous section in connection with the image of the sinking ship, and his "Na kamennyx otrogax Pierii" ("On the Stone Islands of Pieria," 1919). In "The Twilight of Freedom," the ship's wheel turns with difficulty (*Skripučij povorot rulja*, a *creaking* turn of the wheel), and the lyric hero exhorts his fellow men to struggle courageously (*Mužajtes', muži*), whereas in "On the Stone Islands":

> Скрипучий труд не омрачает небо
> И колесо вращается легко.
>
> Creaking labor does not darken the sky
> And the wheel turns easily.

Nilsson interprets the link thus:

> The earlier describes the present situation, the latter a past one, gone forever. The earlier has a note of stoicism (which fits in well with the ship metaphor), the latter ends in a nostalgic call, contrasting past and present: honey, wine, milk and the easily moving wheel belong to a past world; the broken bread, the hard work, the noise and smoke are part of our modern civilization. It is a contrast between the "blessed islands" of Greece and the chaotic Russia after 1917.[22]

Polonskaja's final quatrain contains both the word "courageously" (*mužestvenno*), from the same root as *mužajtes'* and *muži* ("October's ship *courageously* set sail"), and a reference to the milk and honey of the "blessed islands" ("Having left the land of honey, tears, and milk"). Mandel'štam's poem ends:

> О, где же вы, святые острова,
> Где не едят надломленного хлеба,
> Где только мед, вино и молоко,
> Скрипучий труд не омрачает неба
> И колесо вращается легко?
>
> Oh, where are you, sacred islands,
> Where they do not eat broken bread,
> Where there is only honey, wine and milk,
> Creaking labor does not darken the sky
> And the wheel turns easily?[23]

As in "We Were Not Shipwrecked" (see my earlier discussion of *Omens*), in "If Malice Were Greater than Love" Polonskaja uses a subtext from Mandel'štam's "The Twilight of Freedom" with a polemical twist. Instead of leaving a land of milk, *wine*, and honey, her ship leaves one of milk, *tears*, and honey, implying that past blessings were mixed. Guarded in her optimism about Russia's future, Polonskaja nevertheless retains no illusions about its past.

In the second poem of the cycle, "Toržestvennye dni. Ot noči do utra" ("Triumphal Days: From Night until Morning"), revolution is personified as a woman, whose hands are bloody from "the most necessary and burdensome work."[24] However, the third poem, "Tak značit ty dumaeš',—eto konec" ("So, Then, You Think It Is Over"), makes explicit the fact that the work of revolution is far from over. Whereas in the first poem a mother rejoices at her son's pledge of vengeance for centuries of social injustice ("Grief to the fortunate! Grief to the golden ones! / To the silver ones! And thrice death to the rich!"),[25] in the final one:

> Еще нищий липнет у каждой булочной...
> Шныряет карманщик в трамвайной давке...
> Еще не наглядится мальчишка уличный
> На все чудеса игрушечной лавки...
>
> Еще не все передохли безногие,—
> Веселая память Великой Войны,—
> Еще проститутками сделались многие
> Гражданки свободнейшей в мире страны.
>
> A beggar still hovers at every bakery...
> A pickpocket darts in the crush of the tram.
> A street urchin still cannot look his fill
> At all the wonders of a toy shop...

Under a Stone Rain, 1921–23

> The legless still have not died off,—
> The merry memory of the Great War,—
> Many a citizeness of the freest country
> In the world has still become a prostitute.²⁶

Polonskaja's outspoken public criticism of NEP economic policies in particular, which she regarded as a betrayal of the spirit of the Revolution, can be said to begin with the publication of this poem.

Despite her acceptance of the need for social change, Polonskaja's poems repeatedly express dismay at the human cost. The Acmeist motifs of stone, building, and architecture, which appeared earlier in *Omens* ("Petersburg"), are taken up again, with an admixture of blood. In "Stroitel' velikogo bratstva" ("The Builder of a Great Brotherhood"), she acknowledges that "the cathedral will be built upon blood," and:

> Не глиной скрепляются зданья,
> Не камень в основу кладут.
>
> Not with clay are buildings held together,
> Not with stone do they lay a foundation.

The building does not immortalize any human thought or aspiration; instead it consumes countless human lives. This sacrifice is treated as a necessary evil, for:

> ... скажут веселые внуки—
> «Все это уж было не раз;
> Железные надобны руки
> И зоркий, уверенный глаз.»
>
> ... happy grandchildren will say—
> "All this has happened more than once;
> Iron hands are needed
> And a sharp, sure eye."²⁷

Again, we are reminded of lines from Mandel'štam, this time in "Zasnula čern' . . ." ("The Rabble Has Fallen Asleep . . . ," 1913), written during the same year as "Utro Akmeizma" ("The Morning of Acmeism") and the other Acmeist manifestos:

> Курантов бой и тени государей:
> Россия, ты—на камне и в крови—
> Участвовать в твоей железной каре
> Хоть тяжестью меня благослови!
>
> The beating of chimes and shadows of sovereigns:
> Russia,—built on stone and covered with blood—
> Give your blessing, if only with your heaviness
> To my participation in your cruel punishment.²⁸

In Polonskaja's "All Is Confusion: The Years of War," building is also connected with self-sacrifice:

> Но усмиряет день за днем
> Слепых и помнящих обиды,
> И с тайным ропотом кладем
> Мы кирпичи для пирамиды.
>
> Умрем, развеемся как прах,
> Как пыль людской каменоломни,—
> Чтоб силой грозною в веках
> Воздвигся памятник огромный!
>
> И вот лопаты землю бьют
> В ночи душистой и весенней,
> И охраняет мирный труд
> Стена колючих заграждений.
>
> But day after day heals
> The blind, and those who recall grievances,
> And, grumbling in secret, we are laying
> The bricks for the pyramid.
>
> We will die, we will be scattered like ash,
> Like the dust of a human quarry,—
> So that, in the centuries, with terrible strength
> The enormous monument should arise!
>
> And so the shovels beat the earth
> In the fragrant spring night,
> And a wall of thorny barriers
> Protects the peaceful labor.[29]

Without reference to future generations who will supposedly benefit from this labor, the building of the huge monument, which consumes the laborers, acquires a sinister and ultimately futile character, reinforced by the barbed wire surrounding this "peaceful labor." Furthermore, although in the first quatrain of the poem we are told that the memory of the empire (*carstvennoj strany*) has vanished, the monument, product of this immense, all-consuming labor, is called *piramida* (pyramid), echoing the closing lines of Brjusov's sonnet "Egipetskij rab" ("The Egyptian Slave," 1911):

> Я жалкий раб царя, и жребий мой безвестен;
> Как утренняя тень, исчезну без следа,
> Меня с лица земли века сотрут, как плесень;
>
> Но не исчезнет след упорного труда,
> И вечность простоит, близ озера Мерида,
> Гробница царская, святая пирамида.

Under a Stone Rain, 1921–23

> I am a pitiful slave of the emperor, and my fate is unknown;
> Like a morning shadow, I shall disappear without trace,
> The ages shall wipe me from the face of the earth, like mold;
>
> But the trace of my stubborn labor shall not disappear,
> And for eternity there shall stand, by Lake Merida,
> The emperor's tomb, the sacred pyramid.[30]

The corruption of revolution is conveyed also in the stately Alexandrines of "O, Revoljucija, o Kniga meždu knig!" ("O, Revolution, O Book among Books!"), in which "blood and dirt make the lofty pages stick together."[31] The first line of the poem contains a quotation from another sonnet by Brjusov, "Ty ženščina, ty—kniga meždu knig" ("You Are Woman, You Are a Book among Books," 1899), in which woman is both object of desire and source of hellish torment:

> Ты—женщина, ты—книга между книг,
> Ты—свернутый, запечатленный свиток;
> В его строках и дум и слов избыток,
> В его листах безумен каждый миг.
>
> Ты—женщина, ты—ведьмовский напиток!
> Он жжет огнем, едва в уста проник;
> Но пьющий пламя подавляет крик
> И славословит бешено средь пыток.
>
> You are woman, you are a book among books,
> You are a rolled, sealed scroll;
> In its lines an abundance of thoughts and words,
> In its leaves every moment is madness.
>
> You are woman, you are a witch's brew!
> It burns with fire, barely passing the lips;
> But he who drinks the flame stifles a cry
> And madly utters praises amid his torments.[32]

The reader will recall that revolution has been portrayed by Polonskaja as a woman worker (*rabotnica*) elsewhere, in "Triumphal Days." The link between revolution and Brjusov's hellish image of woman reinforces the idea that the ideal of revolution has been betrayed and desecrated in the eyes of Polonskaja's lyric persona; the regime is a travesty of everything it had promised:

> Какая истина в твоей неправде есть?
> Пустыня странствия нам суждена какая?
> Сквозь мертвые пески, сквозь Голод, Славу, Месть
> Придем ли наконец к вратам Небесным рая?

What truth is there in your untruth?
What desert of wandering is fated for us?
Through the dead sands, through Hunger, Glory, Vengeance
Shall we come at last to the gates of Celestial heaven?

After these lines, the final quatrain, although outwardly optimistic, is rendered ironic:

Но все уже равно. Блистательной судьбы
Не избежать стране, тобой благословенной.—
О как счастливы мы! Как нищи! Как слабы!
Счастливей не было и нет во всей вселенной!

But already it is all the same. The country shall not avoid
The splendid fate, blessed by you.—
O how fortunate we are! How destitute! How weak!
There have never been and will not be more fortunate ones
    in the whole universe![33]

The irony is reflected in yet another feminine image: the women of the "freest country in the world" who have become prostitutes in "So, Then, You Think It Is Over" (see earlier text).

Further elaboration of the idea of revolution as a nightmarish betrayal of a noble dream can be found in the three-poem cycle "Petersburg." The first poem, "Čto kryl'ev babočki trepeščuju set'" ("Like the Trembling Web of a Butterfly's Wings"), depicts the sheer terror of the city's residents without reference to political allegiances. The second is a curious piece called "Spjat pobedivšie. Čto im v pobede?" ("The Victors Lie Sleeping. What Have They Won?"), which Marietta Šaginjan called a "pearl of political pathos."[34] The poem bears an epigraph from Puškin's "Skazka o zolotom petuške" ("Tale of the Golden Cockerel") and develops the image of a red cockerel sounding the alarm to defend the capital against a vengeful despot who has returned to reclaim his kingdom while the victors lie sleeping:

... И в глазах у всей столицы
Петушок вспорхнул со спицы,
К колеснице полетел
И царю на темя сел,
Встрепенулся, клюнул в темя
И взвился ...
    Пушкин, «Сказка о золотом Петушке»

Спят победившие; что им в победе?
Подле солдата голодная мать ...
Рокотом трубным и голосом меди
Будут столетия их прославлять.

Кто ж это тайно по городу бродит
В мантии рваной, с дырявым лицом?

Under a Stone Rain, 1921–23

Метит крестами и мелом обводит
Камень за камнем, дворец за дворцом . . .

Или считает хозяин кровавый
Пришлых наследников в мутную рань—
Дерзких правителей из-за заставы,
Сброд разночинный, фабричную рвань . . .

—«Выпито, с'едено все государство,
Все потерял я, а сколько имел . . .
В черной дыре мое пышное царство,
В низком подвале средь тлеющих тел.

Что ж, и последних пора уничтожить,—
Город мятежников, город Не Тронь;
Яд не поможет, железо поможет,
А не поможет—поможет огонь!

Будут вам вопли, и стоны, и скрежет,
Будет набат колокольный в ночи!
Радуйтесь! Всех, кого нож не дорежет,
Жалую властью своей в палачи!»

Спят победившие, спят, не услышат,
Сломлены сном, как трухлявая трость . . .
Только петух запевает на крыше,
С дальней слободки непрошенный гость.

Слушай, бессонная красная птица,
Сторож, дозорный, патруль, часовой!
В цепкие руки попала столица—
Вот он колдует, не мертвый, живой . . .

Трижды пропой! Прокричи свое время!
Сядь ему на плечи, бей, что есть сил
Клювом колючим в плещивое темя,—
Криком пронзительным, взмахами крыл

Дальше гони его,—пусть в агонии,
Ветром взметенный, уносится прочь
Дальше, все дальше по дебрям России,
В страшную, в черную, в вечную ночь!

> Look! The cock whirred off the steeple,
> Swooped upon the coach of state,
> Perched upon the monarch's pate,
> Fluffed his ruff and peck and clink!
> Soared aloft! . . .
>   (tr. Walter Arndt)

The victors lie sleeping; what have they won?
Next to a soldier, a hungry mother . . .

> With a rumble of trumpets and a voice of brass
> The centuries will glorify them.
>
> Who is it that wanders the city secretly
> In a torn mantle, with a face full of holes?
> He is marking with crosses, outlining with chalk
> Stone after stone, palace after palace . . .
>
> Is it the bloody master counting
> His alien heirs in the dull morning—
> Insolent rulers from beyond the gates,
> A classless rabble, factory riffraff . . .
>
> —"The whole state is drunk up, eaten up,
> I've lost everything, but how much I had . . .
> My splendid kingdom is in a black hole,
> In a low cellar among rotting bodies.
>
> Well, it's time to destroy the last of them,—
> The city of rebels, "Touch Me Not" city;
> Poison won't help, iron will help,
> Or if it won't help—there is fire!
>
> You will have howls, and moans, and gnashing,
> There will be alarm bells in the night!
> Rejoice! All whom the knife does not take
> I will turn, by my power, into butchers!"
>
> The victors are sleeping, they sleep, they hear not,
> Broken by sleep, like a rotten stick . . .
> Only the cock starts to sing on the roof,
> Uninvited guest from a distant settlement.
>
> Listen, sleepless red bird,
> Watchman, scout, patrol, sentinel!
> The capital has fallen into powerful hands—
> See how he bewitches, not dead, but alive . . .
>
> Sing out thrice! Cry out your time!
> Perch on his shoulders, beat with all your strength,
> With your sharp beak, on his bald pate,—
> With a piercing cry, with a beating of wings
>
> Drive him further,—be it in agony,
> Swept by the wind, let him take himself hence
> Further, still further through the wilds of Russia,
> Into the terrible, the black, the eternal night![35]

The return of the dead emperor is a frequent theme in Russian literature; the reader need only recall Puškin's "Mednyj Vsadnik" ("The Bronze Horseman"), Lermontov's "The Flying Ship," or Žukovskij's "Nočnoj smotr" ("The Night Inspection") to see a pattern emerge. Petersburg, in particular, is haunted by several imperial ghosts, all murdered. Aleksej Tolstoj's novel *Sestry* (*Sisters*) begins with this chilling portrait of the city: "Petersburg, standing at the edge of the earth, in swamps and woodless tracts, dreamed of limitless glory and power; court coups flashed by in delirious visions, the murders of emperors, triumphs and bloody executions."[36] Thus, the image of Polonskaja's invader draws upon a well-established literary tradition.

At first glance, the dead tsar would appear to be Nikolaj II, but he is actually a composite of several murdered Romanov tsars. *Xozjain krovavyj* (the bloody master) was the epithet applied to Nikolaj II after "Bloody Sunday"; furthermore, the reference to rotting bodies in a low cellar recalls the murder of the imperial family in a cellar in 1917. The figure of Pavel I is suggested by a set of subtexts from Blok's cycle "Pljaski smerti" ("The Dances of Death") which, though written in 1912 to 1914, was first published as a cycle in 1921, in the "canonical" edition of the third volume of his poetry.[37] The first poem in the cycle, "Kak tjažko mertvecu sredi ljudej" ("How Difficult It Is for a Corpse among People," 1912), contains the line, "The living are sleeping. The corpse rises from the grave," as well as clear indications that the setting is Petersburg:

> И в банк идет; и в суд идет, в сенат . . .
> Чем ночь белее, тем чернее злоба . . .
>
> And he goes to the bank, to the court, to the Senate . . .
> The whiter the night, the blacker his malice . . .

There is also a clear link between the *dyrjavoe lico* (face full of holes) of Polonskaja's tsar, with his torn mantle, and the dead king in Blok's fifth poem, "Vnov' bogatyj zol i rad" ("Once Again the Rich Man Is Spiteful and Glad"):

> Шея скручена платком,
> Под дырявым козырьком
>   Улыбается.
>
> His neck bound with a scarf,
> Under a cap full of holes
>   He smiles.[38]

As David Sloane points out, this figure recalls Pavel I, who was strangled with a scarf.[39] Peter III, Pavel's father, was also murdered; the two are buried together in the Peter-Paul Cathedral. Aleksandr II is, of course, another member of this constellation.

The central metaphor in the poem, the attack on the tsar by the red rooster, is an allusion both to Puškin's tale and to the expression *pustit' krasnogo petuxa* (to let out the red rooster), which is understood to mean arson. Arson, or, in many cases, open burning of gentry estates, has historically been the tactic used in peasant uprisings. The image is reinforced by the lines in the fifth quatrain:

> Яд не поможет, железо поможет,
> А не поможет, поможет огонь!

> Poison will not help, iron will help,
> And if it does not, there is fire!

Polonskaja's realization of the metaphor can be traced to another poem by Blok, "Skazka o petuxe i staruške" ("Tale of the Rooster and the Old Woman"). In this poem, written in 1906, an old woman perishes after setting fire to her hut. Blok makes explicit the link between Puškin's golden cockerel and the red cockerel as metaphor for fire:

> Петуха упустила старушка,
> Золотого, как день, петуха!
>
> . . . .
>
> А над кучкой золы разметённой,
> Где гулял и клевал петушок,
> То погаснет, то вспыхнет червонный
> Золотой, удалой гребешок.

> The old woman let out the rooster,
> The rooster, golden as the day!
>
> . . . .
>
> And over a handful of scattered ashes,
> Where the cockerel strolled and pecked,
> Now flickers out, now flares up the crimson
> Golden, bold comb.[40]

As pointed out in the commentary to a recent edition of Blok's poetry, this metaphor has an allegorical significance which is simultaneously folkloric, literary, and political: "Along with the folkloric-mythological subtext (the rooster in folk conceptions is the protector of the hearth from unclean forces) an allegorical meaning is present: a hint at the revolutionary events of 1905 in the country (peasant uprisings, the burning of estates)."[41]

Blok had used the image of a weathercock earlier, in a poem of 1905, "Moej materi" ("To My Mother"):

> Тихо. И будет все тише;
> Флаг бесполезный опущен.
> Только флюгарка на крыше
> Сладко поет о грядущем.

> It is quiet. And all will be even quieter;
> The useless flag has been lowered.
> Only the weathercock on the roof
> Sweetly sings about the future.[42]

Compare this to Polonskaja's lines in the seventh quatrain:

Under a Stone Rain, 1921–23

> The victors are sleeping, they sleep, they hear not,
> Broken by sleep, like a rotten stick . . .
> Only the cock starts to sing on the roof,
> Uninvited guest from a distant settlement.

Blok's entreaty to the tin cockerel, "Sing, tin bird!" is echoed in Polonskaja's line "Sing out thrice! Cry out your time!" The image of Blok's prophetic weathercock was also later paralleled in Axmatova's "Poema bez geroja" ("Poem without a Hero"), in which:

> В Летнем тонко пела флюгарка;
> И серебрянный месяц ярко
> Над серебрянным веком стыл.
>
> In the Summer Garden the weather vane delicately sang;
> And the silver moon brightly
> Froze above the Silver Age.[43]

The parallel between Axmatova's and Blok's use of the image has been noted by V. N. Toporov,[44] and the significance of Axmatova's creation of "a sequence of traditionally vengeful figurines, nemeses of the unrighteous realm" is discussed by Omry Ronen in his book *The Fallacy of the Silver Age*.[45] Polonskaja's poem is a link in the transformation of the image. Her red bird not only warns but avenges.

All of these subtexts to "The Victors Lie Sleeping" support an interpretation of the invader as a murdered tsar and the unrighteous realm as Imperial Russia. The return of the dead tsar may be interpreted as a representation of White forces bent on recapturing the capital. However, the link with "The Dances of Death" also suggests another idea, that of eternal repetition on the historical plane. The second poem in Blok's cycle, "Noč', ulica, fonar', apteka" ("Night, a Street, a Street Lamp, a Pharmacy"), describes the inevitability of repetition and the impossibility of escape, even in death:

> Умрешь—начнешь опять сначала,
> И повторится все, как встарь:
> Ночь, ледяная рябь канала,
> Аптека, улица, фонарь.
>
> You shall die—you shall begin again from the beginning,
> And all will be repeated as of old:
> Night, the icy ripple of the canal,
> The pharmacy, the street, the street lamp.[46]

This endless, inescapable repetition is linked explicitly by Blok with both social injustice and regicide in the fifth poem:

Вновь богатый зол и рад,
Вновь унижен бедный ...

Все бы это было зря,
Если б не было царя
  Чтоб блюсти законы.

Только не ищи дворца,
Добродушного лица,
  Золотой короны.

Он—с далеких пустырей
в свете редких фонарей
  Появляется.

Шея скручена платком,
Под дырявым козырьком
  Улыбается.

Again the rich man is malicious and glad,
Again the poor man is debased ...

All this would have been in vain,
Had there not been a tsar
  To uphold the laws.

Only do not seek the palace,
A good-natured person,
  A golden crown.

He—from distant wastelands,
In the light of rare street lamps
  Shall appear.

His neck bound with a scarf,
Under a cap full of holes
  He smiles.[47]

In David Sloane's view: "These words, which Žirmunskij calls 'prophetic,' presage the recurrence of this event in a new political context (PS V was written on the eve of World War I and the Revolution). At the same time they suggest that such events are ineffectual as agents of historical change. History too is locked in a pattern of meaningless repetitions."[48] Thus, although the red cockerel is called upon to defend the city against the return of empire, there is a suggestion of ultimate futility in the attempt to create a new, socially just state. Revolution and regicide have not broken the eternal cycle of injustice.

There is an additional feature of Polonskaja's invader which renders his identity ambiguous, ambiguous enough to place our interpretation of the poem in an entirely different light. He appears to be a blend of the two main characters from Puškin's tale, the tsar and the sorcerer: "See how he bewitches, not dead, but alive."⁴⁹ Furthermore, there is a puzzling detail in the appeal to the bird to:

> Сядь ему на плечи, бей, что есть сил
> Клювом колючим в плещивое темя....
>
> Perch on his shoulders, beat with all your strength,
> With your sharp beak, on his bald pate....

In Puškin's tale, neither Tsar Dadon nor the sorcerer is described as bald. One member of the composite of murdered tsars, Pavel, fits this description, but there is another, much more conspicuous contemporary figure who also fits: Lenin. This reading is supported by a curious, unpublished poem of Polonskaja's, "Moskva 1922/V moskovskom zamke Černomora" ("Moscow 1922/In the Moscow Castle of Chernomor"), a thematic double to "The Victors Lie Sleeping." In this poem, Lenin is explicitly called a sorcerer:

> И не отбрасывая тени,
> Нетронут пулей, стар и юн,—
> Хозяин местный, входит Ленин—
> Властитель, Ритор, Вождь, Колдун.
>
> And not casting a shadow,
> Untouched by bullets, old and young,—
> The master of these parts, Lenin enters—
> Sovereign, Orator, Leader, Sorcerer.⁵⁰

The image in this poem of a carrion-crows' minuet is another reference to the Dance of Death and thus to Blok's cycle. It also strengthens another subtext to "The Victors Lie Sleeping"—Axmatova's "Čem xuže etot vek predšestvujuščix?" ("How Is This Century Worse than Those Before?"), in which "And here he is marking white houses with crosses" is followed by "And he calls the ravens, and the ravens come."⁵¹

This leaves us with the image of Lenin being set upon by a red cockerel, which returns us to the question of peasant uprising. The antipathy of the peasantry to the urban Bolsheviks is well known, as is a general current of antipeasant sentiment among some of the intelligentsia, who feared the destruction of all culture by the forces of violence and ignorance unleashed by the Revolution. In an article of 1917, "V glubine Rossii" ("In the Depths of Russia"), Maksim Gor'kij predicts the inevitable ascendancy of the peasantry due to their sheer numbers: "The builder of the new state will be peasant Rus'—there is no one else. Where are there other forces? If the working class, small in number and poorly organized, does not disappear in the Civil War,—it will be beaten once and for all by this carnage. The bourgeoisie? The proletariat will not give them a chance to organize for a struggle with the countryside, and with what forces can they oppose tens of millions of peasants, including soldiers? All the conditions indicate that the victor will be rural, peasant Rus'."[52] Gor'kij follows this prediction and ends his article with a pair of chilling anecdotes demonstrating the ignorance and savagery of the Russian peasantry. Šklovskij apparently shared Gor'kij's trepidation. In a letter to Gor'kij dated April 1922, Šklovskij wrote: "My romance with the revolution has been profoundly unhappy.... We, the right socialists, have 'aroused' Russia for the Bolsheviks. But perhaps the Bolsheviks also only 'arouse' Russia, and it is the peasant who will enjoy her."[53]

Given Polonskaja's position as an urban, cultured Jewish intellectual, as well as a student of Šklovskij's and beneficiary of Gor'kij's efforts, it is more than likely that she shared these views. Thus, returning to "The Victors Lie Sleeping" and its subtext in Puškin, we may conclude that the following interpretation is not only possible, but plausible: the sorcerer-tsar, Lenin, whom Polonskaja describes elsewhere as the "chessmaster of popular uprisings,"[54] will become the victim, like Blok's old woman, of the red cockerel which he himself has unleashed.

The final poem in the "Petersburg" cycle, "Igraet med', idut polki" ("The Brass Is Playing, the Regiments Marching"), also ends on a bleak and pessimistic note, and the narrator's attitude toward revolution appears indifferent at best:

> По слову дерзких бедняков,
> Мечтателей, безумцев книжных,
> Здесь в силу воплотилась кровь
> И солнце встало неподвижно.
>
> А ветер с моря сердце рвет
> Пустой и суетной надеждой,
> И медь торжественно поет,
> Как смерть проста и неизбежна.
>
> At the word of insolent peasants,
> Dreamers, and bookish madmen,
> Here blood has been embodied in strength
> And the sun has ceased its motion.
>
> But the wind from the sea tears the heart
> With an empty and vain hope,
> And brass triumphantly sings,
> As simple and unavoidable as death.[55]

TEXTUAL HISTORY

The political harshness in *Under a Stone Rain* is actually considerably milder than Polonskaja originally intended. A partial manuscript and a set of page proofs for *Under the Fatal Point* (1922) have survived, and it is therefore possible to reconstruct some of the changes which were made in its new incarnation as *Under a Stone Rain* in 1923.[56] On inspection of these materi-

Under a Stone Rain, 1921–23

als, it becomes clear that Polonskaja's original conception was altered significantly by the time it appeared in print; the changes reflect an attempt to soften her portrayal of the Bolshevik regime.

A comparison of the two titles and their sources demonstrates a marked shift in emphasis. *Under the Fatal Point* is taken from the poem "Like the Trembling Web of a Butterfly's Wings," the first in the "Petersburg" cycle (described earlier), which did appear in the final version of the collection. The image is of a gilded spire (the Admiralty, or perhaps the spire of the cathedral in the Peter-Paul Fortress) as a needle through the heart of the city, like a pin holding a butterfly to a sheet of paper:

> Что крыльев бабочки трепещущую сеть,
> К бумажному листу насильно пригвожденной,—
> Так сердце города ты можешь рассмотреть
> Под смертным острием иглы позолоченной.

> Like the trembling web of a butterfly's wings,
> Forcibly pinned to a sheet of paper,—
> Thus you may see the heart of the city
> Under the fatal point of a gilded needle.

The poem depicts a city transfixed by terror in a series of images of wind, cold, emptiness, and an oxymoronic scream of silence. Terror itself is personified as a human watchman clad in animal skins:

> А там безмолвие кричит на площадях
> Гортанью сдавленной и ртом обледенелым;
> За сломанной стеной там стражу держит страх,
> В звериной шкуре, с человечьим телом ...

> Пусть ветер повлечет по улицам пустым,
> Пусть покружит тебя по мерзлым перекресткам,
> Чтоб ты насытился и опьянелся им,
> Дыханьем полюса и ночи смертоносным!

> И остановишься, и будешь неживой,
> Обрушишься, как труп, стремительно и сразу,
> Когда из темноты, внезапно, за тобой
> Покажется ревя прожектор одноглазый.

> And there silence screams in the squares
> With a strangled larynx and an ice-covered mouth;
> Behind a broken wall terror stands guard,
> In an animal skin, with a human body ...

> Let the wind rush along empty streets,
> Let it whirl you at frozen crossroads,
> So that you may be sated and intoxicated by it,
> By the breath of the pole and the lethal night!

Serapion Sister

> And you shall stop, and you shall be lifeless,
> You shall fall down at once, headlong, like a corpse,
> When, out of the darkness, suddenly, behind you
> A one-eyed searchlight appears, with a roar.[57]

Unlike the other poems in the cycle, "The Victors Lie Sleeping" and "The Brass Is Playing, the Regiments Marching," which were actually published in journals in 1922,[58] "Like the Trembling Web" never appeared anywhere except in *Under a Stone Rain*. That Polonskaja took the original title of her collection from this terrifying poem suggests that she wished to highlight her depiction of the sheer animal terror experienced by the city's residents.

This emphasis on terror was, apparently, unacceptable to the publisher. The title under which the collection eventually appeared, *Under a Stone Rain,* is taken from the second strophe of Polonskaja's "Though They May Burn Us Up." The phrase itself, as Brett-Harrison points out, is a quotation from Puškin's "Vezuvij zev otkryl—dym xlynul klubom—plamja" ("Vesuvius Opened Its Jaws—Smoke Poured Forth in a Cloud—and Flame," 1834), which was inspired by Karl Brjullov's painting *Poslednij Den' Pompej* (*The Last Day of Pompeii*):

> Везувий зев открыл—дым хлынул клубом—пламя
> Широко развилось, как боевое знамя.
> Земля волнуется—с шатнувшихся колонн
> Кумиры падают! Народ, гонимый страхом,
> Толпами, стар и млад, под воспаленным прахом,
> *Под каменным дождем* бежит из града вон.

> Vesuvius opened its jaws—smoke poured forth in a cloud, and flame
> Spread wide, like a military banner.
> The earth ripples—from the shaken columns
> The idols are falling! The people, driven by terror,
> In crowds, young and old, under the inflamed dust,
> Under a stone rain, flee the city.[59]

Both poems are written in Alexandrines; both depict terror in a city struck by disaster. The residents of Petrograd/Petersburg, however, are not shown fleeing the city. They meet their fate with courage and dignity, thinking not of their own lives, but of their duty to posterity. Amid killing and destruction, the poet speaks of renewal, of the simple biological continuity of human life despite the calamity of war:

> Хотя бы нас сожгли и пепел был развеян
> Из орудийных жерл в пространства вечной тьмы,—
> Мы с жизнью договор наследственный имеем
> И добровольно с ней не разойдемся мы.
>
> Калеки—ползаем, безрукие—хватаем.
> Слепые—слушаем. Убитые—ведем.

Under a Stone Rain, 1921–23

Колеблется земля, и дом уже пылает—
Еще глоток воды! Под каменным дождем . . .

И поцелуй еще! Уже стучат винтовки . . .
—Пора! Прощай!—Прощай! И сына мне оставь,
Чтоб мог ты умереть, конец плотской веревки
Узлом бессмертья туго завязав!

Though they may burn us up and our ashes be scattered
From the cannon's maw into the space of eternal darkness,—
We have a hereditary pact with life
And we will not part with it willingly.

Cripples—we crawl, armless—we clasp.
Blinded—we listen. Murdered—we lead.
The earth shakes, and the house is already blazing—
Another swallow of water! Under a stone rain . . .

And one more kiss! The rifles are already cracking . . .
—It's time! Farewell!—Farewell! And leave me a son,
That you may die, the end of the carnal rope
Having tied into a knot of immortality![60]

Although the poem portrays suffering with great pathos, it has a quality utterly different from that of "Like the Trembling Web." The critic S. Vyšeslavceva singles out this poem as an example of the "vital, strong, biologically obstinate" optimism which "saves" Polonskaja from too strong an association with the "reactionary, un-Soviet lyric of those years, as represented by Axmatova and Radlova, Mandel'štam and Xodasevič."[61] Not surprisingly, it is "Though They May Burn Us Up," not the "Petersburg" cycle, which is not only the source of the collection's title but is also reprinted in all of Polonskaja's subsequent retrospective collections.

The shift in emphasis from the pathos of terror to the resilience of human beings in the face of adversity is further evident when we examine successive versions. Aside from the sorts of editorial changes in the drafts of particular poems which might be expected, there are four provocative political poems which appear in the manuscript and the proofs but not in the final published collection, *Under a Stone Rain*. There are also three poems which appear only in the published version; although not apolitical, they appear less provocative and thus balance out some of the more daring pieces. Thus it is clear that, between this set of proofs and the printed version, censorship was imposed, and the most inflammatory or unorthodox poems were excluded.

The four excluded poems are "Golos" ("The Voice," 1922), "Smirjajem plot' ustalost'ju žestokoj" ("We Subdue Our Flesh with a Cruel Weariness," 1922), "I mudrye pravy i mudrye mudry" ("And the Wise Ones Are Correct and the Wise Ones Are Wise," 1922), and "Kruglyj nož" ("The

Round Knife," 1922). Only one was ever published. "And the Wise Ones" appeared in *Severnoe obozrenie* (*Northern Review*) that year but was never published again.[62]

"The Voice" is a series of imperatives, commanding the addressee to feign weakness and poverty until it is safe to reveal his strength and hatred for a powerful enemy:

> Пусть впалой остается грудь,
> Пусть мышцы дряблы, руки хилы,
> Настанет день, когда нибудь
> Воспрянешь юный, полный силы.
>
> Молчи про верний свой расчет!
> Живи, как подобает нищим!
> Жену и сына, медь и скот
> Скрывай в заплеванном жилище!
>
> И каждый день, и час, и срок
> Наполни ненависти ядом,
> Чтоб враг вздохнуть уже не мог,
> С тобою постречавшись взглядом!
>
> Let your chest remain sunken,
> Your muscles flaccid, your hands weak,
> A day will come, sometime,
> When you will leap up, young and full of strength.
>
> Keep silent about your true reckoning!
> Live as befits a beggar!
> Your wife and son, your copper and cattle—
> Hide them in a dirty dwelling!
>
> And every day, and hour, and moment
> Fill your hatred with venom,
> So that your enemy will be unable to breathe
> Upon meeting your glance![63]

The identities of both lyric persona and addressee are ambiguous; the only hint is a handwritten notation in the proofs. "Golos" ("The Voice"), which is typed above the text, is crossed out, and handwritten above it is an alternative title, "Šejlok" ("Shylock").[64] The allusion is not only to Shakespeare's Shylock, but to Polonskaja's own earlier poem about him, which suggests that the poem is another treatment of anti-Semitism. "The Voice" also plays upon stereotypical images of the Jew in Russian literature as grasping and duplicitous, for example, Gogol's Yankel and his fellow Jews in *Taras Bul'ba*, who command great resources yet live in squalor, dress in dirty rags, and fawn upon gentiles.

"We Subdue Our Flesh with a Cruel Weariness" describes the exhaustion of the day laborer not as heroic but as hideously ugly and somehow sinister; although living, he appears dead ("How ugly he is, still living,—as though dead!"). Furthermore, it ends with an image of a wild, bestial howl that hangs above the houses of the sleepers:

> Но, кто-то по ночам, из глубины великой,
> Кричит сквозь рот его пронзительно и дико.
>
> И в городе, где в каждом доме спящий,
> Унылый вой стоит, как над звериной чащей.
>
> But, someone in the nights, from a great depth,
> Screams through his mouth, piercingly and wildly.
>
> And in the city, where in each house one lies sleeping,
> The gloomy howl hangs, as over a beast's thicket.[65]

"And the Wise Ones Are Correct" is an ironic hymn to the anarchy and violence of revolution, which appear not to have subsided. The wise and their "old God," all-knowing and white-haired, may rule elsewhere, but madness, mob violence, and death still reign here:

> А в нас еще рев и звон и грохот
> Еще колыханье черное толп . . .
> Веселый взвизг выбиваемых стекол,
> Слепящий свет остановленных солнц!
>
> Эй, слушайте там на бумажной карте,
> На глобусе круглом, на плоской земле:—
> Еще у Безумия скипетр на царство
> В веревке намыленной, в крепкой петле!
>
> Да здравствует Карманьола,
> Лучшая из песен!
> Последнего на фонаре,—
> Последнего мудреца,—повесим!
>
> But with us there is still the roar and ringing and thunder,
> Still the black flickering of the crowds . . .
> The merry scream of broken panes,
> The blinding light of halted suns!
>
> Hey, listen, there, on a paper map,
> On a round globe, on the flat earth:—
> Madness still holds the scepter to the kingdom
> In a soaped rope, in a sturdy noose!
>
> Long live the Carmagnole,
> The best of all songs!
> The last one on a lamppost,—
> The last wise one—we shall hang![66]

The last of the censored poems, "The Round Knife," uses the image of a stern, Old Testament God to represent a power which silences the lyric heroine. She expresses a feeling of helplessness before an all-powerful being ("He," "All-knowing") who holds a rounded knife over her, eager to test it on her loved ones. "Child, brother, and mother" was the exact configuration of Polonskaja's family, for whom she was sole support at that time and to whom any politically risky statements of hers could be dangerous. The price of their safety, the poet implies, is her silence and cooperation. The initial admonishment *ne bogoxul'stvuj* (do not blaspheme) is biblical in tone, and the image of the rounded knife resembles the curved blade of the knife in Rembrandt's painting *The Sacrifice of Abraham* (1636), which is in the permanent collection at the Hermitage.[67] Yet the implied sacrifice here comes not as a test of loyalty to God but as a "terrible punishment" for the "blasphemy" of free expression. Furthermore, "He" is never explicitly named as God:

> Над головой твоей, Всеведущ, Мудр и Слеп
> Он держит круглый нож,—ты знаешь—дни и ночи,—
> Ребенка, брата, мать, питье твое и хлеб
> Отнимет, отравит, испытывать охочий!
>
> Поэтому,—молчи! Заткни свой дерзкий рот!
> Безмолвье на уста и воск в пустые уши!
> И дню не доверяй: день здесь, но весь уйдет,—
> А ты останешься и потеряешь душу.

> Above your head, All-knowing, Wise and Blind
> He holds a round knife,—you know—day and night,—
> Child, brother, and mother, your drink and your bread
> He shall take away, shall poison, eager to test you!
>
> Therefore—be silent! Shut your insolent mouth!
> Seal your lips with silence and your empty ears with wax!
> And do not trust the day: day is here, but it shall depart—
> But you will remain and lose your soul.[68]

The image of the knife itself is twofold. In this usage, it corresponds to the round knife held by Abraham in Rembrandt's painting. It also corresponds to the "round knife" in another unpublished poem of that title by Polonskaja, written in 1923. The knife in this poem actually appears to be a cross between a knife and a buzz saw. The first line, "Rukoj ne xvatajsja za kruglyj nož" (Do not take hold of a round knife), refers to the colloquial expression, "Kto tonet, nož podaj, i zá-nož uxvatitsja!" (He who is drowning will take hold of a knife if it is offered!).[69] The poet warns a desperate addressee, perhaps herself, against an act which will not save her. There seems to be no escape from the knife/saw, indifferent and insatiable, which is the poet's life, and which will consume her:

> ... Вертится ремень и пила летит,
> фонтаном кровавая пыль свистит,

Under a Stone Rain, 1921–23

> И, что я сегодня под нож положу—
> Не все ли равно ремню и ножу?
> Затянет ремень и на землю падешь ...
> О, жизнь моя!—Круглый зазубренный нож!

> ...The belt turns and the saw flies,
> A bloody fountain of dust whistles,
>
> And, what shall I place under the knife today—
> Is it not all the same to the belt and the knife?
> The belt will tighten and you fall to the ground ...
> O, my life!—A round buzz saw![70]

The fact that Polonskaja tried to publish the first "Round Knife" poem, as well as the other poems in question, suggests that she was not yet willing in 1922 to accept the impossibility of making such statements; they were a kind of goad, a deliberate provocation to test the limits of the possible. The year 1922 was also the year in which her flippant statement about her inability not to be insolent appeared among the Serapions' autobiographies. As we see in the final version of the collection, by 1923 the limits of the possible had become clear, and Polonskaja had to remove the most "insolent" poems. Her attitude toward this suppression can be inferred from her return to and further development of the image of the round knife.

Somewhere in the course of the editorial process, three poems were added to the collection which do not appear in the publisher's proofs of *Under the Fatal Point*. Two of them, "Legko začat', no trudno budet mne" ("It's Easy to Conceive, But It Will Be Hard for Me") and "Vykup" ("Ransom"), treat the theme of heroic motherhood. "It's Easy to Conceive" is an example of the "biological optimism" described by Vyšeslavceva, a celebration of the role of women in bearing and nurturing not only a new generation but a new sort of person: ("While men struggle in war, / Here women are finishing the job.") "Ransom" is a mother's vow to defy death to protect her child:

> Вот он ползет над страною моей,
> Запах сладимый и хруст костей.
>
> Матери! Встанем живым кольцом!
> К злобному чудищу встанем лицом!
>
> Первая я выступаю вперед:
> «Кто за детеныша выкуп берет?»

> It is crawling over my country,
> A sweetish smell and the crunching of bones.
>
> Mothers! We shall rise up in a living ring!
> We shall rise up to face the evil monster!
>
> I will be the first to step forward:
> "Who will take ransom for our young?"[71]

The selflessness of the heroine, her readiness to give up not only body and blood but also the "joy of my eyes and the black enamel of my braids, bright morning and the scent of dew" for her child is a clear counterpoint to another poem which was part of the original manuscript and remained in the published version. "The Cuckoo Has Brought a Stranger's Chick" presents a very different image of motherhood. This mother, explicitly single and exhausted (there is an echo here of Čexov's "Spat' xočetsja" ["Sleepy"]), both loves her child and resents it with a passion verging on homicidal:

«Кукленок проклятый, оборотень злой,
Я ударю тебя о косяк головой

Я уйду от тебя, пропади совсем!
Будешь ты неподвижен, будешь нем!»

Но жалобно смотрит синий глаз,
И смиряется сердце [в который раз!]
. . . .
«Спи, мое дорогое, спи—живи!
Я тебя охраняю всей злобой любви!»

"Damned doll, evil werewolf,
I will smash your head against the doorframe

I will leave you, be gone forever!
You will be motionless, you will be mute!"

But a blue eye looks at me plaintively,
And my heart gives in [yet again!]
. . . .
"Sleep, my dear, sleep—and live!
I will protect you with all the malice of love!"[72]

"Ransom" appears to be a corrective, a nobler side of the same coin, as it were. Even the formal features of the two poems suggest a link. Both are written in masculine couplets, but whereas the meter of "The Cuckoo" is a loose, four-stressed *dol'nik*, "Ransom" is written in a firm, regular dactylic tetrameter with few deviations, a strong, disciplined meter.

"Ransom" is regarded as one of Polonskaja's finest lyrics, and it was reprinted several times in later collections, whereas "Prinesla Kukuška" was never reprinted. It also became, as A. Anatol'jev remarked, a kind of motto for her, a rule for regarding her own life: "For the poetess, ransom became the immutable law of the time, the law of a generation which was always ready to give its life for the sake of future generations."[73] Like Majakovskij, who "subdued himself, stepping on the throat of his own song," Polonskaja was to pay ransom in her poetry for the life of her child; she began to modify her voice, to go underground, in 1923.

Modification, however, did not necessarily mean complete suppression. As we see in the third poem added to the final version of *Under a Stone*

Under a Stone Rain, 1921–23

Rain, Polonskaja found ways of camouflaging her rebelliousness which were simple but effective. "Ballad of the Fugitive," described previously, is, on its surface, a simple narrative of heroic action in the tradition of Kipling, which had been adopted by a number of her contemporaries, most notably Tixonov. The poem is dedicated to "the memory of the flight of P. A. Krapotkin" (*sic*), implying that its subject is the nineteenth-century anarchist's astonishing escape from the Peter-Paul Fortress. In fact, as Veniamin Kaverin testifies in his memoirs, the real subject of "Ballad of the Fugitive" was not the escape of Kropotkin from a tsarist prison, but that of Viktor Šklovskij from the Bolsheviks in 1922.[74] This piece of information gives the poem an entirely different character; the "two-faced," rapacious, and predatory power ("it wields both terror and punishment") is, in fact, not the tsarist but the Bolshevik state. Furthermore, the speaker reveals her own sympathies:

> . . . Но тот, кому надо скрываться, скрыт.
> Затем что из дома в соседний дом,
> Из сердца в сердце мы молча ведем
> Веселого дружества тайную сеть,
> Ее не нащупать и не подсмотреть!

> . . . But he who needs to hide is hidden.
> Because from house to neighboring house,
> From heart to heart we silently weave
> A secret net of merry friendship,
> You will not see or discover it![75]

If the subject of the poem were really Kropotkin, this *we* would stand out as an inexplicable anachronism, as would the twentieth-century weaponry of the state ("Power has a thousand hands / And more than one machine gun . . .").

Polonskaja's use of the false addressee enabled her to publish this poem not once, but four times. In 1935 she republished it in *Years* in its original form. In 1960, she included it in *Lyric Poems and a Narrative Poem* with two significant changes: a new addressee and a new date, also false. Instead of Kropotkin, it is dedicated to the Bolshevik Jakov Sverdlov and dated June 1917 (the original version was undated).[76] As Brett-Harrison points out, this date places the setting of the poem explicitly in the period of Alexander Kerenskij's provisional government, thus protecting both hero and author even further from identification as anti-Bolshevik sympathizers.[77] The poem appeared in this version in Polonskaja's final collection in 1966, dedicated to Sverdlov but dated simply 1917.[78]

Thus, we see that the publication of *Under a Stone Rain* required a complex negotiation between the poet and the censor. Some of its original sharpness was softened by the removal of a few poems, the shift of emphasis from one poem to another, and, in certain cases, the balancing of more provocative pieces by the addition of apparently less provocative ones. The net result is still a strikingly frank expression of political disillusionment.

Chapter Four

The NEP Period

ROMANTIC COMMUNISM: "KARMEN" AND "V PETLE"

The success of *Under a Stone Rain,* coupled with the *succés de scandale* of the Serapions, established Polonskaja by 1923 as a serious poet with a somewhat reckless reputation. Although unable to publish her most scathing indictments of Bolshevik terror, Polonskaja continued to criticize the contradictions and excesses of the NEP. It was a type of protest she apparently felt she could afford, since it was not so much an anti-Bolshevik stance as an expression of solidarity with the Leningrad-based opposition within the Party, led by Zinoviev and Kamenev, who, according to Boris Frezinskij, was a friend of Polonskaja's.[1] Polonskaja's attacks on NEP reflect what Edward Brown calls "romantic Communism," an idealization of the Revolution itself which underscored the subsequent failure of the regime to live up to its own ideals. Brown, describing Pil'njak's characters in "Krasnoe derevo" ("Mahogany," 1929), stresses the fact that these are people for whom "the finest hour was the Revolution itself and who cannot be at home in the tame construction work of the late twenties."[2] In Polonskaja's work, this phenomenon was most evident in her two major narrative poems, "Karmen" ("Carmen," 1924) and "V Petle" ("In the Noose," 1923).

The heroes of these narratives are devout Communists, idealists, and bold fighters; they represent the antithesis of social order. Although the action in both poems is accompanied by large doses of revolutionary rhetoric, complete with invocations to Lenin in "In the Noose," Polonskaja was chided by critics who reacted with alarm to her "poeticizing of criminals and prostitutes."[3] As Mixail Lučanskij wrote in 1926, "A decrease in the revolutionary romanticism, which had so firmly cemented the strophes of her 'Carmen,' led the author over time to romanticize the heroes of the Ligovka, and not in the figurative or collective sense, but in the most genuine."[4] Because of these two poems, one about a sexually loose woman, the other about a famous criminal, the bandit Len'ka Panteleev, Polonskaja became associated with "hooliganism," a term used to denote not only crime but all manner of phenomena considered socially unhealthy.

The NEP Period

"Carmen," published twice in 1924, is the story of a Russian factory girl saved by the Revolution from the fate of her namesake, Mérimée's heroine:

> Не Хозе вовлекать в беду,
> Не помогать контрабандистам,—
> Кармен в семнадцатом году
> Была в России коммунисткой.
>
> Не к славе цирковых арен,
> Где Эскамильо бьется ловкий,
> Нет, за любовником Кармен
> На Колчака идет с винтовкой . . .
>
> Not luring Jose to his doom,
> Not aiding a smugglers' band,—
> In 1918, Carmen
> Was a Communist in Russia.
>
> Not to the glory of circus rings,
> Where Escamilio deftly battles,
> No, behind her lover Carmen
> Is marching on Kolčak with a rifle . . .[5]

The poem traces the heroine's development from street waif to "wanton factory girl" to rifle-toting rebel in regular quatrains of tight iambic tetrameter. Idly watching a Communist street demonstration, Carmen is awakened from political apathy, her class instinct aroused by hearing "someone fat, with the mug of a dog" snarl at the demonstrators, "You've sung your song, you scum!"

> Тогда, очнувшись, как от сна,
> И медленно сойдя с панели,
> Веселой злобою полна
> Кармен примкнула к тем, кто пели.
>
> Then, as though waking from a dream,
> And slowly stepping down from the sidewalk,
> Full of gay malice
> Carmen joined the ones who were singing.[6]

Because the poem ends with the heroine marching off to fight the White general Kolčak, the reader is given no indication of her attitude once the military phase of revolution has ended; time has frozen for Carmen, as it has for Pil'nyak's Ožogov and his friends, during the time of war communism.

Carmen's inability to adapt to NEP can be inferred from two things: her class solidarity and her powerful, unfettered sexuality. The first guarantees her alienation from the greed and consumerism of neobourgeois society. The second guarantees her alienation from the ideological weapons used by the Party to combat this moral decay. By 1924 the Party, alarmed both at the social chaos created by the sexual revolution and at a resurgence of prostitution, had already initiated what Richard Stites calls the "sexual Thermidor." A campaign against "sexual depravity" was launched in the press, and a theory of "revolutionary sublimation" was developed and advocated by prominent Bolshevik doctors.[7] Carmen, attractive and utterly promiscuous, represents everything the Party was trying to suppress:

> Матрос, армеец, слесарь, вор—
> Она любила не торгуясь,
> И никому до этих пор
> Не отказала в поцелуях...

> Sailor, soldier, locksmith, thief—
> She loved them all without haggling,
> And no one, to this day,
> Has ever been refused her kisses.[8]

The most dangerous feature of Carmen's sexuality, from the Party point of view, is that it appears to have no fatal consequences for anyone. It is, in fact, a kind of metonymy, representing a more general antipathy to any sort of restraint or coercion. Comparison with Blok's 1914 cycle, "Carmen," reinforces our understanding of how Polonskaja has interpreted Carmen. Blok's addressee was not the fictional character but the opera singer Ljubov' Andreeva-Del'mas, with whom he had a love affair after seeing her play the lead in Bizet's opera. Aside from the heroine's name and character, and the idea of love "free as a bird," there are particular echoes from Blok's sixth poem, "Serdityj vzor bescvetnyx glaz" ("The Angry Gaze of Colorless Eyes"), including this one:

> И март наносит мокрый снег.
> And March brings a wet snow.
> (Blok)[9]

> Октябрь. Ты помнишь мокрый снег.
> October. You remember the wet snow.
> (Polonskaja)

The wet March snow refers to the season of Blok's earliest infatuation with Del'mas, when the cycle was written. The juxtaposition of March with October is emblematic of Polonskaja's adaptation of the theme: Carmen is transformed from love heroine to passionate revolutionary. The erotic aspects of the character are no longer central to the narrative; this Carmen's willful sexuality serves as an illustration of her strength and rebelliousness which, far from leading to "an evil death under the gates," lead to victory, long life, and an honored place in posterity.

Some observations by Eric Naiman on the character and function of sexual discourse during NEP are illuminating in this regard. As Naiman writes, during the NEP period, excessive enjoyment of sexual pleasure acquired a suspect character in Party ideology, as did other forms of unregulated consumption: "Excess in eating and excess in sexual behavior were two of the traits that distinguished the bourgeois from his or her hardworking proletarian counterpart.... Protecting one's ideological purity entailed not only controlling one's sexual urges but also refraining from overeating and from surrounding oneself with opulence."[10] Naiman describes the ascetic ideal in Party discourse, often carried to extremes, as a collective rejection of the body in an attempt to curb some of the excesses of NEP. In another article, he explores the use of venereal infection as a metaphor for political corruption, outlining the polemic between those who regarded NEP as a controllable form of social "inoculation" (Stalin, Buxarin) and those who saw the "contamination" as potentially fatal to the future of the Revolution (Kamenev, Zinoviev). He also posits the role of discussions on sexuality in the Party press as an instrument for social control, and literary works as important stimuli to such discussions:

> 1926 saw the publication of several highly publicized tales of sexual depravity, including Pantalejmon Romanov's "Without Cherry Blossoms," Lev Gumilevskij's *Dog Alley* and Sergei Malashkin's "The Moon from the Right Side." These works, when read today, seem didactic, moralizing tracts. But in 1926 and 1927 they were attacked as immoral and slanderous. Nevertheless, or perhaps therefore, these publications aroused enormous interest. Many public discussions were held about them and used to investigate and, in effect, infiltrate the youth's sexual lives. The Komsomol organs in this period endeavored to tease and excite so that they could later condemn and, eventually, control.[11]

These works contain several recurrent themes, such as "the sharing of a woman by two comrades, the direct equation of sexual passion with violent death and the use of infection as metaphor,"[12] and sexual indulgence usually has negative consequences. Polonskaja's Carmen is particularly subversive in this context, because her sexuality, unlike that of her namesake, is fatal to no one, nor does it interfere with her work as a Communist.

Naiman also stresses that the collective rejection of physiology and sexuality had an antifemale bias, which he attributes to certain misogynistic currents in prerevolutionary Russian thought.[13] This "purging of the feminine," he asserts, was practiced not only by men, but also by women, including, oddly enough, Kollontai. The ascetic heroine of her novel *Vasilisa Malygina* (1923) is portrayed as androgynous in appearance and revolted by the voluptuous bodies and blood-red lips of her rivals, the NEP women. According to Naiman: "Political revulsion was becoming unmentionable, while the taboo on sexuality was weakening in accordance with the dictates of a self-consciously materialistic age. In this environment, talk about sex became a metaphor—and symptom—for thoughts about something else:

politics and ideology. In Kollontai's fiction, political disgust with the state of Party policy becomes sexual disgust, and the penetration of Soviet Society by ideological enemies is equated with the defilement—through *normal* physiological processes—of the female body."[14] Thus, Polonskaja's use of an attractive and sexually active woman as emblem of Bolshevik Revolution was bound to be controversial at a time when even Kollontai, long a staunch advocate of sexual freedom for women, used female sexuality as a metaphor for political corruption.

For Polonskaja it is not sexuality itself but traditional constraints upon it which represent the worst aspects of bourgeois culture. Rebellion against traditional marriage is a theme both in "Carmen," whose heroine was born out of wedlock, and in one of her lyrics published that same year, "Lebed'" ("The Swan"). In this poem, the swan-maiden flees the captivity of a suffocating marriage:

> Так унизиться! Так забыться!
> Сыновей носить и блюсти твой дом;
> Пить из блюдечка, мирною птицей
> Прыгать по полу, петь под окном . . .
>
> To so lower myself! To so forget myself!
> To bear sons and look after your house!
> To drink from a saucer, like a peaceable bird,
> Hop along the floor, sing under the window![15]

Kollontai had also insisted on the exploitative nature of bourgeois marriages based on economic dependency; she had long advocated free sexual unions based only on mutual feeling. For Kollontai, however, the satisfaction of the sexual impulse had always been very much a matter of physical and social hygiene; in her "Theses on Communist Morality in the Sphere of Marital Relations," for example, we find the statement, "In the period of the dictatorship of the proletariat, relations between the sexes should be evaluated only according to the criteria . . . [of] the health of the working population and the development of inner bonds of solidarity within the collective."[16] Furthermore, in her essay "Make Way for Winged Eros" (1923), Kollontai stresses the fact that love is not, and never has been, "a 'private' matter concerning only the two loving persons."[17] Polonskaja, on the contrary, writes of love and sex explicitly as matters of individual will and freedom, which often runs directly counter to the norms and interests of the collective.

The critic S. Vyšeslavceva describes "The Swan" as "full of what is so characteristic of Polonskaja, an anarchistic, proud protest against any 'unfreedom' of feeling, against its constraint by daily life or conventional norms (see 'Carmen'). Her love has in it something of the gypsy, it comes and goes unexpectedly, it is a law unto itself."[18] The phrase *sama sebe zakon* (a law unto itself) occurs in the final poem of Blok's "Carmen" cycle, "Net, nikogda moej, i ty nič'ej ne budeš" ("No, Never to Be Mine, and You Shall Belong to No One"): "Sama sebe zakon— letiš', letiš' ty mimo, / K sozvezdijam inym, ne vedaja orbit . . ." (A law unto yourself—you are flying, flying past me, / To other constellations, knowing no orbit . . .)[19] Vyšeslavceva's repetition of it in this context, along with the characterization of Polonskaja's love as "gypsy," emphasizes the fact that, where matters of the heart and the flesh are concerned, Polonskaja has more in common with Blok than with Kollontai.

Even more controversial than "Carmen" was Polonskaja's "In the Noose," based on the story of a contemporary criminal, Len'ka Panteleev. The poem was written in 1923, but Polonskaja did not publish it until 1925. She may have felt emboldened to do so by the Party's cautious declaration of neutrality in literary matters, published in *Pravda* in July of that year. However, despite the fact that the Party refused to show a preference for any particular literary movement, it nevertheless affirmed its intention to "mercilessly fight against counterrevolutionary manifestations in literature, to uncover liberalism of the 'change of landmarks' type and so on."[20] That "and so on" could be interpreted variously, and although Polonskaja's poem purports to be a glorification of the spirit of revolution, it clearly was a kind of glorification that Party critics found unacceptable.

According to Olga Žuk, Polonskaja's poem "somehow absorbed the coexisting official and apocryphal versions of Len'ka's fate."[21] Her Len'ka appears to be a blend of the "real" man, a detective turned criminal and the leader of his own gang, and another famous figure of the same period, Vanja Šorin, a sailor who fell in with a gang and later betrayed them.[22] Polonskaja's Len'ka is a Red sailor who turns to crime, embittered by the social inequities now sanctioned in the name of NEP. In an unpublished poem of 1922, "Vesy i giry, sterlingi i funty" ("Weights and Measures, Sterlings and Pounds"), Polonskaja had protested bitterly against the "loathsome, mercenary, and hateful spirit" of NEP. Her Len'ka robs and murders a drunken NEPman and his woman, takes up with a prostitute, and is finally shot down in his hideout by detectives.

"In the Noose" draws not only upon contemporary urban folklore (Panteleev's story was told not only in newspaper accounts but also in songs)[23] but also on an older tradition. The phrase *bujnaja golova* (untamed spirit), which Len'ka uses to describe himself at the beginning, explicitly links him with the Russian folk song, which includes a long tradition of outlaw-heroes such as Stenka Razin and a host of fabled robbers, many of whom are described with the same phrase. According to Vladimir Propp, there exists an entire category of Russian folk lyrics known as "robber songs," in which the robber is "a fighter for trampled justice. He never robs the poor, only the rich."[24] Thus, by means of a familiar epithet often applied to the heroes of folk songs, sympathy is established for the bandit; the reader is to infer that his crimes are justified because they are committed in the name of social justice.

"In the Noose" also represents the trend toward the "revolutionary adventure" or "red Pinkerton," a term suggested by Nikolaj Buxarin.[25] According to Richard Stites, practitioners of this sort of literature "tried to serve the interests of the state, of the masses, and of their own art by blending propaganda, adventure, and parody. In an obviously self-conscious and good-natured way, they adopted the tricks of popular culture and especially the conventions of silent cinema. Their output was in fact cinematized fiction, another striking example of the mutual fertilization of the popular arts."[26] "In the Noose" is dedicated to Šaginjan, the author of *Mess Mend* (1923–25), which Stites calls "the first and most famous 'red detective story.'"[27] The full title of the poem is "In the Noose: A Lyric Film," and the structure, a montage of eleven numbered scenes placed within a prologue and an epilogue, is indeed reminiscent of a filmed sequence. In keeping with the rapid shifts in setting and action, the formal features of "In the Noose" vary from scene to scene. Some parts are written in more or less regular quatrains with alternating masculine and feminine rhymes, while others are more loosely constructed. Meter varies as well, with some sections in regular trochaic trimeter or tetrameter, some in iambic trimeter, and others in various types of tonic verse. The only unifying formal feature is a strong, driving rhythm which conveys fast-paced action and dramatic tension. Polymetry was common in the 1920s, particularly for a work featuring various voices. However, the formal variety (some might say anarchy) in "In the Noose" also underscores Len'ka's refusal to submit to authority.

In the first scene, which begins, "It's become hard to get bread," the hero describes poverty in the midst of plenty and how the poor still live "gritting their teeth," though there is more than enough bread. It begins with four-stressed *dol'niki* which give way to three-stressed as the monologue progresses. The rhyme also begins erratically and gradually becomes a regular, interlocking *AbAb* pattern as the section builds momentum. Len'ka recalls in a vivid flashback his glory days on the *Aurora* and the storming of the Winter Palace:

> А помнишь, на «Авроре»,
> Ты помнишь пушек гром?
> Шел дождь и был ветер с моря,—
> Мы встали перед дворцом.
> Я первый пошел на приступ
> За волю! за хлеб! за мир!
> Война капиталистам!
> «Погибни старый мир!»

The NEP Period

> And do you remember, on the *Aurora*,
> Remember the cannons' thunder?
> It was raining, and the wind came from the sea,—
> We took our stand in front of the palace.
> I was first in the assault
> For freedom! For bread! For peace!
> War to the capitalists!
> "Die, old world!"[28]

This flashback is a reprise of the second section of "Carmen," also a remembrance of the storming of the palace. It also contains repetitions of the word *pomniš'* (do you remember?), emphasizing the fact that those heroic days are over:

> Ты помнишь стали и свинца
> Борьбу на площади кровавой,
> Когда на штурм ночной дворца
> Внезапно хлынули заставы ...
>
> Do you remember the struggle of steel
> And lead on the bloody square,
> When at the night storming of the palace
> We suddenly rushed the gates ... [29]

The scene then shifts to the present, and Len'ka recounts with bitterness how the struggle is now belittled and mocked:

> Они дрожали, собаки,
> При виде наших знамен!
> А нынче смеется всякий ...
> Матросом гнушается он!
>
> Води пером по странице ...
> Рассчитывай «дважды два» ...
> Может ли с этим мириться
> Буйная голова?
>
> They trembled, the dogs,
> At the sight of our banners.
> And now everyone is laughing ...
> Treating sailors with contempt.
>
> Move your pen across the page,
> Figure "two times two"!
> Can an untamed spirit
> Make his peace with this?[30]

The second scene, beginning "But the city is black and burning with fires," portrays in couplets of four-stressed *dol'niki* the atmosphere of desperate, giddy hedonism in a city just released from the terrors and deprivations of war:

> А на улице говор и женский смех,—
> Кончено! кончено!—смерть не для всех!
> Еще можно любить
> И можно жить,
> И можно сегодня о завтра забыть.
>
> And on the street—chatter and women's laughter,—
> It's over! It's over! Death is not for all!
> You can still love
> And you can live,
> And today you can forget about tomorrow.[31]

In this setting, Len'ka quickly wins fame and admiration for his charm and daring. In scene 3 we see him through the eyes of a prostitute who voices a general sentiment:

> Ленька Пантелеев;
> Сыщиков гроза:
> На руке браслетка,
> Синие глаза...
>   Кто еще так ловок?—
>   Посуди сама!
>   Сходят все девчонки
>   От него с ума!
> Нараспашку ворот
> В стужу и мороз.
> Говорить не надо,—
> Видно, что матрос.
>
> Len'ka Panteleev,
> The terror of detectives:
> Bracelet on his arm,
> Deep blue eyes...
>   Who else is so clever—
>   Judge for yourself!
>   All the broads are losing
>   Their minds over him.
> Collar unbuttoned
> In the cold and frost!
> No need to say it—
> You can see he's a sailor![32]

As in "Carmen," the hero is both a committed Communist and a sex symbol. His blue eyes and open collar drive women to distraction, recalling the figure of the blue-eyed youth in Axmatova's "Rybak" ("The Fisherman," 1911):

The NEP Period

> И всегда, всегда распахнут
> Ворот куртки голубой,
> И рыбачки только ахнут,
> Закрасневшись пред тобой.
>
> And always, always open
> Is the collar of your blue jacket,
> And the fisherwomen only sigh,
> Blushing before you.[33]

It is Len'ka's rebelliousness, aside from his physical charm, which makes him irresistible; like Carmen, he is "a law unto himself." The regular trochaic trimeter of this section, which gives it a songlike quality, shifts abruptly to a final quatrain of alternating tetrameter and trimeter. Having voiced her admiration for Len'ka and announced her intention of taking to the streets, the speaker offers a justification: she has already prostituted herself for bread (her mother's tacit approval is implied), so why not for luxuries as well?

> Все равно, за черный хлеб
> Дочку не сберечь,
> Чтоб ботинки до колен ...
> Серьги бы до плеч ...
>
> It's all the same, for black bread
> To give away your daughter,
> Why not for boots up to my knees ...
> For earrings down to my shoulders ...[34]

Scene 4 shifts again to a voice, presumably Len'ka's, castigating the system by which "leather jackets" protect the "rich and the sated," the jeweler and the wheeler-dealer (*delec*). The trochaic tetrameter/trimeter of the last section is continued here, although in an irregular stanzaic form (two couplets followed by an *abab* quatrain, two more couplets punctuated by repetitions of the metrically anomalous line "Revoljucija tebja oxranjaet" [The Revolution protects you], and a final quatrain). The final warning is given a touch which adds a folk coloring—feminine rhyme alternates with dactylic:

> Миру старому отсрочка
> Перед смертью дадена:
> Пусть последние денечки
> Доживает гадина!
>
> To the old world a postponement
> Is given before death:
> Let them live out
> Their miserable last days, the vermin![35]

Scene 5, written in quatrains of slightly irregular dactylic trimeter, begins with an advertisement for a film depicting a hunt for wild beasts on the Argentine prairie. The excitement and danger of the hunt are then transposed to the city streets, where "you'll catch plenty of game," but the prey is human. Scene 6 depicts the fatal attack, beginning in regular amphibrachic tetrameter with a description of the NEPman-victim. He is portrayed by a synecdoche which doubly dehumanizes him: he is referred to as "the beaver coat" ("The beaver coat walks along, enjoying himself, / The beaver coat is drunk"), not even a live animal, but an inanimate object. It is also a symbol of his wealth, which has attracted his female companion; she is described, in a series of logaoedic lines of dactyl-iamb with caesura (/---/-// /---/), only as a pair of long earrings and a silk shawl. Their relationship is characterized as follows:

> Богатой или нищей,
> Законной или нет,—
> Любовь, немного пищи,
> Да платье, да браслет ...
>
> Rich woman or beggar,
> Lawful or not,—
> Love, a little food,
> A dress, a bracelet ...[36]

The fact that she barters her sexuality (whether as a wife or as a mistress) immediately sets her in contrast with Carmen, who loves "without haggling."

Scene 7 cuts abruptly from the scene of the crime to the dance floor of a seedy nightclub, where Len'ka celebrates his newfound wealth in the arms of a "madcap girl." The dance rhythm is conveyed in quatrains of regular iambic trimeter. In scene 8 he offers her earrings from a corpse and brags of his conquest, which he describes as the rightful redistribution of wealth from pampered aristocrats to "such as I, . . . / Dung and rawhide!" Trochaic tetrameter lines are punctuated by short lines which complete them syntactically:

> Полюби меня немножко,
>   Молодца!
> Подарю тебе сережки
>   С мертвеца!
>
> Love me a little, I'm a fine
>   fellow!
> I will give you earrings
>   from a corpse!

The scene ends with the following lines, set off as a separate couplet in three-stressed *dol'niki* with a dactylic rhyme:

The NEP Period

> Революция еще не кончена!
> Пусть погонаются с гончими!
>
> The revolution is not yet over:
> Let them come after me with hounds!³⁷

These lines, with their equation of crime and revolution, infuriated critic Mixail Lučanskij, who singled them out for attack.³⁸

The final three scenes, in varied *dol'niki*, take place in Len'ka's hideout where, surrounded by detectives, he makes a last stand before being gunned down. In scene 9 the prostitute and a comrade urge him to flee, but he stands his ground. The three-stressed *dol'niki* of this section are accompanied by repetitions of a single line of regular amphibrachic trimeter, like a refrain:

> Убийца сидит за столом ...
>
> Убийца сидит за столом,
> А сыщики тут как тут ...
> Уже окружали дом ...
> Но живым его не возьмут!
>
> The murderer sits at the table ...
>
> The murderer sits at the table,
> But here are the detectives,
> They've already surrounded the house,
> But they won't take him alive!³⁹

In the body of the poem, the main point of view is ostensibly that of the hero, not the author. It is Len'ka, the reader is meant to assume, who regards NEP as corrupt and who thus justifies his banditry, and it is the prostitute who voices her admiration for him in what Sergei Malaxov calls "tones of obvious delight."⁴⁰ The prologue and epilogue express a more measured and politically orthodox, if still somewhat romantic, view of events. In the prologue, Lenin is invoked as the "chessmaster of popular uprisings," who will replace the Bronze Horseman as leader and guiding spirit of the city.⁴¹ In the epilogue, the apparent regression of NEP is described as part of a wise plan engineered by the Chessmaster:

> Но для нас начертал Шахматист
> Схему мудрую новых сражений,—
> Разграфленный квадратами лист
> Наступлений и отступлений.
>
> But for us the Chessmaster has traced out
> A wise scheme of new battles,
> A square-lined sheet
> Of attacks and retreats.⁴²

Retreat is justified as a survival tactic, and the poem closes with a refrain familiar from Polonskaja's earlier poetry:

И когда-нибудь все поймут,—
Умереть—все равно, что сдаться.
Наперекор всему
Надо в живых остаться.

And someday all will understand:
To die is to give in.
In defiance of everything
We must remain among the living.[43]

Critics, however, remained unconvinced, and several insisted that the author's sympathies clearly lie with her hero. According to critics, the "cold lines"[44] about the Chessmaster and his blueprint cannot match the vivid descriptions of the action. Polonskaja's hatred for the class enemy, the bourgeois, is clearly expressed in scene 4 where, as elsewhere in Polonskaja's poetry, he is equated with vermin, a loathsome animal ("Let them live out / Their miserable last days, the vermin"). The bourgeoisie are frequently equated in Polonskaja's poems with dogs, as in the passage quoted from scene 1, where Len'ka calls those who mock him *sobaki* (dogs). In "Carmen," too, we find the heroine radicalized by her hatred for "someone fat, with the mug of a dog," and in another poem, "Sobaki" ("Dogs," 1927), human spectators at a dog race, with "hind-quarters in trousers and hats on their snouts," are compared unfavorably with the animals.[45] Thus, although the passage is spoken in the voice of the hero, the author's attitude is evident.

LITERARY HOOLIGANISM: POLONSKAJA, ESENIN, AND THE CRITICS

Critics expressed alarm over the fact that Polonskaja's Len'ka had captivated not only young girls but also "the inexperienced reader."[46] The issue of *Kovš* which included "In the Noose" also contained Veniamin Kaverin's "Konec Xazy" ("The End of the Gang"), and these two popular works together were seen as a pernicious influence on young people. O. Barabašev observes disapprovingly that "there is a line for it in the libraries . . . the book passes from hand to hand, they are reading it to shreds."[47] L. Baril' echoes Barabašev's concern, in this case about the influence of the two works on other writers: "The Proletarian poets Panfilov and Sadof'jev sing of the criminal street world, as Polonskaja sang of the most left of all lefts, the Leningrad bandit Panteleev, as Kaverin sang of his robbers. What if Sadof'jev, Panfilov, and Polonskaja had the same wide audience as Esenin? Perhaps collapse, rot, and decay will become facts of good order, when proletarian lyricists praise them with their own lips."[48] References to Esenin appear frequently in critical attacks on Polonskaja in the mid-1920s; after the publication of his cycle "Moskva kabackaja" ("Tavern Moscow") in 1924, and increasingly after his shocking suicide in 1925, "Eseninism" became a synonym for "hooliganism" in the press. Lučanskij defines literary "Eseninism" as "poetry of breakdown and spiritual emptiness . . . a cult of the tavern and a glorification of hooliganism."[49] Baril's rebuke to Polonskaja for "poeticizing criminals and—prostitutes"[50] may be read as a reference to Esenin's lines from "Tavern Moscow": "I read verses to prostitutes / And gulp liquor with bandits."[51]

The tradition of *blatnaja romantika* (criminal romanticism) was not created by Esenin, as Žuk points out: "Important here is also public opinion—Russian humanistic thought and folk consciousness, and the criminal's own attitude toward himself and his crime, which coincide in Rus'. The criminal is a sufferer, a victim of his own crime."[52] One need only recall Dostoevskij's Raskolnikov, Leskov's Katerina Izmailovna, or the aforementioned robber songs to see how deeply ingrained is the Russian tradition, both popular and literary, of sympathy for the outlaw, and to realize how receptive a Russian audience would have been to Panteleev. Taverns populated by drunks and prostitutes were Blok's territory years before they were Esenin's. Esenin came to personify the hooligan partly because he himself was famous for his alcoholism, his disorderly personal life, and his penchant for scandalous behavior. His hooligan-poet is not just a poetic mask; he is a pose consciously adopted by the poet in his life as well as his verse, and he admits that the tavern is his refuge from an alien, hostile world:

> Ну кто ж из нас на палубе большой
> Не падал, не блевал и не ругался?
> Их мало, с опытной душой,
> Кто крепким в качке оставался.
>
> Тогда и я
> Под дикий шум,
> Но зрело знающий работу,
> Спустился в корабельный трюм,
> Чтоб не смотреть людскую рвоту.
> То трюм был—
> Русским кабаком.
> И я склонился над стаканом,
> Чтоб, не страдая ни о ком,
> Себя сгубить
> В угаре пьяном

> Well, which of us, on the main deck,
> Has not fallen, has not puked and cursed?
> They are few, the experienced souls
> Who remained strong in this tossing about.

> I too,
> In the wild noise,
> Knowing well what I was doing,
> Went down into the ship's hold,
> So as not to watch people retching.
> That hold was—
> The Russian tavern.
> And I bowed my head over a glass,
> So that, not suffering at all,
> I could ruin myself
> In drunken ecstasy.[53]

Esenin's brand of hooligan actually has little in common with Polonskaja's Len'ka, since he seeks oblivion rather than retribution. His most dangerous and potentially contagious characteristic was not direct political subversion as such, but an incapacitating despair which grew out of his political disillusionment.

Polonskaja's attitude toward Esenin was ambivalent. Her memoir, "Pamjatnaja vstreča: Sergej Esenin" ("Memorial Meeting: Sergej Esenin"), wavers between disapproval of his drunken antics and poetic associations (she did not care much, she says, for his peasant poems or for his "Imagism")[54] and genuine admiration for his lyric gift. In 1924, Polonskaja published a poem, "Sergeju Eseninu" ("To Sergej Esenin"), which expressed her conflicting emotions toward the man and his poetry:

> И цвет волос моих иной,
> И кровь моя горчей и гуще,—
> Голубоглазый и льняной,
> Поющий, плачущий, клянущий.
> Ты должен быть мне чужд как лесть
> Неистовств этих покаянных,
> Ты должен быть мне чужд, но есть
> В твоих светловолосых странах
> Волненье дивное. Меня
> Волной лирической ответной
> Вдруг сотрясает всю, и я,
> Как камертон, едва заметной
> Издалека тебе откликнусь дрожью,
> Затем что не звучать с тобою невозможно.

> And the color of my hair is different,
> And my blood more bitter and thick,—
> Blue-eyed and flaxen-haired one,
> Singing, weeping, and swearing.
> You should be alien to me, but there is
> In your fair-haired lands
> A wondrous agitation. With

The NEP Period

> An answering lyric wave
> It suddenly shakes me utterly, and
> Like a tuning fork, from a distance,
> I respond with a barely perceptible tremor,
> Because not sounding with you is impossible.[55]

The overt references to their physical characteristics—differences in hair color and blood—suggest a reference to Esenin's reputation as an anti-Semite.[56] Polonskaja claims to have avoided meeting him, even at his invitation, and that she saw him for the first time in his coffin.[57] Yet his death, the suicide of a persecuted poet, appears to have affected her deeply; she wrote several elegies to him in 1926, including a draft of a poem, "Kukloj voskovoju on ležal v grobu" ("He Lay in the Coffin Like a Wax Doll"), which contains the following lines: "Ne prostoj pokojnik byl on—dvaždy net— / Byl samoubijca, byl on i poet" (He was no ordinary dead man—twice no,— / He was a suicide and also a poet).[58] The meter of that poem, trochaic hexameter with a strong, constant caesura, recalls the trochaic trimeter of the refrain in which the prostitute declares her admiration for Len'ka Panteleev ("Len'ka Panteleev, / Syščikov groza . . .").[59]

Polonskaja published another poem to Esenin after his death, "Ty byl našej tajnoj ljubov'ju" ("You Were Our Secret Love"), in *A Stubborn Calendar* in 1929, in tandem with the 1924 poem "And the Color of My Eyes Is Different." In this elegy, she expressed a solidarity with Esenin, not only of other poets, but of an "irreverent brotherhood":

> Прощай, златоглавый! Счастливый путь
> Тебе от шутейшего братства!
> Мы все ведь шальные. Когда-нибудь
> И нам надоест притворяться.
>
> Farewell, goldenheaded one! Bon voyage
> To you from the jesting brotherhood!
> For we are all madcaps. Someday
> We too shall grow tired of pretending.[60]

Her admiration, which she retained despite her distaste for various aspects of Esenin's life and work, was inspired not only by his talent but also by his obstinate refusal to conform to political demands which went against his nature. As she wrote in her memoir, "the theoreticians of Marxism could not forgive the *kulak* poet for the willful movements of his heart. . . . In this youth was an insolent spirit, and his struggle with the ideologues of RAPP inspired sympathy in all who loved literature."[61]

The quality of *derzost'* (insolence) had always been precious to Polonskaja. In her memoirs of childhood, she describes the development of a pronounced split between her outward timidity and inner defiance, almost to the point of pugnacity, a split which was reflected in her poetry. When the Serapions published their infamous "autobiographies" in *Literaturnye zapiski* in 1922, Polonskaja's contribution contained the statement, "I was a good student at the gymnasium, but there were three things I never could learn: not to be late to the first lesson, not to look sullen, and not to speak insolently (*ne smotret' ispodlob'ja* [literally 'to look from under my brow'] *i ne govorit' derzostej*)."[62]

These two words, *ispodlob'ja* and *derzost'*, which Polonskaja uses to characterize herself, appear repeatedly in significant places in her poetry from the 1920s. Both are used to describe Carmen:

> Она все та же. Прядь волос
> Тугим кольцом над тонкой бровью,
> И взгляд очей ее раскос
> Из-под косынки, *исподлобья* ...
>
> ... И из глазастой и худой
> Девчонки, *дерзкой* и лукавой,
> Внезапно пышной красотой ...
>
> She is just the same. A lock of hair
> In a tight ring above a delicate brow,
> And the slanting glance of her eyes
> From under the kerchief, *from under her brows* ...
>
> ... And from a large-eyed, skinny
> Little girl, *insolent* and sly,
> Suddenly in splendid beauty
> She blossomed. . . .[63]

Lenin himself, in the prologue of "In the Noose," is shown "sullenly looking sidelong (*ispodlob'ja kositsja*) at the stars."[64] In "Nasledstvo" ("The Legacy," 1924), in which the poet bequeaths her beloved Petersburg to her son, she describes the spirit of the city as follows:

> В нем песни теснились, в нем гибли герои.
> Ценее, чем золото, маузера чтимей,
> В нем *дерзости* творческой дух несмиримый.
>
> In it songs have clustered, heroes have perished.
> More precious than gold, more honored than a Mauser,
> In it is the unconquered spirit of creative *insolence*.[65]

In *A Stubborn Calendar* (1929), the poems to Esenin are followed by "Lavočka velikolepij" ("Little Shop of Splendors"), an affectionate elegy for Lunc, the most irreverent and beloved member of the "irreverent brotherhood."[66] The juxtaposition in the collection emphasizes the kinship perceived by Polonskaja between two "insolent spirits," both of whom died tragically. Lunc represents the obverse of Esenin; he had the poet's impudence without his self-destructiveness. The final lines to Esenin, "For we are all madcaps. Someday / We too will grow tired of pretending," are followed by the opening of the poem to Lunc:

> Так. За прилавком пятый год
> Стоим. Торчим. Базарим ...
>
> So. For the fifth year behind a counter
> We stand. We hang about. We peddle our wares. . . .[67]

The surviving Serapion Brothers, Polonskaja implies, have sold out in adapting to the new literary market, but they still treasure the memory of Lunc, whose infectious laughter and fearlessness before critics made him, in Polonskaja's words, "the most serapionic"[68] among the brothers:

> С воспоминаний сбив замок,
> Достанем из-под спуда
> Что каждый в памяти сберег,
> Что в тайный прятал уголок—
> Усмешку, дерзость, удаль.
>
> Having broken the lock off our memories,
> We shall take out from under a bushel
> That which each has treasured in memory,
> Has hidden in a secret corner—
> A smile, insolence, boldness.[69]

In a five-poem cycle of 1926, "Proščal'naja oda" ("Farewell Ode"), which follows "Little Shop of Splendors" in *A Stubborn Calendar*, Polonskaja bids a resigned, if tongue-in-cheek, farewell to what she calls "idleness" (*prazdnost'*), a term which seems to encompass all of the romantic illusions and caprices of youth embodied in her memories of Paris. Paris is the birthplace of both her verse and her first love; according to Polonskaja's son, drafts of the cycle contain a dedication to Erenburg.[70] The spirit of the city is the animating force of both love and song, and we find Polonskaja once again using the word *derzkij* (insolent), but for the last time:

> Кто стар и бессилен и духом нищ,
> Лишь тот от тебя отречется, Париж!
> Ты нас водил переулком сурочьим
> С песенкой *дерзкой* и сердцем беспечным ...
>
> He who is old and impotent and poor in spirit,
> Only he shall renounce you, Paris!
> You led us down the path of corruption
> With an *insolent* song and a carefree heart.[71]

Contrasted with the merry anarchy of those "wild nights and idle days" is the current reality, in which a clock face has eclipsed the sun, and a relentless bookkeeper enters everything into the "account-book of the fates." The poet bows to historical inevitability, ironically mocking her own nostalgia:

> Утреет. Морозный рассвет.
> И ночь пополам раскололась.
> И трезвых, и будничных лет
> Я слышу насмешливый голос:
>
> «Придет же нелепая дурь
> В пустую башку тунеядца—
> В эпоху сражений и бурь
> За праздною темой погнаться!»
>
> Ну что же! Справедливый упрек!
> Все это излишние бредни.
> Суров мой издатель и цензор мой строг,—
> Простимся, подруга . . . в последний!
>
> Morning comes. A frozen dawn.
> And night has split in two.
> And I hear the mocking voice
> Of sober, workaday years:
>
> "What absurd foolishness will enter
> The empty head of a sponger—
> In the epoch of battles and storms
> To go chasing an idle theme!"
>
> Oh well! It's a fair reproach!
> All this is unnecessary raving.
> My editor is stern and my censor strict,—
> Farewell, dear girlfriend . . . forever![72]

As if to emphasize this farewell, the theme of poetry itself, which appears frequently in Polonskaja's poetry from the early 1920s, largely disappears from her published work after 1924. In "Slovo" ("The Word," 1923), a rare foray into free verse, she had given the joy of words a sensual quality:

> Увидеть—мало! Жадными глазами
> Не обоймешь и не удержишь радость.
> Руками крепкими ее не схватишь.
> Ляг на нее, прижмись к ней алчным телом,
> Смешайся с ней, как муж лежит с женою!
> Она как ветер, как вода в горсти . . .
> Но если ты сумел ее назвать
> По имени и верное названье
> Найти ей среди всех творений мира—
> Она твоя! . . .

The NEP Period

> To see is not enough!
> With greedy eyes
> You will not embrace and will not hold onto joy.
> With strong hands you will not catch her!
> Lie down upon her! Press your greedy body to her,
> Commingle with her, as a husband with his wife!
> She is like the wind . . . like a handful of water . . .
> But if you have contrived to call her
> By name, and a true name
> Have found for her among all creation,—
> She is yours! . . .[73]

In "Imja" ("The Name," 1924), a tribute to Puškin on the 125-year jubilee of his birth, Polonskaja affirms the poet's continuing value and relevance:

> Страна казарм, страна хоругвей,
> Доска, готовая к резьбе;
> Иные проступают буквы,
> Республика, в твоем гербе.
>
> Но смыв державства завитушки:
> «Империя! Россия! Рим!»—
> Мы перепишем имя—«Пушкин»—
> И медь, как память, протравим.
>
> Land of barracks, land of battle flags,
> A board, prepared for carving;
> Other letters show through,
> Republic, in your coat of arms.
>
> But having washed away the flourishes of power:
> "Empire! Russia! Rome!"—
> We will recopy the name—"Puškin"—
> And etch the bronze, like memory.[74]

"Sčast'je / Voem sireny paravoznoj" ("Happiness / With the Wail of the Locomotive Whistle," 1923) also celebrates the joy of words; in it the poet equates happiness with the simple rocking motion of a train which finds its way into the rhythm of verse.[75] The lighthearted "Nočju" ("By Night," 192?) is a playful dialogue between the poet and the moon. These latter two poems did not appear in print until 1929, when they were included in *A Stubborn Calendar*. The power of song is praised in "Pesnja" ("Song," 1925), but it is specifically the "Internationale," played on a tired street organ.[76]

In the final version of "The Legacy" (1924), the legacy in question is the city of Petrograd, which contains "derzosti tvorčeskoj dux nesmirimyj" (the irrepressible spirit of creative insolence). Drafts in the archive express a grander vision, promising not only the city but "the most beautiful toy /

Serapion Sister

Our old earth." There is also a suggestion in some of the drafts and in another poem, "Kolybel'naja," ("Cradle Song," 1922), that the poet bequeaths to her son, along with her boldness and her impudence, the gift of poetry as a talisman to protect him in her absence:

> Зоркий глаз и острый слух,
> Дерзкий смех и смелый дух.
> Да еще, научит мать,—
> Слово на слово низать.
> Если, буду я мертва,—
> Помоги тебе, слова!

> A discerning eye and a sharp ear,
> Insolent laughter and a bold spirit.
> And even more, your mother will teach you—
> The art of threading word to word.
> If I am dead,—
> The words will aid you![77]

From 1925 on, however, the theme of poetry appears in Polonskaja's verse mainly in laments for dead or silenced poets. Aside from her two published lyrics to Esenin, Polonskaja also wrote several other elegies for him. "Serdce eta smert' trevožit" ("This Death Troubles My Heart," January 1926) is a personal response by one poet to the death of another; the heroine is troubled by dreams, awakening with a shiver in the middle of the night:

> ... На стене цветок обойный,—
> Профиль ложный мертвеца.
> Все противно. Все спокойно,—
> Бром в стакане. Жди конца.
>
> ... Схоронили. Придавили.
> Гроб дубовый, глина, лед.
> Вечер. Темная могила.
> Ветер песенки поет.

> ... A wallpaper blossom on the wall
> Mimics the corpse's profile.
> All is repugnant. All is calm.
> Bromide in a glass. Wait for the end.
>
> ... They buried him. They pressed the dirt down.
> An oak coffin, clay, ice.
> Evening. A dark grave.
> The wind sings its songs.[78]

In 1926, Polonskaja also dedicated a poem to Axmatova, whom she described as "the local muse" and "witness of days," who walks unbowed, "with a flying, marble gait."[79]

The NEP Period

For Polonskaja, the figure of the poet is always intimately connected with the idea of history, for he or she transmits historical experience from one generation to another. In the unpublished "Nam budut zavidovat' pokolenija" ("Generations Shall Envy Us," 1926), there is a suggestion of tension between the official version of history and that given by the poet:

> Три тома напишет историк казенный
> О песнях революционных лет.
> По рангу и чину поставит колонны,
> Носящих кличку—поэт.
>
> Ты будешь читать *наши* книги, дитя.
> Дитя, поколенья чужого,
> И ты удивишься, прочтя,
> Иное безумное слово.

> The official historian shall write three volumes
> About the songs of the revolutionary years.
> By rank and class he will set up columns
> Of those bearing the code-name—poet.
>
> You shall read *our* books, child.
> Child of another generation,
> And you shall be surprised, reading
> A different, mad word.[80]

In "Graždanka Smert'" ("Citizeness Death," 1926), perhaps Polonskaja's most direct indictment of the contemporary political situation, she describes the debasement of noble nineteenth-century ideals, to the point where they are no longer worthy of sacrifice:

> Идея—порожденье человечье,—
> Из за нее, в петлю не стоит лезть . . .
>
> . . . Идея, она бушевала,
> И слушать, было неплохо,
> Когда в девятнадцатом, в стекла вокзалов,
> Стучало свинцовым горохом.
>
> А нынче, бродит, медведя ручней,
> И с палкой при ней поводырь,
> И морда в железе, а в шкуре у ней
> Не счесть унижений и дыр.

> The Idea—is a human creation,—
> It is not worth stepping into the noose for it . . .
>
> . . . The Idea, how it raged,
> And it was fine to listen,
> When in the nineteenth century, on the railway station glass,
> It beat like a hail of lead.

> But now it wanders, more tame than a bear,
> And a trainer walks beside it with a stick,
> And it is muzzled in iron, and in its fur
> Are countless holes and degradations.[81]

Although unfinished, this poem is one of the most likely pieces in the archive to have remained unpublished for purely political reasons.

MOTHERS AND GYPSIES: POLONSKAJA'S TREATMENT OF LOVE AND SEXUALITY

Love poetry died harder for Polonskaja during this period. *A Stubborn Calendar* contains an entire section devoted to passionate love lyrics written during these years, but they are not dated, and only the cycle "Ešče ljubov'" ("More Love") had appeared in print before, in 1926.[82] As it happens, "More Love'" stands out for a number of other reasons. Set in an exotic Caucasian locale (Tiflis/Tbilisi), this poem is, as Brett-Harrison points out, one of the very few which portray a moment of sudden and *mutual* passion rather than the separation and loneliness which follow:[83]

> Между небом и городом мы одни,
> Балкон наш причален едва, едва ...
> Ты хочешь, желаньем и волею ночи
> Сниму его с якоря на полет?
> И кровь моя отвечает—хочешь!
> И ветер горячий в голову бьет ...
> ... Срываемся и плывем!

> Between sky and city we are alone,
> Our balcony barely moored ...
> Would you like me, by desire and the freedom of night
> To cut loose from the anchor into flight?
> And my blood answers "You want it!"
> And the hot wind beats in my head ...
> ... We break loose and sail![84]

S. Vyšeslavceva also selects "More Love," and for the same reason, as "the most original and emotionally convincing" of Polonskaja's love lyrics, far superior to her treatments of "painful unrequited love."[85] Actually, "More Love'" does portray a painful separation from the beloved, apparently at the very moment of consummation. In the final lyric, "Otorvan ot ruk moix" ("Torn from My Arms"), he languishes in prison while she pines: "Years and centuries I count, languishing— / For we did not even finish our kiss."[86]

As noted earlier in the discussion of "Carmen," Vyšeslavceva notes the willful, "gypsy" quality of Polonskaja's love poems. She also mentions the "Axmatovian" leitmotif of unrequited love, while at same time contrasting

The NEP Period

Polonskaja's "frank biologism" with the "atmosphere of sickly-sweet mysticism and salon religiosity" of Axmatova.[87] Polonskaja's biologism is accompanied by "a stormy show of temperament and even of atavistic instincts":[88]

> Сжимается рука, а в мыслях нож иль яд,
> И к горлу подступает злоба:
> Как много тысяч лет назад,
> Тебя я задушить готова.

> My hand clenches, and in my thoughts—a knife or poison
> And malice rises in my throat:
> Like many thousand years ago,
> I am ready to strangle you.[89]

According to Vyšeslavceva, Polonskaja's biologism is also the source of her saving grace, a natural optimism connected with the "voice of the blood," of woman's natural calling to continue life.

This facet of Polonskaja's thought is most evident in the poetry of the early 1920s, however, and it is from this period that Vyšeslavceva draws her examples. In Polonskaja's love poetry of the mid-1920s, the maternal instinct is secondary to sexual passion or even antithetical to the heroine's need for self-assertion. In "The Swan" (1924), the lyric heroine flees maternity ("My husband and my home, farewell, my dear chain . . .").[90] In "Aeneas" (192?), the abandoned heroine, who identifies herself with Dido, longs for a child, but this longing is above all to hold on to at least some trace of her faithless lover:

> Беги ему вослед! А корабли далеко
> Уже от пристани в весельи парусов . . .
> О, если бы ребенок твой сегодня
> Под сердцем шевельнулся у меня.

> Run after him! But the ships are far away
> Already from the wharf in the gaiety of sails . . .
> O, if only your child
> Were stirring under my heart today![91]

The concept of the regeneration of humanity through childbearing also becomes more complex in Polonskaja's civic poetry of the mid- to late 1920s. On the one hand, in such poems as "Pervoe maja v Tiflise" ("May 1 in Tiflis," 1925), "Most" ("The Bridge," 1927), and "Stuknuli v okna drevka znamen" ("Flagpoles Were Knocking at the Windows," 1928), children symbolize both biological and social renewal.[92] In "Pionery" (Pioneers, 1924), children defending a pioneer camp are praised as "fruit and seed of the Revolution."[93] The starving beggar child in "The Bridge" is a time bomb waiting to explode into history:

Serapion Sister

> Обернутый в тряпки, прижатый к груди
> Истории малое семя,
> Закинитый в ночь,—подожди, подожди:
> Работает старое Время!
>
> Wrapped in rags, pressed to the breast
> Little seed of history,
> Cast into the night,—wait, wait:
> Old Time is working![94]

"Bol'šoj graždanin" ("The Great Citizen"), a narrative poem of 1929, is the tale of a young student, Marusja, who refuses her lover's demand that she abort their child.[95] When she takes him to court to demand child support, the judge finds in her favor. The law, which "stretches forth its hand to Marusja," is characterized as a woman worker:

> И руку Марусе закон подает,
> Руку работницы с жесткими пальцами,
> Нового мира надежный оплот.
>
> And the law gives her hand to Marusja,
> The hand of a worker woman with hard fingers,
> Trustworthy bulwark of the new world.[96]

Marusja's baby represents that new world, the future, and her refusal to abort, despite her poverty, the resistance of her lover, and her father's curse, is a courageous commitment to that future. Here the reader may recall the lines of Polonskaja's earlier "It Is Easy to Conceive": "While men struggle in wars, / Here women are finishing the job."[97]

On the other hand, Polonskaja also sometimes suggests that the powerful rejuvenating force of youth has a cruel side: revolution becomes a savage act of revenge on the old by the young. "Sčastlivaja žena" ("The Lucky Wife," 1927) is a tale of two mothers and two sons, rich and poor. While the rich mother surrounds her son with love and every comfort, another boy "like the grass of the field, / Grows in empty lots." The two sons are drawn together by fate, which decrees that the poor boy will murder the rich one:

> ... Забыла ты о том, чужом,
> Но за стеной твоей с ножом
> Стоит отверженный и ждет,
> Пока счастливый сын пройдет,
> Чтоб уложить его в постель
> Помягче материнской груди ...
>
> You forgot about that other one, the stranger,
> But behind your wall with a knife
> The outcast stands and waits,

> While the lucky son passes,
> In order to lay him down on a bed
> Softer than a mother's breast.[98]

The "lucky mother'" is left with only her grief and a crushing sense of guilt. Even more cruel is the chilling "Rusalka" ("The Mermaid," 1929), in which a young peasant, just arrived in the city and lured by the dissolute world of the tavern and the brothel, brutally murders his old father. Taken by itself, "The Mermaid" does not belong to the series of poems in which Polonskaja explores themes of social injustice; the coarse young man kills not out of civic motives, or even out of envy or desire for revenge. He kills his father to keep the sick old man from interfering in his pursuit of pleasure.[99] In the context of Polonskaja's poetry of idealized, heroic youth, this poem serves as a sobering reminder of youth's potential for cruelty and egotism.

A STUBBORN CALENDAR: A POETIC DIARY

Polonskaja's third collection, *A Stubborn Calendar* (1929), included selections from the poetry she published during 1924 to 1927 as well as a handful of previously unpublished pieces. Like the first two collections, it is divided along rough thematic lines. The first section contains three narrative poems, "Carmen," "In the Noose," and "Fragments from the Narrative Poem *Plennik* (The Captive)." The second section contains six poems united mainly by their setting, Petrograd. There are poems of social protest ("Dogs," "The Bridge") and colorful portraits of urban life ("Land of Wonders," "Cinema in 1923"), as well as "The Legacy," a hymn to the city's beauty and to poetry. The third part consists of love poetry. The fourth contains a mix of the earlier poems on poetry and the poet, elegies for Esenin and Lunc, "Farewell Ode," in which she bids farewell to free, uncommitted verse, and a handful of others which defy categorization.

Most of the poems in this collection were published earlier and have thus already been discussed. Two of the previously unpublished poems merit particular attention, however. One of these is the fragmentary "Captive," a few sections of which appeared in print in 1925.[100] The title, given for the first time in *A Stubborn Calendar*, is a reference to Puškin's "Kavkazskij Plennik" ("A Captive of the Caucasus"); not only does the poem take place in the Caucasus, but it is also the love story of a Russian man and a Caucasian woman. The similarity ends there. The Russian hero is not a prisoner but a Chekist from Leningrad; the heroine, Nina, a Georgian princess, is the descendent of warriors and oil barons. The Chekist, Gorelov, is blond and blue-eyed, handsome and reckless. In fact, he bears a striking resemblance to Len'ka Panteleev. The setting itself, Tiflis, has been transformed; a new generation has inscribed it with an entirely different kind of romanticism, that of revolution:

Serapion Sister

> Пусть Чацкий спит здесь мирным сном,
> Пошли романтики не те.
> Поправку вносит Закрайком
> К твоей восточной пестроте
> Однообразием диаграмм
> И дробью Интернационала.
> Так, Был твой азиатский хлам
> Здесь в переделке небывалой.
>
> Though Čatskij may still be sleeping peacefully,
> The wrong romantics have gone.
> The *Zakrajkom* is correcting
> Your eastern motleyness
> With the monotony of diagrams
> And the drumming of the Internationale.
> So. Your Asiatic rubbish
> Has undergone an unprecedented alteration.[101]

Because of the fragmentary nature of the piece, it is difficult to draw firm conclusions about Polonskaja's intentions. Even the addressee of the dedication is unclear. In the published version he is identified as "E. B. V.," but according to Mixail L'vovič Polonskij, the drafts in his mother's notebooks are dedicated to "M. S. F." (Mixail S. Ferberg, the lover she met in Tiflis). It is not clear why Polonskaja changed the name, but, as Polonskij points out, she often masked her addressees.[102] The dedication is clearly to a married lover, and again there is the bitter note of unhappy love; the poet sends an offering (the poem) to her beloved, in his peaceful home in the warm south, from which she is barred:

> А мне по праву заказному
> Заказан доступ и огонь,—
> Не пожелай чужого дома,
> Чужого счастия не тронь.
>
> But I am forbidden by law
> From entering, forbidden the fire,—
> Do not covet another's house,
> Do not touch another's happiness.[103]

The other noteworthy poem which appears for the first time in *A Stubborn Calendar* is "Vstreča" ("The Meeting"), in which the poet returns openly, for the first time since *Omens*, to the Jewish theme. "The Meeting," however, is a far cry from the aggressive ethnic pride of "I Cannot Abide the Infant Jesus" or the defiance of "Shylock." In this poem, written in quatrains of *dol'niki* tending toward amphibrachic tetrameter, the assimilated heroine is confronted by her Jewishness in the person of an old beggar woman with a hooked nose, who picks her out of a crowd of passersby and speaks to her in Yiddish. At first the heroine is reluctant to acknowledge the connection; she describes herself as walking "with coat buttoned over her chest, her heart fastened up with a lock and chain." However, she is drawn irresistibly to the old woman:

> И я останавливаюсь на ходу,
> Хоть знаю—нельзя, нельзя,
> И жалкую мелочь ей в руку кладу
> И жадное сердце—в глаза.
>
> And I stop in my tracks,
> Though I know—I must not, I must not,
> And I place some pathetic small coins into her hand
> And my greedy heart—into her eyes.[104]

The heroine insists that there is no obvious connection between them. How then, she asks, could the old woman recognize her so quickly as a Jew? It is her sadness, the woman answers, that identifies her. There is no mistaking Jewish women, for:

> У девушек наших печальный глаз,
> Ленивый и томный шаг.
>
> И смеются они не так, как те,—
> Открыто в своей простоте,—
> Но как луна из-за туч блестит,
> Так горе в улыбке у них сидит.
>
> И пусть ты забыла веру и род,
> А ид из иммер а ид!
> То кровь моя в жилах твоих поет,
> Чужим языком говорит.
>
> Our girls have sad eyes,
> A lazy and languid step.
>
> And they do not laugh like those others,—
> Openly, in their simplicity,—
> But as the moon shines from behind the clouds,
> Thus does grief rest in their smiles.
>
> And though you may have forgotten your faith and your kin,
> A *id iz immer a id!*[105]
> My blood sings in your veins,
> It speaks an alien language.[106]

The "ancient sorrow" of Frug can be heard in these lines; indeed, they sound even more bitter after the raised hopes of the 1920s had been dashed. A year after this poem appeared, the Jewish Section itself was officially disbanded, and a new campaign was launched against "all varieties of

Serapion Sister

Jewish nationalism in a Communist guise,"[107] creating an environment hostile even to such ambivalent expressions of Jewish identity.

Polonskaja later described *A Stubborn Calendar* as her poetic diary of "love, hate, contempt, and pride in the people of our epoch."[108] In the context of the First Five-Year Plan, this collection—with its wayward, gypsy heroines, its bandit-heroes, sad Jews, and passionate, melancholy lovers—was indeed an act of literary stubbornness and courage. It was to be her last stand against the regimentation of the Stalin era. In the years that followed, Polonskaja would eventually submit, at least publicly, to state demands on her art. Just as she had begun to do in *Under a Stone Rain,* she learned to go underground, and she was only occasionally able to insert surreptitious traces of her true voice into the poetry she published in the 1930s and 1940s. In retrospect, there is a chilling prescience in the final lines of "In the Noose":

> Пусть к гортани прилипнет стих,—
> Будут счастливы наши дети!
>
> И когда-нибудь все поймут,—
> Умереть—все равно, что сдаться.
> Наперекор всему
> Надо в живых остаться.

> May verse stick in our throats,—
> Our children shall be happy!
>
> And someday all will understand:
> To die is to give in.
> In defiance of everything
> We must remain among the living.[109]

Chapter Five

Poetry in the Stalinist Period

FROM HER ENTRY into LAPP in 1931 to her evacuation from Leningrad in 1941, Polonskaja worked as a "professional" writer: she gave up practicing medicine and earned her living solely through literary activity. Original poetry was only one of the genres in which she worked. Polonskaja's return to medical practice in evacuation during the war, though it isolated her and reduced her rate of publication, coincides with an increase in her poetic output. Little of her poetry from this period has ever been published, however. From 1946 to 1956, although she was writing steadily, she published no original poetry at all.

The professionalization and regimentation of literature under the First Five-Year Plan left little room for poetry which did not serve its purposes. Polonskaja distinguished this period from the previous one by the fact that, in her "nonprofessional" period, she wrote verse only when exceptionally moved: "when the image of a person or an event arose in my imagination so distinctly and insistently that I felt a physical need to free myself from it."[1] As a literary professional, she could not afford to be so selective, of either subject or genre.

As the scope of her literary activity increased, the range of subject matter and artistic level of her poetry declined, particularly in the 1940s. Aesthetics were subordinated to politically safe content, to the point where even a gypsy is shown holding a volume of Lenin under her arm ("Cyganočka" ["The Gypsy," 1936]).[2] Even such a generally admiring critic as Zara Minc felt obliged to point out that, despite the "ideological-thematic" richness of Polonskaja's poetry from this period, "all the same that unique artistic individuality, which made Polonskaja popular in the first postrevolutionary decade is, at times, a bit less evident in her poems from the 1930s (and especially the 1940s.)"[3] Although the poetry from this period, on the whole, appears less interesting than Polonskaja's earlier work in the aesthetic or philosophical sense, the way in which she conducted her literary career reveals much about the literary-political climate of the period. As A. I. Rubaškin observes, her decision to devote herself full time to the literary profession was an astute one at the time.⁴ The controversial, somewhat reckless reputation she had established in the 1920s, along with her bourgeois background, made refashioning her image as a writer a matter of self-preservation. To do so, she needed to be conspicuous in her acceptance of the new literary bureaucracy. Becoming a full-time *literator* gave her professional legitimacy, and becoming a journalist gave her the opportunity to travel, if not abroad, then at least to the more exotic regions of the Soviet Union. As she states in one memoir, "I was attracted to newspaper work, they offered me interesting trips about the country, and I could not refuse."⁵

Although she conformed outwardly to the demands of socialist realism, Polonskaja continued throughout the 1930s to weave individualistic and subversive threads into her verse. She never abandoned the "woman question," although it had been declared officially solved by Stalin in 1930. In her poetry, as in her journalism, she continued to portray strong, passionate heroines, and her critique of traditional marriage and domesticity continued, albeit in a modified form: she was openly critical only in cases where the setting was outside Soviet Russia, for example, in Muslim Central Asia or "decadent" Europe. In the late 1930s, Polonskaja also used historical subjects, in this case the lives of persecuted nineteenth-century poets Puškin (in "Stixi o Puškine" ["Verses about Puškin," 1937]) and Taras Ševčenko (in "Portret" ["The Portrait," 1939]), to parallel the contemporary situation of the artist in Russia.

Publishing such statements required extreme caution. One of the most remarkable features of Polonskaja's poetry from this period is the way in which it was packaged (in many cases repackaged) to accentuate more politically acceptable features and camouflage more dubious aspects. The repositioning and retitling of certain poems masks their true significance and renders them acceptable to the censor.

THE EARLY 1930S

Polonskaja's work from the early 1930s consists mainly of translations and journalism. Many of her sketches were republished in 1934 in her second prose collection, *Everyday Soviet People*. These pieces, like those in her first collection, *A Trip to the Urals* (1926), portray people Polonskaja encountered on her travels as a correspondent for *Leningradskaja Pravda* and *Krasnaja gazeta*. A remark in a memoir suggests that poetry occupied a secondary position in Polonskaja's work during this period: "I got to know the country and wrote sketches about those features of what was new that I perceived most sharply. And if I could not put something into prose, then I wrote verse."⁶ However, her working notes indicate that she attempted to publish a third collection of verse as early as 1931, and that she submitted it to publishers several times without success. *Goda: Izbrannye stixi* (*Years:*

Selected Poems) did not appear in print until 1935, after prolonged negotiations with more than one publisher.

Years covers more than fifteen years of Polonskaja's poetic output, although, as she wrote to Šaginjan, "it is very mixed and conforms to the demands of the editors. You won't find much of what you know in it."[7] According to Polonskaja's notes, the publisher, Oblit, refused to include "In the Noose," "Shylock," and "Idleness."[8] The book is divided into five sections: "Omens," "Under a Stone Rain," "A Stubborn Calendar," "The New World" (*Novyj Svet*), and "Five Translations." In general, the first three sections represent the collections from which their titles are drawn, although there are a few cases in which Polonskaja has shifted poems from one collection to another or included a poem not previously published. In addition, the section titled "A Stubborn Calendar" is further divided into "Poemy" ("Narrative Poems") "Gljadja na zapad" ("Looking Westward"), "Ešče ljubov'" ("More Love"), and "Vstreči" ("Meetings"). The content of the sections generally corresponds to the arrangement of the original collection; however, the addition of section titles is significant. "Looking Westward" contains poems which, in their original versions, contain no indications that the setting is anywhere but Soviet Russia. They include some of Polonskaja's most strident anti-NEP poems—"Dogs," "The Bridge," and "Night"— under new titles which shift the setting to Western Europe: "Gamburgskij manež" ("The Hamburg Manege"), "Po doroge v Al'tonu" ("Along the Road to Alton"), and "Noč' na Jungfernstuge" ("Night on Jungfernstuge").[9] "The New World" is the only section consisting almost entirely of new poetry. Of the twelve pieces, only two, "The Great Citizen" and "America," were written before 1930 and had not appeared in a previous collection. Most of the poems had appeared at least once in periodicals in the early 1930s.

The tone of these poems is a peculiar mix of optimism and melancholy, nostalgic introspection. The section opens with "America" (1928), in which the "new world" is revealed as no less corrupt than the old; the real "new world" is not America, but Soviet Russia, to which the oppressed masses of America look for salvation:

> ... Всем, кто работать хочет,
> Там место и привет!
> Республика рабочих
> Там строит Новый Свет.
>
> ... For all who want to work
> There is a place and a greeting there!
> The republic of workers
> Is building a New World there.[10]

"Reč" ("The Speech," 1933) describes the power of words "like dry dynamite," which propel the nation into a "great Tomorrow."[11] "Sestra s Vostoka"

Serapion Sister

("Sister from the East," 1932) and "Jangi-kišlak" (1932) portray emancipated Muslim women who have become leaders in their communities and models for the young. Hope for the future is tinged with regret, however; the poet is repelled by aging and decay, yet she feels excluded from the "charmed circle of childhood." This ambivalence is perhaps best expressed in "Kak možno prošloe ljubit'" ("How Can One Love the Past"):

> А вымытый старик
>   почтенен и хорош,
> Он—идол опыта, он кладезь
>   всех познаний,
> И все же голову невольно отвернешь,
> Чтоб не вздохнуть
>   его испорченным дыханием.
> И хочется уйти, со стайкою ребят
> Бродить по городу сквозь ветер, пыль
>   и солнце,
> И улыбаться им, и слушать,
>   как галдят
> Бегущие с обеда комсомольцы,
> И проводить их рой до самой проходной,
> Куда доносится завода гул железный,
> И позавидовать им
>   старшею сестрой,
> Их звонкой юности,
>   напористой и трезвой.
>
> But a well-scrubbed old man,
>   venerable and handsome,
> He is an idol of experience, he is a mine
>   of knowledge.
> And all the same, you involuntarily turn your head away,
> In order not to breathe
>   his rotten breath.
> And you want to run away, with a gang of children,
> Wander the city through wind, dust, and sun,
> And smile at them, and listen to the racket
> Of *komsomols* running from dinner,
> And escort the swarm to the very entrance,
> Where the iron roar of the factory reaches,
> And envy them
>   like an older sister,
> Their resounding youth,
>   energetic and sober.[12]

Whereas earlier her poetic persona spoke as mother to this new generation, here she longs to be part of it herself, to be sister rather than parent; in effect, she wishes to deny her own mortality, to be part of the future rather than the past.

Two poems which express most painfully the poet's consciousness of her own aging are "Na švejnoj fabrike" ("At the Garment Factory") and "Sputniki" ("Companions"). "Companions" is a meditation, in mixed blank iambs, on the stages of life. Each stage is characterized by a taste; the sweetness of childhood, the tartness of youth, the salt of maturity, and, finally, the bitterness of old age:

> Когда же сладость вся уйдет из тела
> И кислоту нейтрализует жизнь,
> Соленой крови ток остынет и ослабнет,
> Тогда приходит к нам
> Четвертый спутник—горечь.

> When all the sweetness leaves the body
> And life neutralizes all our acid,
> The flow of salty blood will weaken and grow cold,
> Then comes our fourth companion—bitterness.[13]

"At the Garment Factory," in which the lyric heroine describes her life to a group of young women, is less distanced. In fact, the voice breaks at one point, giving the reader to understand that a subject has been touched upon which is too painful for words:

> Немецких прописей суровостью простою
> Был детства моего наполнен светлый дом,
> Но серые глаза лучились добротою,
> О мама ... Нет! Давайте о другом!

> The bright house of my childhood was filled
> With the simple severity of German maxims,
> But the gray eyes shone with kindness,
> O Mama ... No! Let's talk of something else![14]

The poem is openly autobiographical; maxims embroidered by her German-educated mother are mentioned in Polonskaja's memoirs of childhood,[15] and the first lover she describes is clearly Erenburg:

> Он жил в плену, в плену у звонких слов,
> Поэзию мы открывали вместе,
> И вместе с ней открыли мы любовь.

> He was a prisoner, a prisoner of ringing words,
> We discovered poetry together,
> And with it we discovered love.[16]

Again, the aging poet seeks sympathy and comfort among the young:

Но сердце сношено. Другого не найдешь.
В родном краю пройду получужою—
Неузнанна, рассеяна, слаба ...
Но девушки заплачут надо мною,
А у стихов—особая судьба.

But the heart is worn out. You will not find another.
I pass through my native land almost a stranger—
Unrecognized, absentminded, weak ...
But girls will cry over me,
And verses have a special fate.[17]

There are only two new love poems in this section, both in a decidedly minor key. The passionate, willful lyric voice of the mid-1920s has given way to a more resigned and wistful one. In "Traktir v Ispanii" ("An Inn in Spain"), the heroine is abandoned after a fleeting encounter. Saddened, she nevertheless recognizes her own part in the outcome, pausing over the words of an old author:

—Любовь,—он говорит,—похожа на трактир
В Испании, а это, друг мой, значит—
В ней можно только то наверное найти,
Что принесешь с собой ...
    И я смеюсь и плачу.

—Love—he says,—is like an inn
In Spain, and that means, my friend,
That in it you surely will only find
That which you bring with you ...
    And I laugh and cry.[18]

"Drugu" ("To a Friend"), a more platonic piece, is dedicated to her cousin Artur. It is both an elegy and a meditation on war and the finality of death; the poet recalls not only the dead man and the circumstances that parted them, but her own youthful self, before war destroyed her illusions:

Мы были так стары,
  мы знали так много—
И все оказалось
Смешно и нелепо—
Мы были так юны,
Мы были так слепы.
И книги ...
   и мудрость ...
Все было обманом.
Не золото
  а пятаком
    оловянным!

> We were so old,
> We knew so much—
> And everything turned out
> Funny and awkward—
> We were so young,
> We were so blind.
> Books . . .
>   and wisdom . . .
> All was deceit.
> Not gold
>   but a tin
>   five-kopek piece![19]

The only trace of the frank sensuality of Polonskaja's earlier lyric heroines is in the final section, "Five Translations." After three poems by Kipling ("The Ballad of East and West," "Mandalay," and "Danny Deever") and Brecht's "Ballad of the Dead Soldier," there is a poem called "Iosif" ("Joseph") which is presented as a translation from an author named E. Bertram. In the poem, Potiphar's wife speaks of her desire for Joseph:

> Счастлива та, к которой он стремится,
> И та, к которой ночью он войдет,
> И та, которая с ним будет биться,
> Пока в беспамятстве пред ним не упадет,
> Кто с ним губами жаркими сольется,
> Чтобы в него желанье перелить . . .
> Кто с ним руками жадными сплетется,
> Чтоб жажду ей сумел он утолить . . .
>
> Lucky is she, to whom he rushes,
> And she, to whom he comes at night,
> And she, who will writhe with him,
> Until she swoons before him,
> Whose hot lips will flow together with his,
> To pour her passion into him . . .
> Whose greedy arms entwine with his,
> So that he might quench her thirst . . .[20]

The original language is not specified. The reader may recall that Elizaveta Bertram was the pseudonym under which Polonskaja published verse in Paris; Polonskaja's son confirms that, in fact, drafts of the poem in her notebooks give no indication that it is a translation.[21]

A similar stratagem can be observed in the claim by Nekrasov that his "Ja za to gluboko preziraju sebja" ("I Deeply Despise Myself for This," 1845) is a translation:

> Nekrasov passed off the poem as a translation from Larra, in order to get around the censor. See the testament of one of his contemporaries: "On cer-

tain of Nekrasov's poems there is an inscription: 'From Larra.' In fact, Larra did not publish verse and was known for his satire in prose. Nekrasov was asked: what does this mean? He would explain with a smile, that this was a stratagem on his part and nothing more: 'In earlier times, he said, some of my other poems would not have been accepted had I not passed them off as translations from some little-known language.'"[22]

The subterfuge was necessary for Nekrasov because of his criticism of the wealthy and powerful classes. In Polonskaja's case, there are two probable reasons for the pretense: the fact that Joseph was a Jew who rose to power in an alien land, and the depiction of a woman overwhelmed by sexual desire. The much-debated image of the "new Soviet woman" of the early 1930s had no place for such an emotion; its portrayal in verse gave rise to sharp criticism from such leading figures as Vera Inber, who wrote in 1933, "The breath of Axmatova wafts even now over women's verse, as it did fifteen to twenty years ago. The notorious 'narrowly personal' obscures for them the widest horizons of our poetry."[23] In the same year, another critic, G. Kolesnikova, praised Feška, a female character in Ščukov's novel *Nenavist'* (*Hatred*), for whom "the personal is always secondary, and [who] is always able to master her feelings." Kolesnikova ends with the following assertion: "We must show woman doing responsible Party work, the woman-engineer, builder, director of plant and factory. It is time for a final break with the traditions of bourgeois literature, which portrayed woman almost exclusively on the biological plane."[24] Polonskaja herself, along with a group of other women writers and their proletarian protégés, signed an appeal to male writers, published in *Izvestija* in 1933, to portray the new Soviet woman in her professional capacity: "You must describe woman in command positions—the former 'kitchen maid' who has learned to govern and to do it successfully. You must show the *komsomol*-girl, the woman Party-member, the woman-organizer and the woman as commander of industry."[25] The appeal calls for Socialist Realism in the depiction of women; writers are asked to portray women not as they are, but as they will be in a "classless socialist society."

Most of Polonskaja's lyric heroines of the 1930s meet all the necessary criteria. Her two Uzbek heroines, Sarra Tašbulatova, the "cotton-farming instructor" who "according to Lenin's word / . . . Abandoned the veil, / The pillows and mothers-in-law, / The captivity of the *ičkari*" ("Sister from the East")[26] and the martyred *komsomolka* Tadžixen ("Jangi-kišlak") are particularly effective examples of the type. The emancipated Soviet woman was also the subject of numerous sketches produced by Polonskaja in the 1930s for *Zvezda, Leningradskaja Pravda,* and *Krasnaja gazeta.* Many of these sketches appeared in her 1934 collection, *Everyday Soviet People.* Polonskaja also had a penchant for portraying budding Soviet youth in various bright, spunky little girls, as in "Arxitektor" ("The Architect," 1931). Yet occasional lapses, such as the melancholy voice in "At the Garment Factory" and Potiphar's wife in "Joseph," persist as alternative feminine images.

THE MID-1930S: *NEW POEMS*

The "narrowly personal" appears again in Polonskaja's next collection, *Novye stixi* (*New Poems*, 1937). In fact, in an ongoing discussion on the place of the lyric in Soviet poetry, reported in *Literaturnaja gazeta,* Polonskaja made the following defense of love poetry as the genre that fosters an individual "personal intonation" which distinguishes the true poet from the hack:

> The most valuable thing in the work of a poet of our day,—says E. Polonskaja, concerning the arguments about the lyric,—is the search for a personal intonation, which allows him to speak about our days in his own way.
>
> Sometimes a youth comes for a literary consultation and begins by reading some high-flown "industrial" verses. Having listened to this blather, we ask the youth to read some love poems. . . . He shyly reads some of his love lyrics, and here we can see whether he has a poetic gift or not: in love poems, the philistine reveals himself immediately.[27]

Even though such pieces do appear in *New Poems,* they are few in number. The majority of the poems in the collection are political, and some are outright propaganda. The first, set apart from the rest, is a panegyric to Kirov who, according to her son, was also a friend of Polonskaja's.[28] It ends on a politically orthodox note; while eulogizing the dead man, the poet simultaneously pays her respects to the living leader:

> На площади Красной, в кремлевской стене,
> Ты в будущее войдешь.
> По-сталински строят в моей стране,
> И ленинский в ней чертеж.
>
> On Red Square, in the Kremlin wall,
> You shall enter the future.
> In my country they are building in Stalin's style,
> And according to Lenin's blueprint.[29]

The sections which follow are "Dorožnaja tetrad'" ("Travel Notebook"), a poetic travelogue with a few love poems; "Portrety" ("Portraits"), a set of poetic portraits of admirable Communist women; "V mojej strane" ("In My Country"), a set of poems on patriotic themes, including a long poem in praise of Stalin and another to Kirov; and "Golosa izdali" ("Voices from Afar"), another set of translations.

"Travel Notebook" begins with three poems set in the Caucasus, where Polonskaja traveled in the early 1930s. "Stancija Allaverdy" ("Allaverdy Station," 1936) is an account of the poet's first impressions of Armenia as seen through the windows of a train en route to Erevan. Stopping briefly at a station, the travelers are greeted with wine, music, and dancing by a group of Armenian miners awaiting the arrival of Kalinin.[30] Kalinin's name also occurs in "Armjanskaja devočka" ("A Little Armenian Girl," 1935), in which a wide-eyed little girl fights her way through crowds to catch a glimpse of the Politburo member. As is typical in Polonskaja's verse, this "black-haired, ruddy little rogue" is not simply a bit of sentimental local color. She represents the future for which so much blood has been spilled, both in her native Armenia and in distant Russia:

> Ведь это для того, чтоб ты росла достойно,
> Чтоб расцвела невиданной красой
> В семье народов сильной и спокойной
> Под пятилучной красною звездой!
>
> For it was so that you might grow up properly,
> So that you might bloom with unprecedented beauty
> In the family of peoples, strong and calm
> Under a five-pointed red star![31]

In "Kanal" ("The Canal," 1935), an ancient inscription by a forgotten ruler on a long since destroyed irrigation canal is recalled by travelers observing a new irrigation project built on the same river. The blossoming of fruit trees in the arid landscape, fed by the new canal, evokes visions not only of the forgotten ruler, one Garistis, but also of Noah tilling the soil of Ararat after the flood:

> А люди бережно склонялись к ней,
> И радостью такой светились лица,
> Как будто ожила старинная легенда
> И землю труд плодотворил впервые.
>
> And the people carefully bent over it,
> And their faces shone with such joy,
> As if the ancient legend had come to life
> And labor had made the earth fruitful for the first time.[32]

The following poems are love lyrics, presumably included in this section because they contain suggestions of exotic locales. In "Sneg v gorax" ("Snow in the Mountains," 1936), a snowy mountaintop recalls the color of a former lover's hair:

> Мне снег
> На черном гребне гор
> Напомнят, знаю я,
> Цвет молодых твоих седин
> И холодность твоя.

Poetry in the Stalinist Period

> Snow
> On the black crest of the mountains
> Reminds me, I know,
> Of the color of your youthful gray hairs
> And your coldness.[33]

"RV-Sakyz" (1936), though ostensibly about a Baku radio station by that name, evokes Polonskaja's connection with Mixail Ferberg, who was living in Baku in the 1930s. The reference to a balcony recalls the airborne balcony of "More Love," reinforcing the association:

> Это, чуть освещено,
> Слабо светится во тьме
> То балконное окно,
> Обращенное ко мне.
>
> It is that same balcony window,
> Barely illuminated,
> Weakly shining in the darkness,
> Turned toward me.[34]

"Gruši" ("Pears," 1936) describes a meeting with a male friend or lover after many years of separation. The taste of wild pears, "grains tasting of sun and sand scraped our teeth,"[35] brings a touch of Polonskaja's characteristic sensuality to the brief meeting.

Finally, there is "Letučaja myš'" ("The Bat," 1933), addressed to an unknown male acquaintance, a native of the Carpathians. The poet responds to his description of a local custom meant to bring happiness to the home: a bat's wing is nailed, unfurled, above the doorway. By chance, a bat becomes entangled in her curtains that very night, but rather than attempting to capture it she takes hold of it only to set it free:

> Так вот оно, как говорится—счастье!
> И сердце дрогнуло . . . но, сдерживая смех,
> Слепую вестницу в распахнутое настежь
> Окно я кинула, как птиц кидают вверх.
>
> So there it is, as they say—happiness!
> And my heart trembled . . ., but suppressing a laugh,
> I flung the blind herald out of the open
> Window, as birds are flung upward.[36]

In releasing the bat and, by implication, the kind of happiness it is meant to ensure, Polonskaja echoes an image used both by Axmatova and by Cvetaeva, namely, the release of birds on Ascension Day as a metaphor for parting from a lover:

Выбрала сама я долю
Другу сердца моего:
Отпустила я на волю
В Благовещенье его.
    (Ахматова, 1915)

I myself chose the fate
Of the friend of my heart:
I gave him his freedom
On Ascension Day.
    (Axmatova, 1915)[37]

Окна настежь распахнуты—
Благовещенье, праздник мой!

В день Благовещенья
Подтверждаю торжественно:
Не надо мне ручных голубей, лебедей, орлят!
Летите—куда глаза глядят
В Благовещенье, праздник мой!
    (Цветаева, 1916)

The windows are thrown wide open—
Ascension, my holiday!

On Ascension Day
I solemnly affirm:
I do not need tame doves, swans, or eaglets!
Fly, follow your nose
On Ascension Day, my holiday!
    (Cvetaeva, 1916)[38]

Cvetaeva's use of the phrase "okna nastež' raspaxnuty" ("the windows are thrown wide open") is repeated almost verbatim in Polonskaja's poem.

The last poem in the section, "Zolotoj dožd'" ("Golden Rain," 1936), is the only one in the collection in which Polonskaja touches upon the Jewish theme. The title refers to a variety of Canadian wheat; the heroine, an agronomist, has chosen to begin sowing the new seed. The scene is "by the steppe river Bira," or, more explicitly, Birobidzhan, the territory declared an autonomous Jewish republic by the Soviet government in 1934. The reference to the river Bira is the closest Polonskaja comes to naming the region. However, the Jewish connection is explicit from the references to Shylock and Ahasuerus:

За бороду седую
Слегка рукой держась,
Шейлок спросил: Какую
Выгоду это даст?

И Агасфер ответил:
—Свет исходил я весь,
И я говорю вам—это
Возможно только здесь!

Lightly pulling
At his gray beard,
Shylock asked: What
Advantage is there in this?

And Ahasuerus answered:
—I have walked the entire earth,
And I say to you—this
Is possible only here![39]

The poem is propaganda for Jewish settlement of the region, which was turning out to be a dismal failure. According to Chimen Abramsky, despite the best efforts of the government, and of Kalinin in particular, the highest percentage of the population ever achieved by Jewish immigrants was 23 percent, at the end of 1935.[40] Polonskaja's letters suggest that she wanted very much to visit Birobidzhan, but there is no indication that she ever succeeded.

The next section, "Portraits," includes two poems published previously in journals and in *Years*, "Sister from the East" and "Jangi-kišlak." The remaining three, "Sokolenok" ("The Falcon Chick"), "Bel'evščica" ("The Laundress," 1936), and "Margarita" (1936), also portray heroic exemplars of the "new Soviet woman"; like most of the heroines of *Years*, they meet all the criteria for propaganda. "The Falcon Chick" is dedicated to the memory of a young parachutist, Nata Babuškina; Polonskaja describes with admiration the reckless bravery of the young woman, while at the same time mourning her death with maternal tenderness.[41] "The Laundress" presents a more self-effacing heroism, that of a laundress in a military hospital. Despite the humble nature of this woman's work, the poet celebrates her efficiency, devotion, and the sense of cheer and well-being she exudes in the face of hardships. The heroine of "Margarita" is a simple working-class German woman who, having lost her husband and son to police brutality, vows to avenge them by serving the Party:

И тогда не ласковой хозяйкой,
Домовитой матерью сынов,—
Ты Валькирией мне кажешься, Германка,
Девой битв средь грозных облаков.

Будет час, к Германии советской
Наконец потянутся домой
С урною, где пепел Клары Цеткин,
Все изгнанники страны твоей родной.

> And then, not a tender housewife,
> Or a thrifty mother to your sons,—
> But a Valkyrie do you seem, German woman,
> A warrior maiden among thunderclouds.
>
> The hour will come, when to a Soviet Germany,
> They will finally return home,
> Bearing an urn with the ashes of Clara Zetkin,
> All the exiles of your native land.[42]

There is not the slightest hint of eroticism in any of these portraits. In fact, in "Sister from the East," Polonskaja critiques the erotic stereotype of Middle Eastern Muslim women as languorous harem slaves who exist only as objects of pleasure. Her Sarra appears in a raincoat, carrying a briefcase, and asserts in her own voice that the reality of her life in no way matches the fantasies of Western (and presumably male) writers:

> Только вовсе не была я
> Той отъявленной лентяйкой,
> Той бездельницей гаремной,
> Про которую писали.
>
> Only I was not at all
> That utter lazybones,
> That harem idler,
> About whom they wrote.[43]

The only traces of sensuality in the whole collection occur in the muted love poetry discussed earlier.

The last set of original poems, "In My Country," contains some of the most propagandistic pieces, including another poem about Kirov's murder and a long poem in praise of Stalin, "The Gardener" (1936). The name of "Comrade Stalin" appears in several of the poems; "Pesnja o politruke" ("Song about a Political Instructor," 1934), though it concerns Kirov, ends with a benevolent Stalin, "our main political instructor," overseeing the work which is carried on in Kirov's name.[44] Tribute is paid to the image of the new Soviet woman in "The Gypsy" (1936), in which a gypsy woman foretells unprecedented opportunities and achievements for her client's little daughter, and in "Pesnja Junosti" ("Song of Youth," 1936).[45] The antifascist note is also sounded in "Synu" ("To My Son," 1935), in the form of a radio broadcast:

> А в рупоре спокойный, твердый голос
> По адресу фашистов произносит
> Убийственный, но вежливый абзац.
>
> But through the speaker a calm, firm voice
> Pronounces, addressed to the Fascists,
> A murderous, but polite paragraph.[46]

Poetry in the Stalinist Period

Despite the appearance of political orthodoxy, however, nuances within certain of the poems suggest an attitude more complex than simple jingoism. The section begins with a reprise of "To a Friend," which had appeared both in journals and in *Years* and which derives its pathos from the fact that it is one side of a dialogue interrupted by death. "To a Friend" ends with the lyric heroine's frustrated desire to show her country to her friend for the first time:

> Но мне не поверить,
>   что это навек,
> Что день не настанет,
>   когда
> Особенно синей
>   покажется мне
> У набережной невской вода.
> И в ветре балтийском,
>   взмывающем флаг,
>   Пристанет большой теплоход,
>   И ты по мосткам
>   торопливо сойдешь.
>   Как школьник—пальто на отлет . . .
> И вместе походкой пройдем молодой,
>   Как в первую нашу весну,
> И я покажу
>   тебе, дорогой,
>   мой дом и мою страну.

> But I cannot believe
>   that this is forever,
> That the day will not come
>   when
> The water by the Neva embankment
>   will seem
> Especially blue to me.
> And in the Baltic wind,
>   whipping the flags,
> A large ship will drop anchor,
> And along the gangway
>   You will hurry down.
> Like a schoolboy—coattails flying . . .
> And together we will go with a youthful step,
>   As into our first spring,
> And I will show
>   you, my dear,
>   My home and my country.[47]

The element of unreality in this wish is heightened by the lyric heroine's vision of herself and this man as not only reunited, but reunited as their youthful selves. By extension, the vision of her country which follows, in "In My Country," is touched with the same air of unreality. Just as the Neva seems "especially blue" in her fantasy meeting with her dead friend, the country she shows the reader in the patriotic poems that follow has an unreal, idealized quality.

Immediately following "To a Friend" is a poem called "Nenavist'" ("Hatred," 1932), apparently an extension of the same speech. The meter, variable amphibrach, is the same; and it has the same slightly ironic tone. The link between the two poems is further suggested by the fact that, when Polonskaja published her retrospective collection *Lyric Poems and a Narrative Poem* in 1960, she published "Hatred" under the heading "To a Friend." This poem is a return to the theme of youthful arrogance; what first brings the heroine and this man together is their hatred of everything smug and false, hatred of whose intensity "only youth is capable":

> От чопорных дур
> До распутных нерях,
> Посредников мелких,
> Ловчайших деляг,
> До крупного хищника
> Мутных вод:
> Мы знали типаж этот
> Наперечет.
>
> From prim fools
> To dissolute slatterns,
> Petty middlemen,
> Deft opportunists,
> To the high-powered shark
> Of muddy waters:
> We knew that type
> Through and through.[48]

Though many years have passed, the heroine's hatred of all that is false, corrupt, and predatory has not mellowed but intensified:

> Ее, как вино,
> Охмеляют года;
> Все крепче, острее настой
> И если друзья
> Предают иногда,
> Враги
> Неизменно со мной.
>
> Like wine, the years
> Grow tipsy upon it;

Poetry in the Stalinist Period

The liquor is ever stronger, sharper.
And if friends
Sometimes betray me,
My enemies
Are with me unfailingly.[49]

The new world, it appears, is little better than the old.

"Iz stixov o Puškine" ("From Verses about Puškin," 1936) also contains nuances more subtle than simple patriotism, or even reverence for the poet. Written for the centennial of Puškin's death, "Gorod" ("The City") and "Ploščad'" ("The Square") both have clear subtexts in Puškin's "The Bronze Horseman." In "The City," the poet speaks of "glorious songs" composed about the city and immediately shifts to the image of poor mad Evgenij and the terrible figure of the Bronze Horseman. "The Square," which begins, "He also loved this square," describes the Field of Mars, of which Puškin writes, in his introduction:

Люблю воинственную живость
Потешных Марсовых полей ...

... I love the military vitality
Of the toy fields of Mars[50]

Puškin's lines

Люблю тебя, Петра творенье,
Люблю твой строгий, стройный вид ...

I love you, Peter's creation,
I love your severe, well-proportioned look.[51]

are echoed by Polonskaja in "The Square":

Он тоже любил эту площадь,—
С тех пор
Она уже стала другой,—
За строгость, за стройность, за даль,
  за простор ...

He also loved this square,—
Since that time
It has already changed—
For its severity, for its harmoniousness, for its distance, for its space ...[52]

The most important echo of "The Bronze Horseman" in Polonskaja's two poems is the image of Petersburg as a blend of beauty and monstrosity, a monumental force which crushes the individual. In "The City" not only Evgenij but also his creator is destroyed by the malevolent forces of the city:

Serapion Sister

> Но тот,
> Кто прекрасную песню сложил,
> Был сам здесь загублен
>   в расцвете сил,
> В рогожную тряпку
> Поспешно зашит,
> И вывезен тайно,
> И ночью зарыт.

> But he
> Who composed the marvelous song,
> Was himself ruined here
>   in the flower of his strength,
> Hastily sewn into a bast cloth,
> And secretly driven away,
> And buried at night.[53]

There is also a more specific subtext which does not come from "The Bronze Horseman." It is the image of blood, specifically the blood of the poet in "The City":

> Властителям царства
> И мертвый поэт
> Казался опасен и страшен:
> Могилы его
> В этом городе нет,
> Но кровь его—
> В городе нашем.

> To the rulers of the kingdom,
> Even dead, the poet
> Seemed dangerous and terrifying:
> He has no grave in this city,
> But his blood—
> Is in our city.[54]

"The Square" also contains this image; in the midst of splendor, the speaker is haunted by the memory of blood in the very stone of the city:

> Не кровь ли здесь вкраплена
> В этот гранит
> И в алую кромку зари?

> Is there not blood sprinkled
> On this granite
> And into the crimson edge of the dawn?[55]

The reader will recall the image of bloodied stone in Polonskaja's "The Builder of a Great Brotherhood" (1922), in which she acknowledges that "the cathedral is built on blood."⁵⁶ That poem is immediately followed by "All Is Confusion: The Years of War" (1922), in which the speaker is one of countless slaves sacrificed in the building of an enormous stone edifice.⁵⁷

Images of building a powerful stone edifice link Polonskaja's earlier poetry both with Brjusov ("The Egyptian Slave"—see discussion in chapter 3) and with the programmatic statements of the Acmeists, such as Mandel'štam's "Morning of Acmeism." However, Polonskaja's use of the imagery turns on a somewhat darker interpretation, linked more closely to an image from Mandel'štam's poem of the same year, "Zasnula čern'" ("The Rabble Has Fallen Asleep," [1913]): "You—Russia, built on stone and covered in blood / Give your blessing, if only with your heaviness, / To my participation in your cruel punishment!"⁵⁸ Polonskaja also draws attention, in "The City," to the fact that the poet whose blood is on the stone of Petersburg has no grave there:

> Могилы его
> В этом городе нет,
> Но кровь его—
> В городе нашем.
>
> His grave
> Is not in this city,
> But his blood—
> Is in our city.⁵⁹

The same can be said of another poet with whom Polonskaja and the Acmeists were connected: Nikolaj Gumilev, the first poet to be executed in Petrograd under the new regime.

UNPUBLISHED POEMS FROM THE 1930S

Polonskaja's unpublished poems from the 1930s, like her published poems, have a different character than the ones she produced during the 1920s. She was generally much more cautious with regard to political and historical questions. Such patriotic verses as "Na sopkax Mančžurii" ("In the Hills of Manchuria," 1935), a hymn to the failed Revolution of 1905, would hardly have given Polonskaja problems with the censor; the fact that they remained unpublished most likely has more to do with the quality of the verse than its content. Polonskaja also wrote a great quantity of patriotic songs during the 1930s, some more successful than others. As mentioned earlier, her "Song about Lina Odena" became extremely popular and was translated into other languages. Others, such as "Mavzolej" ("The Mausoleum," 1937) and "Oktjabr'" ("October," 1937) may have been performed ("October" was set to music by Ljubov' Štrejxer), but they do not appear to have been published anywhere. Her poems on women's concerns, "Vos'moe marta"

Serapion Sister

("March 8," 1931) and "Ženščinam Ispanii" ("To the Women of Spain," 1937) are bland propaganda pieces.

I have seen only one instance of risky, overtly political verse from the 1930s in Polonskaja's archive. As mentioned in chapter 1, the unpublished quatrain of "A Mother Can Be Unjust at Times" (1938–57) reveals Polonskaja's bitterness over the fate of her lover, Mixail Ferberg. However, this poem, above all, is an expression of personal pain over the repression of a loved one, rather than political invective of the sort Polonskaja wrote and even published in the 1920s.

Polonskaja's most potentially problematic unpublished poems from the 1930s are personal meditations, expressions of generalized uneasiness, discouragement, fear of aging, or the nameless terror of a nightmare. Such poems, at odds with the demand for optimism and dismissal of the "narrowly personal," would most certainly have been difficult to publish. In "V poezde" ("In the Train," 1936), the poet describes the rush of darkness into her compartment as she switches off the light; the rushing of the train is a metaphor for her life: "Tak i menja unosit žizn' moja, / Dviženʹje poezdov i večnaja trevoga" (Thus does my life carry me away, / The movement of trains and eternal anxiety).[60]

"Verni moju junost'! Xotja by na čas" ("Give Me Back My Youth! If Only for an Hour," 1937) reflects the poet's nostalgia not only for her own youth but also for the days before "Some betrayed me, and others died. . . ." The most striking of these gloomy personal meditations is the terrifying "Nočnoj košmar" ("Nightmare," 1929–30), in which the speaker wakes with a scream from a macabre dream in which she appears to be struggling with death itself:

> . . . И колокол вдруг начинает бить.
> Ты знаешь это кровь в подземных венах
> В последней гонке бьется в хрупких стенках
> Чтоб просочиться в нежной ткани мозга
> И наконец лишить тебя сознанья.
>
> И наконец лишить тебя сознанья.
> Но яростно и бешенством охвачен,
> Ты начинаешь вдруг кричать—я не хочу!
> Я не хочу, проклятая еще . . .—
> И силы тела все, внезапно пробудясь,
> Бросаешь на борьбу с небытием.
>
> . . . And suddenly a bell begins to strike.
> You know that it is blood in underground veins
> Beating against brittle walls in a final rush
> To leak out into the tender fabric of the brain
> And finally rob you of consciousness.

And finally rob you of consciousness.
But furiously and seized by rage,
You suddenly start to scream—I don't want to!
I don't want to, curse you . . .—
And, the forces of your body suddenly awakening,
You fling yourself into a struggle with nonexistence.[61]

Autobiographical material, mainly connected with love, also fills Polonskaja's unpublished verse in the 1930s; several pieces refer to Lev Polonskij, including "The End" (1932–34), in which she defiantly rejects his belated proposal of marriage, and "The Tale" (1937), a moving address to his deceased wife, Anna (for details, see chapter 1). Polonskaja also composed some love poems at the request of composers who asked for texts to "heart-wrenching romantic songs."[62] Even here, there are traces of Polonskij; in "Černyj agat" ("Black Agate," 1930), the heroine recalls how "Dni prošli i gody prošli, proleteli, / Protekli slovno vody Dnepra" (Days passed, flew by, / Flowed away like the Dnieper's waters).[63] The mention of the Dnieper suggests Kiev, where she met Polonskij and where he remained. In "Sladčajšaja Ljutecija" ("Sweetest Lutetia," 1937), an unfinished, fragmentary piece, the poet returns in a dream to Paris, "That mad, unforgotten city / Where the circle of my love was not completed / (Where you first appeared in my life)."[64] "You" is, of course, Erenburg, who is shown writing verse at a marble table in a café.

THE BEGINNING OF WAR: *VREMENA MUŽESTVA* (*TIMES OF COURAGE*)

Polonskaja suffered from ill health and frayed nerves in the late 1930s and was writing comparatively little original poetry. Her main activity appears to have been translation, particularly from English. Her translation of Shakespeare's *Measure for Measure* was playing at the Novyj Theater, and her translations of Kipling, Robert Browning, Christina Rossetti, and Ernest Dawson were featured in anthologies of English poetry. "David Sassoon," her translation of the Armenian epic, appeared in 1939. Throughout the 1930s she was also translating from Yiddish, mostly folk and children's songs, but also including "Die Schwue" ("The Oath"), the anthem of the Jewish Labor Bund.[65]

In 1939 Polonskaja had a contract with the state publishing house Gosizdat for a collection of poetry, which she had not yet fulfilled; she was finding it more and more difficult to write original verse. On December 22, she wrote to Škapskaja that she did not dare show her face at Gosizdat, since her deadline for the collection had passed.[66] On October 1, 1940, she mentioned the book again to Škapskaja, with the following comment: "The book has made the rounds of the typographical departments and will be called *Vremena mužestva* [*Times of Courage*]. There is no basis for this at all, since there is nothing left in it but rubbish."[67] Ten days later she added the following: "I received word from my editor that he has thought it over and has removed another dozen poems from my collection. Since before that he removed some five poems each of three times he's accepted it, it turns out that not a single poem remains from this year, and thus the title 'Times of Courage' has become completely unnecessary and incomprehensible."[68] *Times of Courage* does indeed appear sparse. It contains only fourteen original lyrics, one translation (from Erich Weinert), and one narrative poem. Unlike any of Polonskaja's previous collections, it is not divided into sections. There are no reviews; the book does not appear to have attracted much critical attention at all.

A few of the poems stand out as historical curiosities, expressions of antifascist sentiments and of growing concern over the threat of war. "Song about Lina Odena," set to music by the composer Viktor Tomilin, became a popular song. Critic Vsevolod Azarov recalled many years later that

> [t]his song became popular in the years when republican Spain began its unequal battle with fascism. And we remember how in Leningrad crowds of thousands, during the October and May demonstrations, would take up its words:
>
> > Robber bands are in Granada,
> > Treachery has opened the door to them.
> > Comrade Lina Odena is leading
> > A *komsomol* division to the city.[69]

Aside from the political sentiments, the poem also contains one of Polonskaja's trademark strong heroines; Odena, outnumbered, shoots herself rather than surrender. "Song about Lina Odena" is immediately preceded by another poem on the theme of the strong woman, "Kolybel'naja dočke" ("Lullaby to My Daughter," 1938). In this piece, perhaps inspired by Lermontov's "Kazač'ja kolybel'naja pesnja" ("Cossack Cradle Song") and Nekrasov's satirical treatment of the same theme, "Kolybel'naja pesnja" ("Lullaby," 1845), a proud mother assures her daughter that her dream of flying will come true.[70]

Polonskaja makes another attempt at treating the Jewish question in "Pravdivaja istorija Doktora Fejgina" ("The Righteous Story of Dr. Fejgin," 1940), but the poem degenerates into hollow propaganda about Soviet nationality policies. The hero, a mild-mannered, devoted Jewish doctor, is fired from his hospital job by anti-Semitic Polish authorities and imprisoned for continuing to practice in his home. Released from prison after the fall of the Polish government, he returns to the hospital to battle a typhus epidemic. When Soviet tanks arrive, he expects the worst, but his impassioned plea, "if I am of Jewish blood, / how are the people to blame?!" is met with fervent assurances of equal treatment for all. Indeed, the Soviet commander appears insulted that anyone would suspect him and his troops of anti-Semitism, and in the end the town erupts into spontaneous, multiethnic outpourings of greeting and song, with Fejgin portrayed as the eternal Jew who can finally rest, "perhaps for the first time / In a thousand years."[71]

The most significant poem in *Times of Courage* is "The Portrait" (1939), which is both a historical piece on the life of the Ukrainian poet Taras Ševčenko and a meditation on the common bond among artists. As in her poems on Puškin, Polonskaja uses a historical subject, the life of a persecuted nineteenth-century poet, to parallel the contemporary situation of artists in Soviet Russia.

Like Polonskaja's other narrative poems, this one resembles a cycle with a plot; the introduction and fourteen sections are written in various meters, the predominant ones being trochaic and amphibrachic tetrameter. The introduction contains an invocation to the muse and a description, sprinkled with Ukrainian words, of the hard life of the young Ukrainian peasant. The boy is seen listening to, and perhaps drawing his inspiration from, the songs of a blind bard. Most of the subsequent sections describe well-known incidents in the poet's life: his discovery by the artist Sošenko, the interest taken in him by Brjullov and Žukovskij, and the purchase of his freedom with money from the sale of the famous portrait; hence the title. The poem ends at the point of Ševčenko's exile, along with the disappearance of the portrait:

> Как будто вдруг в дворцовый вечный праздник
> Ворвался, словно гром, грядущий век ...
> Портрет исчез. Он был подвергнут казни.
> Сожжен иль выслан, словно человек.
>
> As though suddenly, into the eternal holiday of the court,
> The coming age had burst, like thunder ...
> The portrait disappeared. It was executed,
> Burnt, or exiled, like a man.[72]

The occasion for this poem was, no doubt, the 125-year anniversary of Ševčenko's birth in 1939, marked by the publication of a new edition of his works and a number of scholarly studies. One major study was produced by Polonskaja's friend Šaginjan, so it is not surprising that she would also have chosen to write something on the theme. Soviet critical reception of Ševčenko had always been highly politicized, shifting with every change in policy regarding Ukrainian nationalism. According to Petro Odarčenko, the new official Party line, set forth in *Pravda* in 1939, was as follows: "Ševčenko's name was used to propagandize the idea of the political and cultural union between Russia and the Ukraine. *Pravda*'s article stressed the contacts Ševčenko maintained with Russian literature and Russian 'revolutionary democrats' and claimed that 'Ševčenko's poetry reflected the ideals of the Russian revolutionary democrats of the sixties.'"[73] On the most superficial level, Polonskaja's treatment more or less conforms to this image; the episode of the portrait is stressed, emphasizing Ševčenko's indebtedness to two Russians, Brjullov and Žukovskij, for buying his freedom. Furthermore, the final lines, quoted previously, suggest the cult, noted by Odarčenko, of "Ševčenko—the people's poet."[74]

There is more to the poem than official interpretation suggests, however. Section 8 stands out from the rest of the poem and may be a clue to the impetus behind its composition. It contains no explicit references to Ševčenko and could easily stand on its own as a lyric on the natural affinity of all those "whom the muses have loved," which is described as "the strongest union in the world":

> Есть союз, он не отмечен
> Ни в жандармском, ни в охранном,
> Нерушимо человечен
> Через все века и страны.
>
> В нем достоинство людское.
> Крепче в мире нет союза,—
> То содружество простое
> Тех, кого любили музы.
>
> There is a union, not recorded
> Either in the gendarmerie or by the Secret Police,
> It is inviolably humane
> Throughout all ages and countries.
>
> In it there is human dignity.
> There is no stronger union in the world,—
> That simple concord
> Of those whom the muses have loved.[75]

The idea of a bond "not recorded / Either in the gendarmerie or by the Secret Police" echoes Polonskaja's earlier description of the network of "merry friendship" which protected Viktor Šklovskij at the time of his flight (see "Ballad of the Fugitive," 1922). This hymn to an insoluble bond, "the simple concord" of artists, also echoes Lunc's characterization of the Serapions as "not comrades but—Brothers!"[76] The link is confirmed by the date given for the poem. Unlike the other pieces in the collection, which are dated simply by year, this one is dated precisely: February 1, 1939, the official anniversary of the founding of the Serapion Brothers. After such a statement about the solidarity of true artists, the somber note on which the poem ends, with Ševčenko's exile, may be more than simple affirmation of the Ukrainian poet's revolutionary credentials. Such a portrayal of official persecution of an outspoken poetic genius, coming so soon after the purges and the final arrest of Mandel'štam, must be regarded as a statement, however veiled.

UNPUBLISHED POEMS 1940–41

Polonskaja had complained to Škapskaja in 1940 that her editor had removed from *Times of Courage* all the poems written that year. There are, in fact, about twenty unpublished poems from 1940 in the archive, several of which are clearly finished and were probably intended for publication. Of these, about half concerned the war in Europe and the Finnish-Soviet war. The rest are personal or autobiographical, and there are a few interesting meditations. Of the series of six sonnets on the Finnish campaign (1939–40), three were eventually published (separately, not as a cycle) in 1966.[77]

Among the personal poems are a few lyrics to past lovers. "Knigi, radio, uzkij divančik" ("Books, a Radio, a Narrow Little Couch") is Polonskaja's last poem to Lev Polonskij, a reaction to the news of his impending remarriage. In it, she gives her "blessing" to this union, asserting her own independence and speaking contemptuously of the new wife:

> С ней живи, будь ей верным мужем.
> Я люблю лишь любовь да желанья.
> Ты, пожалуй, мне вовсе не нужен,
> А она без тебя увянет.
>
> Live with her, be her faithful husband.
> I love only love and desire.
> I do not need you at all, perhaps,
> But she will wither without you.[78]

Erenburg appears in an unpublished poem from 1940, "Ijun'. Žara. Vojna" ("June. Heat. War"). He was in occupied Paris at the time; Polonskaja wrote "Kak ja rada čto ty vernulsja" ("How Glad I Am That You Have Returned") the following year.[79]

News of the occupation of her beloved Paris brought back memories, and Polonskaja wrote several autobiographical pieces about the city, her student days, and her friends: "Pariž" ("Paris"), "Pariž. Nelli Ljafon" ("Paris. Nellie Lafon"), "Domoj/Sorbonna" ("Homeward/The Sorbonne") (1940–46). "Moej podruge (M. N. Kireeve)" ("To My Girlfriend [M. N. Kireeva]"), though undated, is presumably from the same series. As in "Farewell Ode" (1926), Polonskaja recalls Paris as the setting for a carefree life of love and poetry.

The personal poems also include a pair of elegies, "Zavtra. Pamjati M. A. Fromana" ("Tomorrow. Elegy for M. A. Froman")[80] and "Svetloglazaja devuška. Faine" ("A Bright-Eyed Young Girl. To Faina"),[81] and a curious piece called "Muze (Kogda, slučaetsja, ja tjaželo grušču)" ("To the Muse [When It Happens That I Am Heavy with Sadness"]), a modified version of a lyric written in 1938, "Moej nastavnice (Ty spravedlivaja, i ty ne terpiš' zla)" ("To My Mentor [You Are Just, and You Do Not Tolerate Evil"]). The 1938 version was dedicated to Raisa Grigor'evna Lemberg, "an old Bolshevik woman," Polonskaja's old teacher from the Berlin Marxist youth group; although it is not clearly marked as such, Mixail Polonskij was inclined to see the second variant as dedicated to Polonskaja's mother. It is noticeably darker than the earlier piece. Whereas in the first the speaker says, "I come to you and say:—I want / To leave everything! I do not believe anymore!" in the second her frustration is much more extreme: "I come to you and say:—I want / To hang or even drown myself." Likewise, the older woman's gentle encouragement prompts a somewhat less optimistic response in the second version:

> И ты мне руку на плечо кладешь,
> Приказываешь мне: «Ступай, начни сначала.»
> И, соглашаюсь, думаю:—Ну, что ж!
> За нами правда. То-ль еще бывало!

> And you lay your hand on my shoulder,
> You order me: "Go on! Start over from the beginning."
> And I agree, I think:—Well, all right!
> We have right on our side. (1938)

> И ты мне руку на плечо кладешь,
> Приказываешь мне:—Ступай, начни сначала!—
> И я смеюсь и думаю,—ну, что ж!
> Ведь я жива. Не все уже пропало!

> And you lay your hand on my shoulder,
> You order me: "Go on! Start over from the beginning!"
> And I laugh and think,—well, all right!
> For I am alive. All is not lost yet! (1940)[82]

Polonskaja tried (and failed) to publish this poem in a later collection "Dorogi v buduščee" ("Roads to the Future") in the mid-1960s.

Two meditative lyrics from the spring of 1940 stand out as particularly interesting. "Uborka list'ev" ("Cleaning Up the Leaves"), set in the park at Puškin, shows park workers burning piles of leaves from the previous summer, leaves beneath whose shadow "how many words of love have been heard, / How many songs have been sung, / How much happiness has been promised. . . ." As the smoke spirals upward while the workers rest, the speaker comments:

> Так уборку в сердце сделать,
> Тоже, хорошо бы,

Чтобы дымом разлетелись
И любовь и злоба . . .

To do such a cleanup in the heart
Would also be good,
So that both love and malice
Would fly away like smoke . . .⁸³

"Parki" portrays the three sister-fates, or "Parcae," figures from classical mythology:

И одна сестрица тянет нить,
А второй,—назначена крутить,
Третья,—ножницы свои берет,
Срежет нитку—человек умрет.

And one sister pulls the thread,
But the other has been appointed to wind it,
The third,—takes her scissors,
She cuts the thread—and a person dies.⁸⁴

The speaker, eager for life and new experiences, feels the ominous approach of the shears as "a terrible battle is coming in the world, / We shall not learn its outcome."⁸⁵

THE EARLY 1940S: WAR AND EVACUATION

Times of Courage was not a particularly successful collection, but for Polonskaja it represented the end of a dry spell, a renewal of her creativity which lifted her spirits. As she wrote to Škapskaja in 1941, "At one time I had the feeling that this book would be my last; . . . it has passed, and I want to write much more still. If I could only live and feel well."⁸⁶ She began writing verse again in earnest, and the 1940s proved to be one of the most prolific periods in her life. The challenge, however, was publication; wartime priorities did not favor the sort of introspective lyrics Polonskaja was producing, and her isolation in the Urals made negotiating with publishers even more difficult. Though she spent most of the war in evacuation, far from the front lines, she produced a torrent of verse and songs on the war, many of them extremely moving. None were published until decades later, and many were never published at all.

Although she signed a contract with a publisher in Molotov for a book of poems in 1942 and submitted a manuscript the following year, it did not appear until 1945.⁸⁷ A manuscript, *Kamskij god* (*A Year on the Kama*), mentioned in a letter to Škapskaja in 1943, was lost somewhere between Molotov and Leningrad as she was returning home in 1944. *Kamskaja tetrad'* (*A Kama Notebook*, 1945), a handful of other poems, and two sketches in periodicals are the only pieces Polonskaja was able to publish during the war years, but they represent only a small part of what she wrote. Some other poems were eventually published in the 1960s, in Polonskaja's last two collections. Among them are several of the more subtle and moving pieces she wrote during the war years, poems with less optimism but more pathos than most of those which appeared in *A Kama Notebook*.

One of Polonskaja's first poetic responses to the war was a series of light, humorous verses, which she composed on the train as she traveled east with the ballet academy. These were, most likely, not intended for publication, but to keep up her spirits and those of her companions, whom she gently teased in such verses as "Mnogoobraznye i dorožnye priključenija V. V. Uspenskogo" ("The Diverse Traveling Adventures of V. V. Uspenskij," 22 August 1941)[88] and "Ballada o Čajnike" ("Ballad of a Teapot," 26 August 1941).

Her satirical impulse found expression in ballads and fables, a few of which were published.[89] The German "knights" in "Ballada o rycarskoj ljubvi" ("Ballad of Courtly Love," 1942), who covet their neighbor's wife and property, receive a resounding "whack on the neck" from the outraged husband. In "Vrunu naxodčivost' nužna" ("A Liar Must Have His Wits about Him," 1942), Hitler scolds Goebbels for not being able to match the Soviet information bureau's ample listing of German prisoners' names, ranks, and addresses. The solution:

> Наутро радио немецкое
> Кричало, разевая пасть,
> Что в плен сдалась
>   советская
> Отборная глухонемая часть.

> Next morning the German radio
> Shouted, opening its jaws wide,
> That it had taken prisoner the Soviet
> Crack unit of deaf-mutes.[90]

Polonskaja's touch is somewhat heavier during this period than in the past, her response to the savagery of the Nazis itself a savage grotesque; for example, in "Napoleonovoj vozžaždav slavy" ("Having Thirsted for Napoleonic Glory," 1941), Hitler is portrayed as a bloodthirsty frog who "will burst on our bayonet."[91]

Several of the more serious wartime poems have a similarly ruthless quality, much more so than in anything Polonskaja ever published. The poet calls not only for victory, but also for bloody vengeance in such poems as "Sud prišel" ("The Judge Has Come," 1943), "Etot gorod" ("This City," 1943), and "U našej granicy" ("At Our Border," 1944). Critics have often described Polonskaja's poetic voice as severe, and her muse is particularly fierce with regard to Nazi war atrocities. It is not enough to drive the enemy from the motherland; he must be made to pay for his crimes against humanity. In "Sud' prišel" ("The Judge Has Come"), she speaks of a Soviet tribunal trying "three Hitlerite butchers," swearing to the dead:

> Убитые—в Смоленске, в Таганроге,
> И в древнем Киеве, лежащие во рвах,—
> Мы ваших палачей вернем на те дороги,
> Где в смертной проходили вы тревоге,—
> Они узнают, что такое страх!

> Murdered ones—in Smolensk, in Taganrog,
> And in ancient Kiev, lying in ravines,—
> We shall return your butchers to those roads
> Down which you passed in the agony of death,—
> They will learn what terror is![92]

There is no overt reference in any of these poems (at least, those which have survived) to the specifically anti-Semitic nature of the Nazi campaigns. The absence of overt references to the Holocaust in her wartime poems is striking, given Polonskaja's strong Jewish identity, especially since the campaign against "rootless cosmopolitans" was really a postwar development. Only a verse fragment from 1946, "Narod moj—ulybki skvoz' slezy" ("My People—Smiles through Tears"), in which she exhorts her people to overcome their submissiveness ("Insurrection! Insurrection! Insurrection! / Greatness! Greatness! Greatness!"),[93] appears to allude to a growing despair in the face of anti-Semitism. It is likely that Polonskaja wrote poems on this subject but destroyed them after the war, or that they might have disappeared along with the manuscript of *A Year on the Kama*. Unfortunately, there is no way to verify this.

A Kama Notebook is, as its title suggests, a poetic diary, in twenty-four lyrics, of the author's experience in evacuation. It begins with her departure from Leningrad, in "18 avgusta 1941" ("18 August 1941") and ends with her return, in "Slava Leningradu" ("Glory to Leningrad"). The prevailing tone is one of determined optimism in the face of sorrow, and the range of emotion depicted is narrow. Most of the poems are either descriptions of life in the Urals, with an emphasis on heroic service in the war effort, exhortations to the soldiers of the Red Army, or vows of vengeance against the invaders. A recurring motif is the town artillery factory, where most of the local people work and whose test shots are frequently heard in the background; the factory is mentioned in eight out of the twenty-four poems. The only piece remotely resembling a love lyric is "Pesnja devuški" ("A Young Girl's Song"), a young girl's praise of her beloved, who has been decorated for his military service.

The simple (some might say naive), unreflective nature of the subject matter is complemented by a stylistic adaptation to the geographical setting of the collection. Polonskaja had always been a primarily urban writer; her subjects, lexicon, and intonations reflected highly sophisticated cities, Paris and Leningrad. However, as her travel poems from the 1930s show, she could also adapt her rhythm, vocabulary, and other stylistic features to convey the flavor of an unfamiliar locale or situation. In this case, she chose to portray the people of this remote region in an approximation of the language and cadence of the Russian folk song. Several poems are written in trochaic meters, in some cases complete with dactylic endings and the sorts of lexical repetitions traditionally found in Russian folk songs:

> Ах ты, вьюга-вьюженька,
> Камский синий лед . . .
> А во мне, подруженьки,
> Вся душа поет.
>   («Песня девушки»)

> Oh, you blizzard—little blizzard,
> Blue Kama ice . . .
> But in me, my girlfriends,
> My whole soul sings.
>   ("A Young Girl's Song")[94]

> Жили здесь мастера оружейные,
> Лили пушки они огнестрельные.
>   От времен Суворова
>   Слава велика.
>   Били пушки здорово
>   Немца-пруссака.
>   («Город-городочек»)

> Master gunsmiths lived here,
> They molded fire-shooting-cannons.
>   Since Suvorov's time
>   Their glory has been great.
>   The cannons soundly beat
>   The Prussian-German.
>   ("Town, my little town")[95]

As though in counterpoint, the first and last poems, in which the poet leaves and returns to Leningrad, are written in a more traditionally literary style, without the repetitions, folk meters, and intonations that occur when the speaker is a local person. This is also true of certain other poems which occur in between, in which the image of Leningrad is never far from the thoughts of the poet and other evacuees portrayed, for example, "Doroga na vostok" ("The Road to the East"):

> Уснул малыш. Расстегнут синий ворот.
> А старшие на нарах, лежа в ряд,

Poetry in the Stalinist Period

> Заводят песню про любимый город,
> И звуки песни той летят, летят . . .

> A little one has fallen asleep. His blue collar is undone.
> But the older ones, lying in a row on the plank beds,
> Sing a song about their beloved city,
> And the sounds of that song are flying, flying . . .[96]

There is also a marked change in the depiction of gender roles in this collection. The heroines, unlike those of Polonskaja's earlier poetry, play only supporting roles in the war effort; they are primarily mothers, grandmothers, sisters, wives, and sweethearts of Red Army soldiers. Whether operating a lathe in an ammunition factory ("Devčonka" ["A Lass," 1943]), spinning and weaving cloth for soldiers' shirts ("Naša babuška" ["Our Grandmother," 1943]), sending care packages to the front ("Tri podarka" ["Three Gifts," 1943]), or simply exhorting their men to acts of bravery ("Zaveščanie" ["Testament," 1942]), these women make up the rear guard. There are no Lina Odenas, no fearless female partisans or pilots; the closest any of these women comes to a plane is in "Three Gifts," in which a girl speaks of donating money she has saved for a dress for an airplane.[97] The only poem in the collection with a specific addressee, "Gnezdo" ("The Nest," 1943), is dedicated to one Evdokija Ionovna Ivanova, "mother of fighters." It concerns a woman whose victory is in keeping her home together until her sons return from the front:

> Семья сидит у круглого стола.
> Пьет чай, читает письма фронтовые.
> А мать глядит на них и думает:—Спасла.
> Спасла для них. Все дома. Все живые.
> Спасибо Сталину. Он отстоял Россию.

> The family sits at a round table.
> Drinks tea, reads letters from the front.
> And the mother gazes at them and thinks, "I have saved it.
> I have saved it for them. All are home. All alive.
> Thanks be to Stalin. He has defended Russia."[98]

There are two oblique references to women as more active fighters against the Nazis. In "Stalingrad" (1943) we find, among those who lay down their lives defending the city, "all the sons and daughters of the Fatherland."[99] In "Our Grandmother," the lyric heroine speaks with pride of her sons and daughters at the front. None of these women fighters is the central subject of any of the poems in *A Kama Notebook*.

Polonskaja had not completely abandoned the theme of the strong, active woman, however. In fact, four of her heroines in poems written, but not published, in this period do resemble her earlier ones in physical bravery and sheer moxie. Two of these are Marija Melent'eva and Anna Lysicyna, portrayed in the ballad "Partizanki" ("Partisan Women," 1943), which was not published until 1960. As the two girls are swimming an icy river, Anna is overcome by her wounds; she refuses Marija's help in order not to betray their mission. Marija goes on to complete the mission alone, and both girls, Anna posthumously, are awarded the title of Hero of the Soviet Union.[100] A later, unpublished poem, "Partizanka" ("The Partisan Woman," 1946), features a defiant young girl who dies heroically at the hands of the Germans.[101] The fourth heroine is the female soldier in the unpublished "Kudrjavaja devčonka" ("The Curly-Haired Lass," 1944). She is not only strong and courageous, rescuing a fallen comrade from under enemy fire, she is also delightfully impertinent. Her cap on one side, she answers with ease the taunts of a man who tries to intimidate her with misogynist proverbs:

> Зачем и сам не знаю
> Сказал ей наобум:—
> У бабы, волос долгий,
> Зато, короткий ум.—
>
> Ребята засмеялись,
> А девушка—в ответ:—
> Бывает, парень бритый,
> Ума же,—вовсе нет.

> I said to her,
> Not knowing why myself:—
> A wench has long hair,
> But she's short on brain.
>
> The boys laughed.
> But the girl up and answered:—
> A lad could have a shaved head
> And no brain at all.[102]

Of these pieces, only "Partisan Women" was eventually published.

The overall impression produced by *A Kama Notebook* is one of monotony and of a lapse in Polonskaja's poetic standards. As A. Tarasenkov, the author of the only review of the collection, writes: "The thematic unity and patriotic purposefulness of the majority of the poems in *A Kama Notebook* are not strengthened by artistic wholeness and depth. . . . In E. Polonskaja's book there is not civic indifference, but there is poetic indifference—to the line, to the word, to the image. This is a shame! For it detracts from the greatness of the theme the poet has chosen."[103] If Polonskaja's experience with the editor of *Times of Courage* is any indication, it is likely that some of her more sophisticated and successful poems were simply removed before *A Kama Notebook* was published. Her correspondence with Škapskaja contains hints that her first attempt at a collection, *A Year on the Kama,* had been the subject of much wrangling before it was eventually lost: "The book of my poems, that same long-suffering one, was lost along with Uževič's review somewhere between Molotov and Leningrad. It has been unlucky."[104]

More recent critics, such as Minc and A. Galuškin, have noted a weakening in Polonskaja's verse during the 1940s and the apparent revival of her poetic powers in the collections she published in the 1960s.[105] However, two of the poems described by Minc as particularly fine in her review of *Lyric Poems and a Narrative Poem* ("Duby Sen-Klu" ["The Oaks of St. Cloux"] and "Uvidim vnov' Ulanovu-Žizel'" ["Once Again We Shall See Ulanova-Giselle"]) were actually written during the war.[106] A portion of the final chapter of this book is devoted to Polonskaja's inclusion of previously unpublished wartime poetry in her last two collections.

RETURN TO LENINGRAD

One of Polonskaja's most prominent themes from these years is the hard lot of the refugee and the longing for home. The longing for Leningrad is particularly poignant in such poems as "Toskueš' ty o dal'nem i ljubimom" ("You Yearn for a Distant and Beloved," 1943), "Zapomni vse i vse zapečatlej" ("Remember and Engrave Everything," 1943), and "Leningradskij veter" ("Leningrad Wind," 1943), in which Polonskaja writes:

> Хороши зимовки на Урале,—
> Сини дали, глубоки снега . . .
> Люди здесь—из самой твердой стали,
> Дружба их испытана, долга.
>
> Но тоска, что малахитов камень . . .
> О тебе забыть не в силах я.
> Снится мне тревожными ночами
> Оттепель внезапная твоя.

> The winters are fine in the Urals,—
> The distances blue, the snows deep . . .
> People here are made of the hardest steel,
> Their friendship is long and tested.
>
> But grief is like the stone of malachite . . .
> I have not the strength to forget you.
> In troubled nights I dream
> Of your sudden thaw.[107]

The collection begins and ends with the poet's departure from and return to Leningrad, and references to her distant city are woven throughout the collection. However, nowhere in the published poems is her homesickness expressed with as much pathos as in, for example, "Net, ne golod, i ne xolod, daže" ("No, Not Hunger, Not Even Cold," 1943): "How can you lie down on a stranger's bed? / How can you sit down at a stranger's table?"[108] Also, whereas in *A Kama Notebook* the final poem celebrates her return to the "city of Lenin," one of her first gestures upon returning home was to write "Sankt-Peterburg" (1944), in which she rejoices to find the city intact as it has always been, since long before the Revolution: "You proudly stand, like a century ago . . . / Bullet-riddled, but unbowed!"[109]

In her poems and songs of reconstruction, Polonskaja often focused on the role of women; "Krovel'ščiki" ("The Roofers") and "Xozjajki s našej ulicy" ("The Housewives from Our Street") are two published examples.[110] There are also a few songs in the archive. The heroine in "Čeremuxa" ("Bird Cherry," 1945) dreams of her beloved while painting and plastering, and in "Bojazlivaja žena" ("The Fearful Wife," 1944), a husband returns home to find his formerly timid wife clambering on rooftops.[111] She also published a satirical animal fable, "Lisa na strojke: Basnja" ("The Fox at the Construction Site"), in 1946.[112] It was to be the last original poem she published until 1956, although she was writing steadily.

With victory came a series of triumphant, rather giddy poems and songs, such as "Po slučaju pobedy" ("On the Occasion of Victory," 1945), in which an entire trolley full of people fall to kissing one another out of sheer joy. Yet there are also sober pieces reflecting Polonskaja's anxiety on behalf of her son, who had not yet returned home (for example, "Ne znaju gde, v kakom kraju" ["I Don't Know Where, in What Land," 1945]). Several poems describe the long-anticipated homecoming of a soldier, as in "Skatert' belocvetnuju vynu iz komoda" ("I Will Take a White Tablecloth from the Chest," May 1945) and "Vse čto poverxnostno—unosit veter" ("The Wind Will Carry Off All That Is Superficial," March 1945):

> Зажги огонь и воду вскипяти
> И встреть усталого солдата на пороге
> Хлеб соль на рушнике. Он долго был в пути
> Умой его натруженные ноги.
>
> Light the fire and boil water
> And meet the tired soldier at the threshold
> With bread and salt on a napkin.
> He has been long on the road
> Wash his worn feet.[113]

This note of anxiety for a loved one at a time of general rejoicing marks Polonskaja's return to more intimate, personal verse. She continued, of course, writing politically safe poems, such as "Drug moj, negr" ("Black Man, My Friend," 1947), on a national liberation movement in Africa, and "Iz vsex ego portretov est' odin" ("Of All His Portraits There Is One," 1949), on a portrait of Stalin, as well as a few topical animal fables ("The Fox at the Construction Site" and "Svin'ja, kon' i kolxoznik" ["The Pig, the Horse, and the Kolxoz Worker," 1946], which was never published). However, she also began writing love lyrics again, apparently for the first time since the war began. There are three from the spring of 1946: "Slyšno: tjaželoe s šumom" ("I Can Hear: Heavy with the Noise"); "Ne možet byt', čtob ne bylo ljubvi?" ("Can It Be That There Was No Love?"); and "Predel—za nim ni čuvstv, ne vpečatlenij" ("A Border—Beyond It Neither Feelings nor Impressions"). A later love lyric, "My pis'ma pisat' perestali" ("We Ceased Writing Letters," c. 1949), is dedicated to Erenburg. In it she recalls the early days of their acquaintance in Paris:

> Вы мне открыли тайное тайных—
> Созревание тела и духа . . .
> Наша встреча была не случайна,—
> Хотв мучительно стала разлука.

> You showed me the secret of secrets—
> The maturing of body and spirit . . .
> Our meeting was not accidental,—
> Though our parting became a torment.[114]

Polonskaja also turned to another intimate subject in her verse: the death of her mother in January 1946, about which she wrote eleven extremely moving lyrics in 1946 and 1947. There is no evidence that she ever intended to publish any of these; none of them appears on any of the lists of proposed contents for either *Lyric Poems and a Narrative Poem* or "Dorogi v buduščee" ("Roads to the Future"), a collection she never succeeded in publishing. They were an expression of her grief, an instance of emotion so strong that it had to be put into such tender verses as "Mama, dorogaja, ja s toboju vmeste" ("Mama, Dear, Together with You," 1946):

> Мама, дорогая, я искала счастья,
> Я узнала цену жизни и людей,
> Лишь в тебе, нашла я ласку и участье,—
> Не было подруги у меня—верней.

> Mama, dear, I searched for happiness,
> I learned the worth of life and people,
> Only in you did I find caress and caring,
> I never had a truer friend.[115]

This loss appears to have prompted Polonskaja to renewed meditation on her own mortality, a subject which had already begun to appear in her poetry in the 1930s. Several poems from the late 1940s express sadness, even pessimism, about the prospect of her own death. "Segodnja na viske u syna" ("Today at My Son's Temple"), which appeared in her last two collections, was written in 1948; there is an alternate draft as well as the final version. "Ostalis' gody, možet byt', minuty" ("Years Remained, or Perhaps Minutes,"

1946) is somewhat darker, as is the sonnet "V detstve, esli tebe" ("If You in Childhood," 1947):

> Вот и зрелые годы прошли.
> Боль утрат и горечь измен.
> Слово бьется, как птица средь каменных стен.
> Только запах весенней земли . . .
>
> Отсеки, отруби, отдели
> Горе сердца и горе уму,
> Умирать одному . . .
>
> Thus did my mature years also pass.
> The pain of losses and the bitterness of betrayals.
> The word beats, like a bird within stone walls.
> There is only the smell of the spring earth . . .
>
> Cut off, chop off, separate
> Grief of the heart and grief of the mind,
> To die alone . . .[116]

Polonskaja was able at times to retain some of her characteristic irony even in the face of aging, however. In "Mne skazali segodnja v tramvae" ("Someone Said to Me in the Tram Today," 1946), she responds to a stranger's calling her *babuška* (granny): "For I know I am young, / But, all the same, I'm a bit offended."[117]

Polonskaja also turned her irony on her own penchant for celebrating the feminine in verse. In 1946 she wrote "V šutku skazat'" ("In Jest"), in which the speaker states her exasperation with the entire subject of sisterhood:

> Никогда сестры я не имела
> И даже, пожалуй, не хотела;
> Очень плохо—младшей быть сестрою,
> Но старшею родиться—хуже двое.
>
> Я за братьев. Даже за кузенов,
> Хоть бы до четвертого колена,—
> За двоюродных и четвероюродных.
> Без сестры мне обойтись нетрудно!
>
> I never had a sister
> And I never even wanted one;
> It's very bad to be the younger sister,
> But to be the older is twice as bad.
>
> I'm for brothers. Even for cousins,
> Second and fourth, even.
> I can get along very well without sisters![118]

She did, nonetheless, continue producing such examples of the genre as "Kamen'ščik" ("The Mason," 1949), about a female stonemason, "Martovskij večer" ("March Evening," 1949–50), a commemorative poem for International Women's Day, and "O ženščiny, o sestry dorogie" ("O Women, O My Dear Sisters," 1949).

A theme which appears shortly after the war, and which was to become increasingly important in Polonskaja's late verse, is nature. The starting point for this trend is around 1946, when she wrote "Vesennaja skazka" ("Spring Fairy Tale"), a whimsical personification of spring as a young woman come to clean up the mess left behind at winter's feast, and "Detskoe selo" ("Children's Village"). The latter is only a four-line poem, a fragmentary evocation of a familiar setting. Its significance comes from its position as a link in a series of unpublished poems, begun in 1920, dedicated to this place. During the summer of 1920, Polonskaja worked as a doctor at a hospital in Detskoe Selo (formerly known as "Tsarskoe Selo," or Tsar's Village, the summer home of the royal family), where an orphanage had been established. At that time she produced a draft, "Children's Village," in which she described an idyllic haven for children:

> Светло и солнечно, и тихо, и тепло.
> Плодов невиданных цветут сухие гряды,
> Как будто вправду здесь не Царское Село,
> А сказочной страны капустная рассада.
>
> О, сколько маленьких и от каких отцов,
> И матери их родили какие?—
> Огромный выводок беспомощных птенцов
> Великой и большой трудящейся России.
>
> It is bright and sunny, and quiet, and warm.
> The dry garden beds bloom with unprecedented fruits,
> As though this really were not Tsar's Village,
> But the cabbage patch of a fairy-tale land.
>
> O, how many little ones, and of what fathers,
> And what mothers bore them?—
> An enormous brood of the helpless chicks
> Of great and large laboring Russia.[119]

In "Raj" ("Heaven," 1922), she had described a green heaven "Only for little ones, for children, / Grown-ups are not allowed here at all." In 1955, she produced another draft, this time called "Detskoe Selo," ("Children's Village"), a slightly modified version of "Heaven"; this time, the idyllic portrayal of the garden is placed within a historical frame:

> Да, в двадцатые годы, в обнищалом крае
> Неверящие в бога мечтали о рае: . . .
> . . . .
> Так в голодные годы, в обнищалом крае,
> В коммунизм поверив, но пути не зная,

Мы Романовых логово, бывший царский дом,
Называли ласково «Детским Селом».

Yes, in the twenties, in a beggared land
Those who did not believe in God believed in heaven: . . .
. . . .
Thus, in hungry years, in a beggared land,
Believing in Communism, but not knowing the way,
We tenderly called "Children's Village"
The Romanov lair, the tsar's former home.[120]

The image of an Eden populated only by children underwent a transformation in Polonskaja's late verse. In order to rework her concept of the garden, Polonskaja had to return herself, not as a child but as an aging woman. It was in 1949 that she returned to Tartu, the scene of her youth, for the first time since she had studied there in 1915. She recorded the event in a short poem, "Zdravstvuj Tartu, staryj drug" ("Hello, Tartu, Old Friend"), greeting the town after a long separation, during which "the salt of the sciences, / Has soaked into the black enamel of my hair." From 1949 on, Polonskaja and her family spent their summers not far from Tartu, in the tranquil little town of El'va, which figures heavily in her late verse. The "garden" becomes not Detskoe Selo, the utopian fantasy of a children's heaven, but El'va, the haven of the poet's own declining years. The transition can be traced in several unpublished "Detskoe Selo poems" and the beginning of Polonskaja's long and fruitful creative focus on El'va.

POLONSKAJA'S POSTWAR POETIC SILENCE

A note from Polonskaja's account book from October 1946, regarding her translation of Calderón, reads: "I was delayed with this work, and now, in connection with the 'resolution on *Zvezda*' everything is being put off."[121] In addition to the fallout from Ždanov's attack on Zoščenko, the postwar years were also a period of increased anti-Semitism; the murder of Solomon Mikhoels, head of the Jewish Anti-Fascist Committee, in 1948, the campaign against "rootless cosmopolitans," the execution of most of the major Yiddish writers in 1952, and the incident of the "Doctors' Plot" in 1953 made the years leading up to Stalin's death a particularly difficult time for a Jewish writer, particularly one who was also a doctor.

Polonskaja kept a low profile during those years. She no longer frequented the Poets' Section of the Writers Union, spending most of her time with the Translators' Section, which she headed for a few years in the 1950s. An innocuous book of sketches about the bravery of Red Cross nurses during the war, which she published in two editions in 1948, appears to be a direct response to a passage in Ždanov's famous speech, in which he specifically asks why Leningrad writers have not taken up the theme of Soviet woman, "particularly Leningrad girls . . . who *shouldered* the enormous burden of the war years."[122] Polonskaja's title, *Na svoix plečax* (*On Their Own Shoulders*), is a direct quotation from the passage, which reads in Russian: "kotorye vynesli *na svoix plečax* ogromnye trudnosti voennyx let."[123]

Polonskaja's attempt at a novel, *The City*, about the reconstruction of Leningrad (discussed in chapter 1), was ultimately unsuccessful, but she was able to establish herself as a regular writer for the journal *Gudok*. It was only after Stalin's death, in the more liberal atmosphere of the Thaw, that she was able to find venues for publishing original verse. That period will be discussed in my final chapter.

Chapter Six

Poetry in the Post-Stalinist Period

POLONSKAJA'S ATTEMPTS to publish her poetry between the end of the war and Stalin's death can be reconstructed from various documents in her archive. Her account book from 1946 contains a note about a collection, *Poterjannyj i vozvraščennyj dom* (*The Lost and Recovered Home*), submitted to the publisher Sovetskij pisatel' and returned to her for reworking. On November 10, 1951, she noted that she had finished a book of poems, and in January 1953 she submitted a request to the Poets' Section of the Writers Union for a consultation on a collection which they themselves had approved for publication two years earlier. Polonskaja stated in her request that she had no contract with Sovetskij pisatel' and that the directions she had been given by the publisher regarding the first variant were "unclear and imprecise." She therefore requested that a member of the Poets' Section be assigned to consult with her on "content, thematics, sections, the proportion of old to new verse, etc." "With the help of a consultant, chosen by the Bureau of the Poets' Section," she wrote, "I could have the book ready to go to press in three months, that is, around March or April of 1953."[1]

The proposed collection was never published, at least not in the form envisioned by the author in 1953. It was not until 1956, the year when Stalin was officially denounced, that Polonskaja was finally able to publish two poems in a Leningrad almanac, *Den' poeta* (*Day of the Poet*); from then on, she published new poetry regularly, though not in great quantity, until her final illness in 1967, producing two more collections, *Stixotvorenija i poema* (*Lyric Poems and a Narrative Poem*, 1960) and *Izbrannoe* (*Selected Poems*, 1966), and appearing in numerous periodicals. Several more poems were published with a memorial tribute in *Den' poezii* (*Day of Poetry*) in 1969, the year of her death.

Polonskaja's late poetry was warmly received by critics, who wrote admiringly of its "deep historicism,"[2] of its "bright, life-affirming motifs,"[3] and of the "kindness and self-sacrifice [which] are the foundations of the severe world of Elizaveta Polonskaja."[4] Meditations on aging and death are often warmed by thoughts of nature, music, children, "the joy of the heart, of the body.... No, I did not want to die yet!" ("Ja razljubila vse, čto serdcu milo"

["I Have Fallen Out of Love with All That Was Dear to My Heart"], 1958).[5] As in Polonskaja's earlier work, children represent the future of humanity; furthermore, the harshness of some of her earlier political invective is tempered by a more universal, maternal concern for all human life in an age of global wars. In the words of Zara Minc, "It is now in particular that the leading theme of her poetry can be felt as a humanitarian one. She has brought to life a new tradition—a Puškinian one, the bright and harmonious 'Puškinian' worldview has been organically reconceptualized as the all-embracing feeling of the contemporary mother."[6]

According to A. Galuškin, the lyric hero (*sic*) of Polonskaja's late poetry has something in common with that of her poetry from the 1920s: a sense of moral obligation to preserve cultural and historical memory through the poetic word.[7] The poet's duty to bear witness is clearly stated in "Vospominanija" ("Memories," 1958), in which the dead address her:

«...Захочешь, мы в небытие,
Как все прекрасное на свете,
Уйдем, и дело не твое,
И ты за это не в ответе.

Но если любишь ты смелей,
Превозмогая сон покоя,
Из царства мертвых, как Орфей,
Ты уведешь нас за собою».

If you wish, we shall cease to exist,
Like everything beautiful on earth,
And it is no affair of yours,
And you are not to blame.

But if you love more bravely,
Overcoming the dream of peace,
From the kingdom of the dead, like Orpheus,
You shall lead us behind you.[8]

Prose memoirs were a major part of Polonskaja's late work, particularly memoirs of friends and colleagues from the 1920s whose names were taboo or simply forgotten, such as Zoščenko, Gumilev, David and Emma Vygodskij, Mixail Lozinskij, Škapskaja, and others. Fellow poets are also memorialized in Polonskaja's late poetry, most notably Majakovskij and Axmatova, whom she called "the glorious muse of Russian verse."[9]

Despite the loosening of constraints on writers after Stalin's death, Polonskaja found herself once again compelled to modify her image in exchange for the privilege of being allowed to publish original verse. Those who praised her poetry in the 1960s tended to minimize the controversial aspects of her early work, emphasizing instead its formal beauty and profound humanism. In general, the tone is one of respect for "one of the oldest Soviet poetesses";[10] there are cryptic allusions to her "complex path of ideological-artistic development,"[11] but after *Omens* she is said to have resolved her political uncertainties. Some of these same critics admit that Polonskaja's poetry from the 1920s is aesthetically superior to her output from the 1930s and 1940s, but they are obliged to point out the "ideological-thematic enrichment" of her poetry in the 1930s and during the war.[12] The cumulative effect of these reviews is to camouflage Polonskaja's early rebelliousness behind a mask of venerable, but oddly neutral, respectability; she became a literary grandmother figure who enjoyed a surge of popularity before receding into benign neglect after her death.

THE LATE 1950S: RETURN TO PUBLISHING

Polonskaja's first new poems appeared in print in 1956, and they share some of the spirit of liberalism which emerged in the wake of the Twentieth Party Congress. In "Svideteli velikix potrjasenij" ("Witnesses of Great Upheavals"), the heroine imagines the world's next great poet in the future, who will take his deepest inspiration from the carefully preserved records of those who witnessed the major upheavals of the age:

> О мужестве и верности любимых,
> О доблести суровой матерей
> Прочтет он в письмах, бережно хранимых,
> Залитых кровью баснословных дней.
>
> Задумается он, как жили люди,
> Как для отчизны жертвовали всем ...
> И сердце дрогнет в нем, и это будет
> Прекраснейшая из людских поэм.
>
> About the courage and loyalty of loved ones,
> About the stern valor of mothers
> He will read in letters, carefully preserved,
> Stained with the blood of legendary days.
>
> He will start to think about how people lived,
> How they sacrificed everything for the fatherland ...
> And his heart will shudder, and this will be
> The most marvelous of human poems.[13]

The nationality of the future poet is indeterminate and ultimately unimportant ("In what country, I do not know . . . Ovid, / Hugo or Puškin, Goethe or Shakespeare"), an affirmation of Polonskaja's characteristic position on the brotherhood of artists superseding national boundaries.

One year later, Polonskaja published "Bereza-belogrudka u verandy" ("A White-Breasted Birch by the Veranda"), in which a birch's sudden burst into leaf is a herald of spring and an affirmation of life in a hostile, wintry

Poetry in the Post-Stalinist Period

world. The birch becomes a sentient being with an individual will which goes against the grain of her chilly surroundings:

> По радио сказали: плюс четыре.
> Луна висела над соседним бором,
> Бежали облака в небесной шири.
> Заснули мы,—теперь весна не скоро!
> Проснулись, а она зазеленела,
> Стоит в зеленом пламени убора.
> Что ж, может быть луна ее пригрела:
> Она так сильно расцвести хотела!

> They said on the radio—four degrees above freezing.
> The moon hung above the neighboring wood,
> Clouds were running in celestial space.
> We fell asleep—now spring will not come soon!
> We awoke—and she had already turned green,
> She stands in the green flame of her attire.
> Well, perhaps the moon warmed her:
> She wanted so badly to blossom![14]

The birch's reckless insistence on unfurling her leaves despite the cold suggests a metaphor for the situation of the Soviet artist in the late 1950s, after the scandal surrounding the *Literaturnaja Moskva* anthology in 1956 had made clear the limits of the thaw. The poem, undated on its appearance in *Priboj* (*Surf*), was dated 1951 when it appeared in *Lyric Poems and a Narrative Poem*. However, Polonskaja's dating of her poetry was often fluid, changing to suit her sense of political necessity, particularly when she republished earlier pieces which might be retrospectively construed as questionable. It is possible that she changed the date of this poem to avoid its being connected with the year when it was first published. Such changes of date are particularly noticeable in *Lyric Poems and a Narrative Poem*.

Four of Polonskaja's poems were published in a large anthology of Soviet poetry in 1957: "Fairy Tale," "1919," "Isn't It Strange That We Shall Forget Everything," all from *Omens,* and a previously unpublished poem, "Belomorsk (aprel')" ("Belomorsk [April]," 1943). The latter portrays a little girl sent alone on an errand to town, who sings to herself as she runs:

> Не потому поет она,
> Что весел день вчерашний,
> А потому, что ночь, война
> И ей немного страшно.

> She does not sing because
> Yesterday was merry,
> But because it is nighttime, wartime
> And she is slightly terrified.[15]

This is the first of Polonskaja's unpublished wartime poems to appear in the post-Stalinist period. Unlike the pieces in *A Kama Notebook*, these lyrics vividly portray not only patriotism and determination but also the weariness and terror of the war experience. It is hardly surprising that Polonskaja had to wait not only for the end of the war but for the end of the Ždanov era to publish such poems; as Hugh McLean and Walter Vickery point out, optimism was mandatory during that period, and even in depictions of the war, "Soviet people were not to be depicted as in any way pessimistic, weary or sorrowing; Soviet man was made of superhuman heroism and devotion to duty."[16] Several other of Polonskaja's wartime poems published only in the 1960s share this emotional honesty; they are far more powerful and dignified than most of the patriotic exhortations in *A Kama Notebook*.

A few other poems published by Polonskaja during the late 1950s have a more cautious, conventionally optimistic focus. The poet looks to the future in "V čem priznak novogo? Uželi" ("What Signifies the New? Is It Really") in which the new person, the person of the future:

> Сам осознал свое призванье
> И, времени поняв закон,
> В могучем счастье созиданья
> Сам ускоряет бег времен.

> Having recognized his calling
> And, having understood the law of time,
> He himself, in the powerful happiness of creation
> Speeds the flight of time.[17]

The only note of mild ambivalence is in "Svetloglazyj umnyj mal'čik" ("Bright-Eyed, Clever Boy"), in which the heroine restrains herself from discouraging a young boy's restless desire for challenge and danger, though she knows he will encounter sorrow:

> Что ж! Лети на волю! Разжимаю молча руки,
> Стиснув зубы, улыбаюсь. Улыбаюсь гордо. Пусть!
> Без колоды карт я знаю: суждены года разлуки,
> Сыновьям и дочкам нужно знать борьбу, победу, грусть.

> Well then! Fly freely! I fold my arms in silence,
> I smile with gritted teeth. I smile proudly. Let it be!
> I know without a deck of cards: years of separation are fated,
> Our sons and daughters must know struggle, victory, and sorrow.[18]

LYRIC POEMS AND A NARRATIVE POEM

Polonskaja's first postwar collection, *Lyric Poems and a Narrative Poem*, appeared in 1960 to generally positive reviews. The editorial history of the collection, however, reveals the extent to which this "representative of the

Poetry in the Post-Stalinist Period

oldest generation of Soviet lyricists"[19] still had to adapt to the "censor-muse." This book is presented as a summary of Polonskaja's work, and new pieces are preceded by several sections representing earlier phases of her career. However, as in *Years*, the republished poems are not entirely faithful to the original versions; the political corrections from *Years* are retained, and there are even some additional revisions and rearrangements. As Nikolaj Braun wrote in an internal review of an early version of the manuscript, "Polonskaja's poetry has not been published for a long time. We must take into account that some of the poems in the book were published at one time in editions of five hundred to one thousand, and they are unfamiliar to the young and even to the older reader."[20] Precisely because the original versions of many of these poems had appeared many years before in small editions, significant changes go unremarked, and the image of the poet is distorted yet again to fit the demands of a different historical period.

The very title of the collection is the result of censorship. The original title was to be *Lyric and Narrative Poems*, since Polonskaja's original intention was to include "Carmen" (1924), "The Great Citizen" (1929), and "The Portrait" (1939). The final version contains only one *poema*, "The Portrait." "The Great Citizen," the tale of an abandoned single mother's fight for justice, was the first to go, apparently because the editors felt it was "noticeably lower [in quality] than E. Polonskaja's other works."[21] This change was made in February 1959. In November of that year, the poems being considered for inclusion had still included "Carmen,"[22] but a pair of undated internal memos reveal that it was removed for other reasons. The first, from one I. Abramenko to a Evgenija Markovna, asks her to give the proofs to the editor, Ninov, and to have him look specifically at two pieces, "Carmen" and the lyric "Kamskij golubok" ("A Kama Dove"), both of which were eventually removed. "A Kama Dove," which had originally appeared in *A Kama Notebook*, is referred to here as "verses about an artillery factory"; it was cut because of its description of the artillery factory in Perm.[23] The reasons for excluding "Carmen" become clear in a fragment of another note (the names of author and addressee are missing): "Elizaveta Grigor'evna . . . suggests that instead of replacing 'Carmen,' we remove four lines from it (p. 135—"Sailor, soldier . . ." and so on). Could we do it that way?"[24] The lines in question are:

> Матрос, армеец, слесарь, вор—
> Она любила не торгуясь
> И никому до этих пор
> Не отказала в поцелуях.

> Sailor, soldier, locksmith, thief—
> She loved them all without haggling,
> And no one, to this day,
> Has been refused her kisses.

This strategy was unsuccessful, but its implications are clear; in the 1960s, as in the late 1920s, portrayal of open and easy sexuality was unacceptable in a poem about a Bolshevik heroine. Even without these four lines, the heroine remains "neither mother nor wife"; her streetwise allure has as much to do with her impudence as it does with her physical charm. In her review of the collection, Minc notes the absence of this poem, "in which was created one of the first images in our poetry of woman as fighter for the Soviets."[25] "A Kama Dove" was obscure enough not to be missed, but "Carmen's" absence would certainly have been felt by anyone familiar with Polonskaja's earlier work.

More noticeable than "Carmen's" absence, however, is the selection and arrangement of poems, in particular the extremely scanty representation of Polonskaja's first two collections, *Omens* and *Under a Stone Rain*, which are not even named. The first section, called "From the First Books," contains four poems from *Omens* and one from *Under a Stone Rain*. The absence of the two collection titles would not be noticeable were it not for the fact that every other section (there are six) bears the title of a previous collection or cycle. "From the First Books" is followed by "From the Book 'Years,'" "From the Cycle 'The New World,'" "From the Books 'A Stubborn Calendar' and 'Times of Courage,'" "From the Book 'A Kama Notebook,'" and "From the Cycle 'Roads to the Future.'" "Roads to the Future" is followed by "The Portrait" (1939), the one narrative poem to survive the editorial process. "From the Book 'Years'" contains poems on love and art, several of which did not actually appear in *Years* or appeared for the first time in *A Stubborn Calendar*. *A Stubborn Calendar*, in turn, is lumped together with *Times of Courage*, although they appeared eleven years apart, with two other collections in between; only two poems from *A Stubborn Calendar* are included in that section, and both are printed not as they appeared in 1929, but with the titles given to them in *Years*, "The Hamburg Manege" and "Along the Road to Alton" (original titles: "Dogs" and "The Bridge"). Four of the eleven poems in this section had actually never been published before. The same is true of the following section, "From the Book 'A Kama Notebook,'" in which five out of the eight poems were either unpublished previously or had not appeared in the collection named.

In certain cases, the rearrangement of the poems gives thematic unity to a section, as, for instance, with the love lyrics or the wartime pieces, but the specific titling of those sections (by collection) is misleading. The most obvious result of all this shifting and retitling is that the importance of Polonskaja's earliest, most controversial verse is minimized. The selection of poems in "From the First Books" is extremely conservative: "With a Soft Sponge, with Warm Water" and "Fairy Tale" are two of her celebrated poems on maternity; "Isn't It Strange That We Shall Forget Everything" and "1919" portray the heroism of the civil war years; "Ballad of the Fugitive," previously made respectable by the dedication to Kropotkin, is here given an even more orthodox addressee: the first Soviet president, Jakov Sverdlov.[26] The poem is also given a significant new date, June 1917, which places it during the period of the provisional government; it was actually written in 1922. There are also significant changes in "With a Soft Sponge" which render it more innocuous: it is dated 1916, as though to suggest that it was inspired by World War I rather than the Revolution,[27] and the final strophe has been changed in a way which reduces its original searing pathos, producing a gentler impression more in keeping with the "life-affirming" qualities attributed to Polonskaja's poetry in the 1960s. The original reads "I still feel your feeble mouth / Upon my emptied breast." It has been replaced by "I can feel your feeble mouth / Draw life from my burning breast." As for *A Stubborn Calendar*, its defiant character is masked by placing its most characteristic poems under another less controversial heading. *Years* had been highly praised by critics, whereas *A Stubborn Calendar* had been attacked for its perceived glorification of unruly passions and the criminal underworld.

On the other hand, previously unpublished later poems which had not been allowed to appear were presented as having already done so. Some of the war poems could not possibly have appeared in their time, portraying as they do the weariness, uncertainty, and desolation of war. For example, "Zdes' včera ešče ljudi žili" ("Yesterday People Still Lived Here," dated 1940) contains a pathetic image of skeletal chimneys in vacant lots, where "The corpses of solid iron stoves / Hang in the blue ether."[28] "Russkuju peč' ja zakryla" ("I Have Closed the Russian Stove," 1941–42) is a desperate plea to the muse for strength:

> Не уходи. Я так обездолена,—видишь
> Плечи согбенные, пряди седые волос ...
> В сердце мое загляни, и в бездну ты внидешь.
> Мужество дай мне, молю,—не посылай мне слез.
>
> Don't go. I'm unlucky enough,—look,
> Bent shoulders, strands of gray hair ...
> Look into my heart, and you enter the abyss.
> Give me fortitude, I pray,—don't send me tears.[29]

These poems are integrated into the sections representing the two published wartime collections. In addition, Polonskaja has given *A Kama Notebook* two of her trademark strong heroines who do not appear in it originally: Marija Melent'eva and Anna Lisicina, decorated Heroes of the Soviet Union from "Partisan Women" which, though written in 1946, does not appear in print until now (see chapter 5).

The section "From the Cycle 'Roads to the Future'" consists mostly of postwar poems appearing in print for the first time; the few which had been published had appeared only in periodicals in the 1950s. In keeping with the section's title, several concern the end of the war, the rebuilding of Leningrad, and the future, which is embodied in children. The artist's moral obligation to preserve memory is expressed in "Memories," published for the first time here. "Witnesses of Great Upheavals" is reprinted here, along with "What Signifies the New," "Song of Our Country," and "Bright-Eyed, Clever Boy."

Though the subject of maternity is not new, the focus shifts in Polonskaja's late verse from direct experience of motherhood to a more distanced portrayal. Mother-love no longer has the fierce, almost bestial quality of some of the earliest poems; the lyric heroine's concern encompasses not only her own child, but all children, viewed from the perspective of old age. These pieces also have none of the didactic tone of the poems from the 1930s and 1940s, in which the names of various Bolshevik leaders are invoked and their dedication to children proclaimed. The most personal of the poems on children is the charming "Saše" ("To Saša," 1957), written for her grandson Aleksandr. "Deti" ("Children," 1945) portrays a school outing to the Neva; the poet reflects on the future these children will inherit. Side by side are "Ljublju tetrad' s kosymi v tri linejki" ("I Love a Notebook with Three Slanting Lines," 1958) and "U malen'kix lastoček pervyj urok" ("The Little Swallows Have Their First Lesson," 1958), in which the poet observes with affection the first efforts of a young generation:

> И сад наш сегодня—детский сад,
> На каждом дереве слетки.
> А если дождь? А если град?
> Корми их! Прячь их! Работка . . .
>
> And our garden is a kindergarten today,
> There are little classes on every tree.
> And if it rains? And if it hails?
> Feed them! Hide them! An assignment . . .[30]

Also reprinted here is "Litoj rešetkoj ogorožen" ("Fenced with a Cast-Iron Grate," first published in 1956), in which a row of infants sleeping in their carriages is equated with a garden planted on a bombed-out building site:

> Где бомбой срезан угол дома,
> Там молодой посажен сад,
> И малыши под шум и гомон
> В колясках безмятежно спят.
>
> Как бы зеленый полустанок
> Средь серых каменных громад,
> Руками наших горожанок
> Там молодой посажен сад.

Poetry in the Post-Stalinist Period

> Where the corner of a house was torn off by a bomb,
> There a young garden is planted,
> And little ones, through noise and hubbub,
> Are sleeping peacefully in their carriages.
>
> Like a little green station
> Among gray stone masses,
> By the hands of our city's women
> A young garden has been planted.³¹

Several important thematic lines in Polonskaja's verse intersect in this poem. Here, as in Polonskaja's early verse, women complete the task of building a new world: in the bombed-out ruins of the old world they bear children, seeds of the future. However, unlike the early verse, where the child was often presented as an animal, sometimes wild, crude, and bestial ("Fairy Tale," "All That Year Was Difficult and Cruel," "The Fire-God"), in these poems the natural images are botanical: the child has gone from wild cub to tender shoot. This image of humanity as a garden tended for the future had appeared first in "The Gardener" (1936), Polonskaja's epic on Stalin; however, it became specifically connected with children somewhat later in an unpublished poem, "Malyš—kak tugo svernutaja počka" ("A Child Is Like a Tightly Furled Bud," 1946):

> Малыш—как туго свернутая почка:
> В нем поколенья жизни молодой.
> Побеги пустит, выпустит листочки,
> Даст плод и цвет, оденется корой.
>
> Сомкни вокруг него скорее руки!
> Как детские нам удержать сердца?
> Уже шумят сыны твои и внуки,
> Теснится роща вместо деревца.
>
> A child is like a tightly furled bud:
> In him are generations of young life.
> He puts forth sprouts, he puts out little leaves,
> Gives fruit and blossom, clothes himself with bark.
>
> Put your arms around him quickly!
> How can we hold children's hearts?
> Your sons and grandsons are already clamoring,
> A grove clusters where a sapling stood.³²

In general, Polonskaja expresses a much greater feeling for nature, particularly trees, in her late poetry than she did in her youth. Most of her early verse is set in cities, particularly Petrograd, and she tends to portray the natural world as a setting for reflection of the struggles taking place in the human one. The one nature poem she published in the 1920s, "Mirtut'" (1929), begins with a lyrical description of the Finnish landscape but ends with an abrupt shift to a mother's reunion with her child.[33] In the 1930s, exotic landscapes form a backdrop for love poetry and even some political verse, as in the Central Asian and Armenian poems; in the 1940s, Siberian nature is a setting for the war effort. "Duby Sen-Klu" ("The Oaks of St. Cloux," 1940), published for the first time in *Lyric Poems and a Narrative Poem* (in the section "From the Books 'A Stubborn Calendar' and 'Times of Courage'"), is an exception. It portrays the French trees as subjects rather than setting, heroic martyrs in the fight against the Germans:

> Вы взяли их в кольцо древесных полчищ,
> Где с полумглою схож зеленый день.
> Вы дали им прохладой насладиться,—
> И пламя преградило путь убийцам,
> Ваш черный дым плывет под небеса . . .
> В раскатах взрывов, в самом пекле боя,
> Вы умираете бесстрашно, стоя,
> Дубы Сен-Клу, узорчатые клены,
> Густые липы Севра и Медона . . .
> Пылают Франции леса.

> You took them into a ring of wooden hosts,
> Where the green day was like half-darkness.
> You let them enjoy your coolness—
> And flame blocked the murderers' path,
> Your black smoke sails under the sky . . .
> In peals of explosions, in the very heat of battle,
> You die without fear, standing,
> Oaks of St. Cloux, patterned maples,
> Thick lindens of Sevres and Medon . . .
> France's forests are blazing.[34]

In the 1950s, a tree also functions as heroine in "A White-Breasted Birch by the Veranda" (discussed earlier), which also appears here. The focus of "Akvarel'" ("Watercolor," 1955), dedicated to the painter E. P. Jakunina, is a painting in which a huge, century-old tree recalls the image of the elderly artist herself, whose gnarled hand holds a branchlike fan of brushes.

The theme of aging had appeared in Polonskaja's verse already in the 1930s, when she was entering middle age. In her sixties and seventies she naturally continued to write on this theme, and her published poetry contains little evidence of bitterness or fear. Nikolaj Braun, in his internal review, expressed some reservations about "Svoevremennye mysli" ("Timely Thoughts," 1958), which he regarded as "not quite corresponding to the life-affirming principle of the book,"[35] but the cycle was kept, no doubt due to its beauty and gentle humor, particularly in "Today at My Son's Temple," in which the poet is saddened by the first signs of gray in her son's hair:

Poetry in the Post-Stalinist Period

> А он, взглянув, сказал шутя:
> —Подумаешь! Какая малость.
> Ах, мама, ты еще дитя!
>
> But glancing at me, he said, jokingly:
> Just think of it! What a trifle.
> Ah, Mama, you're still a child![36]

Minc describes as "programmatic for this period" the poem "I Have Fallen Out of Love with All That Was Dear to My Heart," in which the "despised" world of chimerical dogmas is contrasted with the world of genuinely high human values: nature, children, art, pride "in people, in long, tenacious labor, unknown yesterday but fruitful tomorrow," the joys of "thought, of the heart, of the body," of this earthly world."[37] This collection also marks a return to Polonskaja's celebration of the strength and beauty of women; several other pieces, some from the 1940s, depict women in various active roles. The reader will recall that, in *A Kama Notebook*, the heroines were mainly portrayed in supporting roles, tending homes and factories for absent men. It is only in *Lyric Poems and a Narrative Poem* that Polonskaja is able both to republish some of her earlier poems on strong, independent women ("The Swan," "Jangi-kišlak," "Lullaby to My Daughter," "Song about Lina Odena") and to publish poems from the war and early postwar period which portray women as active fighters and builders. "Partisan Women" (1946), mentioned earlier, belongs to this category. "Roofers" (1945) and "The Housewives from Our Street" (1944) depict women energetically rebuilding Leningrad after the blockade:

> ... Так, пройдя года блокады,
> Видя правды торжество,
> Лечат раны Ленинграда
> Дочки младшие его.
>
> Thus, having gone through the blockade years,
> Seeing the triumph of truth,
> Leningrad's younger daughters
> Are healing her wounds.[38]

The heroines in this collection are engaged in creative as well as military and practical work. As always in Polonskaja's writing, art is presented as a powerful elevating and humanizing force; the muse can be frustratingly elusive, but she can also inspire courage and strength. Besides the painter Jakunina, Polonskaja celebrates another woman artist, the ballerina Galina Ulanova ("Uvidim vnov' Ulanovu-Žizel'" ["Once Again We Shall See Ulanova-Giselle," 1946]), and an unnamed ballerina who inspires the Russian troops by performing for them at the front ("Lebedinoe ozero" ["Swan Lake,"

1945]).³⁹ "Prazdnik pesni v Estonii" ("Festival of Song in Estonia," 1954) also celebrates the artistry of Estonian women, their songs, and their exquisite costumes, lovingly woven and embroidered by their grandmothers.

Not included in the collection are Polonskaja's darker poems on aging from the 1950s, such as "A možet byt' zasneš'" ("And Perhaps You Will Fall Asleep," 1951), about the different sorts of dreams that come with age, dreams of youth, in which "you will fly like a bird," and those of death and horror: "Tormented faces / Of deceased friends." In "Esli vyjti iz vorot" ("If You Go Out from the Gate," 1955), Polonskaja meditates on the futility of struggle in life when the end of all roads is inevitably the same:

> Исчерпаешь силы и мечты,
> И печальным старцем станешь ты.
> Уходить из дома или нет—
> Все равно ты глаз утратишь свет.
>
> Подожди еще совсем, совсем немного,
> Все равно тебе одна дорога.
>
> You will exhaust your strength and dreams,
> And you will become a sad old man.
> Whether you leave home or not—
> All the same you will lose the light of your eyes.
>
> Wait just the littlest bit longer,
> All the same there is only one road for you.⁴⁰

At the same time, the poet is unwilling to let go of what little precious time she has left; in "Ja prinjala snotvornoe i noč'" ("I Took a Sleeping Tablet, and the Night," 1955–57), she regrets having taken a soporific because it has robbed her of one of her few remaining dawns:

> Мне стало грустно, словно потеряла
> Я друга верного. Но ведь нельзя помочь:—
> Проходит безвозвратно каждый час,
> И в сердце, словно, что-то оборвалось . . .
>
> I became sad, as though I had lost
> A true friend. Yet there's no help for it:—
> Each hour passes irrevocably,
> And in my heart it feels as though something has snapped . . .⁴¹

There is a trace of regret at the fading of her sexuality, as in "Tak nedavno, ja byla moja" ("So Recently I Was My Own," 1957):

> Крашу волосы и щеки мажу,
> Но ничья рука, на грудь не ляжет.
> Повернула голову—и жизнь прошла,
> А ведь я не старше,—я все та-же.

Poetry in the Post-Stalinist Period

> I dye my hair and rouge my cheeks,
> But no one will lay his hand upon my breast.
> I turned my head—and my life had passed,
> Yet I am no older—I am still the same.⁴²

As illness became a more constant feature of her life, it became more prominent in her verse, along with sober thoughts about death, as in "Poka ešče ty dyšiš'" ("While You Still Breathe," 1955), "V razgare našix junyx let" ("In the Heat of Our Young Years," 1957), "Čudo v Peredel'kine" ("Miracle at Peredel'kino," 1957), and "Na bol'ničnoj kojke" ("On a Sickbed," 1957). It is likely that most of these pieces remain unpublished above all because of their pessimism.

Polonskaja spent a good part of the winter of 1957 at the writers' colony at Peredel'kino, during which time she produced three interesting poems devoted to her aging friends and colleagues. On February 1, she and the Kaverins went to the home of Vsevolod Ivanov to celebrate February 1, the Serapion anniversary; also present were Fedin and Zoja Nikitina, one of the original "Serapionic Maidens."⁴³ Not long after that, Polonskaja renewed her old habit of commemorating Serapion gatherings in verse and wrote, "Pozabyli my dorogi v staryj mir" ("We Have Forgotten the Paths to the Old World"), a bittersweet paean to old ties of literary friendship:

> У одних—штакетник возле дачи,
> У других—и не было удачи.
> Встретимся с тобой порой у сада:
> —«Здравствуй!»—
> —«Здравствуй!»—
> —«Рад тебе!»—
> —«Я рада.»—
>
> И пахнет внезапно, чем то милым,
> Прежнею любовью, юным миром.

> One has a fence by his dacha,
> Others—had no success.
> I meet you sometimes by the garden:
> "Hello!"—
> "Hello!"
> "I'm glad for you!"
> "I am glad."
>
> "And suddenly it smells of something dear,
> Of our former love, the world of our youth.⁴⁴

In March 1957, she wrote an affectionate and humorous tribute to Kornej Čukovskij on the occasion of his seventy-fifth birthday:

> Я Вас люблю Корней Иваныч,
> Я Вас люблю с далеких лет,

> И даже с Ив Монтаном «за ночь»,
> Ваш взгляд не променяю, нет!
>
> За то, что Вы не сноб, не нытик,
> Сопротивлялись, что есть сил,
> И ни один ученый критик
> Еще «с катушек», Вас не сбил.
>
> I love you, Kornej Ivanyč,
> I've loved you for many years,
> And I wouldn't trade your glance, oh no,
> For a night with Yves Montand!
>
> Because you are not a snob or a whiner,
> You resisted as much as you could,
> And not one learned critic
> Has yet "knocked you off your reel."[45]

According to Polonskaja, age had not been so kind to Nikolaj Tixonov. In "Poetu" ("To a Poet: So This Is What You Have Become, My Dear," 1957) she laments the change in her old friend from young and brash to "indifferent, gray, malicious," and in his verse, which has become "monotonous and limp." In closing, she expresses hope that he will come to his senses:

> Но сродни поету пламя.
> Опровергнешь мой упрек
> И взлетешь, взмахнув крылами,
> Из под пепла скушных строк!
>
> But flame is kin to the poet.
> You will refute my reproach
> And fly up, having flapped your wings,
> From the ashes of tedious verse.[46]

THE MID-1960S: CLIMATIC CHANGES

After the appearance of *Lyric Poems and a Narrative Poem*, Polonskaja continued publishing regularly. She was a regular contributor to the Leningrad almanac *Den' poezii*, and her poems also appeared in *Zvezda* and *Neva*. Between 1961 and 1963, twelve new poems by Polonskaja were published, and many more composed. Yet, when she presented a manuscript containing fifty-four lyrics for a collection of new poems, "Dorogi v buduščee" ("Roads to the Future") to Sovetskij pisatel' in 1963, she received a disappointing response. An internal review by V. Orlov, dated March 1963, praises several of the new poems but declares a number of them inferior and even trivial. Orlov suggests that Polonskaja might augment the best of the new poems with some of her best previously published ones in order to fill out the collection.[47]

Poetry in the Post-Stalinist Period

In June 1963, Polonskaja wrote to Erenburg, "I am sending you a few of my old poems, since it has become clear that I will not see them in print in the next few years."[48] However, in October of that year she noted, once again to Erenburg, "I have been noticing some small climatic changes— Anna Andreevna's [Axmatova's] poems in *Literaturnaja gazeta,* Evtušenko's poems in *Junost' (Youth)*. . . ."[49] These were hopeful signs, since Orlov's complaints had contained specific objections to Polonskaja's "To Anna Axmatova," which he called "an excessive apologia to A. Axmatova," and "To a Poet," dedicated to Evtušenko, which he declared "incorrect in its 'pathos' and its conclusions. About some fashionable poet it is said that he has 'honorably taken on no more and no less than the "stewardship of Russia."'"[50] Emboldened, no doubt, by such "climatic changes" as the publication of Axmatova and Evtušenko, Polonskaja submitted the manuscript a second time without following all of Orlov's suggestions. In January 1964 she received a tart response from one Maren'kov, who reproached her for ignoring Orlov's recommendations and informed her that the publisher would prefer to wait until she could provide a reasonable number of acceptable new poems.[51] "Roads to the Future" was, in effect, going nowhere, and was never published.

Polonskaja did eventually succeed in publishing another volume, *Izbrannoe* (*Selected Poems*), in 1966, though not with Sovetskij pisatel'; it was published by Xudožestvennaja Literatura. It includes only a handful of previously unpublished poems, about half of which were written before 1960. Thus, most of the new poetry published by Polonskaja in the 1960s (about twenty poems) was never included in a collection but appeared only in journals and in *Den' poezii,* an almanac published, ironically, by Sovetskij pisatel'.

Most of these are lyrics celebrating the beauty of the northern landscape, not just as a metaphor but for its own sake. Polonskaja writes with an almost mystical reverence for the life force in nature, particularly in trees. In "Ilana" (1962), the poet describes a pine tree whom she has named and with whom she converses in the early mornings.[52] In an unpublished poem, "Ja podružila s molodoj sosnoju" ("I Befriended a Young Pine," 1961), she describes the tree as "like a generous forest deity"; its branches are a haven for hundreds of birds, and though "she already belongs to the azure, / She is also kind to human fate."[53] "V lesu" ("In the Forest," 1961) portrays the pines as linking earth and sky; they stand straight and tall "in the consciousness of their duty," while the poet observes them in silent awe:

> И с неба падает на травы,
> Позвякивая, свысока
> Дождь крупный, теплый, величавый,
> И тренькают стволы слегка.
> Шаг муравья, кукушки клики . . .

Serapion Sister

> Трепещут радостно кусты ...
> И тайно я учусь музыке
> Ультравысокой частоты.

> And from the sky onto the grass,
> Tinkling, from above
> A heavy rain falls, warm, stately,
> And lightly strums the trunks.
> The stride of an ant, the cuckoo's calls ...
> The bushes tremble joyfully ...
> And I secretly study the music
> Of ultrahigh frequency.[54]

Polonskaja's most passionate declaration of love for nature, "Čem starše delajus', tem ja ljublju sil'nej" ("The Older I Become, the More Strongly I Love," 1962), ends with the lyric heroine pressing her cheek to the trunk of a tree to feel the stubborn life beneath the rough bark:

> Чем старше делаюсь, тем я люблю сильней,
> Не с пылкостью влюбленного подростка,
> Не с жаждой зрелых лет, властительной и острой,
> Но с верностью познавших жизнь людей.
>
> ... И прикоснуться я люблю щекою
> К большому дереву, березе иль сосне,
> И вдруг почувствовать: оно живое—
> Там, под корой шершавой, в глубине.

> The older I become, the more strongly I love,
> Not with the ardor of a lovelorn youth,
> Not with the thirst of mature years, domineering and sharp,
> But with the faithfulness of people who have known life.
>
> ... And I love to lay my cheek
> Against a big tree, a birch or a pine,
> And suddenly feel: it is alive—
> There, under the shaggy bark, in its depths.[55]

This focus on the life force in nature reflects both Polonskaja's failing health and her surroundings. As she became more prone to debilitating bouts of illness, she spent more time in the country, either at the writers' community in Komarovo, outside Leningrad, where she lived for extended periods in the winters, or in the little Estonian river town of El'va, where, from 1949 on, she spent every summer with her family. El'va in particular, in Polonskaja's descriptions, takes on an idyllic, almost mythical quality, as in one of the unpublished poems of the period, "Ne Bramsa sonatu prošu povtorit'" ("Not Brahms Did I Ask to Repeat the Sonata," 1967):

> Мы наняли домик и маленький сад
> В долине зеленого рая:

Poetry in the Post-Stalinist Period

> Мой брат незабвенный и двое внучат,
> И няня, пестунья седая.

> We rented a house and a little garden
> In the valley of a green heaven:
> My unforgettable brother and two grandsons,
> And their nanny, a gray-haired mentor.[56]

As though to emphasize the primal innocence and purity of this green heaven, Polonskaja peoples it almost exclusively with children and the elderly who, having learned to appreciate the earth "with the faithfulness of people who have known life," will soon be peacefully reunited with it. The three adults, Polonskaja, her brother Aleksandr, and their elderly housekeeper, Anastasija Petrovna, live together in a close but sexless accord. Both Aleksandr and Anastasija Petrovna ("Naka," as she was called by the family) are the subjects of affectionate verse portraits: "Golubka naša" ("Our Darling") and "Ottepel'" ("Thaw") appeared together in *Zvezda* in 1963.[57] The poem "Not Brahms Did I Ask to Repeat the Sonata" is a variant of "Pamjati Karla Rooziorga" ("In Memory of Karl Rooziorg," 1966), in memory of another elderly sibling pair, Polonskaja's Estonian landlord and his sister Adela, who lived together and patiently tended the cottage garden.

In the published poems about El'va, it is the children who predominate, perhaps due to the preference of editors for a more overtly optimistic and "life-affirming" tone. "V zelenoj El've" ("In Green El'va," 1961) presents a rainwashed landscape in which little boys are flying model airplanes;[58] in "Plotina v Pjeedu" ("The Dam at Pjeedu," 1963) a boy ignores his mother's warnings about undertows in the flooded river El'va and returns from a night's fishing with a bucket full of trout.[59] Finally, "Prazdnik pesni v El've" ("Festival of Song in El'va," 1964) depicts an open-air festival at which adults are moved to tears by the singing of children.[60]

However, the innocence of these children is accompanied by heedless arrogance destined to be short-lived; they must eventually leave the garden. The boys in "In Green El'va" will soon forsake their model airplanes for real ones, just as one of the daughters in "Skazka dlja sebja" ("Fairy Tale for Myself," 1960–64) finds that "there was not enough space on the planet— / She flew off into the sky and perished."[61] At one time a symbol of freedom in Polonskaja's poetry (see "Lullaby for My Daughter," 1937), the airplane becomes much more ambiguous, a jarring intrusion of technology into the garden. In one of several drafts of an unpublished poem of 1960, Polonskaja calls the airplane "a symbol of death . . . resembling a dove."[62] It is only the old who are entirely at peace on the "green planet," having no desire to leave any sooner than necessary. Adam and Eve in this garden are not the children, but old Karl Rooziorg, tenderly watering his peonies, and the lyric heroine listening to the music of the pines.

There are several unpublished poems to younger generations from Polonskaja's last years. Some, such as "Antenny televizorov stremjatsja" ("The Television Antennas Strive," 1961), in which children, "sons of the cosmic age," are mesmerized by televised images, and "Molodye otcy" ("Young Fathers," 1962), in which the poet sympathizes with the hard lives of young parents in a less-than-perfect world, are more or less in keeping with her published statements. They are expressions of mingled hope and apprehension for the future these children will inherit. In fact, "Young Fathers" is among the poems Polonskaja had hoped to publish in "Roads to the Future." There are also a few poems, however, which express a more troubled vision, an assumption of the worst and of resignation to the impossibility of warning or protecting young people from harm and disillusionment. This idea had appeared previously in some of Polonskaja's published poems, for example, "Bright-Eyed, Clever Boy" (1958). However, it had never reached the level of pessimism found in "Vse neustojčivo, vse neverno" ("All Is Unstable, All Is Uncertain," 1966), in which the heroine, despairing at life's emptiness and futility, suggests to her friend that they spare the children by keeping this knowledge to themselves:

> Будем делать вид по прежнему,—
> Детям не надо знания.
> Пусть-же отчаянье—будет последним
> Классом в школе познанья.
>
> We will pretend all is just as before,—
> Our children do not need to know.
> Let despair be the last
> Class in the school of their knowledge.[63]

Other poems touching on this theme are "Kak trudno rasskazat' mne molodeži" ("How Difficult It Is for Me to Tell the Young," 1963) and "Mne xorošo, čto ja žila na svete" ("I Am Glad That I Lived in This World," 1966).

The perspective of age is also reflected in Polonskaja's last love lyrics, which exhibit some of the passionate sensuality characteristic of her earliest verse but are also tempered with more gentleness and insight. "Orbity raznye, no ellips ili krug" ("Different Orbits, but an Ellipse or a Circle," 1960) is a declaration in sonnet form of enduring love for an old friend from whom she is separated by physical distance and the presence of another woman, but to whom she still feels extremely close mentally and emotionally:

> И как возвратный тиф, меня томит недуг,
> Ночами думаю:—Пускай моложе
> Она, и ты любил ее ... Так что же!
> Мне мысли, мне! А ей отдай досуг.

Poetry in the Post-Stalinist Period

> Твои враги—мои враги навеки,
> Твоя борьба,—навек моя борьба.
> И, чтоб не плакать, опускаю веки . . .
> Так суждено. Изменница—судьба.
>
> Но если, ты узнал победы хмель,
> Я рядом,—хоть за тридевять земель.

> And like recurring typhus, this ailment torments me,
> I think at night:—So she is younger,
> And you loved her . . . What of it!
> Give your thoughts to me, to me! And to her, your spare time.
>
> Your enemies are my enemies forever,
> Your struggle is forever my struggle.
> And, to keep from crying, I lower my eyelids . . .
> It is fated thus. Fate is a traitor.
>
> But if you have known the intoxication of victory,
> I am by your side, though at the other end of the world.[64]

The addressee is quite possibly Erenburg, with whom she maintained an affectionate correspondence in the 1960s.[65] Erenburg may also be the addressee of "Vse propalo," in which the poet expresses an intensely physical passion which only death will end:

> Запах тела, запах плоти,
> Не уходит, ходит, ходит . . .
> И тебя везде находит,
> Резок, ощутим и плотен.
>
> В нем и острый вкус укуса,
> Чуть тошнотный запах крови . . .
> Раскусить я не беруся,
> Что в нем от твоей любови . . .

> The smell of the body, the smell of flesh,
> Does not vanish, it moves, it moves . . .
> And finds you everywhere,
> Sharp, palpable and dense.
>
> In it is also the sharp taste of a bite,
> The slightly sickening smell of blood . . .
> I will not presume to distinguish
> What in it is from your love . . .[66]

In "Tebe by nužno ženščinu inuju" ("You Would Need a Different Woman," 1966), Polonskaja's heroine muses with some regret on the willfulness which, she fears, has made her unsuitable as a partner to her beloved. Such willfulness is, in fact, a quality which Polonskaja had always prized in her own heroines, but which is not conducive to happiness in love.[67]

SELECTED POEMS

Polonskaja's last collection, *Selected Poems*, has an author's preface, "To My Readers," in which she outlines her poetic career. It is an odd, uneven piece, containing some striking factual errors; for example, *New Poems* is stated to have preceded *A Stubborn Calendar*, and "The Lost and Recovered Home" is described as a collection (*sbornik*), although it was never published as such.[68] Much space is devoted to Polonskaja's career as a translator of poetry; indeed, she says more about her translations than she does about her original poetry. She also emphasizes the most politically safe aspects of her work: her antifascist songs and wartime lyrics, for example, as well as her postwar translations from the languages of the "countries of the people's democracy," that is, Poland and Czechoslovakia. The piece ends on a curious note, a description of Polonskaja's last major journey, to Prokop'jevsk, in the Kuznec coal-mining region, in 1951. Although she wrote several poems about this trip, none were ever published, and she does not appear even to have published any sketches about the trip. Yet she uses her observations on the city's remarkable growth and modernization as a bridge to a summary of the historical relevance of her writing: "Yes, everything about which I wrote was an echo of what was taking place in my country, in everything was the spirit of my people, which had burst into freedom, onto the wide road of October."[69]

This introduction is a combination of assertion of Polonskaja's credentials and pretext for her to present parts of her memoirs of the 1920s, which she had begun publishing in journals in 1963. The passages on Gumilev and the Serapions are condensed versions of those sections of her "The Early Twenties," which had appeared in the journal *Prostor* in 1964.[70] There is also a detailed description of Kornej Čukovskij as a teacher of translation, which segues into a description of Polonskaja's own beginnings as a translator. These passages, which make up almost half the introduction, stand out vividly from the bland, schematic outlines of the rest of the piece. Publishing her memoirs was a matter of great urgency for Polonskaja, as we see in these lines from a letter to Erenburg from 1966: "Now I am working on reminiscences, it is not easy, but I have to do it . . . above all, I am afraid of becoming helpless not only mentally, but also practically."[71] Including memoir material in the introduction to a collection released by a major publisher (Xudožestvennaja Literatura) in a publishing run of thirty-seven thousand assured its reaching a fairly large audience—much larger, no doubt, than the readership of *Prostor*.

Polonskaja had tried to include in "Roads to the Future" a cycle of poems, written in 1949 and 1950, to her friend Emma Vygodskaja, a children's writer and the wife of critic David Vygodskij. Vygodskij, as mentioned earlier, was purged, died in 1943, and was posthumously rehabilitated. His widow died in Leningrad in 1949. In "Po beregu reki zabvenii" ("Along the Shore of the River of Oblivion," 1949–50), the lyric heroine recalls her friend with affection and a sense of having failed in her own obligations:

> Как быстро ты перелистала
> Всей жизни пеструю тетрадь!
> А я должна была—я знала—
> Тебя за руку удержать.
>
> How quickly you leafed through
> The motley notebook of your whole life!
> And I knew I should have
> Taken your hand and held you back.[72]

"Idut goda, a my s toboj v razluke" ("The Years Pass, and We Are Apart," 1950–51) is a farewell gathering of the heroes of Vygodskaja's historical novels for children. In 1956, Polonskaja produced another poem in memory of Vygodskaja, "S mysl'ju o Cervantese" ("With Thoughts of Cervantes"), a reference to Vygodskaja's first novel, *Alžirskij plennik* (*The Prisoner of Algiers*), a portrait of Cervantes. Polonskaja clearly regarded it as her duty to preserve the memory of the Vygodskijs. She began her memoir, "David and Emma Vygodskij," which was to have appeared in *Meetings*, with the following statement: "I should write about the Vygodskijs not only because they were my friends and contemporaries. While other representatives of their generation fought for the Revolution with rifles in their hands, the Vygodskijs shouldered the best values of human culture and intellect, and preserved them for the future."[73] The cycle, as well as the prose memoir, remained unpublished.

Selected Poems appears to have pleased Polonskaja. As she wrote to Erenburg in the letter cited earlier, "My editor was a good one, a bit fearful, but with good taste."[74] The selection and arrangement of the poems is both more generous and less contradictory than in *Lyric Poems and a Narrative Poem*. As before, the titles of *Omens* and *Under a Stone Rain* do not appear in the section headings, but both are better represented. The first section, "Poems from the Early Years," contains seven poems from each, as well as two previously unpublished poems written before 1917. Furthermore, opposite the table of contents is a bibliography which is almost complete; the only title missing is that of Polonskaja's first collection of sketches, *A Trip to the Urals*. The first section also includes Polonskaja's notorious narrative poem "In the Noose," a bold choice even in 1966. The next section, "Times of Courage," contains poems from several collections, from the 1920s through 1940, and also several previously unpublished lyrics from 1940 which, most likely, had been removed from the manuscript of *Times of Courage.* "The Lost and Recovered Home" contains poems on evacuation from and return to Leningrad, all of which had been published before. The final section, "Roads to the Future," presumably represents the collection Polonskaja had tried and failed to publish with Sovetskij pisatel'. It contains poetry from the late 1940s, 1950s, and 1960s, including eight poems appearing for the first time.

The first two poems in the first section, both previously unpublished, were actually written during Polonskaja's years in France. Taken together, they illustrate the shift in her verse from the imitative, intimate lyrics of her youth to the beginning of a more mature civic verse. "Davno eto bylo" ("It Was Long Ago," 1913), the tale of a childhood love, like most of Polonskaja's early love poems, shows the influence of Axmatova; narration and dialogue are interwoven throughout.

> «На старый пруд пойдем. Возьми жакет».
> Осенний дождь. «Как пахнет здесь грибами . . .
> В последний раз прощаемся мы с Вами.
> Мы женимся с тобой через шесть лет.
> Ты подождешь меня!»—«Клянусь!» И он кланется.
> В двенадцать лет как весело живется.

> "Let's go to the old pond. Take a jacket."
> An autumn rain. "How it smells of mushrooms here . . .
> For the last time I say farewell to you.
> I will marry thee in six years.
> Thou wilt wait for me!"—"I swear!" And he swears.
> How jolly it is to be twelve.[75]

The youth and innocence of the lovers, their immersion in a world inaccessible to adults, and the precise syllabotonic meter (iambic pentameter) also recall Cvetaeva's early lyrics. The second, "Under the Apple Trees of Lorraine" (1915; see chapter 2), is autobiographical, describing her wartime medical service. The thematic shift from love poetry to civic verse begins with this poem.

The republication of poems is subject to the same precautions here as in earlier versions, particularly with regard to the dates given. Most of the early poems were not dated when first published, so their actual dates of composition are difficult to establish. However, in certain cases it is clear that a change has been made. The date changes in "Ballad of the Fugitive" and "With a Soft Sponge" are the same here as in *Lyric Poems and a Narrative Poem,* discussed previously. In addition, *Under a Stone Rain* was originally subtitled *1921–1923,* yet some of the other poems which first appeared there are dated earlier here, as though to suggest that the harsh reality they depict was from the time of World War I or the civil war, not the early NEP period. On the other hand, the love lyric "You Ask Me Why" is dated 1931, although it first appeared (in an identical version) in 1929, in *A Stubborn Calendar*.

Polonskaja—or, more likely, her editor—seems to have been particularly concerned with camouflaging and toning down *A Stubborn Calendar*, her most controversial collection from the 1920s. The six poems reprinted here are altered in various ways, from date changes (as in "You Ask Me Why") to the addition of an apologetic foreword to "In the Noose," in which the reader is assured that the erroneous point of view in the poem is that of the misguided hero, not the author:

> And by the very construction of the poem everything in it, with the exception of the prologue and epilogue, is shown through the eyes and narrated in the intonations of the hero. And even the "noose" itself existed only in the imagination of the hero, in reality turning out to be not a wire noose but a fatal aerial loop.
>
> The Author[76]

Some of the lyrics from *A Stubborn Calendar* have been rather obviously pruned, for example, the elegy to Esenin, whose last two lines, "For we are all madcaps. Someday / We too will grow tired of pretending," have been lopped off, leaving in place of a quatrain an unrhymed couplet: "Farewell, golden-headed one! Bon voyage / To you from the irreverent brotherhood!"[77] Likewise, the final section of "More Love," in which the lover languishes in prison, has been removed.[78]

Even more significant, and more subtle, however, is the presentation of two poems originally from *A Stubborn Calendar*, "Along the Road to Alton" and "The Hamburg Manege," both dated 1934 here. In their original form, they were provocative for their portrayal of the crasser aspects of NEP society. As mentioned earlier, the original titles were simply "The Bridge" and "Dogs"; they acquired their European titles, along with certain corresponding textual alterations, in the 1930s, when they appeared in *Years* under the heading "Looking Westward" (see chapter 5). These altered versions were republished in *Lyric Poems and a Narrative Poem*. In this instance, however, though the titles match those of the 1934 versions, the texts are practically identical to the originals which appeared in 1929, in *A Stubborn Calendar*. In the case of "Along the Road to Alton," the match is exact. In "The Hamburg Manege," a few minor details differ, but the most significant alteration has been removed. The line "Thus invisibly *we* uphold property," changed in the 1930s to "Thus invisibly *they* protect *their* property," is restored to its original wording (emphases mine). Close reading of these two poems reveals that, essentially, these are the original 1929 texts from *A Stubborn Calendar*. Only the titles and dates remain from the altered versions, and it was probably those altered external features which enabled the poems to pass the censor.

Four poems dated 1940 appear for the first time in the section "Times of Courage." Three are sonnets depicting simple but moving scenes of human generosity and courage shown by women during wartime. "U starogo Finljandskogo vokzala" ("By the Old Finland Station") is a farewell scene between a mother and her son, who is leaving with his regiment:

> Ты перед ним не плакала, о нет!
> Ты даже улыбалась. Ты шутила.
> «Мамаша молодец!» сказал сосед.
>
> Но острой болью сердце защемило.
> И поезд отошел. Уйти скорей!
> О мужество простое матерей!
>
> You did not cry in front of him, oh no!
> You even smiled. You joked.
> "Good for you, little mama!" said your neighbor.
>
> But a sharp pain clenched your heart,
> And the train moved away. Go quickly!
> Oh, the simple courage of mothers![79]

"Kak v eti dni my nežnost'ju bogaty" ("How Rich in Tenderness We Are These Days") depicts the fervor of female volunteers wishing to serve in military hospitals.[80] Perhaps most moving is "Metel' i temnota. Ideš' s raboty" ("Blizzard and Darkness. You Are Coming from Work"), in which the heroine is briefly distracted from her own fears for loved ones at the front by the plight of a frail old woman on the icy pavement:

> «Переведите, люди, на панель!
> Не покидайте!»—Выпростаешь руку—
> Здесь бабка древняя. И вдруг метель
>
> Утихнет как-то. И чужую муку
> Поняв, ты успокоишься. Идешь
> Уверенно, и старую ведешь.
>
> "Guide me, people, along the pavement!
> Don't abandon me!"—You work your hand free—
> Here is an ancient crone. And suddenly the blizzard
>
> Dies down somewhat. And comprehending
> Another's pain, you become calmer. You walk
> With confidence, and lead the old woman.[81]

The fourth of these four poems from 1940, "Sapogi" ("Boots"), is one of Polonskaja's last published references to the Jewish question. The title refers to boots worn by gentiles, as opposed to the wooden shoes worn by Jews in the Polish ghetto:

> В Польше стук деревянных подошв,
> Кожаной обуви там не найдешь.
> Женщины, дети и старики,
> Девушки, нежные как цветки,
> Стучат деревяшками для приметы,
> Проходя по улицам современных гетто.
>
> In Poland is heard the knocking of wooden soles,
> You will not find leather shoes here.
> Women, children, and old men,
> Young girls, tender as blossoms,
> Clatter their wooden feet as a sign,
> Moving through the streets of modern ghettos.[82]

The poem ends with the threatening tread of leather boots: "Boots are standing on the throat of Europe." Polonskaja's only previous published reference to the Jewish experience during the war, "The Righteous Story of Dr. Fejgin" (1940), had appeared in *Times of Courage* (see chapter 5). Though they were apparently written in the same year, "Boots" differs from "Dr. Fejgin" in that it treats the subject of Jewish experience much less openly, and with less optimism. The word "Jew" itself is not mentioned but implied by "ghetto." The same is true of a later poem, "Tartu" (1964), published in *Den' poezii,* in which Polonskaja refers to her old friend and colleague from Tartu, Bronislava (Bronka) Fejgina, who died defending the Warsaw Ghetto:

> Где вы, друзья, товарищи былые?
> Я ваши имена встречала в книгах,—
> Свою вы верно выполнили клятву.
> А ты, веселая, с печальными глазами,
> Делившая со мной и труд и отдых,
> Ты микроскоп сменила на винтовку:
> В бою с фашистами, в варшавском гетто
> Сражаясь, пала ты как честный воин.
>
> Where are you, friends, comrades of old?
> I have seen your names in books,—
> You have faithfully fulfilled your oath.
> And you, gay one, with sad eyes,
> Who shared with me both rest and labor,
> You traded your microscope for a rifle:
> In battle with Fascists, in the Warsaw Ghetto
> Fighting, you fell like an honorable soldier.[83]

Polonskaja's last reference to the fate of the Jews appears in the final section of *Selected Poems,* "Roads to the Future." The poem is "Madonna Rembrandta" ("Rembrandt's Madonna," 1965), a somber reflection on history and the future not only of Jews but of all humanity. Looking at the idyllic portrait of a nursing mother, the lyric heroine muses on the fate of a child in the world of her own historical experience, in which the Nazi death camps represent the worst possible extreme:

> Я не знаю, что ждет его дальше на свете.
> Бухенвальдских печей тошнотворная вонь ...
> Иль он в космос подымется в мощной ракете
> Добывать для собратьев небесный огонь ...
>
> I don't know what awaits him in this world.
> The sickening stench of Buchenwald ovens ...
> Or perhaps he will rise to the cosmos in a mighty rocket
> To get the heavenly fire for his fellows ... [84]

She refers also to biblical figures, again, not only Old Testament Jews, but also Christ:

> Я не знаю, какая грозит ему доля,
> Кто его вознесет, чем он будет убит.
> Авраам ли его для порядка заколет?
> Иль Иуда ему поцелуй подарит?
>
> I don't know what kind of fate threatens him,
> Who shall lift him up, by whom he shall be killed.
> Will Abraham stab him to keep the peace?
> Or will Judas bestow on him a kiss? [85]

Ultimately, the heroine feels she must beg this child's forgiveness, presumably for her own part in creating the world which awaits him. The historical optimism of "The Bridge" (1929), in which the "cruel world" will certainly become worthy of the child, "a little seed of history," is revealed as false; the "brave new world" envisioned by Polonskaja's generation has turned out to contain new, unheard-of nightmares:

> Но хочу перед ним я упасть на колени
> И прощенья просить за себя и людей.
> О, дитя, сын несчастных людских поколений,
> На руках у счастливейшей мати твоей!
>
> But I want to fall on my knees before him
> And beg forgiveness for myself and mankind.
> O, child, son of hapless human generations,
> In the arms of your most fortunate mother! [86]

Aside from these few references, Polonskaja was largely silent on the Jewish theme in the 1960s. Her poem to Evtušenko, "Ty načal veselo i šumno" ("You Started Out Gaily and Noisily," 1962), is another veiled statement which never made it into print. In it she goes so far as to assert his moral guardianship over Russia, no doubt in reference to the controversy

Poetry in the Post-Stalinist Period

over his poem "Babij Yar" (1961), in which he not only reflects on the tragedy of the Jewish fate during the war but also confronts both Russian anti-Semitism and the appeal to such sentiments to stir up antagonism against liberal tendencies.[87] Polonskaja remarked privately in a letter to Erenburg of 1961, "I love this author, but I am afraid that a section of 'Judaizers' is forming among us. Well, let it form!"[88]

As mentioned before, the third section of *Selected Poems*, "The Lost and Recovered Home," consists entirely of reprints, including "I Have Closed the Russian Stove," "Belomorsk, April," "Roofers," and "Swan Lake." All the truly new poetry in the collection appears in the final part, "Roads to the Future," along with a careful selection of pieces from *Lyric Poems and a Narrative Poem* and Polonskaja's journal publications. Representing her published works are "Witnesses of Great Upheavals," "Memories," "Timely Thoughts," "What Signifies the New?" and a few others. Several of the eight new poems, including "Rembrandt's Madonna," touch upon Polonskaja's major themes of childhood, motherhood, aging, and the life cycle. For example, "Naš mal'čik' vozvratilsja v dom" ("Our Little Boy Has Returned Home," 1947) takes a small child's joyous return home from the hospital as the starting point for a meditation on all the other challenges and obstacles he will face. The poem is based upon an incident involving Polonskaja's grandson, Igor', hospitalized with scarlet fever in 1946.[89] The boy is compared with a sparrow, and his antics with those of a bird learning to fly. The image dovetails nicely with "The Little Sparrows Have Their First Lesson," also included in this section.

A more metaphorical examination of the mother-child relationship is "At Times a Mother Can Be Unjust" (1957), which, like "Rembrandt's Madonna," is really a dark historical reflection, in this case on the emotional torments suffered by the abused children of the motherland:

> Бывает мать несправедлива
> К своим сынам. И вот тогда
> Любви и горькой и ревнивой
> Для них приходит череда.
>
> Им не забыть. Им не расстаться.
> Ты не любовница, ты мать.
> Им песни детства ночью снятся,
> И этих песен не отнять.
>
> Им снится юность буревая,
> Огонь твоих гражданских битв.
> И рана старая, сухая
> Опять в ночи кровоточит.
>
> И сердце бьется так тревожно,
> И холод смерти давит грудь.

> Проклясть тебя им невозможно
> И невозможно обмануть.
>
> At times a mother can be unjust
> To her sons. And then
> A sequence will come to them
> Of love both bitter and jealous.
>
> They cannot forget. They cannot leave you.
> You are a mother, not a lover.
> At night they dream their childhood songs,
> And those songs can never be taken away.
>
> They dream of a stormy youth,
> The fire of your civil battles.
> And the old, dry wound
> Bleeds again in the night.
>
> And the heart beats in such alarm,
> And death's cold crushes the breast.
> It is impossible for them to curse you
> And impossible to deceive.[90]

As mentioned in chapter 1, the original draft of this poem, dated 1938, is titled "Otčizni-materi" ("To the Fatherland-Mother," an ambiguous title); it is dedicated to Mixail Ferberg, who had been arrested and exiled.

Also included here, as always, are several statements on art, among them the previously suppressed poem to Axmatova, a reverent portrait of the "glorious muse of Russian verse,"[91] and "Tolmač" ("The Interpreter," 1965), an admission of her own ambivalence about the role of translator:

> Не буду тратить чувства на других,
> Чужим не стану озаряться светом!
> Луна я, что ли? Для чего свой стих
> Иноязычным отдаю поэтам?...
>
> ... Довольно! Стоп!
>   Но попадется вдруг
> Такое на глаза и запоет так больно,
> Что у меня захватывает дух
> И льются русские стихи невольно...
>
> I will not waste my feelings on others,
> I will not shine with a stranger's light!
> What am I, a moon? Why should I give
> My verse to poets of other tongues?
>
> ... Enough! Stop!
>   But suddenly something
> Meets my eye and starts to sing so painfully,
> That it seizes my mind
> And Russian verses pour out involuntarily...[92]

The collection ends with "Kto ty, čitatel'? Vek, mogučij škval" ("Who Are You, Reader? The Age, a Powerful Squall," 1965) in which the poet reflects on the passing of her generation and the coming of a new one which will know her through her verse:

> Задумается над моей строкой
> Горячая, колючая девчонка.
> И даже критик, слишком молодой,
> С иронией меня отметит тонкой.
>
> А жизнь идет. Ей—ни добра, ни зла . . .
> Мы даже с нею не были в разладе.
> И все же я недаром прожила:
> На дне останусь тоненькой тетради.

> A fiery, sharp girl shall grow
> Pensive over a line of mine.
> And even a critic, too young,
> Will mention me with subtle irony.
>
> But life goes on. For her—there is no good or evil . . .
> I did not even disagree with her.
> And all the same I did not live in vain:
> I shall remain at the bottom of a slender notebook![93]

"COMES AN END TO ALL LABORS AND TROUBLES": POLONSKAJA'S LAST PUBLISHED POEMS

After *Selected Poems* and before her death, Polonskaja published a few more poems in *Den' poezii*. In 1967, the almanac published one of her nature poems, "Karel'skij pejzaž" ("Karelian Landscape," undated), and two of her early poems from *Under a Stone Rain*, from the cycle "Oktjabr'," were reprinted in a *Biblioteka poeta* volume, *Oktjabr' v sovetskoj poezii* (*October in Soviet Poetry*).[94]

Polonskaja remained preoccupied with the themes of poetry and the poet. Her archive also contains several pieces about verse itself, in particular the sonnet form, which she had always favored. "Uslyšannyj razgovor" ("An Overheard Conversation," 1965) is a meditation in sonnet form on the superiority of the sonnet over prose as a form of expression:

> Угодливая проза нам противна.
> Где тон найти для мысли благородной?
> Засалено скороговоркой модной
> Любые словеса—звучат фиктивно.
>
> К сонету возвращаюсь инстинктивно.
> Оружие старинное пригодно.
> Не подается трепке ежегодно.
> Поет, как птица,—просто, переливно.

> Obsequious prose is repulsive to us.
> Where can we find the tone for noble thought?
> Soiled by a fashionable patter
> Any words sound false.
>
> I return instinctively to the sonnet.
> The time-honored weapon still suits.
> It does not yield to yearly scolding.
> It sings like a bird,—simply, with modulations.[95]

Another sonnet, "Prozaiku, pletuščemu korzinki" ("To a Prose Writer Weaving a Basket," 1965), the poet compares writing a sonnet to weaving a basket: "Winding the reeds in a tight circle, / I fasten tercinas and quatrains . . . / . . . In baskets and sonnets there are many rules. . . ." Polonskaja also experimented with poetic form in "Starye stixi vozvraščajutsja ko mne" ("My Old Verses Come Back to Me," 1966), in which eight of the twelve lines are taken whole from her other poems. A modified form of this piece was published in *Den' poezii* in 1969.

Appearing in the 1966 volume of *Den' poezii* were two new poems to other writers whom Polonskaja admired. "Ol'ge Berggol'c" ("To Ol'ga Berggol'c") is an admiring portrait of the poet whose wartime *Leningradskaja tetrad'* (*Leningrad Notebook*) is echoed in the title of Polonskaja's own *A Kama Notebook*:

> . . . На Урале, в зиму запоздалую,
> Прорывалась через лед и тлен,
> Прозвучал нам силой небывалою
> Голос ваш из ленинградских стен.
>
> Трудной мерой ваша жизнь измерена.
> Не сбылись девические сны.
> Но любовь родной страны вам вверена.
> И земные звезды вам даны.
>
> Оленька, рожденная в метелицу,
> Русской сказкой стали вы для нас:
> «Ступит—горе под ногами стелется.
> Молвит слово—выронит алмаз».

> In the Urals, into a delayed winter,
> You burst through ice and rot,
> Your voice rang out to us
> With unprecedented strength from the walls of Leningrad.
>
> Your life has been meted out by a difficult measure.
> Your girlish dreams were not fulfilled.
> But you have been entrusted with the love of your native land.
> And earthly stars have been given to you.

Poetry in the Post-Stalinist Period

> Olen'ka, born in a blizzard,
> You became for us a Russian fairy tale:
> "She takes a step—and grief spreads out beneath her feet.
> She utters a word—and drops a diamond."[96]

"Pozdnee priznan'je" ("A Belated Confession"), though lacking an addressee in print, is clearly dedicated to Erenburg, with whom she maintained a warm correspondence throughout the 1960s until his death:

> Вижу вновь твою седую голову,
> Глаз твоих насмешливых немилость,
> Словно впереди вся наша молодость,
> Словно ничего не изменилось.
>
> Да, судьба была к тебе неласкова,
> Поводила трудными дорогами.
> Ты и сам себя морочил сказками,
> Щедрою рукою роздал многое.
>
> Не раздумывала я, не мерила.
> Жизнь прошла как будто миг единственный . . .
> Ну а все-таки, хоть все потеряно,
> Я тебя любила, мой воинственный.
>
> I see your gray head once more,
> The severity of your mocking eyes,
> As though all our youth were before me,
> As though nothing had changed.
>
> Yes, fate was not kind to you,
> It led you on difficult paths.
> You fooled yourself with fairy tales,
> You gave much, with a generous hand.
>
> I did not ponder, I did not measure.
> Life passed like a single moment . . .
> But all the same, though all is lost,
> I loved you, my militant one.[97]

This poem had been included in the rejected manuscript of "Roads to the Future" in 1963.[98] In April 1967, Polonskaja sent Erenburg a slightly modified version of this poem in a letter.[99] She was not to hear from him again. According to her son, upon hearing of his death that autumn, Polonskaja fell ill and took to her bed, where she remained until her death in January 1969.[100] "A Belated Confession" was the last new poem to appear during Polonskaja's life. The latest unpublished poem in her archive (of those I have seen), "Poroj ešče prixodjat" ("At Times They Still Come"), is dated June 28, 1967.

Polonskaja was honored after her death in the 1969 volume of *Den' poezii* with a eulogy by her contemporary, the Leningrad poet Ljubov' Popova, accompanied by six of her previously unpublished poems, all from the late 1950s and 1960s: "Spring Suite," "Fairy Tale for Myself," "Festival of Song" (a variant of "Festival of Song in El'va"), "To the Motherland, "Moi slova" ("My Words"), and "Buduščee" ("The Future"). Some of these have been described earlier. The first three belong to the series of nature lyrics composed, for the most part, in El'va. The latter three are a blend of reminiscence and rather optimistic meditation on Russia and the future. In the latest of these, "My Words," dated 1966, Polonskaja writes:

> Моих наставников благодарю я низко,
> Но их уж нет, до них мне не достать ...
> Хочу я в прошлое послать записку,
> Но лучше в будущее посылать!

> I bow deeply to my mentors,
> But they are gone, I cannot reach them ...
> I want to send a note to the past,
> But it's better to send it to the future![101]

Popova's introduction stresses Polonskaja's revolutionary credentials, her ties with the Serapions and the House of Arts, and her commitment to mentoring young Soviet writers. No mention is made of the critical attacks on Polonskaja in the 1920s or the difficulties she faced in trying to publish her poetry in the late 1940s and 1950s.

Popova's characterization of Polonskaja is more or less in line with those of most critics in the 1960s. As mentioned before, she is usually presented as a venerable representative of the oldest generation of Soviet poets, worthy of respect not only for her literary achievements but also as a former Bolshevik activist and veteran of revolution, civil war, and two world wars. Those features which had made her earlier poetry controversial—her rebelliousness and fascination with the criminal underworld and her portrayal of independent, unconventional heroines and reckless, even selfish, passion—are ignored. Reviews from the 1960s are often inconsistent with earlier critical statements and present a distorted picture of Polonskaja's early verse. They stress the themes of motherhood and love of children as central, whereas in the early 1920s several reviewers describe Polonskaja's central themes as civic and political. Moreover, critical stress on these themes deflects attention from another specifically feminine, but less acceptable, theme in Polonskaja's early verse: female rebellion against marriage and domesticity. This is particularly evident in the case of the editors' refusal to republish "Carmen," even with changes that would make the heroine's promiscuity less obvious. There is little mention of the severity and "masculinity" which were frequently noted (and often praised) by earlier critics. Whereas Ol'ga Forš, in her novel *Sumasšedšij korabl'* (*The Mad Ship*), had characterized Polonskaja emphatically as "a woman and a poet—not a poetess,"[102] critics in the 1960s almost invariably refer to Polonskaja as "poetess." When Polonskaja's characteristic severity is mentioned, it is attributed to external factors, specifically the influence of Gumilev's training at the Literary Studio and the harsh realities of life in the revolutionary period. A. Anatol'jev writes: "It is possible that internal precision, even severity, is in Polonskaja's character. . . . But the fundamental and most difficult lessons of stern endurance and self-discipline were taught by the revolution."[103]

In only one case does a critic from the 1960s focus on the less orthodox aspects of Polonskaja's verse. In a 1963 critical essay, the sole negative piece on Polonskaja from this period, Grigorij Solov'ev attacks her for including her "decadent" early love poetry and formal experiments in *Lyric Poems and a Narrative Poem*. Vera Inber, he says, also wrote fashionably decadent poetry early in her career. "But the poetess had the good taste, tact, and common sense to leave all of that not only outside the borders of her 'Selected Poems,' but out of her mature verse altogether."[104] Solov'ev does not use the word "poetess" to refer to Polonskaja; he calls her simply "author." In a striking reversal of an earlier tendency in Soviet criticism, when female poets were praised for not being too "feminine," and "poetess" was a term of derision, Solov'ev's use of a masculine or gender-neutral term to describe a woman poet signifies disapproval, whereas *poetessa* is a term of respect, which he gives to Inber and withholds from Polonskaja.[105] Solov'ev's treatment of Polonskaja may not be approving, but he does at least mention significant aspects of her work which are downplayed by other critics.

Polonskaja's literary epitaph, which appeared in *Literaturnaja gazeta* shortly after her death, contains a curious misrepresentation symptomatic of the distortion of her literary reputation. This piece, written by several of her colleagues, contains the following statement: "The last years of Elizaveta Polonskaja were almost completely devoted to literary translation."[106] Translation certainly remained an important facet of Polonskaja's work to the end of her life, but it is an exaggeration to say that it was practically her sole activity during the years when she was actively producing and publishing both new verse and memoirs. Such misrepresentations were to continue in the decades that followed.

Conclusion

AS I HAVE DEMONSTRATED, Polonskaja's career as a poet was both long and distinguished, and she was recognized during her lifetime as one of the more significant figures in the Leningrad literary community. Yet because of the difficulties she faced in publishing her poetry, even in the early 1920s, many of her most interesting poems have never been accessible to readers. Political circumstances led to a forced flattening of her literary biography, particularly in the 1960s, which has rendered her more politically acceptable but less interesting to younger generations unfamiliar with the original versions of her edited poems. Her unremarkable fate has contributed to this flattening, and the problem is compounded by the lack of a critical edition of her work and of any large-scale attempt at scholarly analysis of her poetry. Even Brett-Harrison's thesis, valuable as it is, consists more of biography than poetic analysis. Since Polonskaja's death, her significance as a daring political poet, particularly in the 1920s, has largely been overshadowed by her image as a benevolent grandaunt of Soviet literature.

Polonskaja's role as "Serapion Sister" and her popularity as a memoirist have also contributed to her obscurity as a poet, since some of her greatest literary successes toward the end of her life were her reminiscences of the Serapions and others connected with the House of Arts. When her name has appeared in print in recent years, it has often been in connection with her membership in the Serapion Brotherhood rather than with her poetry. The question of Polonskaja's significance in Russian poetry has been raised several times in the press but has yet to be answered.[1]

Reprints of Polonskaja's poems in the years following her death have been rare. In 1973, three of her poems from the 1920s—"Šejlok," "Vstreča," and "Agar'"—were included in an anthology of poetry on Jewish subjects.[2] However, this volume was published in the United States. Appearances in Russia in the 1970s and 1980s have been limited to one poem from *Under a Stone Rain* ("October" ["If Malice Were Greater than Love"]) in an anthology called *Oktjabr' v sovetskoj poezii* (*October in Soviet Poetry*)[3] in 1987 and three poems ("We Learn to Love" [1920], "Isn't It Strange That We

Conclusion

Shall Forget Everything" [1921], and "Who Are You, Reader? The Age, a Powerful Squall" [1965]) published along with a short critical article by A. Galuškin in *Medicinskaja gazeta* the same year.[4]

Since 1969, a few more poems from the archive have appeared in print. In 1981, A. I. Rubaškin, in collaboration with M. L. Polonskij, published seven, including pieces from the 1940s ("Derevjannye bogi" ["Wooden Gods," 1944], "Doč' rodiny slavnoj moej" ["Daughter of My Glorious Homeland," 1942–44], "Čtecu" ["To a Reciter," 1949]), the 1950s ("Jubilejnoe, S. Ja. Maršak" ["Jubilee, to S. Ja. Maršak," 1957]), and one from the early 1920s, ("Ty spiš', moe ditja, edinstvennyj moj klad" ["You Are Sleeping, My Child, My Only Treasure," 1921]). Like Popova in her eulogy, Rubaškin emphasizes Polonskaja's revolutionary background, even citing the same lines from her "To My Readers" that Popova cites in her eulogy: "I count the chronology of my literary work from the October Revolution. The October Revolution gave me the opportunity to learn a new profession while continuing to work in the 'old one.'"[5] Unlike Popova, however, Rubaškin does specifically address, albeit briefly, Polonskaja's more intimate lyrics, citing "You Are Sleeping, My Child" as a moving example. Even here, however, Rubaškin is quick to point out those qualities in Polonskaja's lyric which link it to her civic poetry: "But her lyric is inseparably linked with the general, the intimate—with the civic. We recall: it was the same with Anna Axmatova."[6]

In 1985, Mixail Polonskij, in collaboration with B. Ja. Frezinskij, published yet another set of poems from his mother's archive, "Veet veter bezrassudnyj" ("The Reckless Wind Wafts," 1922), "Anne Axmatovoj" ("To Anna Axmatova," 1926), "Ne ržaveet [N. Tixonovu]" ("It Does Not Rust [To N. Tixonov]," 1937), "Na dal'nem severe zimuet drug" ("My Friend Is Wintering in the Far North," undated), and "Vnuku (O tex godax bor'by upornoj)" ("To My Grandson [About Those Years of Stubborn Struggle]," 1952). Their introduction, though brief, represents a departure from the previous ones, avoiding repetition of the obligatory references to Polonskaja's statements on the October Revolution and explicitly mentioning *A Stubborn Calendar* as one of her collections which are "absolutely in keeping with their time."[7] The inclusion of "My Friend Is Wintering in the Far North" is also significant, since the poem is addressed (though not in print) to a cousin of Polonskaja's, Boris Viktorovič Aš, who was purged in the 1930s. This is the only poem in the group which is not dated; it was written in 1938.[8] Polonskij and Frezinskij have also published a collection of Polonskaja's epigrams and "Serapionic odes" in 1993, along with an outline of her career as a satirist.[9]

Mixail Polonskij spent several years during the 1980s preparing a selection of 166 of his mother's poems (many unpublished), with commentary, for a proposed *Biblioteka poeta* edition of poetry from the 1920s and 1930s. The volume was to have included Polonskaja and five or so other poets. For reasons which are not entirely clear (most likely financial), the collection never materialized. The same fate befell a proposed edition of her memoirs, which he prepared and edited with Frezinskij.

All of these gaps, oversights, and distortions make evaluating Polonskaja's place in the canon of Russian literature a complicated and painstaking task. As demonstrated in my analysis, however, the originality and complexity of her poetry, particularly in the 1920s, amply reward the effort. In her verse Polonskaja actively engaged both the poetic traditions and the history of Russia, weaving an intricate web of political and aesthetic insights which not only draw upon, but in some cases influence, the verse of other poets. In the words of Rubaškin, "She did not have a famous name, but the book of Soviet poetry would be incomplete without Polonskaja's verse."[10]

Polonskaja's current absence from the canon is particularly striking at a time when scholarly interest in overlooked women writers is increasing steadily, both in Russia and in the West. Even recent works on Russian women writers contain little or nothing on Polonskaja. A recent Russian anthology, *Caricy muz (Queens of the Muses)*, completely omits her, although it includes her contemporaries Šaginjan and Škapskaja, and even Larisa Reisner, who was better known as a journalist and political figure than as a poet.[11] Discussion of Polonskaja in some recent Western reference works on Russian women writers is incomplete and frequently inaccurate. For example, Catriona Kelly, in her *History of Russian Women's Writing*, places Polonskaja, for the wrong reason, in the category of writers from what she questionably calls the "petty intelligentsia": "people of relatively humble origins (the children of provincial teachers, priests, factory workers, or peasants) who had been given new educational and professional opportunities—as teachers, Party workers, engineers, journalists—by Bolshevik rule. Understandably grateful to the new Soviet regime for the change in their lives, they were also enthusiastic supporters of Stalin."[12] This characterization, Kelly's only statement about Polonskaja, is probably based on a rather literal interpretation of the poet's statement in "To My Readers" that "October gave me the opportunity to learn a new profession without abandoning the old,"[13] which is a calculated exaggeration on the part of the author. Another recent reference article, from the 1994 *Dictionary of Russian Women Writers*, also appears to derive most of its information from an uncritical reading of "To My Readers," which, as I have shown in chapter 6, is a carefully crafted piece of self-promotion rather than a reliable autobiographical source.[14] Thus, even among scholars currently involved in the reclaiming of forgotten women writers, Polonskaja remains a little-known and misunderstood figure.

Polonskaja's place among the various poetic movements of the period is problematic and ultimately unimportant. The major influence on her style appears to be Acmeism or, more specifically, the Guild of Poets; however, when she began publishing regularly in 1921, there was a new Guild of Poets which was quite different from the original one. The most important similarities between her poetics and that of Mandel'štam and Axmatova, specifically her ideas about the function of poetry as preserver of cultural memory in the twentieth century, belong to the later period of those poets' work. Polonskaja's affinity with Esenin is more temperamental than stylistic; it has more to do with the raw emotionalism of some of her lyrics and the subject matter of her *poemy* of the mid-1920s than with the poetics of Imaginism, which she herself claimed to have disliked.[15] Polonskaja's closest literary tie was with the Serapions, who did not constitute a school. Some stylistic influence of Tixonov is evident, particularly in her ballads, but Tixonov was the only other poet in the Serapion Brotherhood. In general, the bond between the Serapions was a common commitment to excellence and originality regardless of style or ideology.

This bond also transcended nationality, as evidenced by the multiethnic character of the group. As a Russian Jewish writer, Polonskaja could feel especially close to Slonimskij, Kaverin, and particularly Lunc, but she was valued and respected by all of the Serapions at a time when certain critics were quick to characterize her as an alien writing in a language not her own. The vehemence of critics on this point makes Polonskaja an excellent test case for the question of whether a separate Russophone Jewish literature does exist and to what extent it is a fiction created by Russian chauvinism and based on content rather than language. Close linguistic study of her poetry in this context will, no doubt, prove illuminating, particularly since, unlike Mandel'štam, she did not represent the first generation in her family to achieve a high level of literacy in Russian.

In 1994, the Moscow publishing house Vysšaja škola released a volume called *Serapionovy brat'ja* (*The Serapion Brothers*), which contains both a translation of Hoffmann's *Die Serapionsbrüder* and a reprint of the contents (prose only) of the Petrograd edition of the Serapions' *Almanax pervyj*, as well as several articles by various members of the group.[16] In March 1995, an international conference on the Serapion Brothers was held in St. Petersburg.[17] These events mark an important shift in Russian critical reception of the Serapions; after decades of ambivalence, they are being treated as an important literary phenomenon, rather than as a somewhat disreputable early association of certain otherwise respectable writers. Polonskaja is barely mentioned in the 1994 volume, which contains only prose. She is, however, the subject of a conference paper by Svetlana Timina, "Elizaveta Polonskaja v krugu 'Serapionovyx brat'jev'," which, though brief, contains none of the inaccuracies which characterize the other recent articles previously mentioned.[18]

Timina draws particular attention to an image conceived by critic Jakov Braun, in 1924, of Tixonov and Polonskaja as "Adam and Eve, arisen from the primordial biblical chaos of our new world,"[19] an image which she describes as "a truly new aesthetic conception of the world, displayed in the poetess's gifted verse."[20] Timina closes with the following assertion:

> "The Serapion Brothers" entered the twentieth century of Russian literature as an example of a unique community, having unfolded on the pages of their works the perspective, possibilities, and variety of the paths of a new art. Each talented master in this union was the bearer of the strongest creative impulse.
>
> The clearly undervalued place of Elizaveta Polonskaja's poetry in the circle of this marvelous brotherhood deserves the attention of researchers, and the poetry itself—escape from oblivion.[21]

Thus, still following the established tradition, it is in the specific context of scholarship on the Serapion Brotherhood that we find the beginnings of serious scholarly attention in Russia to Elizaveta Polonskaja, who, of course, deserves individual attention.

Notes

INTRODUCTION

1. Boris Ejxenbaum, "Recenzija na sborniki V. Roždestvenskogo i E. Polonskoj," *Knižnyj ugol* 7 (1921): 41.

2. D. S. Mirsky, *Contemporary Russian Literature 1881–1925* (1926; reprint, New York: Kraus Reprint Co., 1972), 279.

3. Joy Brett-Harrison, "Dichterin in bewegter Zeit. Leben und Werk der Elizaveta Polonskaja (1890–1969)" (master's thesis, University of Zurich, 1990).

4. A. I. Rubaškin, personal interview, St. Petersburg, 23 June 1993.

5. A translator and younger colleague of Polonskaja, Svjatoslav Pavlovič Svjatskij, expressed in a personal conversation with me his belief that Polonskaja's Jewish nationality and non-Party status may have been the reasons for her abrupt dismissal from her position as head of the Translators' Section of the Writers' Union in the late 1950s. S. P. Svjatskij, personal interview, St. Petersburg, June 1993.

6. A. Metčenko, "Istorizm i dogma," *Novyj mir* 12 (1956): 229.

7. Wolfgang Kasack, "Elizaveta Polonskaya," *Dictionary of Russian Literature since 1917* (New York: Columbia University Press, 1988), 315.

8. Elizaveta Polonskaja, *Uprjamyj kalendar': stixi i poemy 1924–1927* (Leningrad: Izdatel'stvo Pisatelej v Leningrade, 1929), 87–89.

9. Aleksandr Rubaškin, "Ne sotvori kumira," *Literaturnaja gazeta*, 10 April 1991.

10. For example, the archives of Tixonov and Zoščenko at the Institute of Russian Literature and Art (IRLI, or Puškin House) were listed as closed in 1993.

11. "Serapionovy brat'ja o sebe," *Literaturnye zapiski* 3 (1922): 25.

12. V. Etov, "Sovetskaja literatura i ee amerikanskije istolkovateli," *Voprosy literatury* 11 (1966): 87.

13. Maksim Gor'kij, "Gor'kij o molodyx," *Žizn' iskusstva* 22 (1923): 19. Reprinted from a letter sent by Gor'kij to the editor of the Belgian journal *Le Disque Vert*, along with translations of Fedin's "Sad" and Zoščenko's "Viktorija Kazimirovna." See also *Gor'kij i Sovetskie pisateli: Neizdannaja*

perepiska, vol. 70 of *Literaturnoe Nasledstvo* (Moscow: Izdatel'stvo Akademii Nauk, 1963), 561–63.

14. Gary Kern and Christopher Collins, eds., *The Serapion Brothers: A Critical Anthology* (Ann Arbor, Mich.: Ardis, 1975), xxix.

15. Leon Trotskij, *Literature and Revolution* (Ann Arbor: University of Michigan Press, 1968), 217.

16. Viktor Šklovskij, *A Sentimental Journey: Memoirs, 1917–1922,* trans. Richard Sheldon (Ithaca, N.Y.: Cornell University Press, 1970), 189.

17. Ibid., 190.

18. Elizaveta Polonskaja, "K moim čitateljam," in *Izbrannoe* (Moscow and Leningrad: Izdatel'stvo Xudožestvennaja literatura, 1966), 10–11.

19. Evgenij Zamjatin, "The Serapion Brethren," *A Soviet Heretic: Essays by Evgenij Zamjatin,* ed. and trans. Mirra Ginsburg (Chicago: University of Chicago Press, 1970), 79.

20. Ibid., 78.

21. For a detailed discussion of this conflict, see Richard Sheldon, "Šklovsky, Gor'kij, and the Serapion Brothers," *Slavic and East European Journal* 12, no. 1 (1968): 1–13.

22. Konstantin Fedin, *Gor'kij sredi nas* (Moscow: Sovetskij pisatel', 1977), 79. Cited in Kern and Collins, *Serapion Brothers,* xvii.

23. Gary Kern, "Lev Lunc: Serapion Brother" (Ph.D. diss., Princeton University, 1969), 77.

24. Zamjatin, "Maxim Gorky," *A Soviet Heretic: Essays by Evgenij Zamjatin,* 255.

25. Fedin, *Gor'kij sredi nas,* 29.

26. Kern, "Lev Lunc: Serapion Brother," 76.

27. "'Sredy' Doma Literatorov," *Literaturnye zapiski* 2 (1922): 22.

28. *Peterburgskij sbornik 1922: Poety i belletristy* (St. Petersburg: Publishing House of the Journal *Letopis' Doma Literatorov,* 1922), 3.

29. Sergej Gorodetskij, "Zelen' pod plesen'ju," *Izvestija* no. 42 (22 February 1922).

30. "Otvet Serapionovyx Brat'jev Sergeju Gorodetskomu," *Novaja Rossija* 1 (1922): 160.

31. *Serapionovy Brat'ja: Almanax pervyj* (St. Petersburg: Alkonost', 1922).

32. Jurij Tynjanov, review of *Serapionovy Brat'ja. Al'manax pervyj,* in *Kniga i revoljucija* 6 (1922): 62–64; Aleksandr Voronskij, review of *Serapionovy Brat'ja. Al'manax pervyj,* in *Krasnaja nov'* 3 (1922): 265–68.

33. "Serapionovy brat'ja o sebe," 25–31.

34. Ibid., 31.

35. For an overview of the controversy, see William Edgerton, "The Serapion Brothers: An Early Soviet Controversy," *The American Slavic and East European Review* 8 (1949): 47–64.

36. Trotskij, *Literature and Revolution*, 218.
37. Cited in A. Metčenko, "Istorizm i dogma," 230.
38. "O politike partii v oblasti xudožestvennoj literatury (Rezoljucija CK RKP[b])," *Pravda*, no. 147 (3078), 1 July 1925, 6. Translation by Jan Eichelis, in Carl R. Proffer et al., eds., *Russian Literature of the Twenties: An Anthology* (Ann Arbor, Mich.: Ardis, 1987), 553.
39. Lev Lunc, "Na Zapad! Reč' na sobranii Serapionovyx Brat'jev 2-ogo dekabrja 1922 g.," in *Lev Lunc: Rodina i drugie proizvedenija*, ed. M. Vainštein (Jerusalem: Serija "Pamjat'," 1981), 291–306. The article was originally published by Gor'kij in his Berlin journal *Beseda*, no. 3 (1923): 259.
40. Viktor Šklovskij, "Serapionovy brat'ja," *Knižnyj ugol* 7 (1921): 18–21.
41. *Gor'kij i sovetskie pisateli, neizdannaja perepiska*, vol. 70 of *Literaturnoe nasledstvo*, 473.
42. *Pervyj Vsesojuznyj S'jezd Sovetskix Pisatelej 1934: Stenografičeskij Začet* (Moscow: Sovetskij pisatel', 1990), 230.
43. Vjačeslav Vsevolodovič Ivanov, literary scholar and the son of Vsevolod Ivanov.
44. Vjačeslav Vs. Ivanov, "Sud'ba 'Serapionovyx brat'jev' i put' Vsevoloda Ivanova," *Literaturnaja gruppa "Serapionovy brat'ja": istoki, poiski, tradicii, meždunarodnyj kontekst. Tezisy dokladov*, 19, International Conference, St. Petersburg, 13–16 March 1995; Mixail Zoščenko, Diary entry in *Mixail Zoščenko: Uvažaemye graždane* (Moscow: Izdatel'stvo Knižnaja Palata, 1991), 63.
45. Ivanov, "Sud'ba 'Serapionovyx brat'jev' i put' Vsevoloda Ivanova," 20. The image of "whips and gingerbread" (*knut i prjanik*) is attributed to one A. Kron, who used the phrase in his article "Zametki pisatel'ja (Notes of a Writer)," in *Literaturnaja Moskva* 2 (1956): 789.
46. *The Central Committee Resolution and Ždanov's Speech on the Journals 'Zvezda' and 'Leningrad'. Doklad T. Ždanova o žurnalax 'Zvezda' i 'Leningrad'*, bilingual edition, trans. Felicity Ashton and Irina Tidmarsh (Royal Oak, Mich.: Strathcona Publishing Company, 1978), 13.
47. "Serapionovy brat'ja o sebe," 28. Cited in ibid., 12.
48. "Serapionovy brat'ja o sebe," 31. Cited in *Central Committee Resolution*, 13.
49. *Doklad Ždanova*, 29–30.
50. Metčenko, "Istorizm i dogma," 230.
51. *Očerk istorii russkoj sovetskoj literatury*, part 1 (Moscow: Izdatel'stvo AN SSSR, 1954), 101.
52. K. D. Muratova, *M. Gor'kij v bor'be za razvitie sovetskoj literatury* (Moscow and Leningrad: Izdatel'stvo AN SSSR, 1958), 170.
53. A. Metčenko, A. Dement'jev, and G. Lomidze, "Za glubokuju razrabotku istorii sovetskoj literatury," *Kommunist* 12 (1956): 86.

54. Ibid., 86.
55. Muratova, M. Gor'kij v bor'be za razvitie sovetskoj literatury, 167.
56. Ibid., 158.
57. "Lev Lunc i 'Serapionovy brat'ja': Publikacija i kommentarii Gari Kerna," Novyj žurnal 82 (March 1966): 136–92; "Lev Lunc i 'Serapionovy brat'ja': Publikacija i kommentarii Gari Kerna," Novyj žurnal 83 (June 1966): 132–84.
58. Etov, "Sovetskaja literatura i ee amerikanskije istolkovateli," 88.
59. M. V. Minokin, "Serapionovy brat'ja' v zarubežnyx istolkovanijax," Russkaja literatura 1 (1971): 184.
60. Edward Brown, *Russian Literature since the Revolution* (New York: Collier Books, 1963), 135; N. Anastas'jev, "Formula nepravdy (po povodu pis'ma Professora E. Brauna)," Voprosy literatury 10 (1967): 105.
61. Ju. V. Tomaševskij, "Zoščenko i ego 'serapionovy' brat'ja," *Literaturnaja gruppa "Serapionovy brat'ja": istoki, poiski, tradicii, meždunarodnyj kontekst*, 34.
62. Veniamin Kaverin, "An Open Letter to Konstantin Fedin" (English translation), Survey 68 (July 1968): 188.
63. Veniamin Kaverin, *Epilog: Memuary* (Moscow: Moskovskij rabočij, 1989), 255–57.
64. Elizaveta Polonskaja, "Iz literaturnyx vospominanij," 375–89.
65. Zoja Nikitina, letter to E. G. Polonskaja, 30 November 1963, Private Archive of E. G. Polonskaja.
66. Elizaveta Polonskaja, "Načalo dvadcatyx godov," Prostor 6 (1964): 110–19.
67. Veniamin Kaverin, *"Ždravstvuj, brat. Pisat' očen' trudno"* Moscow: Sovetskij pisatel', 1965).
68. Mixail Slonimskij, *Kniga vospominanij* (Moscow and Leningrad: "Sovetskij pisatel'," 1966).
69. Veniamin Kaverin, *Ždravstvuj, brat. Pisat' očen' trudno*, 192–93.
70. Polonskaja, "Načalo dvadcatyx godov," 116.
71. Veniamin Kaverin, *Sobranie sočinenij: Osveščennye okna. Trilogija* (Moscow: Xudožestvennaja literatura, 1983), 532.
72. Kaverin, *Epilog*, 448–49.
73. Ibid., 443–57.
74. *Lev Lunc ("Serapionov brat") Vne zakona: p'jesy, rasskazy, stat'ji* (St. Petersburg: Izdatel'stvo 'Kompozitor,' 1994). A similar collection had already appeared in Israel in 1981: *Lev Lunc: Rodina i drugie proizvedenija* (Jerusalem: Serija Pamjat', 1981).
75. Kaverin, *Epilog*, 458–59.
76. Ibid., 468. This statement, in the epilogue to *Epilog*, is dated 1981.
77. Kornelia Ičin, from Belgrad, presented "'Obez'jany idut' L'va Lunca," and Janina Sałajczyk, from Gdansk, presented "'Vosstanie veščej'

L'va Lunca v rusle katastrofičeskoj literatury XX veka," 63–64, *Literaturnaja gruppa "Serapionovy brat'ja": istoki, poiski, tradicii, meždunarodnyj kontekst*, 1995.

CHAPTER ONE

1. According to her son, the foreign languages she mastered during her lifetime included Polish, German, French, English, Italian, Spanish, Bulgarian, Estonian, Greek, and Latin. M. L. Polonskij, personal interview, St. Petersburg, July 1993.
2. Polonskaja, "Otkuda vzjalis' stixi" (ts.), Private Archive of E. G. Polonskaja, St. Petersburg, 1–2.
3. Polonskaja, "Žanna Niko" (ts.), Private Archive of E. G. Polonskaja, 2.
4. Polonskaja, "Lodz" (ts.), Private Archive of E. G. Polonskaja, 13.
5. Polonskaja, "Žanna Niko," 2–3.
6. Polonskaja, "Iz černovikov pis'ma k literaturnomu kritiku. 1924–1926 gg." (ts.), prepared with notes by M. L. Polonskij, Private Archive of E. G. Polonskaja, 8.
7. For a detailed description of this period, see E. G. Polonskaja, "Do oktjabrja ešče desjat' let," *Zvezda* 7 (1965): 143–57.
8. E. G. Polonskaja, "1908 god. Zanjatija Medicinoj. Novyje Druz'ja" (ts.), Private Archive of E. G. Polonskaja, 9.
9. Il'ja Erenburg, *Ljudi, gody, žizn'* (Moscow: Sovetskij pisatel', 1961), 114.
10. Marija Kireeva, "Iz vospominanij (I. Erenburg v Pariže 1909 g.)," *Voprosy literatury* 9 (1982): 154.
11. E. G. Polonskaja, "Russkij bal/ 1909/" (ts.), Private Archive of E. G. Polonskaja, 2.
12. M. Polonskij and B. Frezinskij, "Serapionovskie ody i epigrammy Elizavety Polonskoj," *Voprosy literatury* 6 (1993): 356.
13. Kireeva, "Iz vospominanij," 153.
14. I. G. Erenburg, "Pis'ma," publication of A. I. Rubaškin, *Voprosy literatury* 12 (1987): 175–76.
15. Ibid., 177.
16. Fond 1204, Erenburg, op. 2, e.x. 2055, TsGALI (Moscow), l. 24. Polonskaja later wrote about her talk at the *Vol'fila* in a memoir on Jurij Tynjanov, in 1966. This memoir is in her private archive.
17. E. G. Polonskaja, "Iz knigi 'Vstreči,'" *Neva* 4 (1987): 195–97.
18. E. G. Polonskaja, "Vstreči," *Neva* 1 (1966): 185.
19. Polonskaja, "Proščal'naja Oda," *Uprjamyj kalendar*, 82. The poem, a fond farewell to Paris and youth, appeared first in the almanac *Kovš*, Kniga 4, 1926. In a letter to Marietta Šaginjan, postmarked "15.V.26,"

Polonskaja lamented, "The French won't allow me into Paris," referring to her failure to obtain a French visa. E. G. Polonskaja, letter to Marietta Saginjan, 15 May 1926 (ts., photocopy), Private Archive of E. G. Polonskaja.

20. Polonskaja, "Iz černovikov pis'ma k literaturnomu kritiku," 11.

21. For details, see Brett-Harrison, "Dichterin in bewegter Zeit," 21–22.

22. Some contradictions arise in various accounts of this period; according to Brett-Harrison, Polonskaja remained in Petrograd with her son and found work there as a municipal doctor for the poor in 1916. Brett-Harrison, however, does not appear to have had access to Polonskaja's memoirs "Moe vozvraščenije s fronta" and "Petrograd 1917–1918 gg." in Polonskaja's private archive. These two memoirs are themselves contradictory with respect to certain details, but both indicate that Polonskaja did indeed return to the front after the birth of her son, returning to Petrograd sometime in the spring of 1917.

23. Polonskaja, "Petrograd 1917–1918 gg." (ts.), Private Archive of E. G. Polonskaja, 5.

24. Boris Ejxenbaum, "Recenzija na sborniki V. Roždestvenskogo i E. Polonskoj," *Knižnyi ugol* 7 (1921): 40–41.

25. E. G. Polonskaja, *Znamen'ja* (Petrograd: Erato, 1921).

26. Polonskaja, "Iz literaturnyx vospominanij," Trudy po russkoj i Slavjanskoj filologii 6. Učenye zapiski, 384–85.

27. Viktor Šklovskij, "Serapionovy Brat'ja," 19.

28. Polonskaja, "Serapionovy brat'ja o sebe," 29.

29. See B. Frezinskij and M. Polonskij, "Serapionovskie ody i epigrammy Elizavety Polonskoj."

30. Svjatoslav Pavlovič Svjatskij, personal interview, St. Petersburg, June 1993.

31. See B. Frezinskij and M. Polonskij, "Serapionovskie ody i epigrammy E. G. Polonskoj."

32. M. L. Polonskij, personal interview, St. Petersburg, 17 June 1993.

33. M. L. Polonskij confirms that, of all the Serapions, Lunc was dearest to his mother. Personal interview, St. Petersburg, 17 June 1993.

34. Lev Lunc, "Detskij smex," *Žizn' iskusstva*, 29–30 November 1919.

35. Polonskaja, "O detskix avtorax, detskix p'jesax, i detskom teatre," *Žizn' iskusstva*, 10 February 1920.

36. Gary Kern uses the date of Polonskaja's article to suggest that "Na Zapad!" may have been written as early as 1919. Kern, "Lev Lunc: Serapion Brother," 164–65.

37. Polonskaja, "O detskix avtorax."

38. Veniamin Kaverin, interview in Brett-Harrison, "Dichterin in bewegter Zeit," 128.

39. Kern, "Lev Lunc i 'Serapionovy Brat'ja'," *Novyj žurnal* 82: 177.

40. Ibid., 178.

41. Svetlana Timina, "Elizaveta Polonskaja v krugu 'Serapionovyx brat'ev'," in *Literaturnaja gruppa 'Serapionovy Brat'ja': Istoki, poiski, tradicii, meždunarodnyj kontekst,* 65, International Conference, St. Petersburg, 13–16 March 1995.

42. Evgenij Švarc, *Živu bespokojno . . . Iz dnevnikov* (Leningrad: Sovetskij pisatel', 1990), 292–93.

43. "Lev Lunc i "'Serapionovy brat'ja': Publikacija i kommentarija Gari Kerna," *Novyj žurnal* 82 (1966): 191.

44. E. G. Polonskaja, *Pod kamennym doždem, 1921–1923* (St. Petersburg: Poljarnaja zvezda, 1923).

45. Švarc, *Živu bespokojno . . . Iz dnevnikov,* 293.

46. Ibid.

47. M. L. Polonskij, personal interview, St. Petersburg, May 1993.

48. E. G. Polonskaja, *Poezdka na Ural* (Leningrad: Priboj, 1927).

49. Polonskaja, "K moim čitateljam," 10.

50. Ibid., 9–10.

51. Polonskaja, *Zajčata* (Petrograd and Moscow: Raduga, 1923). The book appeared in three more editions in 1924 and two in 1926.

52. Ljubov' Štrejxer, *Časy: Detskaja opera—igra,* Tekst Elizavety Polonskoj (Moscow: Gosudarstvennoe Izdatel'stvo, Muzykal'nyj Sektor, 1927).

53. Polonskaja, *Znamen'ja,* 31–32.

54. Polonskaja, "V petle: Liričeskij fil'm," *Kovš* (Leningrad, 1925), 108–19.

55. O. Barabašev, "Naletčiki na Revoljuciju ili o tom, kak Gosizdat izdal zamečatel'noe posobie k rasprostraneniju xuliganstva," *Leningradskaja pravda* 59 (12 March 1925): 7.

56. Polonskaja, "Karmen," *Nedra* 4 (1924): 215–18.

57. L. Baril', "Literaturnye zametki," *Priboj* 1 (1928): 40–42.

58. Polonskaja, "Konec" (1932–34) (ts.), Private Archive of E. G. Polonskaja.

59. Polonskaja, "Povest'" (1937) (ts.), Private Archive of E. G. Polonskaja.

60. Aleksandra Kollontai, "*Novaja ženščina, Novaja moral' i rabočij klass* (Moscow: Izdatel'stvo VCIK, 1919), 24. Cited in Richard Stites, *The Women's Liberation Movement in Russia: Feminism, Nihilism and Bolshevism, 1860–1930* (Princeton, N.J.: Princeton University Press, 1978), 350.

61. M. Čumandrin, "Polnocennaja zajavka," *Večernaja krasnaja gazeta,* 11 June 1935.

62. Polonskaja, *Pod kamennym doždem,* 32.

63. Polonskaja, *Goda: Izbrannye stixi* (Leningrad: Izdatel'stvo pisatelej v Leningrade, 1935), 72.

64. Polonskaja, "K moim čitateljam," 10.

65. Robert Maguire, *Red Virgin Soil* (Princeton, N.J.: Princeton University Press, 1968), 388.
66. A. I. Rubaškin, personal interview, St. Petersburg, 23 June 1993.
67. Polonskaja, *Ljudi sovetskix budnej* (Leningrad: Izdatel'stvo pisatelej v Leningrade, 1934).
68. Barbara Heldt, "Motherhood in a Cold Climate: The Poetry and Career of Mariia Shkapskaia," *Russian Review* 51 (1992): 160.
69. Polonskaja, "K moim čitateljam," 11.
70. Polonskaja, *Goda: Izbrannye stixi.*
71. Polonskaja, *Novye stixi* (Leningrad: Xudožestvennaja Literatura, 1937).
72. *Sobranie sočinenij Mol'era*, vol. 1 (Leningrad: Academia, 1935).
73. Z. Minc, "E. G. Polonskaja i ee literaturnye vospominanija. Priloženija. Osnovnye proizvedenija E. G. Polonskoj," *Trudy po russkoj i slavjanskoj filologii* 6, *Učenye zapiski tartusskogo universiteta* 139 (1963): 377.
74. Polonskaja, "Stixi, rasskazy, poemy," *Literaturnyj Leningrad* 40, no. 185 (1936): 3.
75. Polonskaja, "Iz prixodo-rasxodnoj literatury 1937" (ts.), excerpted by M. L. Polonskij, Private Archive of E. G. Polonskaja, 2.
76. Polonskaja, "Iz prixodo-rasxodnoj literatury 1936" (ts.), excerpted by M. L. Polonskij, Private Archive of E. G. Polonskaja, 2. Polonskaja notes: "May— . . . Looked over L. Štrejxer's Uzbek Symphony at the Composers' Union; the newspapers make absolutely no mention of my text."
77. Polonskaja, memoir on Jurij Tynjanov (ts.), prepared with notes by M. L. Polonskij, Private Archive of E. G. Polonskaja. See note 23. According to this note, "Ottorvan ot ruk moix" was originally part of the unfinished "Plennik," dedicated to Mixail Ferberg.
78. M. L. Polonskij, personal interview, St. Petersburg, 17 June 1993.
79. Polonskaja, letter to Marietta Šaginjan, postmarked "15.V.26" (ts., photocopy), Private Archive of E. G. Polonskaja.
80. Polonskaja, "K moim čitateljam," 8.
81. Polonskaja, "Načalo dvadcatyx godov," 116.
82. See Vera Luknickaja, *Pered toboj zemlja* (Leningrad: Lenizdat, 1988), 50, 53, for samples of such reports, in which Polonskaja's opinions on the poetry of Pavel Luknickij, Nikolaj Braun, and Marija Kommisarova are recorded.
83. Polonskaja, "Kak i tridcat' let nazad," *Vsevolod Ivanov—pisatel' i čelovek* (Moscow: Sovetskij pisatel', 1975), 99.
84. Luknickaja, *Pered toboj zemlja*, 51.
85. Polonskaja, letter to Marietta Šaginjan, postmarked 25 June 1931 (ts., photocopy), Private Archive of E. G. Polonskaja.
86. Fond 2182, Škapskaja, op. 1, e.x. 436, TsGALI (Moscow), ll. 79–82.

87. Polonskaja, letter to Marietta Šaginjan, 30 December 1938 (ts., photocopy), Private Archive of E. G. Polonskaja.

88. Polonskaja, "Žurnal 'Rabotnica i krest'janka.' Lidija Čarskaja," 14, Leningrad–Komarovo 1967 god. (ts.), Private Archive of E. G. Polonskaja.

89. Polonskaja, "David i Emma Vygodskie" (ts.), Private Archive of E. G. Polonskaja, 9.

90. Ibid., 10.

91. Polonskaja [listed erroneously as "K. Polonskaja"], "Govorit Ispanija," *Literaturnoe obozrenie* 16 (1938): 53–56.

92. Polonskaja, memoir on Jurij Tynjanov, Private Archive of E. G. Polonskaja.

93. Polonskaja, "Sadovnik, Otryvok iz poemy," *Literaturnyj Leningrad*, 29 August 1936.

94. Polonskaja, "Sadovnik," *Novye stixi, 1932–1936* (Leningrad: Goslitizdat, 1937), 79–90.

95. Polonskaja, letter to Marietta Šaginjan, 14 October 1936 (ts., photocopy), Private Archive of E. G. Polonskaja.

96. M. L. Polonskij, personal interview, St. Petersburg, 17 June 1993.

97. Polonskaja, "Otčizni-materi," ms., Notebook 35 P12, p. 52, Private Archive of E. G. Polonskaja.

98. Fond 2182, Škapskaja, op. 1, e.x. 436, TsGALI (Moscow), l. 68.

99. Polonskaja, *Vremena mužestva: Stixi; Portret: poema* (Leningrad: Goslitizdat, 1940).

100. Fond 2182, Škapskaja, op. 1, e.x. 436, TsGALI (Moscow), ll. 83–84.

101. See Erenburg's letter of 30 January 1943 to the president of the Molotov City Soviet, Fond 602, Polonskaja, no. 532, RNB.

102. Polonskaja, "Zolotye polja," *Zvezda.* Perm', 1942. 3 October; "Druz'ja, spešite!" *Prikam'je* 5 (1942): 46; "Spasibo, ural'cy!" *Prikam'je* 6 (1942): 179; "Nataša," *Rabotnica* 6/7 (1943): 5.

103. E. G. Polonskaja, *Kamskaja tetrad'* (Molotov: Molotovgiz, 1945). This collection appears to have undergone some major changes between the time it was contracted (early 1942) and its appearance in 1945. Polonskaja wrote to Škapskaja on 27 August 1943 that she had turned in the book to Molotovgiz and that it was to be called *Kamskij god* (*A Year on the Kama*). In the same paragraph she mentions another book of poems, including a narrative poem, which she plans to bring to Moscow. On 14 September 1944 she wrote that her collection, "that same long-suffering one," had been lost somewhere between Molotov and Leningrad. These details on the history of this collection are found in Fond 2182, Škapskaja, op. 1, e.x. 437, TsGALI (Moscow), ll. 7, 43, 58.

104. Fond 2182, Škapskaja, op. 1, e.x. 437, TsGALI (Moscow), l. 19.

105. Ibid., l. 58.

106. Polonskaja, letter to Škapskaja, 21 January 1946. Fond 2182, Škapskaja, op. 1, e.x. 437, TsGALI (Moscow), l. 63.

107. Polonskaja, "Materi" (ts.), Source in Notebook T-4, 11. Private Archive of E. G. Polonskaja.

108. Polonskaja, *Gorod* (ts.), Private Archive of E. G. Polonskaja.

109. M. L. Polonskij, personal interview, St. Petersburg, 17 June 1993.

110. Brett-Harrison, "Dichterin in bewegter Zeit," 126 (interview with B. Ja. Frezinskij).

111. Ibid., 101.

112. M. L. Polonskij, personal interview, St. Petersburg, 17 June 1993.

113. Brett-Harrison, "Dichterin in bewegter Zeit," 101–2.

114. R. Fedorov, "Devuški našego goroda," *Večernij Leningrad* 242, no. 869 (13 October 1948).

115. See introduction, note 5.

116. M. L. Polonskij, personal interview, St. Petersburg, 17 June 1993.

117. Polonskaja, *Stixotvorenija i poema* (Leningrad: Sovetskij pisatel', 1960).

118. A. Galuškin, "U stixov osabaja sud'ba," *Medicinskaja gazeta*, 16 January 1987; Minc, "Polonskaja i ee literaturnye vospominanija," 375.

119. Fond 1204, Erenburg, op. 2, e.x. 2055, TsGALI, (Moscow), l. 14.

120. For more details on these poems, see the discussion in chapter 6.

121. A. Anatol'jev, review of *Izbrannoe*, *Zvezda* 10 (1966): 219–20.

122. Polonskaja, *Stixotvorenija i poema*, 126.

123. Fond 2182, Škapskaja, op. 1, e.x. 436, TsGALI (Moscow), ll. 49–51.

124. Fond 1204, Erenburg. op. 2, e.x. 2055, TsGALI (Moscow), l. 14.

125. Zoja Nikitina, letter to E. G. Polonskaja, 30 November 1963, Private Archive of E. G. Polonskaja.

126. Kornej Čukovskij, letter to E. G. Polonskaja, 7 November 1963, Private Archive of E. G. Polonskaja.

127. Marietta Čudakova, personal interview, Moscow, 4 September 1992.

128. Polonskaja, "Do oktjabrja ešče desjat' let," *Zvezda* 7 (1965): 143–57.

129. Polonskaja, "Iz knigi Vstreči," *Neva* 4 (1987): 193–97.

130. Polonskaja, letter to Erenburg, 6 August 1966, Fond 1204, Erenburg, op. 2, e.x. 2055, TsGALI, (Moscow), l. 37.

CHAPTER TWO

1. Ju. I. Levin et al., "Russkaja semantičeskaja poetika kak potencial'naja kul'turnaja paradigma," *Russian Literature* 7–8 (1974): 50–51.

2. Polonskaja, *Pod kamennym doždem*, 36.

3. See Kireeva, "Iz vospominanij," page 153.
4. Ibid., 148.
5. Victor Žirmunskij, "Poetika Aleksandra Bloka," *Teorija literatury, poetika, stilistika (Izbrannye Trudy)* (Leningrad: Nauka, 1977), 212–17.
6. Polonskaja, "U nix byla verbnaja subbota" (ts.), Private Archive of E. G. Polonskaja.
7. Aleksandr Blok, *Sobranie sočinenij v vos'mi tomax, tom pervyj* (Moscow and Leningrad: Gosudarstvennoe Izdatel'stvo Xudožestvennoj literatury, 1960), 290.
8. Vladimir Dal', *Tolkovyj slovar' živago velikorusskago jazyka, tom četvertyj P-V.* (1882; reprint, Moscow: "Russkij jazyk," 1991), 270.
9. Jeanmarie Rouhier-Willoughby, personal communication, 9 March 1995.
10. Polonskaja, "Proščal'naja Oda," *Uprjamyj kalendar'*, 81.
11. Polonskaja, "Na švejnoj fabrike," *Goda: Izbrannye stixi*, 137.
12. Kireeva, "Iz vospominanij," 154.
13. M. L. Polonskij, personal interview, St. Petersburg, June 1993.
14. Samuel Cioran, "The Russian Sappho: Mirra Lokhvitskaya," *Russian Literature Triquarterly* 9 (1974): 334.
15. Nikolaj Pojarkov, *Poety našix dnej* (Moscow: I. M. Kholchev and Co., 1907), 83. Cited in Temira Pachmuss, *Women Writers in Russian Modernism: An Anthology* (Urbana and Chicago: University of Illinois Press, 1978), 88.
16. Polonskaja, "Polden' l'jetsja v komnatu kak sladkij med" (ts.), Private Archive of E. G. Polonskaja.
17. Polonskaja [E. Bertram], *Večera: ežemesjačnik stixov* 2 (1914): 8–11.
18. Sonia Ketchian, "Anna Axmatova," in *Handbook of Russian Literature*, ed. Victor Terras (New Haven, Conn.: Yale University Press, 1985), 15.
19. Polonskaja, "Ja kogda-to byla veselaja" (ts.), Private Archive of E. G. Polonskaja.
20. Polonskaja, "Da, v etot večer ja odna ostalas'" (ts.), Private Archive of E. G. Polonskaja.
21. Polonskaja, *Izbrannoe*, 19.
22. Polonskaja, "Načalo dvadcatyx godov," 112. The poem, which was never published, is in the private archive.
23. Brett-Harrison, "Dichterin in bewegter Zeit," 35.
24. Polonskaja, "Načalo dvadcatyx godov," 112.
25. Zinovij Davydov, "Na pamjat' o tjaželom gode," *Sovremennoe obozrenie* 2 (November 1922): 5–6.
26. Ejxenbaum, "Recenzija na sborniki V. Roždestvenskogo i E. Polonskoj," 41.

27. Osip Mandel'štam, "Sumerki svobody," *Sobranie sočinenij v dvux tomax, tom pervyj* (Moscow: Xudožestvennaja literatura, 1990), 122.
28. Ibid., 122–23.
29. Levin et al., "Russkaja semantičeskaja poetika kak potencial'naja kul'turnaja paradigma," 50.
30. Ibid.
31. S. Averincev, introduction, in Mandel'štam, *Sobranie sočinenij v dvux tomax, tom pervyj*, 41–42.
32. Polonskaja, *Znamen'ja*, 4.
33. "Slovo o pl'ku Igoreve, Igorja syna Svjat'slavlja, vnuka Ol'gova," *Anthology of Old Russian Literature*, ed. A. D. Stender-Petersen and Stephan Congrat-Butler (New York: Columbia University Press, 1962), 154. Translation from Sergei A. Zenkovsky, ed., *Medieval Russia's Epics, Chronicles and Tales*, rev. and enl. ed. (New York: E. P. Dutton, 1963), 170.
34. Polonskaja, *Znamen'ja*, 7–8.
35. Ibid., 10.
36. Ibid., 11.
37. Ibid., 21.
38. Ibid., 24.
39. Voronskij, review of *Serapionovy Brat'ja. Al'manax pervyj*, 266.
40. Polonskaja, *Znamen'ja*, 13–14.
41. Ibid., 22.
42. Ibid., 24.
43. Ibid., 29.
44. Ibid.
45. Maurice Friedberg, "The Jewish Search in Russian Literature," *Prooftexts* 4 (1984): 98.
46. Alice Stone Nakhimovsky, *Russian-Jewish Literature and Identity* (Baltimore: Johns Hopkins University Press, 1992), 18–19.
47. Zvi Gitelman, *A Century of Ambivalence: The Jews of Russia and the Soviet Union, 1881 to the Present* (New York: Schocken Books, 1988), 116, 120.
48. Friedberg, "The Jewish Search," 98.
49. Nakhimovsky, *Russian-Jewish Literature and Identity*, 20.
50. V. L'vov-Rogačevskij, *A History of Russian Jewish Literature*, ed. and trans. Arthur Levin (Ann Arbor, Mich.: Ardis, 1979), 173.
51. Polonskaja, *Znamen'ja*, 31.
52. Ibid., 32.
53. Ibid., 33
54. Gitelman, *Century of Ambivalence*, 112.
55. R. D. Timenčik, "Evrejskie motivy v russkoj poezii načala XX veka (Tri predvaritel'nyx zamečanija)," *Tynjanovskij sbornik: Pjatye Tynjanovskie Čtenija* (1994): 178.

56. Polonskaja, "Načalo dvadcatyx godov," 113.
57. Timenčik, "Evrejskie motivy v russkoj poezii načala XX veka," 175.
58. Ibid., 178.
59. Clare Cavanagh in *Osip Mandelstam and the Modernist Creation of Tradition* (Princeton, N.J.: Princeton University Press, 1995), 208. Gorodetskij expressed this view in his review of Mandel'štam's *Kamen'* (reprinted in Osip Mandel'štam, *Kamen'*, ed. L. Ja. Ginzburg et al. [Leningrad: Nauka, 1990], 228).
60. P. Guber, "Novye sborniki stixov," *Letopis' Doma Literatorov* 3 (1921): 14.
61. Mixail Kuzmin, "Parnasskie zarosli," *Zavtra: Lit.-krit. sbornik pod red. Evg. Zamjatina, M. Kuzmina, i M. Lozinskogo* 1 (1923): 119.
62. Georgij Ivanov, "Elizaveta Polonskaja. Znamen'ja. Erato: Petrograd," *Cex poetov* no. 3 (Pg.): 67.
63. Mixail Pavlov, review of *Znamen'ja*, by Elizaveta Polonskaja, *Letopis' Doma Literatorov*, 25 February 1922, 9.
64. A. Baxrax, review of *Znamen'ja*, by Elizaveta Polonskaja, *Dni* (Berlin) 11 February 1923, 14.
65. Il'ja Erenburg, review of *Znamen'ja*, by Elizaveta Polonskaja, and *Dvor čudes*, by Irina Odoevceva, *Novaja russkaja kniga* 3 (1922): 9.
66. Vera Alexandrova, "Jews in Soviet Literature," in *Russian Jewry 1917–1967*, ed. Gregor Aronson et al. (New York: Thomas Yoseloff, 1968), 311.
67. Polonskaja, "Izrail'" (ts.), Private Archive of E. G. Polonskaja.
68. Polonskaja, "O, deti naroda moego" (ts.), Private Archive of E. G. Polonskaja.
69. L'vov-Rogačevskij, *History of Russian Jewish Literature*, 142.
70. Ibid., 134.
71. Polonskaja, "O, Rossija, zlaja Rossija" (ts.), Private Archive of E. G. Polonskaja.
72. Shmuel Ettinger, "The Jews in Russia at the Outbreak of the Revolution," in *The Jews in Soviet Russia since 1917*, ed. Lionel Kochan (New York: Oxford University Press, 1970), 17.
73. Vjačeslav Popov and Boris Frezinskij, *Il'ja Erenburg: Xronika žizni i tvorčestva v dokumentax, pis'max, vyskazyvanijax i soobščenijax pressy, svidetel'stvax sovremennikov. Tom I 1891–1923* (St. Petersburg: Izdatel'stvo "Lina," 1993), 301.
74. Zamjatin, "Serapionovy brat'ja," 8.
75. Ibid.
76. Cited by M. Vejnštejn in "Golos, preodolevšij desjatiletija" (afterword), *Rodina i drugie proizvedenija*, 318–19. Translation by Kern, "Lev Lunc: Serapion Brother," 132–33.

77. Lev Lunc, "Novye poety," *Irida, lit. gazeta, pod red. A. G. Fomina,* 1922, ms., Fond 568, op. 1, no. 125, IRLI (St. Petersburg).
78. Brett-Harrison, "Dichterin in bewegter Zeit," 26–28.
79. Četvertaja kniga Moiseeva 10:9. *Biblija. Knigi Svjaščennago Pisanija Vetxago i Novago Zaveta Kanoničeskija,* ed. and trans. B. Gece (Warsaw: Izdatel'stvo B. Gece, 1939).
80. Vtoraja kniga Moiseeva 15:17.
81. Ejxenbaum, "Recenzija na sborniki V. Roždestvenskogo i E. Polonskoj," 41.
82. Lunc, "Obez'jany idut!" *Rodina i drugie proizvedenija,* 228–29.
83. Polonskaja, "Iz černovikov pis'ma k literaturnomu kritiku," 2.
84. Ibid., 5.
85. Polonskaja, *Znamen'ja,* 37.
86. Ibid., 48.
87. Ibid.
88. Ibid.
89. Anna Axmatova, *Sočinenija v dvux tomax, tom pervyj* (Moscow: Xudožestvennaja literatura, 1986), 82.
90. Ibid., 79.
91. Polonskaja, *Znamen'ja,* 48.
92. A. Baxrax, review of *Znamen'ja,* 14.
93. Polonskaja, *Znamen'ja,* 38.
94. Ibid., 40.
95. Ibid., 44–45.
96. Osip Mandel'štam, "Slovo i kul'tura," *Sobranie sočinenij v trex tomax. Tom vtoroj: Proza,* eds. G. P. Struve and B. A. Fillipov (New York: Inter-Language Literary Associates, 1971), 226–27.
97. Mandel'štam, Sobranie sočinenij v dvux tomax. Tom pervyj, 124.

CHAPTER THREE

1. *Serapionovy Brat'ja. Zagraničnyj al'manax* (Berlin: Izdatel'stvo "Russkoe tvorčestvo," 1922).
2. Polonskaja, *Pod kamennym doždem,* 40.
3. Ibid., 45–46.
4. Polonskaja, *"Pojdu ja v magazin Kornilova na Nevskom"* (ts.), Private Archive of E. G. Polonskaja.
5. Polonskaja, "Pro knigi," *Vorobej* 2/5 (1924): 25.
6. Polonskaja, *Pod kamennym doždem,* 35.
7. Ibid., 34.
8. Polonskaja, "B'jet dožd' v lico, i veter brodit p'janyj," *Pod kamennym doždem,* 32.
9. Stites, *Women's Liberation Movement in Russia,* 333.

10. A. Kollontai, *Ženščina na perelome (psixologičeskie etjudy)* (Moscow, 1923), which includes the autobiographical novella *Bol'šaja ljubov'* and two other stories, and *Ljubov'pčel trudovyx* (Moscow, 1923), which includes "Vasilisa Malygina," "Sestry," and "Ljubov' trex pokolenij."

11. Polonskaja's translation of Kipling's "Ballad of East and West" was published by Čukovskij in the first issue of the journal *Sovremennyj zapad* in 1922. See Polonskaja, "K moim čitateljam," 10.

12. Polonskaja, *Pod kamennym doždem*, 17–18.

13. David Vygodskij, review of *Pod kamennym doždem*, *Kniga i revoljucija* 3 (1923): 76.

14. M. Gutner, "Gody poeta," *Literaturnyj Leningrad*, 8 June 1935, 3.

15. Innokentij Oksenov, review of *Pod kammenym doždem*, *Petrogradskaja pravda*, 17 June 1923, 5.

16. Polonskaja, *Pod kamennym doždem*, 25.

17. Mixail Čumandrin, "Polnocennaja zajavka," *Večernaja krasnaja gazeta*, 11 June 1935.

18. Ibid.

19. The theme of the return of a dead emperor does in fact arise in *Pod kamennym doždem* and will be discussed subsequently.

20. Mandel'štam, *Sobranie sočinenij v dvux tomax. Tom pervyj*, 88.

21. Ibid., 121.

22. N. A. Nilsson, "'Proslavim, brat'ja' and 'Na Kamennyx otrogax': Remarks on Two Poems by Osip Mandel'štam," *Slavic Poetics: Essays in Honor of Kiril Taranovskij* (The Hague and Paris: Mouton, 1973), 297.

23. Mandel'štam, "Čerepaxa," *Sobranie sočinenij v dvux tomax. Tom pervyj*, 125.

24. Polonskaja, *Pod kamennym doždem*, 26.

25. Ibid., 25.

26. Ibid., 28–29.

27. Ibid., 15.

28. Mandel'štam, "Zasnula čern'. Zijaet ploščad' arkoj," *Kamen'*, ed. L. Ja. Ginsburg et al. (Leningrad: Nauka, 1990), 47.

29. Polonskaja, *Pod kamennym doždem*, 16.

30. Valerij Brjusov, *Sočinenija v dvux tomax. Tom pervyj* (Moscow: Xudožestvennaja literatura, 1987), 287.

31. Polonskaja, *Pod kamennym doždem*, 14.

32. Brjusov, *Sočinenija v dvux tomax*, 85.

33. Polonskaja, *Pod kamennym doždem*, 14.

34. Marietta Šaginjan, "Post Scriptum," *Sobranie sočinenij v devjati tomax. Tom vtoroj* (Moscow: Xudožestvennaja literatura, 1986), 739.

35. Polonskaja, *Pod kamennym doždem*, 10–12.

36. Aleksei Tolstoj, "Sestry," *Polnoe sobranie sočinenij, Tom Sed'moj* (Moscow: Gosudarstvennoe izdatel'stvo xudožestvennoj literatury, 1947), 8.

37. David A. Sloane, *Aleksandr Blok and the Dynamics of the Lyric Cycle* (Columbus, Ohio: Slavica Publishers, 1988), 277.
38. Blok, *Kniga tret'ja*, 45.
39. Sloane, *Aleksandr Blok*, 283.
40. Aleksandr Blok, *Stixotvorenija. Kniga vtoraja (1904–1908)*, ed. Ju. K. Gerasimov (St. Petersburg: Severo-Zapad, 1994), 88–89.
41. N. Ju. Grjaklovaja and O. A. Kuznecova, commentary to Blok, *Kniga vtoraja*, 389.
42. Blok, *Kniga vtoraja*, 87.
43. Axmatova, *Sočinenija. Tom pervyj: Stixotvorenija i poemy*, 287.
44. V. N. Toporov, *Axmatova i Blok (k probleme postroenija poetičeskogo dialoga) Modern Russian Literature and Culture* 5 (Berkeley, Calif.: Berkeley Slavic Specialties, 1981), 133.
45. Omry Ronen, *The Fallacy of the Silver Age in Twentieth Century Russian Literature* (Amsterdam: Harwood Academic Publishers, 1997), 26–27.
46. Blok, *Kniga tret'ja*, 42.
47. Ibid., 44–45.
48. Sloane, *Aleksandr Blok*, 286.
49. Polonskaja, *Pod kamennym doždem*, 11.
50. Polonskaja, "Moskva 1922" (1923) (ts.), Private Archive of Elizaveta Polonskaja.
51. Axmatova, *Sobranie sočinenij v dvux tomax*, 131.
52. Maksim Gor'kij, "V glubine Rossii," *Polnoe sobranie sočinenija. Tom šestnadcatyj. Povest', rasskazy, očerki, stixi 1917–1924* (Moscow: Nauka, 1973), 402.
53. Viktor Šklovskij, *Gamburgskij sčet. Stat'ji—vospominanija—esse 1914–1933* (Moscow: Sovetskij pisatel', 1990), 507.
54. Polonskaja, "V petle. Liričeskij fil'm," *Uprjamyj kalendar'*, 13.
55. Polonskaja, *Pod kamennym doždem*, 13.
56. RNB Fond 602, op. 1, no. 7, *Pod smertnym ostriem. Stixotvorenija.* 1921–1922, 11 pp. (ms.); RNB Fond 602, op. 1, no. 8: *Pod smertnym ostriem. Stixotvorenija. Pravl. verstka s avtografom—daritel'noj nadpis'ju Mariette* (Šaginjan) 1921–1922, 27 pp. (page proofs).
57. Polonskaja, *Pod kamennym doždem*, 9.
58. Polonskaja, "Igraet med', idut polki," *Literaturnaja nedelja. Pril. k gaz. 'Petrogradskaja Pravda'* 6 (1922): 1; "Peterburg" (Spjat pobedivšie . . .)," *Krasnaja nov'* 6 (1922): 92–93; "Peterburg (Spjat pobedivšie . . .)," *Literaturnaja nedelja. Priloženie k gazete "Petrogradskaja Pravda"* 18 (1922): 5.
59. A. S. Puškin, *Polnoe sobranie sočinenij v desjati tomax. Tom tretij: Stixotvorenija 1827–1836* (Moscow: Izdatel'stvo Akademii Nauk SSSR, 1957), 522. Cited in Brett-Harrison, "Dichterin in bewegter Zeit," 49.
60. Polonskaja, *Pod kamennym doždem*, 37.

61. S. Vyšeslavceva, "15 let poetičeskoj raboty," *Xudožestvennaja literatura* 10 (1935): 7.
62. Polonskaja, "I mudrye pravy i mudrye mudry," *Severnoe obozrenie* 1 (1922): 4.
63. Fond 602, Polonskaja, op. 1, no. 7, *Pod smertnym ostriem 1921–1922* (ms.), RNB (St. Petersburg), l. 5.
64. Fond 602, Polonskaja, op. 1, no. 8, *Pod smertnym ostriem. Stixotvorenija* (page proofs), l. 15.
65. Fond 602, Polonskaja, op. 1, no. 8, *Pod smertnym ostriem* (page proofs), l. 10.
66. Fond 602, Polonskaja, op. 1, no. 8, *Pod smertnym ostriem* (page proofs), l. 11.
67. The resemblance was noted by Omry Ronen.
68. Fond 602, Polonskaja, op. 1, no. 8, *Pod smertnym ostriem* (page proofs), l. 17–18.
69. Dal', *Tolkovyj slovar', tom vtoroj*, 553.
70. Polonskaja "Kruglyj nož" (1923) (ts.), Private Archive of E. G. Polonskaja.
71. Polonskaja, *Pod kamennym doždem*, 38–39.
72. Ibid., 44.
73. A. Anatol'jev, review of *Izbrannoe*.
74. Kaverin, *Epilog*, 29–31.
75. Polonskaja, *Pod kamennym doždem*, 19.
76. Polonskaja, *Stixotvorenija i poema*, 5–7.
77. Brett-Harrison, "Dichterin in bewegter Zeit," 56.
78. Polonskaja, *Izbrannoe*, 21–23.

CHAPTER FOUR

1. B. Ja. Frezinskij, personal interview, St. Petersburg, 7 July 1995.
2. Brown, *Russian Literature since the Revolution*, 110–11.
3. Baril', "Literaturnye zametki," 41.
4. Mixail Lučanskij, "Ščepki," *Komsomolija* 10 (1926): 53.
5. Polonskaja, "Karmen," *Nedra* (1924): 218.
6. Ibid.
7. Stites, *Women's Liberation Movement in Russia*, 376–91.
8. Polonskaja, "Karmen," 217.
9. Blok, *Kniga tret'ja*, 267.
10. Eric Naiman, "Revolutionary Anorexia (NEP as Female Complaint)," *SEEJ* 37, no. 3 (1993): 306.
11. Eric Naiman, "The Case of Chubarov Alley: Collective Rape, Utopian Desire and the Mentality of NEP," *Russian History/Histoire Russe* 17, no. 1 (spring 1990): 8–9.

12. Ibid., 9 (fn).
13. See also his article "Historectomies: On the Metaphysics of Reproduction in a Utopian Age," in *Sexuality and the Body in Russian Culture,* ed. Jane Costlow, Stephanie Sandler, and Judith Vowles (Stanford, Calif.: Stanford University Press, 1993), 255–76.
14. Naiman, "Revolutionary Anorexia," 317.
15. Polonskaja, "Lebed'," *Krasnyj žurnal dlja vsex* 4 (1924): 246.
16. A. Kollontai, *Selected Writings of Alexandra Kollontai,* trans. with an introduction and commentary by Alix Holt (Westport, Conn.: Lawrence Hill and Co., 1977), 229.
17. Ibid., 279.
18. Vyšeslavceva, "15 let poetičeskoj raboty," 8.
19. Blok, *Kniga tret'ja,* 272.
20. "O politike partii v oblasti xudožestvennoj literatury (Rezoljucija CK PKP[b])," *Pravda,* 1 July 1925, 6.
21. O. A. Žuk, "'Čertovo koleso' i gorodskaja kul'tura," *Kinovedčeskie zapiski* 7 (1990): 57.
22. Ibid.
23. Ibid.
24. Vladimir Propp, "O russkoj narodnoj liričeskoj pesne," *Narodnye liričeskie pesni* (Leningrad: Sovetskij pisatel', 1961), 35.
25. Richard Stites, *Russian Popular Culture: Entertainment and Society since 1900* (Cambridge and New York: Cambridge University Press, 1992), 42–43.
26. Ibid., 43.
27. Ibid.
28. Polonskaja, "V petle: liričeskij fil'm," *Kovš* 1 (1925): 114.
29. Polonskaja, "Karmen," 216.
30. Polonskaja, "V petle," 114.
31. Ibid.
32. Ibid., 114–15.
33. Axmatova, *سočinenija. Tom pervyj,* 42.
34. Polonskaja, "V petle," 115.
35. Ibid.
36. Ibid., 116. The previous four lines do not contain the initial unstressed syllable; therefore, I am treating this as anacrusis.
37. Ibid., 117.
38. Lučanskij, "Ščepki," 53–54.
39. Polonskaja, "V petle," 117.
40. Sergei Malaxov, review of *Uprjamyj kalendar',* *Krasnaja nov'* 4 (1929): 231.
41. Polonskaja, "V petle," 113.
42. Ibid., 119.

43. Ibid.
44. G. Lelevič, "Pervyj akt materialističeskoj kritiki (metodologičeskie zametki)," *Pečat' i revoliucija* 1 (1928): 37.
45. Polonskaja, "Sobaki," *Koster* (Leningradskij Sojuz Poetov, 1927), 63.
46. Barabašev, "Naletčiki na Revoljuciju," 7.
47. Ibid.
48. Baril', "Literaturnye zametki," 41–42.
49. Lučanskij, "Ščepki," 50.
50. Baril', "Naletčiki na Revoljuciju," 41.
51. Sergej Esenin, "Da! Teper' rešeno. Bez vozvrata" (1922), *Stixotvorenija i poemy. Biblioteka poeta. Bol'šaja serija, Izdanie tret'je* (Leningrad: Sovetskij pisatel', 1986), 168.
52. Žuk, "'Čertovo koleso' i gorodskaja kul'tura," 58.
53. Sergej Esenin, "Pis'mo k ženščine" (1924), *Stixotvorenija i poemy*, 219.
54. Polonskaja, "Pamjatnaja vstreča (Sergej Esenin)" (ts.), Private Archive of E. G. Polonskaja, 4.
55. Polonskaja, "Sergeju Eseninu," *Žizn' iskusstva* 20 (1924): 5.
56. In a highly publicized incident of November 1923, Esenin and three other poets were briefly jailed after a drunken tavern brawl, in which the word *žid* (Yid) was used frequently. Similar incidents had occurred during his visit to America earlier that year. According to Gordon McVay, "Esenin was not a consistent anti-Semite. . . . Nevertheless, especially when intoxicated, he was prone to crudely anti-Semitic outbursts, which were clearly one aspect of his 'Great Russian' nationalism." Gordon McVay, *Esenin: A Life* (Ann Arbor, Mich.: Ardis, 1976), 200, 232–34.
57. Polonskaja, "Pamjatnaja vstreča," 4, 6.
58. Polonskaja, "Iz nabroskov k stixotvoreniju ob Esenine" (ts.), Private Archive of Elizaveta Polonskaja.
59. Polonskaja, "V petle," 114.
60. Polonskaja, *Uprjamyj kalendar'*, 76.
61. Polonskaja, "Pamjatnaja vstreča," 3.
62. "Serapionovy brat'ja o sebe," 29.
63. Polonskaja, "Karmen," 215. Emphasis mine.
64. Polonskaja, V petle," 8.
65. Polonskaja, "Nasledstvo," *Leningrad* 21, no. 36 (1924): 5. Emphasis mine.
66. An abridged version of the poem appeared in *Leningrad* 18 (1925): 13.
67. Polonskaja, *Uprjamyj kalendar'*, 77.
68. Kern, "Lev Lunc i 'Serapionovy brat'ja,'" *Novyj žurnal* 82 (March 1966): 177.

69. Polonskaja, *Uprjamyj kalendar'*, 77.
70. M. L. Polonskij, personal interview, St. Petersburg, June 1993.
71. Polonskaja, "Proščal'naja oda," *Kovš* 4 (Moscow, 1926), 134.
72. Polonskaja "Proščal'naja oda," 135. "Girlfriend" refers to *prazdnost'* (idleness), which is feminine.
73. Polonskaja, "Slovo," *Krasnyj žurnal dlja vsex* 1–2 (1923): 2.
74. Polonskaja, "Imja," *Leningrad* 11 (1924): 5.
75. This poem appears elsewhere as "Sčast'je" (Happiness).
76. Polonskaja, "Pesnja," *Prožektor* 21 (1925): 22.
77. Polonskaja, "Kolybel'naja," private archive, 1922.
78. Polonskaja, "Serdce eta smert' trevožit," private archive, 1926.
79. Polonskaja, "U Nevy (Anne Axmatovoj)" (1926), *Poezija* 42 (1985): 121–22.
80. Private Archive of Elizaveta Polonskaja. Emphasis mine.
81. Ibid.
82. Polonskaja, "Ešče ljubov'," *Sobranie stixotvorenij* (Leningrad: Leningradskij otdel vserossijskogo sojuza poetov, 1926), 40–43.
83. Brett-Harrison, "Dichterin in bewegter Zeit," 71.
84. Polonskaja, "Ešče ljubov'," 41–42.
85. Vyšeslavceva, "15 let poetičeskoj raboty," 8.
86. Polonskaja, *Uprjamyj kalendar'*, 62.
87. Vyšeslavceva, "15 let poetičeskoj raboty," 6.
88. Ibid.
89. Polonskaja, "Ljubov'," *Uprjamyj kalendar'*, 52.
90. Polonskaja, "Lebed'," 1924.
91. Polonskaja, *Uprjamyj kalendar'*, 58.
92. Polonskaja, "Pervoe maja v Tiflise," *Leningrad* 15 (1925): 7; "Most," *Leningradskij rabočij* 7 (1927): 15; "Stuknuli u okna drevka znamen," *Novyj mir* kn. 4, April 1928, 72.
93. Polonskaja, "Pionery," *Petrograd* 1 (1924): 11.
94. Polonskaja, "Most," *Leningradskij rabočij* 7 (1927): 15.
95. "Bol'šoj graždanin" did not appear in *Uprjamyj kalendar'*, which contains only poetry written between 1923 and 1927. It was included in her next collection, *Goda* (1935).
96. Polonskaja, "Bol'šoj graždanin," *Nedra* 17: 129.
97. Polonskaja, *Pod kamennym doždem*, 24.
98. Polonskaja, "Sčastlivaja žena," *Zvezda* 6 (1927): 41.
99. Polonskaja, "Rusalka," *Zvezda* 9 (1927): 104.
100. Polonskaja, "Otryvki iz poemy," *Leningradskaja Pravda*, 1 January 1925, 5; Polonskaja, "Pervoe maja v Tiflise," *Leningrad* 15 (1925): 7.
101. Polonskaja, *Uprjamyj kalendar'*, 28.
102. M. L. Polonskij, personal interview, St. Petersburg, 17 June 1993.
103. Polonskaja, *Uprjamyj kalendar'*, 23.

104. Ibid., 88.
105. A Jew is always a Jew!
106. Polonskaja, *Uprjamyj kalendar'*, 88.
107. Gregor Aronson, "The Jewish Question during the Stalin Era," in *Russian Jewry 1917–1967*, ed. Gregor Aronson et al. (New York, South Brunswick, and London: Thomas Yoseloff, 1967), 179.
108. Polonskaja, "K moim čitatel'jam, 11.
109. Polonskaja, "V petle," 119.

CHAPTER FIVE

1. Polonskaja, "K moim čitateljam," 7.
2. Polonskaja, *Goda. Izbrannye stixi*, 71–72.
3. Minc, "E. G. Polonskaja i ee literaturnye vospominanija," 374–75.
4. Aleksandr Rubaškin, personal interview, St. Petersburg, 23 June 1993.
5. Polonskaja, "Iz literaturnyx vospominanij (O Tynjanove)" (ts.), Private Archive of E. G. Polonskaja, 14.
6. Polonskaja, "K moim čitateljam," 11.
7. Polonskaja, letter to Marietta Šaginjan, 12 May 1935 (ts., photocopy), Private Archive of E. G. Polonskaja.
8. Polonskaja, "Iz prixodo-rasxodnoj literatury, 1935 g." (ts.), Private Archive of E. G. Polonskaja, 1.
9. "Noč' na Jungfernstuge," which was written in 1929 but did not actually appear in *Uprjamyj kalendar'*, was originally called simply "Noč'." It contained the lines "V prostore ulic gorodskom / *Neva* trevožno protekla" (In the urban space of streets / The *Neva* flowed agitatedly); the published version is "V prostore ulic gorodskom / *Reka* trevožno protekla" (In the urban space of streets / The *river* flowed agitatedly). "Noč'" (ts.), Private Archive of E. G. Polonskaja.
10. Polonskaja, *Goda*, 100–1.
11. Ibid., 103.
12. Ibid., 134–35.
13. Ibid., 132–33.
14. Ibid., 136.
15. E. G. Polonskaja, "Mama" (ts.), Private Archive of E. G. Polonskaja, 5.
16. Polonskaja, *Goda*, 137.
17. Ibid.
18. Ibid., 131.
19. Ibid., 140.
20. Ibid., 165.
21. M. L. Polonskij, personal interview, St. Petersburg, June 1993.

22. M. Vatson, "Iz Larry," *Vestnik Evropy* 5 (1878): 194. Cited in N. A. Nekrasov, *Polnoe sobranie sočinenij v 15 tomax. Tom I* (Leningrad: Nauka, 1981), 583.

23. Vera Inber, "O ženskix stixax," *Literaturnaja gazeta* 45, no. 232–33 (29 January 1933): 7.

24. G. Kolesnikova, "Obraz novoj ženščiny v xudožestvennoj literature," *Literaturnaja gazeta* 11, no. 239 (March 1933): 5.

25. "Proletarki Leningrada pred'javljajut sčet sovetskoj literature: obraščenie ženščin Leningrada ko vsem rabotnikam literatury, teatra i kino," *Izvestija*, no. 108 (24 April 1933): 4.

26. Polonskaja, *Goda*, 38.

27. "Poetičeskaja diskussija v Leningrade," *Literaturnaja gazeta*, no. 4, 567 (20 January 1936).

28. According to her son, they were on a first-name basis. M. L. Polonskij, personal interview, St. Petersburg, June 1993.

29. Polonskaja, *Novye stixi*, 4.

30. Ibid., 11.

31. Ibid., 13.

32. Ibid., 19.

33. Ibid., 20.

34. Ibid., 23.

35. Ibid., 24–25.

36. Ibid., 27.

37. Axmatova, *Sočinenija. Tom pervyj*, 111.

38. Marina Cvetaeva, *Stixotvorenija i poemy* (Leningrad: Sovetskij pisatel', 1990), 93. The poem itself contains no external clues as to the nature of the metaphor, but as Omry Ronen has demonstrated, its meaning was understood clearly by Mandel'štam, who was one of her "ručnye golubi, (tame doves)." See Omry Ronen, "'Bednye Izidy': Ob odnoj vol'noj šutke Osipa Mandel'štama," *Literaturnoe obozrenie* 11 (1991): 92.

39. Polonskaja, *Novye stixi*, 28.

40. Chimen Abramsky, "The Biro-Bidzhan Project, 1927–1959," in *The Jews in Soviet Russia since 1917*, ed. Lionel Kochan (New York: Oxford University Press, 1970), 72.

41. Polonskaja, *Novye stixi*, 35.

42. Ibid., 54.

43. Ibid., 37–38.

44. Ibid., 78.

45. Ibid., 73.

46. Ibid., 69.

47. Ibid., 59–60.

48. Ibid., 61.

49. Ibid., 62–63.

50. Puškin, "Mednyj vsadnik," *Polnoe sobranie sočinenij v desjati tomax, tom 4* (Moscow: Izdatel'stvo Akademii Nauk SSSR, 1957), 382.
51. Ibid., 381.
52. Polonskaja, *Novye stixi,* 65.
53. Ibid.
54. Ibid.
55. Ibid., 67.
56. Polonskaja, *Pod kamennym doždem,* 15.
57. Ibid., 16.
58. Mandel'štam, *Kamen',* 47.
59. Polonskaja, *Novye stixi,* 65.
60. Private Archive of E. G. Polonskaja.
61. Ibid.
62. "Romans. (Ja ždu ego. Proxodit tixij večer.)" (c. 1930), commentary by M. L. Polonskij. Private Archive of E. G. Polonskaja.
63. Private Archive of E. G. Polonskaja.
64. Ibid.
65. "Kljatva" ("Die Schwue"), music by Ljubov' Štrejxer, words by Elizaveta Polonskaja (Leningrad: Triton, 1930).
66. Fond 2182 (Škapskoj), op. 1, e.x. 436, TsGALI (Moscow), ll. 59–62.
67. Ibid.
68. Ibid., 71.
69. Vsevolod Azarov, "Glazami molodymi," *Leningradskaja Pravda,* 31 August 1966, 3.
70. Polonskaja, *Vremena mužestva,* 37.
71. Ibid., 21.
72. Ibid., 76.
73. *Pravda,* 6 March 1939. Cited in Petro Odarčenko, "Ševčenko in Soviet Literary Criticism," *Taras Ševčenko 1814–1861: A Symposium,* ed. Volodymyr Mijakovs'kyj and George Y. Shevelov on behalf of the Ukrainian Academy of Arts and Sciences in the United States (S-Gravenhage: Mouton and Co., 1962), 274.
74. Ibid.
75. Polonskaja, *Vremena mužestva,* 67.
76. Lunc, "Počemu my Serapionovy brat'ja," 31.
77. Polonskaja, "U starogo Finljansdkogo vokzala," "Metel' i temnota. Ideš' s raboty," "Kak v eti dni my nežnost'ju bogaty," *Izbrannoe* 97, 98, 99.
78. Private Archive of E. G. Polonskaja.
79. Polonskaja, *Izbrannoe,* 102.
80. M. A. Froman was the husband of the poet Ida Nappel'baum.
81. Faina Statina was a writer connected with the literary circle at *Rabotnica i krest'janka.*
82. Private Archive of E. G. Polonskaja.

83. Ibid.
84. Ibid.
85. Ibid.
86. Fond 2182 (Škapskoj), op. 1, e.x. 436, TsGALI (Moscow), ll. 83–84.
87. Polonskaja, *Kamskaja tetrad'* (Molotov: Molotovgiz, 1945).
88. A literary scholar and teacher in the ballet academy.
89. Polonskaja, "Vzbesivšijsja volk"; "Razgovor v adu," *Leningrad* 16 (1941): 12.
90. Private Archive of E. G. Polonskaja.
91. Ibid.
92. Ibid.
93. Ibid.
94. Polonskaja, *Kamskaja tetrad'*, 44.
95. Ibid. Polonskaja actually mocked such pseudofolk versification in a 1943 letter to Škapskaja. Describing the participants in a conference, *Ural v literature* (The Urals in Literature), she wrote:

Kamenskij praises himself, and I have written a parody of him.

> Я на Камушке сижу
> Я стихи горожу,
> Их на музыку ложу.
> Ах ты Кама Камушка!
> А хвалю их сам уж как!

> I sit by the little Kama
> I spout verses,
> I set them to music.
> Oh you, Kama, little Kama!
> And I certainly do praise them myself!

I borrowed the last rhyme [Kamuška / sam už kak] from him.

Fond 2182 (Škapskaja), op. 1, e.x. 437, TsGALI (Moscow), l. 40.
96. Polonskaja, *Kamskaja tetrad'*, 9.
97. Ibid., 18.
98. Ibid., 41.
99. Private Archive of E. G. Polonskaja.
100. Polonskaja, *Stixotvorenija i poema*, 90.
101. Polonskaja, "Partizanka" (1946) (ts.), Private Archive of E. G. Polonskaja.
102. Polonskaja, "Kudrjavaja devčonka" (1944) (ts.), Private Archive of E. G. Polonskaja.
103. A. Tarasenkov, "Nevoploščennaja tema," *Literaturnaja gazeta*, 17 November 1945.
104. Fond 2182 (Škapskoj), op. 1, e.x. 436, TsGALI (Moscow), l. 58.

105. Z. Minc, "E. G. Polonskaja i ee literaturnye vospominanija," 375; A. Galuškin, "U stixov osobaja sud'ba," *Medicinskaja gazeta*, 16 January 1987.

106. Z. Minc, review of *Stixotvorenija i poema*, *Zvezda* 11 (1960): 217.

107. Private Archive of E. G. Polonskaja.

108. Ibid.

109. Ibid.

110. Polonskaja, "Krovel'ščiki," "Xozjajki s našej ulicy," *Leningrad* 10/11 (1944): 15.

111. Polonskaja, "Krovel'ščiki," "Xozjajki s našej ulicy," "Da my trudilis. Nenavist' k vragu," *Leningrad* 10/11 (1944): 15.

112. Polonskaja, "Lisa na strojke: Basnja," *Večernyj Leningrad*, 14 November 1946.

113. Private Archive of E. G. Polonskaja.

114. Ibid.

115. Ibid.

116. Ibid.

117. Ibid.

118. Ibid.

119. Ibid.

120. Ibid.

121. Polonskaja, "Prixodo-rassxodnaja literatura, 1946, October 21." Private Archive of E. G. Polonskaja.

122. *Doklad Ždanova*, 59–60.

123. *Central Committe Resolution*, 23.

CHAPTER SIX

1. E. G. Polonskaja, "V Sekciju Poetov LO SSP" (letter, ts.), Private Archive of E. G. Polonskaja.

2. Minc, "E. G. Polonskaja i ee literaturnye vospominanija," 375.

3. Zelig Štejnman, "Bol'šoe darovanie. 70-letie Elizavety Polonskoj," *Večernij Leningrad* 157, no. 4469 (1 July 1960): 4.

4. A. Anatol'jev, review of *Izbrannoe*.

5. Polonskaja, *Stixotvorenija i poema*, 123.

6. Minc, "E. G. Polonskaja i ee literaturnye vospominanija," 375.

7. Galuškin, "U stixov osobaja sud'ba."

8. Polonskaja, *Stixotvorenija i poema*, 126.

9. Polonskaja, *Izbrannoe*, 153.

10. Ju. Meškov, review of *Izbrannoe*, *Neva* 10 (1967): 195.

11. Minc, review of *Stixotvorenija i poema*, 217.

12. Minc, "E. G. Polonskaja i ee literaturnye vospominanija," 374.

13. Polonskaja, *Den' poeta* (Leningrad, 1956), 89. This poem's date is given as 1950 in Polonskaja's next collection, *Stixotvorenija i poema;* however, according to M. L. Polonskij, it was actually written in 1940 and concerns the First World War rather than the Second.

14. Polonskaja, "Bereza-belogrudka u verandy," *Priboj: sbornik proizvedenij leningradskix pisatelej* (Leningrad: Gosudarstvennoe Izdatel'stvo Xudožestvennoj Literatury, 1957), 222.

15. Polonskaja, "Belomorsk (aprel')," *Antologija russkoj sovetskoj poezii 1917–1957. T. 1.* (Moscow: GIXL, 1957), 299.

16. Introduction, *The Year of Protest, 1956: An Anthology of Soviet Literary Materials*, trans. and ed. Hugh McLean and Walter Vickery (New York: Vintage Books, 1961), 13.

17. Polonskaja, "V čem priznak novogo? Uželi," *Den' poeta* (Leningrad: Lenizdat, 1958), 80.

18. Polonskaja, "Svetloglazyj umnyj mal'čik," *Priboj: sbornik proizvedenij leningradskix pisatelej* (Leningrad: Gosudarstvennoe Izdatel'stvo Xudožestvennoj Literatury, 1959), 154.

19. Minc, review of *Stixotvorenija i poema*, 217.

20. Nikolaj Braun, "Recenzija na knigu Elizavety Polonskoj 'Stixotvorenija i poemy,'" 17 September 1958. Fond 344, op. 2, delo 636: Recenzii na rukopisi avtografov na bukvy P-Ja. Leningradskoe otdelenie Izdatel'stva Sovetskij pisatel', TsGALI (St. Petersburg), l. 13.

21. A. Ninov, "Elizaveta Polonskaja. Stixotvorenija i poemy," 20 February 1959. Fond 344, op. 2, delo 671, Leningradskoe otdelenie Izdatel'stva Sovetskij pisatel', Redakcionnyj otdel, TsGALI (St. Petersburg), ll. 4–5.

22. Fond 344, op. 2, delo 671, TsGALI (St. Petersburg), l. 15.

23. According to Mixail Polonskij, a military engineer, this reference was actually seen as a threat to military security. Personal conversation, St. Petersburg, June 1993.

24. Fond 344, op. 2, delo 671, TsGALI (St. Petersburg), l. 11.

25. Minc, review of *Stixotvorenija i poema*, 218.

26. Polonskaja, *Stixotvorenija i poema*, 5.

27. Braun, in his review, written 17 September 1958, states that the earliest poem in the collection was dated 1917; he was, no doubt, referring to "Ballada o beglece." This suggests that the backdating of "Mjagkoj gubkoj" may have come later. Fond 344, op. 2, delo 636, TsGALI (St. Petersburg), l. 14.

28. Polonskaja, *Stixotvorenija i poema*, 78.

29. Ibid., 82.

30. Ibid., 121.

31. Ibid., 107, dated 1950; originally in *Den' poezii* (Leningrad: Sovetskij pisatel', 1956), 90, undated.

32. Polonskaja, "Malyš—kak tugo svernutaja počka" (ts.), Private Archive of E. G. Polonskaja.
33. Polonskaja, *Uprjamyj kalendar'*, 85–86.
34. Polonskaja, *Stixotvorenija i poema*, 75–76.
35. Fond 344, op. 2, delo 636, TsGALI (St. Petersburg), l. 14.
36. Polonskaja, *Stixotvorenija i poema*, 122.
37. Minc, "E. G. Polonskaja i ee literaturnye vospominanija," 375.
38. Polonskaja, *Stixotvorenija i poema*, 96–97.
39. Ibid., 102.
40. Private Archive of E. G. Polonskaja.
41. Ibid.
42. Ibid.
43. Polonskaja, "Kak i tridcat' pjat' let nazad," 100–1.
44. Private Archive of E. G. Polonskaja.
45. Private archive.
46. Ibid.
47. V. Orlov, "Elizaveta Polonskaja. Dorogi [sic] v buduščee." 24 March 1963. Fond 344, op. 3, delo 215, Leningradskoe otdelenie Izdatel'stva Sovetskij pisatel', Recenzii na rukopisi, 1963. TsGALI (St. Petersburg), ll. 144–46.
48. Fond 1204, Erenburg, op. 2, e.x. 2056, TsGALI (Moscow), l. 7.
49. Ibid., 10.
50. Fond 344, op. 3, delo 215, TsGALI (St. Petersburg), l. 146.
51. Fond 344, op. 3, delo 293, Perepiska s central'nym izdatel'stvom, avtorami i drugimi o dejatel'nosti izdatel'stva, TsGALI (St. Petersburg), l. 3.
52. Polonskaja, "Ilana." *Den' poezii* (Leningrad: Sovetskij pisatel', 1962), 162.
53. Polonskaja, "Ja podružila s molodoj sosnoju" (ts.), Private Archive of Elizaveta Polonskaja.
54. Polonskaja, "V lesu," *Neva* 6 (1964): 134. Dated according to a typescript in the Private Archive.
55. Polonskaja, "Čem starše delajus', tem ja ljublju sil'nej," *Den' poezii* (Moscow and Leningrad: Sovetskij pisatel', 1962), 181.
56. Polonskaja "Ne Bramsa sonatu prošu povtorit'" (1967) (ts.), Private Archive of E. G. Polonskaja.
57. Polonskaja, "Golubka naša"; "Ottepel'," *Zvezda* 1 (1963): 45.
58. Polonskaja, "V zelenoj El've," *Den' poezii* (Leningrad: Sovetskij pisatel', 1961), 159.
59. Polonskaja, "Plotina v Pjeedu," *Zvezda* 3 (1964): 48.
60. Polonskaja, "Prazdnik pesni v El've," *Den' poezii* (Leningrad: Sovetskij pisatel', 1964), 189.
61. Polonskaja, "Skazka dlja sebja," *Den' poezii* (Leningrad: Sovetskij pisatel', 1969), 119.

62. Polonskaja, "V zimnem nebe" (1960) (ts.), Private Archive of E. G. Polonskaja.
63. Private Archive of E. G. Polonskaja.
64. Ibid.
65. There is no addressee in the original typescript of the poem, but according to M. L. Polonskij's commentary, "There can be no doubt about the addressee."
66. Private Archive of E. G. Polonskaja.
67. Ibid.
68. Polonskaja, *Izbrannoe*, 11, 13.
69. Polonskaja, "K moim čitateljam," 14.
70. Polonskaja, "Načalo dvadcatyx godov," *Prostor* 6 (1964): 110–19.
71. Fond 1204, Erenburg, op. 2, e.x. 2056, TsGALI (Moscow), l. 39.
72. Private Archive of E. G. Polonskaja.
73. Polonskaja, "David i Emma Vygodskie," 1.
74. Fond 1204, Erenburg, op. 2, e.x. 2056, TsGALI (Moscow), l. 39.
75. Polonskaja, *Izbrannoe*, 18.
76. Ibid., 41.
77. Ibid., 61.
78. Ibid., 57.
79. Ibid., 97.
80. Ibid., 98.
81. Ibid., 99.
82. Ibid., 92.
83. Polonskaja, "Tartu," *Den' poezii*, 1964, 188. Details about Polonskaja's friendship with Fejgina can be found in her unpublished memoir, "Gorod Jur'jev," in the Private Archive.
84. Polonskaja, *Izbrannoe*, 154.
85. Ibid.
86. Ibid.
87. Brown, *Russian Literature since the Revolution*, 289–90.
88. Fond 1204, Erenburg, op. 2, e.x. 2056, TsGALI (Moscow), l. 23.
89. Polonskaja, *Izbrannoe*, 131.
90. Ibid., 136.
91. Ibid., 153.
92. Ibid., 152.
93. Ibid., 155.
94. *Oktjabr' v sovetskoj poezii*, ed. V. N. Orlov (Leningrad: Sovetskij pisatel', 1967), 172.
95. Private Archive of E. G. Polonskaja.
96. Polonskaja, "Ol'ge Berggol'c," *Den' poezii* (Leningrad: Sovetskij pisatel', 1966), 15.

97. Polonskaja, "Pozdnee priznan'je," *Den' poezii* (Leningrad: Sovetskij pisatel', 1966), 15.
98. Fond 344, op. 3, delo 293, Perepiska s central'nym izdatel'stvom, avtorami i drugimi o dejatel'nosti izdatel'stva, TsGALI (St. Petersburg), l. 3.
99. Fond 1204, Erenburg, op. 2, e.x. 2056, TsGALI (Moscow), l. 41.
100. M. L. Polonskij, personal interview, St. Petersburg, May 1993.
101. Polonskaja, "Moi slova," *Den' poezii* (Leningrad: Sovetskij pisatel', 1969), 118.
102. Ol'ga Forš, *Sumasšedšij korabl': roman, rasskazy* (Leningrad: Xudožestvennaja literatura, 1988), 138.
103. A. Anatol'jev, review of *Izbrannoe*, 219.
104. Grigorij Solov'ev, "Ol'xa i v poezii ne v česti," *Otvetstvennost' pered vremenem: sbornik kritičeskix statej* (Moscow: Sovetskaja Rossija, 1963), 101–4.
105. See L. Dorfman, "Serapionova Sestra: Elizaveta Polonskaja i kritičeskoe vosprijatie 'ženskoj liriki'," *Preobraženie* 4 (1996).
106. D. Granin et al., "Pamjati E. G. Polonskoj," *Literaturnaja gazeta*, 22 January 1969, 5.

CONCLUSION

1. See Rubaškin, "Ne sotvori kumira"; Galuškin, "U stixov osobaja sud'ba."
2. *Neopalimaja kupina: evrejskie sjužety v russkoj poezii,* ed. Aleksandr Donat (New York: New York University Press, 1973), 311–12.
3. *Oktjabr' v sovetskoj poezii (1917–1987)* (Leningrad, 1987), 172–73.
4. A. Galuškin, "U stixov osobaja sud'ba."
5. A. I. Rubaškin, "Vernost' poezii," *Den' poezii* (Leningrad: Sovetskij pisatel', 1981), 348.
6. Rubaškin, "Vernost' poezii," 349.
7. M. L. Polonskij and B. Ja. Frezinskij, *Poezija. Al'manax No. 42* (Moscow, 1985), 121.
8. M. L. Polonskij, personal interview, St. Petersburg, June 1993.
9. M. Polonskij and B. Frezinskij, "Serapionovskie ody i epigrammy Elizavety Polonskoj," 1993.
10. Rubaškin, "Vernost' poezii," 318.
11. V. V. Učenova, ed. *Caricy muz: russkie poetessy XIX-načala XX vekov* (Moscow, 1989).
12. Catriona Kelly, *A History of Russian Women's Writing 1820–1992* (Oxford: Clarendon Press, 1994), 234.
13. Polonskaja, *Izbrannoe*, 8. This collection is, in fact, the only work by Polonskaja listed in Kelly's bibliography.

14. Elena Trubilova, "'Polonskaia,' Elizaveta Grigor'evna," trans. Jill Roese, in *Dictionary of Russian Women Writers*, ed. Marina Ledkovsky, Charlotte Rosenthal, and Mary Zirin (Westport, Conn., and London: Greenwood Press, 1994), 512–14.

15. Polonskaja, "Pamjatnaja vstreča (Sergej Esenin)," 4.

16. *Serapionovy brat'ja* (Moscow: Vysšaja škola, 1994).

17. *Literaturnaja gruppa "Serapionovy brat'ja'": istoki, poiski, tradicii, meždunarodnyj kontekst. Tezisy dokladov*, 13–16 March 1995, St. Petersburg.

18. Timina, "Elizaveta Polonskaja v krugu 'Serapionovyx brat'jev'," 64–66. Due to illness, Timina was not able to present this paper at the conference itself.

19. Jakov Braun, "Devjat' strannikov v 'osjazaemoe ničto'." *Sibirskie ogni* 1 (1924): 226.

20. Timina, "Elizaveta Polonskaja v krugu 'Serapionovyx brat'jev'," 66.

21. Ibid.

Bibliography

PRIMARY SOURCES: PUBLISHED

Verse Collections by E. G. Polonskaja

Znamen'ja. St. Petersburg: Erato, 1921.
Pod kamennym doždem, 1921–1923. St. Petersburg: Poljarnaja zvezda, 1923.
Uprjamyj kalendar': stixi i poemy, 1924–1927. Leningrad: Izdatel'stvo pisatelej v Leningrade, 1929.
Goda: izbrannye stixi. Leningrad: Izdatel'stvo pisatelej v Leningrade, 1935.
Novye stixi, 1932–1936. Leningrad: Goslitizdat, 1937.
Vremena mužestva: stixi; Portret: poema. Leningrad: Goslitizdat, 1940.
Kamskaja tetrad': stixi. Molotov: Molotovskoe Oblastnoe Izdatel'stvo, 1945.
Stixotvorenija i poema. Leningrad: Sovetskij pisatel', 1960.
Izbrannoe. Moscow and Leningrad: Xudožestvennaja Literatura, 1966.

Verse for Children

Zajčata. Petrograd, Moscow: Raduga, 1923.

Poems Published Individually

"Ulybnulsja izdali, možet byt' ne mne"; "Nad rešetkoj vašego okna"; "U tebja pri každom rezkom slove"; "Kogda ja budu staroj, ja ujedu." *Večera. Ežemjesjačnik stixov* 2 (1914): 8–11. (Published under the pseudonym Elizaveta Bertram.)
"I mudrye pravy i mudrye mudry." *Severnoe obozrenie* 1 (1922): 4.
"Igraet med', idut polki . . ."; "Odni roptali, plakali drugie." *Literaturnaja nedel'ja. Pril. k gazete, Petrogradskaja Pravda* 6 (1922): 1.
"Na pamjat' o tjaželom gode"; "Suxoj i gulkij šelknul baraban." *Serapionovy Brat'ja: Zagraničnyj Al'manax.* Berlin: Izdatel'stvo 'Russkoe tvorčestvo', 1922.
"Peterburg (Spjat pobedivšie)." *Literaturnaja nedel'ja. Priloženie k gazete, Petrogradskaja Pravda* 18 (1922): 5.

Bibliography

"Smešalos' vse. Goda vojny." *Peterburgskij sbornik 1922. Poety i belletristy*. St. Petersburg: Izdatel'stvo Žurnala 'Letopis' Doma Literatorov', 1922.
"Slovo." *Krasnyj žurnal dlja vsex* 1–2 (1923): 2.
"Imja." *Leningrad* 11 (1924): 5.
"Karmen." *Nedra* 4 (1924): 215–18.
"Karmen." *Zaboj* 3 (1924): 5.
"Lebed'." *Krasnyj žurnal dlja vsex* 4 (1924): 246.
"Nasledstvo." *Leningrad* 21, no. 36 (1924): 5.
"Pionery." *Petrograd* 1 (1924): 11.
"Pro knigi." *Vorobej* 2/5 (1924): 25.
"Sergeju Eseninu." *Žizn' iskusstva* 20 (1924): 5.
"Lavočka velikolepij." *Leningrad* 18 (1925): 13.
"Otryvki iz poemy." *Leningradskaja pravda*, 1 January 1925, 5.
"Pervoe maja v Tiflise." *Leningrad* 15 (1925): 7.
"Pesnja." *Prožektor* 21 (1925): 22.
"V petle: Liričeskij fil'm." *Kovš* Kn. 1. (1925), 108–19.
"Ešče ljubov'." *Sobranie stixotvorenij*. Leningrad: Leningradskij Otdel Vserossijskogo Sojuza Poetov, 1926; 40–43.
"Proščal'naja oda." *Kovš* Kn. 4. (1926), 133–35.
"Most." *Leningradskij rabočij* 7 (1927): 15.
"Rusalka." *Zvezda* 9 (1927): 103–4.
"Sobaki." *Koster*. Leningrad: Leningradskij Sojuz Pisatelej, 1927; 63.
"Ščastlivaja žena." *Zvezda* 6 (1927): 40–42.
"Stuknuli v okna drevka znamen." *Novyj mir* Kn. 4. April 1928, 72.
"Bol'šoj graždanin." *Nedra* 17 (1929): 120–30.
"Sadovnik. Otryvok iz poemy." *Literaturnyj Leningrad,* 29 August 1936.
"'Vzbesivšijsja volk'; 'Razgovor v adu'." *Leningrad* 16 (1941): 12.
"Druz'ja, spešite!" *Prikam'je* 5 (1942): 46.
"Spasibo, ural'cy!" *Prikam'je* 6 (1942): 179.
"Zolotye polja." *Zvezda (Perm')*, 3 October 1942.
"Nataša." *Rabotnica* 6/7 (1943): 5.
"'Krovel'ščiki'; 'Xozjajki s našej ulicy'; 'Da, my trudilis'. Nenavist' k vragu.'" *Leningrad* 10/11 (1944): 15.
"Lisa na strojke (Basnja)." *Večernij Leningrad,* 14 November 1946.
"Svideteli velikix potrjasenij"; "Litoj rešetkoj ogorožen." *Den' poeta*. Leningrad: Sovetskij pisatel', 1956; 89–90.
"Belomorsk (aprel')." *Antologija russkoj sovetskoj poezii 1917–1957*. Moscow: Gosudarstvennoe Izdatel'stvo Xudožestvennoj Literatury, 1957; 299.
"Bereza-belogrudka u verandy." *Priboj: sbornik proizvedenij leningradskix pisatelej*. Leningrad: Gosudarstvennoe Izdatel'stvo Xudožestvennoj Literatury, 1957; 222.
"V čem priznak novogo." *Den' poeta*. Leningrad: Lenizdat, 1958; 80.

"Svetloglazyj umnyj mal'čik." *Priboj: sbornik proizvedenij leningradskix pisatelej.* Leningrad: Gosudarstvennoe Izdatel'stvo Xudožestvennoj Literatury, 1959; 154.
"V zelenoj El've." *Den' poezii.* Leningrad: Sovetskij pisatel', 1961; 159.
"Čem starše delajus', tem ja ljublju sil'nej." *Den' poezii.* Moscow and Leningrad: Sovetskij pisatel', 1962; 181.
"Ilana." *Den' poezii.* Leningrad: Sovetskij pisatel', 1962; 162.
"'Golubka naša'; 'Ottepel'." *Zvezda* 1 (1963): 45.
"Plotina v Pjeedu." *Zvezda* 3 (1964): 48.
"Prazdnik pesni v El've." *Den' poezii.* Leningrad: Sovetskij pisatel', 1964; 189.
"Tartu." *Den' poezii.* Leningrad: Sovetskij pisatel', 1964; 187–89.
"V lesu." *Neva* 6 (1964): 134.
"Ol'ge Berggol'c." *Den' poezii.* Leningrad: Sovetskij pisatel', 1966; 15.
"Pozdnee priznan'je." *Den' poezii.* Leningrad: Sovetskij pisatel', 1966; 15.
"Oktjabr'." *Oktjabr' v sovetskoj poezii.* Ed. V. N. Orlov. Leningrad: Sovetskij pisatel', 1967; 172.
"Rodine"; "Moi slova"; "Skazka dlja sebja"; "Vesennjaja sjuita"; "Prazdnik pesni"; "Buduščee." *Den' poezii.* Leningrad: Sovetskij pisatel', 1969; 118–19.
"Šejlok"; "Vstreča"; "Agar'." *Neopalimaja kupina: evrejskie sjužety v russkoj poezii.* Ed. Aleksandr Donat, 311–12. New York: New York University Press, 1973.
"U Nevy (Anne Axmatovoj)"; "Veet veter bezrassudnyj"; "Ne ržaveet (N. Tixonovu)"; "Na dal'nem severe zimuet drug"; "Vnuku." *Poezija* 42 (1985): 121–22.
"My naučaemsja ljubit'"; "Ne stranno li, čto my zabudem vse"; "Kto ty, čitatel'? Vek, mogučij škval." *Medicinskaja gazeta,* 16 January 1987.
"Oktjabr'." *Oktjabr' v sovetskoj poezii (1917–1987).* Leningrad, 1987; 172–73.
"Serapionovskie ody i epigrammy Elizavety Polonskoj." Prep. M. L. Polonskij and B. Ja. Frezinskij. *Voprosy literatury* 6 (1993): 356–66.

Libretti
Ljubov' Štrejxer. *Časy: Detskaja opera—igra.* Tekst Elizavety Polonskoj. Moscow: Gosudarstvennoe Izdatel'stvo, Muzykal'nyj Sektor, 1927.

Translations
"Sumasbrod, ili vse nevpopad." *Sobranie sočinenij Mol'era,* vol. 1. Leningrad: Academia, 1935.

Memoirs
"Iz literaturnyx vospominanij." Fwd. Z. Minc. *Trudy po russkoj i slavjanskoj filologii* 6. *Učenye zapiski tartusskogo universiteta* 139 (1963): 375–89.

"Načalo dvadcatyx godov." *Prostor* 6 (1964): 110–15.
"Do oktjabrja ešče desjat' let." *Zvezda* 7 (1965): 143–57.
"K moim čitateljam." Introd. *Izbrannoe*. Moscow and Leningrad: Xudožestvennaja literatura, 1966; 7–14.
"O Konstantine Fedine." *Tvorčestvo Konstantina Fedina*. Moscow: Izdatel'stvo "Nauka," 1966; 450–54.
"Vstreči." *Neva* 1 (1966): 184–90.
"Na pamjat' o podvorotnjax'." *Ol'ga Forsh v vospominanijax sovremennikov*. Leningrad: Sovetskij pisatel', 1974; 94–100.
"Kak i tridcat' pjat' let nazad." *Vsevolod Ivanov–pisatel' i čelovek*. Moscow: Sovetskij pisatel', 1975; 96–101.
"Moi referat." Memoir. *Vospominanija o Kornee Čukovskom*. Ed. M. Ja. Malxazov, 73–75. Moscow: Sovetskij pisatel', 1977.
"Moe znakomstvo s Mixailom Zoščenko." *Mixail Zoščenko v vospominanijax sovremennikov*. Moscow, 1981; 129–36.
"V Dome Iskusstv." *Vospominanija o Konstantine Fedine*. Moscow, 1981; 48–51.
"V Tiflise (iz vospominanij)." *Bratstvo: Stixotvorenija poetov bratskix respublik. Vospominanija. Zametki*. Fwd. A. Amsterdam, 459–66. Leningrad, 1982.
"Nezabyvaemye vstreči." *Vospominanija o N. Tixonove*. Comp. I. I. Kotov and M. I. Gaglov, 143–50. Moscow: Sovetskij pisatel', 1986.
"Iz knigi 'Vstreči'." Prep. M. L. Polonskij and B. Ja. Frezinskij. *Neva* 4 (1987): 193–97.
"Iz vospominanij." [o Tynjanove] *Znamia Truda Darba Karogs: Gazeta Goroda Rezekne i Rezeknenskogo Raiona*, 9 June 1990.
"Moe znakomstvo s Mixailom Zoščenko." *Vspominaja Mixaila Zoščenko*. Leningrad, 1990; 147–54.
"Iz Literaturnyx vospominanij [o Lidii Čarskoj]." Prep. V. S. Baxtin. *Čas Pik* 37, no. 237 (21 September 1994): 15.

Articles on Literature

"O detskix avtorax, detskix p'jesax i detskom teatre." *Žizn' iskusstva* 367 (10 February 1920).
Autobiography. "Serapionovy Brat'ja o sebe." *Literaturnye zapiski* 3 (1922): 25–31.
"Proletarki Leningrada pred'javljajut sčet sovetskoj literature: Obraščenie ženščin Leningrada ko vsem rabotnikam literatury, teatra i kino." *Izvestija* 108 (24 April 1933): 4.
"Poetičeskaja diskussija v Leningrade." *Literaturnaja gazeta* 4, no. 567 (20 January 1936).
"Stixi, rasskazy, poemy." *Literaturnyj Leningrad* 40, no. 185 (1936): 3.
"Govorit Ispanija." Review. *Literaturnoe obozrenie* 16 (1938): 53–56.

Bibliography

Prose

Poezdka na Ural. Leningrad: Priboj, 1927.
Ljudi sovetskix budnej. Leningrad: Izdateľstvo Pisatelej v Leningrade, 1934.
Na svoix plečax: Očerki. Moscow: Ispolkom Sojuza Obščestv Krasnogo Kresta i Krasnogo Polumesjaca SSSR, 1948.
Na svoix plečax: Rasskazy. Leningrad: Lenizdat, 1948.

PRIMARY SOURCES: UNPUBLISHED

Poems from the Private Archive

1908–19

Da, v etot večer ja odna ostalas' (1911–14)
Israel (July 1919)
Ja kogda-to byla veseloj (1911–14)
Nad rešetkoj vašego okna (1914)
Polden' ľjetsja v komnatu kak sladkij med (1911–14)
U nix byla verbnaja subbota (undated)
V litejnoj masterskoj starik rabočij (December 1919)
V okne starevščika na Ekateringofskoj (1911–15)

1920–24

Carskoe selo (summer 1920)
Esli eto konec, esli my umrem (April 1921)
Golos (16 March 1922)
Kruglyj nož (Ne bogoxuľstvuj . . .) (23 August 1922)
Kruglyj nož (Rukoj ne xvatajsja za kruglyj nož) (15 April 1923)
Moskva 1922 (V moskovskom zamke Černomora) (14 January 1923)
Nasledstvo (Drafts): Ditja, ty, rodilsja v izmenčivom marte (1924)
    Ja gorod podarju tebe (1924)
    Ja ostavlju tebe v nasledstvo (1924)
O deti naroda moego (10 July 1921)
O Rossija, zlaja Rossija (19 April 1922)
Pojdu ja v magazin Kornilova na Nevskom (15 May 1921)
Raj (Postroit' by dom, ustroit' by sad) (25 June 1922)
Sčasťje 1923 (15 August 1923)
Smirjaem ploť užalosťju žestokoj (29–30 June 1922)
Tiflis (October 1924)
Vesy i giry, sterlingy i funty (May 1922)

1925–29

Eseninu (1926)
Graždanka Smerť (1926)

Bibliography

Kukloj voskovoj on ležal v grobu (1926)
Nam budut zavidovat' pokolen'ja (1926)
Serdce eta smert' trevožet (January 1926) [To Esenin]

1930–35

Černyj agat (1930)
Konec (Vrag moj, drug moj, muž moj nevenčannyj) (1932–34)
Na sopkax Mančžurii (1935)
Nočnoj košmar (1929–30)
Romans (Ja ždu ego. Proxodit tixij večer) (1930)

1936–39

Mavzolej (pesnja) (1937)
Moej nastavnice (Ty spravedlivaja, i ty ne terpiš' zla) (1938)
Povest' (Ty tože byla nesčastlivoj, Anna) (23 April 1937)
Sladčajšaja Ljutecija (1937)
V poezde (Ja vyključila lampu u stola) (May 1936)
Verni moju junost'! Xotja by na čas (September 1937)

1940–44

Ballada o čajnike (26 August 1941)
Ballada o čužom dobre (undated)
Ballada o rycarskoj ljubvi (1942)
Basnja (Napoleonovoj vozžaždav slavy) (September 1941)
Basnja (Vrunu naxodčivost' nužna) (1942?)
Bojazlivaja žena (4 October 1944)
Dom/Sorbonna (Pod sen' Latinskogo kvartala) (1940–46)
Etot gorod (Mnogie drugie ljubjat etot gorod (4–8 June 1943)
Gul samoletov slyšen v otdalenii (20 August 1941)
Ijun'. Žara. Vojna (1940)
Knigi, radio, uzkij divančik (22 July 1940)
Kto solnce svet uvidel na Urale (1943)
Kudrjavaja devčonka (1944, after June)
Leningradskij veter (25 February 1943)
Mnogoobraznye i dorožnye priključenija V. V. Uspenskogo (22 August 1941)
Moej podruge (M. N. Kireeve) (undated)
Muze (Kogda, slučaetsja, ja tjaželo gruščú (1940)
Net, ne golod i ne xolod, daže (February 1944)
Pariž (Etot gorod ja ljubila s detstva (August 1940)
Pariž. Nelli Ljafon (5 August 1940)
Parki (Gde-to v mire tri sestry živut) (11 June 1940)
S toboj načinali my put' (May 1942)

Bibliography

Sankt-Peterburg (Vot, značit, kakim ja tebja zastaju) (1944)
Sud prišel (My slyšali, my kulaki sžimali) (20 December 1943)
Svetloglazaja devuška. Faine. (September–October 1940)
Toskueš' ty o dal'nem i ljubimom (January 1943)
U našej granicy (Drožite, podlye ubijcy) (28 February 1944)
Uborka list'jev (11–22 May 1940)
Zapomni vse i vse zapečatlej (1943)
Zavtra (Pamjati M. A. Fromana) (22 June 1940)

1945–49

Čeremuxa-pesnja (Vysoko nad krovlej gorodskoj) (1945)
Detskoe Selo (1946)
Iz vsex ego portretov est' odin (19 June 1949)
Kamenščik (1949)
Malyš—kak tugo svernutaja počka (1946)
Martovskij večer (Kak radostno, sestry, sodružestvo naše) (8 March 1949)
Materi (Mama, dorogaja, ja s toboju vmeste) (1946)
Mne segodnja skazali v tramvae (1946)
My pis'ma pisat' perestali (1949)
Narod moj—ulybki skvoz' slezy (1946)
Ne možet byt', čtob ne bylo ljubvi (23 April 1946)
Ne znaju gde, v kakom kraju (1945)
Ni dlja odnogo ljubovnika na svete (6 April 1946)
O ženščiny, o sestry dorogie (1949)
Ostalis' gody, možet byt', minuty (20 February 1946)
Partizanka (26 October 1946)
Po slučaju pobedy (1945)
Segodnja na viske u syna (variants) (1948)
Skatert' belocvetnuju vynu iz komoda (21 May 1945)
Slyšno: tjaželoe s šumom (8 April 1946)
Svin'ja,kon' i kolxoznik (Basnja) (1946)
V detstve, esli tebe (1947)
V šutku skazat' (Počemu-to govorjat o bratstve) (6 March 1946)
Vesennaja skazka (Kogda zima ustanet pirovat') (8–18 March 1946)
Vse čto poverxnostno—unosit burja (1 March 1946)
Zdravstvuj Tartu, staryj drug (September 1949)

1950–54

A možet byt' zasneš' (1951)
Idut goda, a my stoboj v razluke. Pamjati E. Vygodskoj (1950–51)
Pamjati Emmy Vygodskoj (1950–51)
Po beregu reki zabvenij. Pamjati E. Vygodskoj (1949–50)

Bibliography

1955–59

Čudo v Peredelkine—neizvestnomu tovarišču (2 March 1957)
Detskoe Selo (1955?)
Esli vyjti prjamo iz vorot (1955)
Ja ešče ne umerla, ja ešče živaja! (14–24 July 1957)
Ja prinjala snotvornoe i noč' (1955–57)
Korneju Ivanoviču Čukovskomu ko 75-letiju (25 March 1957)
Na bolničnoj kojke (19 April 1957)
Nikak (Pozabyli my dorogi v staryj mir) (February 1957)
Poet (Vot kakim ty stal, moj milyj) (22–27 January 1957)
Poka ešče ty dyšiš' (December 1955)
S myslju o Cervantese. Pamjati E. Vygodskoj (20 September 1956)
Tak nedavno, ja byla moja (8 October 1957)
V razgare našix junyx let (1957)

1960–64

Antenny televizorov stremjatsja (27 April 1961)
Ja podružila s molodoj sosnoju (17 June 1961)
Kak trudno rasskazat' mne molodeži (15 December 1963)
Minuvšee leto (Ne Gajdna sonatu prošu povtorit') (1960)
Molody otcy s golubymi koljaskami (29 November 1962)
Peredo mnoj tvoe lico živoe. Pamjati Emme Vygodskoj (September 1964)
Plotina v Peedu (August 1963)
Poetu. Evtušenko. (Ty načal veselo i šumno) (June 1962)
Priznanie (Čem starše delajus', tem ja ljublju sil'nee) (5 February 1962)
Sonnet (Orbity raznie, no ellips ili krug) (14 July 1960)
V zimnem nebe nad toboju (20 December 1960)

1965–67

Moi slova (Slova, kotorye pisala ja kogda to) (June 1966)
Na beregax reki zabvenij. Pamjati E. Vygodskoj (22 October 1966)
Nabrosok stixotv. o D. I. Vygodskom (1963–67)
Ne Bramsa sonatu prošu povtorit' (18 January 1967)
Pamjati Karla Roziorga (My nanjali domik . . .) (17 April 1966)
Pavlu Ivanoviču Petuninu (Prozaiku, pleteščemu korzinki) (April 1965)
Poroj ešče prixodjat (28 June 1967)
Pozdnee priznanie (Vižu vnov' tvoju seduju golovu) [variant] (1967 in a letter)
Starye stixi vozvraščajutsja ko mne (August 1966)
Tebe by nužno ženščinu inuju (1966)
Uslyšannyj razgovor (Ugodlivaja proza nam protivna) (October 1965)
Vse neustojčivo, vse neverno . . . (10 July 1966)
Vse propalo, tol'ko zapax (13 July 1966)

Bibliography

Prose

"Gorod. Povest'." Ts. St. Petersburg: Private Archive of E. G. Polonskaja.

Memoirs

"Mama." Ts. St. Petersburg: Private Archive of E. G. Polonskaja.
"Otkuda vzjalis' stixi." Ts. St. Petersburg: Private Archive of E. G. Polonskaja.
"Žanna Niko." Ts. St. Petersburg: Private Archive of E. G. Polonskaja.
"Lodz." Ts. St. Petersburg: Private Archive of E. G. Polonskaja.
"1908 god. Zanjatie medicinoj. Novye druz'ja." Ts. St. Petersburg: Private Archive of E. G. Polonskaja.
"Russkij bal/1909." Ts. St. Petersburg: Private Archive of E. G. Polonskaja.
"Gorod Jur'jev." Ts. St. Petersburg: Private Archive of E. G. Polonskaja.
"Moe vozvraščenie s fronta." Ts. St. Petersburg: Private Archive of E. G. Polonskaja.
"Petrograd 1917–1918 gg." Ts. St. Petersburg: Private Archive of E. G. Polonskaja.
"Pamjatnaja vstreča (Sergej Esenin)." Ts. St. Petersburg: Private Archive of E. G. Polonskaja.
"Žurnal 'Rabotnica i Krest'janka'. Lidija Čarskaja." Ts. St. Petersburg: Private Archive of E. G. Polonskaja, 1967.
"Jurij Tynjanov." Ts. Ed. and with commentary by M. L. Polonskij. St. Petersburg: Private Archive of E. G. Polonskaja.
"David i Emma Vygodskie." Ts. St. Petersburg: Private Archive of E. G. Polonskaja.
"Iz knigi vospominanij 'Vstreči'." Ts. Ed. M. L. Polonskij and B. Ja. Frezinskij. St. Petersburg: Private Archive of E. G. Polonskaja.

Letters from E. G. Polonskaja

Iz černovikov pis'ma k literaturnomu kritiku. 1924–1926 gg. Ts. Prep. M. L. Polonskij. St. Petersburg: Private Archive of E. G. Polonskaja.
Letters to Il'ja Erenburg. Ličnyj Fond Erenburga, 1204, op. 2, e.x. 2055. TsGALI (Moscow).
Letters to Marietta Šaginjan. Photocopy of typescript from correspondence of E. G. Polonskaja and Marietta Šaginjan. St. Petersburg: Private Archive of E. G. Polonskaja.
Letters to Marija Škapskaja. Ličnij Fond Marii Škapskoj, 2182, op. 1, e.x. 436: 5 Avg. 1924–31 Dek. 1941 G. TsGALI (Moscow).
Letters to Marija Škapskaja. Ličnyj Fond Marii Škapskoj 2182, op. 1, e.x. 437: 1942.I.14–1951.XII.13. TsGALI (Moscow).
"V Sekciju Poetov LO SSP." Ts. St. Petersburg: Private Archive of E. G. Polonskaja.

Bibliography

Letters to E. G. Polonskaja

Čukovskij, Kornej. Letter to E. G. Polonskaja, 7 November 1963. St. Petersburg: Private Archive of E. G. Polonskaja.

Maren'kov, A. Letter to E. G. Polonskaja. January 1964. Fond 344, op. 3, delo 293, Perepiska s Central'nym Izdatel'stvom, Avtorami i Drugimi o Dejatel'nosti Izdatel'stva Sovetskij pisatel', TsGALI (St. Petersburg).

Nikitina, Zoja. Letter to E. G. Polonskaja. 30 November 1963. St. Petersburg: Private Archive of E. G. Polonskaja. Possession of M. L. Polonskij.

Miscellaneous Archival Documents

From the Private Archive of E. G. Polonskaja, St. Petersburg

"Iz prixodo-rasxodnoj literatury, 1935." Ts. Prep. M. L. Polonskij.
"Iz prixodo-rasxodnoj literatury, 1936." Ts. Prep. M. L. Polonskij.
"Iz prixodo-rasxodnoj literatury, 1937." Ts. Prep. M. L. Polonskij.
"Iz prixodo-rasxodnoj literatury, 1946, October 21."

From the Manuscript Room of the Rossijskaja Nacional'naja Biblioteka, St. Petersburg

Fond 602, op. 1, e.x. no. 7: *Pod smertnym ostriem. Stixotvorenija 1921–1922.* Ms.

Fond 602, op. 1, e.x. no. 8: *Pod smertnym ostriem. Stixotvorenija 1921–1922.* Pravl. verstka s avtografom-daritel'noj nadpis'ju Mariette (Šaginjan).

SECONDARY SOURCES ON ELIZAVETA POLONSKAJA

Anatol'jev, A. Review of *Izbrannoe. Zvezda* 10 (1966): 219–20.

Azarov, Vsevolod. "Glazami molodymi." *Leningradskaja Pravda,* 31 August 1966, 3.

Barabašev, O. "Naletčiki na revoljuciju ili o tom, kak Gosizdat izdal zamečatel'noe posobie k rasprostraneniju xuliganstva." *Leningradskaja Pravda* 59 (12 March 1925): 7.

Baril', L. "Literaturnye zametki." *Priboj* 1 (1928): 40–42.

Baxrax, A. "Elizaveta Polonskaja, *Znamen'ja.*" Review of *Dni* (Berlin), 11 February 1923, 14.

Braun, Jakov. "Desjat' strannikov v 'osjazaemoe ničto'." *Sibirskie ogni* 1 (1924): 201–40.

Braun, Nikolaj. "Recenzija na knigu Elizavety Polonskoj 'Stixotvorenija i poemy,' 9/17/1958." Fond 344, op. 2, delo 636: "Recenzii na rukopisi avtografov na bukvy P-Ja. Leningradskoe otdelenie izdatel'stva 'Sovetskij pisatel'." TsGALI (St. Petersburg).

Brett-Harrison, Joy. "Dichterin in bewegter Zeit. Leben und Werk der Elizaveta Polonskaja (1890–1969)." Lizentiatsarbeit der Philosophischen

Fakultät der Universität Zürich. Master's thesis, University of Zurich, 1990.

Čumandrin, M. "Polnocennaja zajavka." Rev. *Večernaja krasnaja gazeta*, 11 June 1935.

Davydov, Zinovyj. "Na pamjat' o tjaželom gode." *Sovremennoe obozrenie* 2 (1922): 5–6.

Dligač, Lev. "O novyx stixax E. Polonskoj." *Literaturnaja gazeta*, 15 June 1937.

Dorfman, Leslie. "Elizaveta Polonskaia." *Russian Women Writers*. Ed. Christine Tomei, 1053–83. New York: Garland Press, 1999.

———. Dorfman, L. "Serapion Sister: The Poetry of E. G. Polonskaja." Ph.D. dissertation. University of Michigan, 1996.

———. "Serapionova Sestra: Elizaveta Polonskaja i kritičeskoe vosprijatie 'ženskoj liriki'." *Preobraženie* 4 (1996).

Ejxenbaum, Boris. "Recenzija na sborniki V. Roždestvenskogo i E. Polonskoj." *Knižnyj ugol* 7 (1921): 37–42.

"Elizaveta Grigor'jevna Polonskaja." *Russkie sovetskie pisateli: Poety (sovetskij period)*. Bibliografičeskij ukazatel'. Tom 19. St. Petersburg: Rossijskaja Nacional'naja Biblioteka 1996, 134–55.

Erenburg, Il'ja. "Elizaveta Polonskaja, *Znamen'ja*; Irina Odoevceva *Dvor čudes*." *Novaja russkaja kniga* 3 (1922): 9.

———. *Ljudi, gody, žizn'*. Moscow: Sovetskij pisatel', 1961.

———. "Pis'ma." Prep. A. I. Rubaškin. *Voprosy literatury* 12 (1987).

Fedorov, R. "Devuški našego goroda." Rev. *Večernij Leningrad* 242, no. 869 (13 October 1948).

Forš, Ol'ga. "Sumasšedšij korabl'." *Sumasšedšij korabl': Roman, rasskazy*. Ed. T. Mel'nikova and T. Stepanova. Leningrad: Gosudarstvennoe Izdatel'stvo Xudožestvennoj Literatury, 1988.

Frezinskij, B. Ja., and V. Popov, eds. *Il'ja Erenburg: Xronika žizni i tvorčestva v dokumentax, pis'max, vyskazyvanijax i soobščenijax pressy, svidetel'stvax sovremennikov*. Tom I 1891–1923. St. Petersburg: Izdatel'stvo "Lina," 1993.

Galuškin, A. "U stixov osobaja sud'ba." *Medicinskaja gazeta*, 16 January 1987.

Granin, D., et al. "Pamjati E. G. Polonskoj." *Literaturnaja gazeta*, 22 January 1969, 5.

Guber, P. "Novye sborniki stixov." *Letopis' Doma Literatorov* 3 (1921): 14.

Gutner, M. "Gody poeta." Rev. *Literaturnyj Leningrad*, 8 June 1935, 3.

Ivanov, Georgij. "Elizaveta Polonskaja. Znamen'ja. Erato: Petrograd." Rev. *Cex poetov* 3 (1922): 67.

Ivanov, Vjačeslav. "Sud'by Serapionovyx Brat'jev i put' Vsevoloda Ivanova." In *Literaturnaja gruppa "Serapionovy Brat'ja: istoki, poiski, tradicii, meždunarodnyj kontekst. Tezisy dokladov*," 3–21. International conference, St. Petersburg, 1995.

Kasack, Wolfgang. *Dictionary of Russian Literature since 1917.* New York: Columbia University Press, 1988.
Kaverin, Veniamin. *Epilog. Memuary.* Moscow: Moskovskij Rabočij, 1989.
Kelly, Catriona. *A History of Russian Women's Writing 1820–1992.* Oxford: Clarendon Press, 1994.
Kern, Gary. "Lev Lunc: Serapion Brother." Ph.D. diss., Princeton University, 1969.
———, comp. and ed. "Lev Lunc i 'Serapionovy brat'ja': Publikacija i kommentarii Gari Kerna." Letters. *Novyj žurnal* 82 (March 1966): 136–92.
———, comp. and ed. "Lev Lunc i 'Serapionovy brat'ja': Publikacija i kommentarii Gari Kerna." Letters. *Novyj žurnal* 83 (June 1966): 132–84.
Kern, Gary, and Christopher Collins, eds. *The Serapion Brothers: A Critical Anthology.* Ann Arbor, Mich.: Ardis Publishers, 1975.
Kireeva, M. "Iz vospominanij (Il'ja Erenburg v Pariže 1909 goda)." Introd. B. Ja. Frezinskij. *Voprosy literatury* 9 (1982): 144–57.
Kuzmin, Mixail. "Parnasskie zarosli." *Zavtra: Literaturno-kritičeskij sbornik pod red. Evg. Zamjatina, M. Kuzmina, i M. Lozinskogo* 1 (1921): 114–22.
Lelevič, G. "Pervyj akt materialističeskoj kritiki (metodologičeskie zametki)." *Pečat' i revoljucija* 1 (1928): 32–44.
Lučanskij, Mixail. "Ščepki." *Komsomolija* 10 (1926): 48–57.
Luknickaja, Vera. *Pered toboj zemlja.* Leningrad: Lenizdat, 1988.
Lunc, Lev. "Na Zapad! Reč' na sobranii Serapionovyx Brat'jev 2-ogo dekabrja 1922 G." In *Lev Lunc: Rodina i drugie proizvedenija.* Serija "Pamjat'," 1981.
———. "Novye Poety." *Irida, literaturnaja gazeta, pod red. A. G. Fomina.* Fond 568, A. G. Fomin, op. 1, e.x. 125 (1922). St. Petersburg: IRLI.
Malaxov, Sergej. Review of *Uprjamyj kalendar'*. *Krasnaja nov'* Kn. 4 (1929): 230–32.
Meškov, Ju. "Izbrannoe." *Neva* 10 (1967): 195.
Minc, Z. "E. G. Polonskaja i ee literaturnye vospominanija." *Trudy po russkoj i slavjanskoj filologii* 6. *Učenye zapiski tartusskogo universiteta* 139 (1963): 374–78.
———. "E. Polonskaja, *Stixotvorenija i poema.*" *Zvezda* 11 (1960): 217.
Mirsky, D. S. *Contemporary Russian Literature 1881–1925.* 1926. Reprint. New York: Kraus Reprint Co., 1972.
Ninov, A. "Elizaveta Polonskaja. Stixotvorenija i poemy, 2/20/59." Fond 344, op. 2, delo 671, "Leningradskoe Otdelenie Izdatel'stva 'Sovetskij pisatel'," Redakcionnyj otdel," TsGALI (St. Petersburg).
Oksenov, Innokenty. *"Pod kamennym doždem." Petrogradskaja Pravda,* 17 June 1922, 5.
Orlov, V. "Elizaveta Polonskaja. Dorogi v buduščee, 3/1963." Fond 344, op. 3, delo 215, "Leningradskoe Otdelenie Izdatel'stva 'Sovetskij pisatel', Recenzii na rukopisi," TsGALI (St. Petersburg).

Bibliography

Pavlov, Mixail. "Elizaveta Polonskaja, *Znamen'ja.*" *Letopis' Doma Literatorov,* 25 February 1922, 9.
Polonskij, Mixail, and Boris Frezinskij. Fwd. to Publication of Poems by E. Polonskaja. *Poezija. Al'manax* 42 (1985): 121.
Popova, Ljubov'. "Elizaveta Polonskaja." *Den' poezii.* Leningrad: Sovetskij pisatel', 1969; 117–18.
Rubaškin, A. I. "Ne sotvori kumira." *Literaturnaja gazeta,* 10 April 1991, 10.
———. "Vernost' poezii." *Den' poezii.* Leningrad: Sovetskij pisatel', 1981; 348.
Šaginjan, Marietta. "Post Scriptum." *Sobranie sočinenij v devjati tomax. Tom vtoroj.* Moscow: Xudožestvennaja Literatura, 1986; 735–39.
Šklovskij, Viktor. *A Sentimental Journey. Memoirs, 1917–1922.* Trans. Richard Sheldon, 267–68. Ithaca and London: Cornell University Press, 1970.
———. "Serapionovy Brat'ja." *Knižnyj ugol* 7 (1921): 18–21.
Solov'jev, Grigorij. "Ol'xa i v poezii ne v česti." *Otvetstvennost' pered vremenem: sbornik kritičeskix statej.* Moscow: Sovetskaja Rossija, 1963; 97–108.
"'Sredy' Doma Literatorov." *Literaturnye zapiski* 2 (1922): 22.
Štejnman, Zelig. "Bol'šoe darovanie. 70-letie Elizavety Polonskoj." *Večernij Leningrad* 50, no. 4469 (1 July 1960): 4.
Švarc, Evgenij. *Živu bespokojno . . . iz dnevnikov.* Leningrad: Sovetskij pisatel', 1990.
Tarasenkov, A. "Nevoploščennaja tema." *Literaturnaja gazeta,* 17 November 1945.
Timenčik, R. D. "Evrejskie motivy v russkoj poezii načala XX veka (Tri predvaritel'nyx zamečanija)." *Tynjanovskij sbornik: Pjatye Tynjanovskie Čtenija,* 1994.
Timina, Svetlana. "Elizaveta Polonskaja v krugu 'Serapionovyx brat'ev'." *Literaturnaja gruppa "Serapionovy brat'ja": istoki, poiski, tradicii, meždunarodnyj kontekst. Tezisy dokladov,* 64–66. International Conference, St. Petersburg, 13–16 March 1995.
Trotskij, Leon. *Literature and Revolution.* Ann Arbor: University of Michigan Press, 1968.
Trubilova, Elena. "Polonskaia, Elizaveta Grigor'evna." *Dictionary of Russian Women Writers.* Ed. Marina Ledkovsky, Charlotte Rosenthal, and Mary Zirin, 512–14. Westport, Conn., and London: Greenwood Press, 1994.
Vygodskij, David. "Pod kamennym doždem. Review." *Kniga i revoljucija* 3 (1923): 76.
Vyšeslavceva, S. "15 let poetičeskoj raboty." Review of *Goda. Xudožestvennaja literatura* 10 (1935): 5–10.

Žuk, O. A. "'Čertovo koleso' i gorodskaja kul'tura." *Kinovedčeskie zapiski* 7 (1990): 56–61.

OTHER MATERIALS CITED

Abramsky, Chimen. "The Biro-Bidzhan Project, 1927–1959." Ed. Lionel Kochan, 62–75. *The Jews in Soviet Russia since 1917.* New York: Oxford University Press, 1970.

Alexandrova, Vera. "Jews in Soviet Literature," *Russian Jewry 1917–1967.* Ed. Gregor Aronson, Jacob Frumkin, Alexis Goldenweiser, and Joseph Levitan. New York: Thomas Yoseloff, 1968.

Anastas'jev, N. "Formula nepravdy (po povodu pis'ma Professora E. Brauna)." *Voprosy literatury*, no. 10 (1967): 97–114.

Aronson, Gregor. "The Jewish Question during the Stalin Era." *Russian Jewry 1917–1967.* Ed. Gregor Aronson, Jacob Frumkin, Alexis Goldenweiser, and Joseph Levitan, 171–208. New York, South Brunswick, and London: Thomas Yoseloff, 1967.

Averincev, S. "Sud'ba i vest' Osipa Mandel'štama." Introd. to Osip Mandel'štam, 5–64. *Sobranie sočinenij v dvux tomax.* Moscow: Xudožestvennaja literatura, 1990.

Axmatova, Anna. *Sobranie sočinenij v dvux tomax.* Moscow: Xudožestvennaja literatura, 1986.

———. *Sočinenija. Tom pervyj.* Munich: Inter-Language Literary Associates, 1965.

Bjalyj, G. A., ed. *Poety 1880–1890-x godov.* Leningrad: Sovetskij pisatel', 1972.

Blok, Aleksandr. *Sobranie sočinenij v vos'mi tomax. Tom pervyj.* Moscow and Leningrad: Gosudarstvennoe Izdatel'stvo Xudožestvennoj literatury, 1960.

———. *Stixotvorenija v trex tomax.* St. Petersburg: Severo-Zapad, 1994.

Brjusov, Valerij. *Sočinenija v dvux tomax.* Moscow: Xudožestvennaja literatura, 1987.

Brown, Edward. *Russian Literature since the Revolution.* New York: Collier Books, 1963.

Cavanagh, Clare. *Osip Mandelstam and the Modernist Creation of Tradition.* Princeton, N.J.: Princeton University Press, 1995.

The Central Committee Resolution and Ždanov's Speech on the Journals 'Zvezda' and 'Leningrad'. Doklad T. Ždanova O žurnalax 'Zvezda' I 'Leningrad'. Bilingual ed. Trans. Felicity Ashton and Irina Tidmarsh. Royal Oak, Mich.: Strathcona Publishing Company, 1978.

Cioran, Samuel. "The Russian Sappho: Mirra Lokhvitskaya." *Russian Literature Triquarterly* 9 (spring 1974): 317–35.

Cvetaeva, Marina. *Stixotvorenija i poemy.* Biblioteka Poeta. Leningrad: Sovetskij pisatel', 1990.

Dal', Vladimir. *Tolkovyj slovar' živago velikorusskago jazyka*. 1882. Reprint. Moscow: Russkij Jazyk, 1990.
Edgerton, William. "The Serapion Brothers: An Early Soviet Controversy." *American Slavic and East European Review* 8, no. 1 (1949): 47–64.
Esenin, Sergej. *Stixotvorenija i poemy*. Biblioteka Poeta. Bol'šaja Serija, Izdanie tret'je. Leningrad: Sovetskij pisatel', 1986.
Etov, V. "Sovetskaja literatura i ee amerikanskie istolkovateli." *Voprosy literatury* 11 (1966): 87.
Ettinger, Shmuel. "The Jews in Russia at the Outbreak of the Revolution." *The Jews in Soviet Russia since 1917*. Ed. Lionel Kochan. New York: Oxford University Press, 1970.
Fedin, Konstantin. *Gor'kij sredi nas*. Moscow: Sovetskij pisatel', 1977.
Friedberg, Maurice. "The Jewish Search in Russian Literature." *Prooftexts* 4 (1984): 93–105.
Gece, B., ed. *Biblija: Knigi Svjaščennago Pisanija, Vetxogo i Novago Zaveta, Kanoničeskija*. Warsaw: Religioznoe Izdatel'stvo B. Gece, 1939.
Gitelman, Zvi. *A Century of Ambivalence: The Jews of Russia and the Soviet Union, 1881 to the Present*. New York: Schocken Books, 1988.
Gor'kij i sovetskie pisateli: neizdannaja perepiska. Vol. 70 of *Literaturnoe nasledstvo*. Moscow: Izdatel'stvo Akademii Nauk, 1963.
Gor'kij, Maksim. "Gor'kij o molodyx." *Žizn' iskusstva* 22 (1923): 561–63. Repr. in *Gor'kij i sovetskie pisateli: neizdannaja perepiska*, vol. 70 of *Literaturnoe nasledstvo*. Moscow: Izdatel'stvo Akademii Nauk, 1963.
———. "V glubine Rossii." *Polnoe sobranie sočinenij. Tom šestnadcatyj. Povest', rasskazy, očerki, stixi 1917–1924*. Moscow: Nauka, 1973.
Gorodetskij, Sergej. "Zelen' pod plesen'ju." *Izvestija*, no. 42 (22 February 1922).
Gumilev, N. S. "Anatomija stixotvorenija." *Sobranie sočinenij v 4-x tomax*. T. 4. Ed. G. P. Struve and B. A. Fillipov, 185–89. Washington, D.C.: Kamkin, 1968.
Heldt, Barbara. "Motherhood in a Cold Climate: The Poetry and Career of Mariia Škapskaia." *Russian Review* 51 (1992): 160–71.
Ičin, Kornelija. "'Obez'jany idut' L'va Lunca." In *Literaturnaja gruppa 'Serapionovy Brat'ja': istoki, poiski, tradicii, meždunarodnyj kontekst. Tezisy Dokladov*, 63. International Conference, St. Petersburg, 1995.
Inber, Vera. "O ženskix stixax." *Literaturnaja gazeta* 45, no. 232–33 (29 January 1933): 7.
Kaverin, Veniamin. "An Open Letter to Konstantin Fedin." *Survey* 68 (1968): 187–88.
———. *Osveščennye okna: Trilogija*. In *Sobranie sočinenij. Tom sed'moj*. Moscow: Xudožestvennaja literatura, 1983.
———. *"Zdravtsvuj, Brat! Pisat' očen' trudno . . ."* Moscow: Sovetskij pisatel', 1965.

Ketchian, Sonia. "Anna Axmatova." Ed. Victor Terras, 15. *Handbook of Russian Literature.* New Haven, Conn.: Yale University Press, 1985.

Kolesnikova, G. "Obraz novoj ženščiny v xudožestvennoj literature." *Literaturnaja gazeta* 11, no. 239 (5 March 1933).

Kollontai, Aleksandra. "Novaja ženščina." *Novaja moral' i rabočij klass.* Moscow: Izdatel'stvo VCIK, 1919.

———. *Selected Writings of Alexandra Kollontai.* Westport, Conn.: Lawrence Hill and Co., 1977.

———. *Ženščina na perelome (psixologičeskie etjudy).* Moscow, 1923.

Kron, A. "Literaturnye zapiski." In *Literaturnaja Moskva,* vol. 2. Moscow, 1956.

Levin, Jurij I., D. M. Segal, R. D. Timenčik, V. N. Toporov, and T. V. Civ'jan. "Russkaja semantičeskaja poetika kak potencial'naja kul'turnaja paradigma." *Russian Literature* 7–8 (1974): 47–82.

Literaturnaja gruppa "Serapionovy Brat'ja": istoki, poiski, tradicii, meždunarodnyj kontekst. Tezisy Dokladov. International Conference—Abstracts, St. Petersburg, 1995.

Lunc, Lev. "Detskij smex." *Žizn' iskusstva,* 29–30 November 1919.

———. "Počemu my Serapionovy Brat'ja." *Literaturnye zapiski* 3 (1922): 31.

———. *Rodina i drugie proizvedenija.* Ed. M. Vajnštejn. Jerusalem: Pamjat', 1981.

L'vov-Rogačevskij, V. *A History of Russian Jewish Literature.* Ed. and trans. Arthur Levin. Ann Arbor, Mich.: Ardis, 1979.

Maguire, Robert A. *Red Virgin Soil: Soviet Literature in the 1920s.* Princeton, N.J.: Princeton University Press, 1968.

Mandel'štam, Osip, L. Ja. Ginsburg, et al., eds. *Kamen'.* Leningrad: Nauka, 1990.

———. "Slovo i kul'tura." *Sobranie sočinenija v trex tomax. Tom vtoroj: Proza.* New York: Inter-Language Literary Associates, 1971, 222–27.

———. *Sobranie sočinenij v dvux tomax.* Moscow: Xudožestvennaja literatura, 1990.

McLean, Hugh, and Walter Vickery. Introd. to *The Year of Protest, 1956: An Anthology of Soviet Literary Materials,* 3–34. New York: Vintage, 1961.

McVay, Gordon. *Esenin: A Life.* Ann Arbor, Mich.: Ardis, 1976.

Metčenko, A. "Istorizm i dogma." *Novyj mir* 12 (1956): 223–38.

Metčenko, A., A. Dement'jev, and G. Lomidze. "Za glubokuju razrabotku istorii sovetskoj literatury." *Kommunist,* no. 12 (1956): 83–100.

Minokin, M. "'Serapionovy Brat'ja' v zarubežnyx istolkovanijax." *Russkaja Literatura,* no. 1 (1971): 177–86.

Muratova, K. D. *M. Gor'kij v bor'be za razvitie sovetskoj literatury.* Moscow and Leningrad: Izdatel'stvo Akademii Nauk SSSR, 1958.

Naiman, Eric. "The Case of Chubarov Alley: Collective Rape, Utopian Desire and the Mentality of NEP." *Russian History/Histoire Russe* 17, no. 1 (1990): 1–30.

———. "Historectomies: On the Metaphysics of Reproduction in a Utopian Age." Ed. Jane Costlow, Stephanie Sandler, and Judith Vowles. *Sexuality and the Body in Russian Culture.* Stanford, Calif.: Stanford University Press, 1993, 255–76.

———. "Revolutionary Anorexia (NEP as Female Complaint)." *Slavic and East European Journal* (1993): 305–25.

Nakhimovsky, Alice Stone. *Russian-Jewish Literature and Identity.* Baltimore: Johns Hopkins University Press, 1992.

Nekrasov, N. A. *Polnoe sobranie sočinenij v 15 tomax. Tom I.* Leningrad: Nauka, 1981.

Nilsson, N. A. "'Proslavim, brat'ja' and 'Na kamennyx otrogax': Remarks on Two Poems by Osip Mandel'štam." *Slavic Poetics. Essays in Honor of Kiril Taranovskij.* The Hague and Paris: Mouton, 1973, 295–97.

"O politike partii v oblasti xudožestvennoj literatury (Rezoljucija CK RKP(b))." *Pravda,* 1 July 1925, 6.

Očerk istorii russkoj sovetskoj literatury, Čast' I. Moscow: Izdatel'stvo Akademii Nauk SSSR, 1954.

Odarčenko, Petro. "Ševčenko in Soviet Literary Criticism." Ed. Volodymyr Mijakovsk'kyj and George Y. Shevelov. *Taras Ševčenko 1814–1861: A Symposium.* Ukrainian Academy of Arts and Sciences in the United States. 'S-Gravenhage: Mouton and Co., 1962.

"Otvet Serapionovyx Brat'jev Sergeju Gorodetskomu." *Novaja Rossija,* no. 1 (1922): 160.

Pachmuss, Temira, ed. and trans. *Women Writers in Russian Modernism: An Anthology.* Urbana: University of Illinois Press, 1978.

Pervyj vsesojuznyj s'jezd sovetskix pisatelej 1934. Stenografičeskij otčet. Moscow: Sovetskij pisatel', 1990.

Peterburgskij sbornik 1922. Poety i Belletristy. St. Petersburg: Izdatel'stvo žurnala "Letopis' Doma Literatorov," 1922.

Proffer, Carl, et al., eds. *Russian Literature of the Twenties: An Anthology.* Ann Arbor, Mich.: Ardis, 1987.

Propp, Vladimir. *Narodnye liričeskie pesni.* Leningrad: Sovetskij pisatel', 1961.

Puškin, A. S. *Polnoe sobranie sočinenij v desjati tomax.* Moscow: Izdatel'stvo Akademii Nauk SSSR, 1957.

Ronen, Omry. "'Bednye Izidy': Ob odnoj vol'noj šutke Osipa Mandel'štama." *Literaturnoe obozrenie* 11 (1991): 91–92.

———. *The Fallacy of the Silver Age in Twentieth Century Russian Literature.* Amsterdam: Harwood Academic Publishers, 1997.

Salajczyk, Janina. "'Vosstanie veščej' L'va Lunca v rusle katastrofičeskoj literatury XX veka." In *Literaturnaja gruppa "Serapionovy Brat'ja": istoki,*

poiski, tradicii, meždunarodnyj kontekst. Tezisy Dokladov, 64. International Conference, St. Petersburg, 1995.
Serapionovy Brat'ja. Comp. and ed. A. A. Gugnin. Moscow: Vysšaja škola, 1994.
Serapionovy Brat'ja: Almanax pervyj. St. Petersburg: Alkonost', 1922.
"Serapionovy Brat'ja o sebe." *Literaturnye zapiski* 3 (1922): 25–31.
Sheldon, Richard. "Šklovskij, Gor'kij, and the Serapion Brothers." *Slavic and East European Journal* 12, no. 1 (1968): 1–13.
Šklovskij, Viktor B. "Probniki." *Gamburgskij sčet: stat'ji, vospominanija, esse.* Moscow: Sovetskij pisatel', 1990; 186–87.
———. "Serapionovy Brat'ja." *Knižnyj ugol,* no. 7 (1921): 18–21.
Sloane, David. *Aleksandr Blok and the Dynamics of the Lyric Cycle.* Columbus, Ohio: Slavica Publishers, 1988.
Slonimskij, Mixail. *Kniga vospominanij.* Moscow and Leningrad: Sovetskij pisatel', 1966.
Stender-Peterson, A. D., and Stephan Congrat-Butler, eds. *Anthology of Old Russian Literature.* New York: Columbia University Press, 1962.
Stites, Richard. *Russian Popular Culture: Entertainment and Society since 1900.* Cambridge and New York: Cambridge University Press, 1992.
———. *The Women's Liberation Movement in Russia: Feminism, Nihilism and Bolshevism, 1860–1930.* Princeton, N.J.: Princeton University Press, 1978.
Tolstoj, Aleksej. "Sestry." *Polnoe sobranie sočinenij.* Moscow: Gosudarstvennoe Izdatel'stvo Xudožestvennoj Literatury, 1947.
Tomaševskij, Jurij. "Zoščenko i ego 'Serapionovy Brat'ja'." In *Literaturnaja gruppa "Serapionovy Brat'ja": istoki, poiski, tradicii, meždunarodnyj kontekst. Tezisy Dokladov,"* 33–34. International Conference, St. Petersburg, 1995.
Toporov, V. N. *Axmatova i Blok (k probleme postroenija poetičeskogo dialoga).* Modern Russian Literature and Culture 5. Berkeley, Calif.: Berkeley Slavic Specialties, 1981.
Tynjanov, Jurij. "Serapionovy Brat'ja. Al'manax pervyj." Rev. *Kniga i revoljucija* 6, no. 18 (1922): 62–64.
Učenova, V. V. *Caricy muz: russkie poetessy XIX-načala XX vekov.* Moscow, 1989.
Vatson, M. "Iz Larry." *Vestnik Evropy* 5 (1878). Cited in N. A. Nekrasov, *Polnoe sobranie sočinenij v pjatnadcati tomax. Tom I.* Leningrad: Nauka, 1981.
Voronskij, Aleksandr. "Serapionovy Brat'ja. Al'manax Pervyj." Rev. *Krasnaja nov'* 3 (1922): 265–67.
Zamjatin, Evgenij. "Serapionovy Brat'ja." *Literaturnye zapiski* 1 (1922): 8.
———. *"A Soviet Heretic:" Essays by Evgenij Zamjatin.* Trans. Mirra Ginsburg. Chicago: University of Chicago Press, 1970.

Bibliography

Zenkovsky, Sergei, ed. *Medieval Russia's Epics, Chronicles and Tales*. Rev. and enl. ed. New York: E. P. Dutton, 1963.

Žirmunskij, Viktor. "Poetika Aleksandra Bloka." *Teorija literatury, poetika, stilistika (Izbrannye trudy)*. Leningrad: Nauka, 1977; 212–17.

Zoščenko, Mixail. *Uvažaemye graždane: parodii, rasskazy, fel'etony, satiričeskie zametki, pis'ma k pisatel'ju, odnoaktnye komedii*. Moscow: Izdatel'stvo Knižnaja Palata, 1991.

Index

Abramenko, I., 179
Abramsky, Chimen, 147, 234
Acmeism, 8, 58, 85, 153, 210
Aleksandr II, 91
Alexandrova, Vera, 64, 225
Anastas'ja Petrovna, 42–43, 191
Anastas'jev, N., 14, 216
Anatol'ev, A., 43, 104, 207, 222, 229, 237, 241
Andreev, Leonid, 21
Andreeva-Del'mas, Ljubov', 108
anti-Semitism, 2, 3, 12, 19, 20, 45, 47, 60–70, 100, 121, 156–57, 163, 172, 201, 211, 213, 221, 231
Appollinaire, 22
architecture, 58, 85–87
Aronson, Gregor, 225, 233
Arvatov, Boris, 9
Aš, Boris, 209
Averbax, Leopold, 33
Averincev, S., 55, 224
Axmatova, Anna, 7, 8, 40, 46, 51–52, 55, 70–72, 78, 93, 95, 99, 114, 126–29, 133–34, 142, 145–46, 175, 189, 196, 202, 209, 211, 223, 226, 228, 230, 232, 234
Azarov, Vsevolod, 156, 235

Babuškina, Nata, 35, 147
Bal'mont, Konstantin, 21
Barabašev, O., 118, 219, 231
Baril', L., 118–19, 219, 229, 231
Baudelaire, Charles, 48
Baxrax, Aleksandr, 63–64, 225, 226
Belinskij, Vissarion, 19
Belyj, Andrej, 68, 77–78
Berggol'c, Ol'ga, 204–5, 240
Bertram, Elizaveta, 25, 141, 223
Beseda (Conversation) [Berlin], 215

Biblical sources, 3, 19, 64–65, 68–70, 72, 81, 101–2, 141–42, 144, 191, 200, 211–12, 226
Birobidzhan, 146–47, 234
Bizet, Georges, 108
Blok, Aleksandr, 20, 21, 48–49, 53, 70, 72–73, 91–96, 108, 111, 119, 223, 228–30
Bolsheviks, 2, 8, 9, 11, 20–23, 26, 32, 36, 45, 47, 60, 62, 95–97, 105, 106, 108, 110, 160, 180, 182, 206, 210
Brahms, Johannes, 190–91, 239
Braun, Jakov, 211–12, 242
Braun, Nikolaj, 179, 184, 220, 238
Brecht, Bertold, 27, 35, 141
Brett-Harrison, Joy, 1, 40, 53, 68–69, 98, 105, 128, 208, 213, 218, 222, 223, 226, 228, 229, 232
Brjullov, Karl, 98, 157–58
Brjusov, Valerij, 21, 77–78, 86–87, 153, 227
Brown, Edward, 5, 14, 106, 216, 229, 240
Browning, Robert, 27, 155
Buxarin, Nikolaj, 109, 112

Calderón, 27, 172
Carmen, 28, 106–11, 113–16, 118, 122, 128, 131, 179–80, 206, 219, 229, 230, 231
Čarskaja, Lidija, 221
Caucasus, 128–29, 131–33, 143
Cavanagh, Clare, 62–63, 225
Čexov, Anton, 104
Čikovani, 44
Cioran, Samuel, 223
Civil war, 24, 45, 52, 56, 58, 67, 77, 95, 196, 206
classical mythology, references to, 54–56, 129, 161

Index

Collins, Christopher, 214
Costlow, Jane, 230
Crusoe, Robinson, 54–55
Čudakova, Marietta, 44–45, 222
Čukovskij, Kornej, 1, 6, 27, 44, 45, 187–88, 194, 222, 226, 227
Čumandrin, Mixail, 36, 82, 219, 227
Cvetaeva, Marina, 145–46, 196, 234

Dal', Vladimir, 223, 229
Daniel, Julij, 15
Davydov, Zinovij, 223
Dawson, Ernest, 155
de Gabriak, Čerubina, 45
Dement'jev, A., 12–13, 215
Den' poeta (*Day of the Poet*), 42, 174, 238
Den' poezii (*Day of Poetry*), 42, 174, 188, 189, 199, 203–4, 206, 238, 239, 240, 241
Dni (*Days*) [Berlin], 225
Donat, Alexander, 241
Dorfman, Leslie, 241
Dostoevskij, Fjodor, 119

Edgerton, William, 214
Ejxenbaum, Boris, 1, 24, 54, 69, 73, 213, 218, 223, 226
Erenburg, Il'ja, 1, 15, 20–22, 24, 30, 38, 42, 44, 45, 48, 50, 63–64, 67, 68, 123, 139, 155, 159, 169, 189, 193–95, 201, 205, 217, 221, 222, 225, 239, 240, 241
Esenin, Sergej, 5, 45, 118–22, 126, 131, 197, 211, 231, 242
Etov, V., 216
Ettinger, Shmuel, 225
Evtušenko, Evgenij, 189, 200–1

Fadeev, Aleksandr, 38
fascism, 35, 148, 156, 172, 194
Fedin, Konstantin, 1, 2, 4, 5–7, 10–16, 44, 67, 187, 213, 214, 216
Fedorov, R., 41, 222
Fejgina, Bron'ka, 199, 240
Fellow Travelers, 5, 9–10
Ferberg, Mixail, 30, 34, 37, 132, 145, 154, 202, 220
Fillipov, B. A., 226
First Congress of Soviet Writers, 11, 33, 215
folklore (Russian), 58, 92–95, 110–12, 115, 119, 164
Fomin, A. G., 226
Forš, Ol'ga, 44, 207, 241

Fort, Paul, 22
Frezinskij, Boris, 106, 209–10, 217, 218, 222, 225, 229, 241
Friedberg, Maurice, 61, 224
Froman, Mixail, 159, 235
Frug, Semen, 66, 133

Galuškin, Aleksandr, 42, 167, 175, 209, 222, 237, 241
Gerasimov, Ju. K., 228
Gerasimov, Mixail, 22
Ginzburg, L. Ja., 225, 227
Gitelman, Zvi, 60, 62, 224
Goebbels, P. J., 162
Goethe, Johann W., 176
Gogol', Nikolaj, 100
Gor'kij, Maksim, 2, 5–8, 10–12, 68, 95–96, 213, 214, 215, 216, 228
Gorodetskij, Sergej, 8, 13, 62, 214, 225
Granin, Daniil, 241
Grjaklova, N. Ju., 228
Gruzdev, Il'ja, 4, 6, 24, 76
Guber, P., 63, 225
Gudok (*Train Whistle*), 40, 173
Gumilev, Nikolaj, 2, 6, 15, 24, 33, 44, 53, 62–63, 153, 175, 194, 207
Gumilevskij, Lev, 109
Gutner, Mixail, 81, 227

Heine, Heinrich, 19
Heldt, Barbara, 32, 220
Hitler, Adolf, 162–63
Hoffman, E. T. A., 6, 211
House of Arts, 6, 8, 10, 15, 24–26, 33, 44, 45, 206, 208
House of Scholars, 6
House of Writers, 6–8, 10, 44, 76
Hugo, Victor, 3, 176

Ibsen, Henrik, 20, 27
Ičin, Kornelia, 216
Inber, Vera, 22, 28, 142, 207, 234
Irida, 226
Ivanov, Georgij, 63, 225
Ivanov, Vjačeslav 11, 215
Ivanov, Vsevolod, 1, 2, 4–8, 10–13, 26, 33, 44, 67, 187, 215
Izvestija, 8, 11, 142, 214, 234

Jakunina, A. P., 184–85
Jammes, Francis, 22

264

Index

Jewish Question, 2–3, 12, 18, 19, 20, 27–28, 36, 47, 59–70, 100, 132–34, 142, 146–47, 156–57, 163, 172, 198–201, 208, 211, 224–25, 233
journalism, 2, 27, 31, 32, 41, 136
Judenič', Nikolaj (General), 69
Junost' (Youth), 189

Kalinin, Mixail, 144, 147
Kamenev, Lev, 32, 106, 109
Kasack, Wolfgang, 2–3, 213
Kaverin, Veniamin, 1, 2, 4, 6, 7, 12–16, 26, 27, 38, 45, 67, 68, 105, 118, 187, 211, 216, 218, 229
Kelly, Catriona, 210, 241
Kennedy, John F., 42
Kerenskij, Aleksandr, 105
Kern, Gary, 5, 8, 13, 14, 214, 216, 218, 219, 225–26, 231–32
Ketchian, Sonia, 51, 223
Kipling, Rudyard, 26, 27, 80, 105, 141, 155, 227
Kireeva, Marija, 21, 48, 50, 159, 217, 223
Kirov, Sergej, 32, 143, 148
Kiselev, Igor' N., 40, 191, 120
Kniga i revoljucija (Revolution and the Book), 214, 227
Knižnyj ugol (Book Corner), 213, 215, 218
Kochan, Lionel, 225, 234
Kolčak, Aleksandr (General), 28, 107
Kolesnikova, G., 142, 234
Kollontai, Aleksandra, 3, 30, 79, 109–11, 219, 227, 230
Komarovo, 190, 221
Kommisarova, Marija, 220
Kommunist, 215
Komsomolija, 229
Kovš (The Dipper), 217, 218, 219, 230, 232
Krasnaja gazeta (Red Gazette), 136, 142
Krasnaja nov' (Red Virgin Soil), 8, 10, 214, 228, 230
Krasnyj žurnal dlja vsex (Red Journal for All), 230, 232
Kron, A., 215
Kropotkin, Petr, 105, 181
Kuzmin, Mixail, 8, 63, 225
Kuznecova, O. A., 228

La Fon, Nellie, 159
Lay of Igor's Campaign (Slovo o pl'ku Igoreve), 56, 224

Ledkovsky, Marina, 242
Lelevič, G., 231
Lemberg, Rozalija Grigor'jevna, 19, 160
Lenin, Vladimir, 5, 20, 21, 95–96, 106, 117, 122, 135, 142, 143, 168
Leningrad, 4, 11, 32, 215, 231, 232, 236, 237
Leningrad Association of Proletarian Writers (LAPP), 33, 135
Leningradskaja pravda, 27, 32, 136, 142, 219, 232, 235
Leningradskij rabočij (Leningrad Worker), 232
Leninskie iskry (Lenin's Little Sparks), 27
Lermontov, Mixail, 82, 90, 156
Lesinski, Oscar, 22
Leskov, Nikolaj, 119
Letopis' Doma Literatorov (Chronicle of the House of Literateurs), 225
Levin, Jurij, 55, 222, 224
Libedinskij, Jurij, 36
Literary Studio, 6, 15, 44, 53, 207
Literaturnaja gazeta, 35, 143, 189, 207, 213, 234, 236, 241
Literaturnaja Moskva (anthology), 14, 177, 215
Literaturnoe obozrenie (Literary Review), 35, 221, 234
Literaturnye zapiski (Literary Notes), 8, 9, 89, 122, 213, 214
Literaturnyj Leningrad, 36, 220, 221, 227
Lomidze, G., 12–13, 215
Longfellow, Henry Wadsworth, 41
love lyrics, 28–31, 48–52, 70–75, 78–79, 128–32, 140, 143–46, 155, 169, 192, 197
Loxvitskaja, Mirra, 50, 72, 223
Lozinskij, Mixail, 6, 45, 175, 225
Lučanskij, Mixail, 106, 117, 119, 229, 230, 231
Luknickaja, Vera, 220
Luknickij, Pavel, 220
Lunačarskij, Anatolij, 22
Lunc, Lev, 4, 6, 7, 9–11, 13–17, 25–26, 45, 67–70, 122–23, 131, 158, 211, 214, 215, 216–18, 219, 225–26, 231–32, 235
L'vov-Rogačevsky, 61, 66, 224, 225
L'vova, Nad'ja, 21, 224
Lysicina, Anna, 166, 181

Maguire, Robert, 31, 220
Majakovskij, Vladimir, 5, 81, 104, 175

265

Index

Malaškin, Sergej, 109
Malaxov, Sergej, 117, 230, 231
Mandel'štam, Osip, 7, 46–47, 54–56, 62–63, 74–75, 80, 81–85, 99, 153, 159, 211, 224, 225, 226, 227, 234, 235
Marlowe, Christopher, 41
Maršak, Samuil, 44, 209
Marxist critics, 3, 4, 8, 9, 26, 121
McLean, Hugh, 178, 238
McVay, Gordon, 231
medicine, 20, 23, 24, 26, 31, 32, 38–39, 45, 52, 135, 156–57, 196
Medicinskaja gazeta, 209, 222, 237, 241
Medvedev, Pavel, 19, 22, 70
Mejlax, Sofija, 18
Melent'jeva, Marija, 166, 181
memoirs, 1, 15, 18, 20, 40, 42, 44–45, 48, 120–21, 136, 159, 175, 194, 208, 217–18
Mérimée, Prosper, 107
Meškov, Jurij, 237
Metčenko, A., 2, 12–14, 213, 214, 215
Metropol (anthology), 4, 16
Mikhoels, Solomon, 172
Minc, Zara, 135, 167, 175, 180, 185, 220, 222, 233, 237, 238, 239
Minokin, M. V., 216
Minskij, Nikolaj, 22
Mirskij, D. S., 1, 213
Molière, Jean-Baptiste, 27, 32, 220
Montand, Yves, 188
Moréas, Jean, 22, 48
motherhood (as theme), 28, 37, 56–59, 77–79, 81, 103–4, 129–31, 175, 180–84, 198, 200–1, 206
Movšenson, Aleksandr, 19, 23, 38, 42, 191
Movšenson, Charlotta, 18, 19, 23, 38, 40, 44, 139, 160, 169
Movšenson, Grigorij, 18, 19, 23
Muratova, K. D., 12–14, 215, 216

"Na zapad!" ("Go West!"), 10, 13, 15, 16, 25, 215, 218
Nadson, Semen, 19, 20
Naiman, Eric, 108–10, 229–30
Nakhimovsky, Alice, 61, 224
Napoleon, 82, 162
Nappel'baum, Ida, 235
Narodnyj Kommissariat Vnutrennyx Del (NKVD), 11, 14
Nazis, 61, 162–63, 165, 200
Nedra (*Depths*) 26, 219, 229, 232

Nekrasov, Nikolaj, 3, 18, 19, 20, 141–42, 156, 234
Neva, 45, 188, 217, 222, 237, 239
New Economic Policy (NEP), 5, 28, 36, 76, 85, 106–34, 137, 196, 197, 229
Nicault, Jeanne, 18, 217
Nikitin, Nikolaj, 4, 6–8, 10, 13, 14, 26, 45, 67
Nikitina, Zoja, 15, 44, 187, 216, 222
Nikolaj II, 91
Nilsson, Nils A., 83, 227
Ninov, Aleksandr, 179, 238
Novaja rossija (*New Russia*), 8, 214
Novaja russkaja kniga (*New Russian Book*), 225
Novyj mir (*New World*), 44, 213, 232
Novyj Robinzon, 27
Novyj žurnal (*New Journal*), 14, 216, 218, 219, 231

Odarčenko, Petro, 157–58, 235
Odena, Lina, 35, 153, 156, 165, 185
Odoevceva, Irina, 225
Offenbach, Jacques, 32
Oksenov, Inokentij, 81, 227
Orlov, V., 188–89, 239, 240
Orpheus, 42–44, 175
Ostrovskaja, Nadežda, 23
Oulanoff, Hongor, 5
Ovid, 176

Pachmuss, Temira, 223
Panteleev, Lenka, 28, 106, 111–21, 131
Pasternak, Boris, 14
Pavel I, 91, 95
Pavlov, Mixail, 63, 225
Pečat' i revoljucija (*The Press and Revolution*), 231
Peguy, Charles, 22
Peredelkino, 187
Peter I, 83
Peter III, 91
Peterburgskij sbornik (*A Petersburg Collection*), 8, 10, 76, 214
Petrograd, 232
Petrogradskaja pravda, 227, 228
Pil'njak, Boris, 5, 68, 106, 107
Plexanov, Georgij, 21
Podol'skij, S. S., 16
Poets' Section, 172–74
Poets' Union, 24, 33

Index

Poezija, 232
pogroms, 19, 45, 60, 64, 66
Pojarkov, Nikolaj, 223
Poljanskij, Valerian, 9
Polonskij, Aleksandr M., 182, 191
Polonskij, Lev Davidovič, 23, 28–30, 155, 159
Polonskij, Mixail L'vovič, 23, 36, 38, 40, 41, 42, 45, 50, 126, 132, 141, 143, 148, 160, 168, 169, 184–85, 205, 209, 217–23, 232–35, 238, 240, 241
Popov, Vjačeslav, 225
Popova, Ljubov', 206, 209
Pozner, Vladimir, 6, 80
Pravda, 111, 157–58, 215, 230, 235
Priboj (*Surf*), 42, 177, 219, 238
Prikam'je (*By the Kama*), 38, 221
Proffer, Carl, 215
Proñektor (*Searchlight*), 232
Propp, Vladimir, 111, 230
Prostor (*Expanse*), 194, 216, 240
purges, 34–36
Puškin, Aleksandr S., 55, 88–96, 98, 125, 131, 136, 151–52, 157, 175, 176, 228, 235

Rabotnica (*Worker Woman*), 38, 221
Rabotnica i krest'janka (*Worker Woman and Peasant Woman*), 32, 35, 221, 235
Radlova, Anna, 99
Razin, Stenka, 111
Reisner, Larissa, 44, 210
Rembrandt, 42, 102, 199–201
Remizov, Aleksej, 8, 68
Romanov, Pantalejmon, 109
Ronen, Omry, 93, 228, 229, 234
Rooziorg, Karl and Adela, 191
Rosenthal, Charlotte, 242
Rossetti, Christina, 155
Rouhier-Willoughby, Jeanmarie, 223
Roždestvenskij, V., 213, 218, 223, 226
Rubaškin, Aleksandr, 3, 31, 135–36, 209–10, 213, 217, 220, 233, 241
Russian Academy, 22
Russian Association of Proletarian Writers (RAPP), 10, 121
Russian Social Democratic Party, 20, 22

Šaginjan, Marietta, 33–34, 36, 40, 45, 88, 112, 137, 157, 210, 217–18, 220, 221, 227, 228, 233

Sałajczyk, Janina, 216
Sandler, Stephanie, 230
Sappho, 78
Sel'vinskij, I., 28
Serapion Brothers, 1–17, 24–27, 33, 36, 44, 45, 58, 67, 68, 76, 79–80, 103, 106, 122–23, 158, 187, 194, 206, 208, 209, 211–12, 213–19, 224, 225, 226, 231, 232, 235, 241, 242
Ševčenko, Taras, 136, 157–59, 235
Severnoe obozrenie (*Northern Review*), 100, 229
Shakespeare, William, 20, 27, 32, 62, 100, 155, 176
Sheldon, Richard, 214
Shylock, 59, 62–64, 100, 132, 137, 146–47, 208
Sibirskie ogni (*Siberian Fires*), 242
Sinjavskij, Andrej, 15
Škapskaja, Marija, 22, 32, 34, 37, 38, 39, 44, 45, 155, 159, 161, 166, 175, 210, 220–22, 235–37
Šklovskij, Viktor, 1, 5–7, 10, 16, 24–25, 44, 45, 67, 96, 105, 158, 214, 215, 218, 228
Sloane, David, 91, 94, 228
Slonimskij, Mixail, 4, 6–8, 10, 12, 13, 15, 16, 38, 67, 211, 216
Socialist Realism, 11, 12, 136, 142
Sologub, Fedor, 8
Solov'ev, Grigorij, 207, 241
Solženicyn, Aleksandr, 14
Sovremennoe obozrenie (*Contemporary Review*), 223
Sovremennyj zapad (*Contemporary West*), 27, 227
Spanish Civil War, 35
Stalin, Josef, 2, 4–5, 11, 12, 26, 36–37, 44, 47, 61, 109, 134, 136, 143, 148, 165, 168, 172–75, 178, 183, 210, 233
Statina, Faina, 160, 235
Štejnman, Zelig, 237
Stites, Richard, 108, 112, 219, 226, 229, 230
Štrejxer, Ljubov', 27, 32, 153, 219, 220, 235
Struve, G. P., 226
Švarc, Evgenij, 1, 26, 219
Sverdlov, Jakov, 105, 181
Svjatskij, Svjatoslav, 213, 218

Tadžixen, 142
Talov, Mark, 22

Index

Tarasenkov, A., 166, 236
Tartu, 23, 172, 199, 240
Tašbulatova, Sarra, 142, 148
theatre work, 32, 155
Timen ik, R. D., 62–63, 224–25
Timina, S. I., 25–26, 211–12, 219, 242
Tixonov, Nikolaj, 2, 4–8, 11–14, 16, 44, 67, 76, 80, 105, 188, 209, 211, 213
Tjutčev, Fedor, 81
Tolstoj, Aleksej, 91, 227
Tomaševskij, Jurij, 14, 216
Tomilin, Viktor, 156
Toporov, V. N., 93, 228
translations, 2, 26, 27, 32, 33, 41, 42, 48, 76, 80, 136–37, 141–42, 155–56, 194, 202, 207
Translators' Section (Leningrad Writers' Union), 41, 172, 213
Translators' Studio, 6, 24
Trotskij, Lev, 5, 9, 21, 214, 215
Trubilova, Elena, 241
Twentieth Party Congress, 37, 176
Tynjanov, Jurij, 1, 9, 36, 38, 214, 217, 220, 221, 224, 233
Tynjanovskie čtenija, 224

Učenova, V. V., 241
Ulanova, Galina, 167, 185
Uspenskij, V. V., 162
Utesov, Leonid, 33

"V petle" ("In the Noose"), 106, 111–18
Vatson, M., 234
Večernaja krasnaja gazeta (*Evening Red Gazette*), 32, 219, 227
Večernyj Leningrad (*Evening Leningrad*), 222, 237
Vejnštejn, M., 215, 225
Verhaeren, Émile, 41
Verlaine, Paul, 22, 48
Vickery, Walter, 178, 238
Vol'fila (Free Philosophical Society), 22, 217
Voprosy literatury (*Literary Questions*), 213, 216, 217
Vorobej (*Sparrow*), 27
Voronskij, Aleksandr, 9, 10, 58, 214, 224
Vowles, Judith, 230

Vygodskaja, Emma, 45, 175, 194–95, 221, 240
Vygodskij, David, 34, 45, 81, 175, 195, 221, 226, 227, 240
Vyšeslavceva, S., 99, 103, 110, 128–29, 229, 230, 232

Weinert, Erich, 35, 156
"Why We Are the Serapion Brothers" ("Počemu my Serapionovy Brat'ja"), 9, 13–14, 16, 26, 235
Woman Question, 2–3, 28–30, 35, 47, 79, 110, 136, 142, 147–48, 153–54, 165–66, 168, 170–71, 179–80, 185–86, 206–7, 210
World Literature, 6, 33
World War I, 22–23, 52, 56, 85, 94, 181, 196, 206, 238
World War II, 26, 37–41, 159, 161–67, 178, 181–85, 198–99, 206, 238
Writers' Union, 2, 11–13, 16, 33, 41, 172, 174, 213

Xodasevič, Vladislav, 8, 99
Xudožestvennaja literatura (*Artistic Literature*), 229

Yiddish, 3, 12, 33, 60–61, 133, 155, 172

Zamjatin, Evgenij, 6–8, 67, 68, 214, 225
Ždanov, Andrej, 2, 11–14, 16, 17, 172–73, 178, 215, 237
Zemljačka, Rozalija Samojlovna, 20
Zenkovsky, Sergei, 224
Zetkin, Clara, 147–48
Zinoviev, Grigorij, 106, 109
Zirin, Mary, 242
Žirmunskij, Viktor, 48, 94, 223
Žizn' iskusstva (*Life of Art*), 25, 213, 218, 231
Zoščenko, Mixail, 1, 2, 4, 6–8, 11–15, 24, 40, 44–45, 67, 172, 175, 213, 215, 216
Žuk, Ol'ga, 111, 119, 230, 231
Žukovskij, Nikolaj, 90, 157–58
Zvezda [Perm'], 38, 221
Zvezda (*Star*), 4, 11, 32, 43, 45, 142, 172, 188, 191, 215, 217, 222, 232, 237, 239

OHIO UNIVERSITY LIBRARY

Please return this book as soon as you have finished with it. In order to avoid a fine it must be returned by the latest date stamped below. All books are subject to recall after two weeks or immediately if needed for reserve.

CF